MW00625207

Titles in the Series

The History of Military Aviation

PAUL J. SPRINGER, EDITOR

This series is designed to explore previously ignored facets of the history of airpower. It includes a wide variety of disciplinary approaches, scholarly perspectives, and argumentative styles. Its fundamental goal is to analyze the past, present, and potential future utility of airpower and to enhance our understanding of the changing roles played by aerial assets in the formulation and execution of national military strategies. It encompasses the incredibly diverse roles played by airpower, which include but are not limited to efforts to achieve air superiority; strategic attack; intelligence, surveillance, and reconnaissance missions; airlift operations; close-air support; and more. Of course, airpower does not exist in a vacuum. There are myriad terrestrial support operations required to make airpower functional, and examinations of these missions is also a goal of this series.

In less than a century, airpower developed from flights measured in minutes to the ability to circumnavigate the globe without landing. Airpower has become the military tool of choice for rapid responses to enemy activity, the primary deterrent to aggression by peer competitors, and a key enabler to military missions on the land and sea. This series provides an opportunity to examine many of the key issues associated with its usage in the past and present, and to influence its development for the future.

REAR ADMIRAL HERBERT V. WILEY

A Career in Airships and Battleships

M. Ernest Marshall

NAVAL INSTITUTE PRESS
Annapolis, Maryland

This book has been brought to publication with the
generous assistance of Edward S. and Joyce I. Miller.

Naval Institute Press
291 Wood Road
Annapolis, MD 21402

Library of Congress Cataloging-in-Publication Data is available.
978-1-68247-317-7 (hardcover)
978-1-68247-318-4 (eBook)

⊗ Print editions meet the requirements of ANSI/NISO z39.48-1992 (Permanence of Paper).
Printed in the United States of America.

27 26 25 24 23 22 21 20 19   9 8 7 6 5 4 3 2 1
First printing

Map by Chris Robinson.

This work is dedicated to the visionaries
in the early days of manned flight who
devoted themselves with great courage
and sacrifice to the science and
engineering of lighter-than-air ships.

The romance of the air is fast replacing the romance of the seas, so fast, in fact, that we scarcely think of the romance of the seas at all, our minds being constantly stimulated and thrilled by aerial exploits as some particularly daring and spectacular deed links up distant and little-known parts of the earth with the beaten tracks of men and ships. . . . Romance is still with us although science has dulled the keen edge of its mystery.

—*Adm. William A. Moffett*

CONTENTS

ACKNOWLEDGMENTS

With deep gratitude the author acknowledges the people and agencies whose assistance made this book possible. The National Archives and Records Administration (NARA), National Personnel Records Center, St. Louis, Missouri, provided the military records of Herbert Victor Wiley, Charles Emery Rosendahl, and Adm. William A. Moffett. Copies of the logbooks of the USS *Shenandoah*, USS *Los Angeles*, USS *Akron*, and USS *Macon* were provided by NARA, Washington, D.C. Logbooks, action reports, war diaries, and damage reports of the USS *West Virginia* were obtained from NARA, College Park, Maryland.

Special appreciation is expressed for David D'Onofrio, Special Collections Librarian, Nimitz Library, U.S. Naval Academy, Annapolis, Maryland, for providing numerous documents, including the court of inquiry proceedings related to the 1915 "cheating scandal." John Ball, Library Associate Senior, The University of Akron—Archival Services, Akron, Ohio, supplied records related to technical aspects of the USS *Akron* and *Macon*. Herbert V. Wiley's daughter, Marie Wiley Ross, through her son, Ian N. Ross, made available letters from the family collection that offered insights into the private life and thoughts of Wiley. Liberal use has been made of newspaper articles from the major press services relating to events and people described in this book. A number of extensive excerpts from newspapers, letters, and government documents are given, both to suggest what the public knew and thought during the early days of manned flight and to display their eloquence and expressiveness, the kinds of which have been eroded over the years.

Gratitude is extended to Elizabeth E. Engel, Certified Archivist, Senior Archivist for the State Historical Society of Missouri, for providing material from that transcript collection and to Lisa Crunk, Photographic Archivist at the Naval History and Heritage Command.

The famed lighter-than-air (LTA) historian and author William F. Althoff has made available to researchers his research materials, including transcripts of oral histories taken from numerous LTA personnel, by donating them to the William F. Althoff Oral History Library, Smithsonian Libraries / National Air and Space Museum, Washington, D.C. I am grateful to Phil Edwards of the National Air and Space Museum for allowing that library to be referenced as the source of this material during the early days of its organization.

Appreciation is expressed for Capt. Paul Huber, USN (Ret.), and attorney Allen Klein—both renowned philatelists—who provided elusive details relating to the incident of the mailbag drop from planes of the *Macon* to President Franklin D. Roosevelt on board the USS *Houston.*

Special gratitude is expressed to Dr. Paul J. Springer, professor, Air Command & Staff College, Maxwell Air Force Base, Montgomery, Alabama, for his editorial advice, which made this a better book. Appreciation is expressed also to Paul Merzlak, editorial director; Chris Robinson, cartographer; and Rachel Crawford, production editor, of the Naval Institute Press for their contributions and guidance; and to Pel Boyer for his editorial skills.

Finally, I reserve my deepest gratitude for my wonderful wife, Lisa, who has created for us a life that allows me to pursue my passions for historical research and writing. This book could not have been written without her.

Introduction

Herbert Victor Wiley was the product of small-town life in Missouri. After leaving his hometown to attend the Naval Academy, he never returned to live there, but the town, its people, and its values were always part of him. He was the town's hero and, vicariously, its people shared with pride in his achievements. Gifted with a military bearing, he was the stereotypical strong, quiet type that expressed itself better in deeds than words. His was a life of honor and devotion—to family and the Navy. His life is a study in steadfastness and leadership. He was an anchor to his family in dire economic times and later a solid reassurance to his men in crises. He exhibited great courage, but his is not so much the tale of a storied hero as one of a leader and of the things that molded him.

Wiley was born into a world of rapidly changing technology. Early in his Navy career, he volunteered for the germinal lighter-than-air (LTA) service, founded at Lakehurst Naval Air Station in New Jersey. Manned flight too was in its infancy, and the world looked on as rapid advances were being made in both heavier-than-air (HTA—i.e., airplanes) and LTA flight. The Navy's LTA program was a small, intimate community with relatively few officers and men compared to other elements of the Navy. It began as a volunteer service that attracted men with a sense of adventure and a vision of the future of manned flight. In its history, the Navy was to have only four of the giant airships—the USS *Shenandoah*, *Los Angeles*, *Akron*, and *Macon*, in that order. The airships (dirigibles) were huge yet remarkably fragile vessels, and every flight was a learning experience for their officers and crews. Danger was ever present. In the early days the men of the American airship service were, for the most part, inexperienced in this mode of flight; it was with the *Shenandoah*—the first of three of the airships to crash—that the Navy learned its earliest lessons and first analyzed the causes of an airship disaster to make future flights safer. Wiley experienced and survived two of the three crashes and lived to see the end of the great airship era.

Manned flight was still a novelty, and the public was interested in news of the men and machines that took to the air. Perhaps because there were far fewer airships than airplanes, these behemoths possessed a particular, romantic appeal. Almost every flight of the Navy's airships received detailed press coverage, and because of this the names and faces of the senior airship officers became widely recognizable. In the perspective of history, the LTA program made up only a small part of the timeline of Navy aviation. It was to be a path not taken, but until airplanes established themselves as the technology of the future, it had to be explored. The history of the airship era is rich in stories of the lives of the men who brought it to life and sustained it to the very end, always believing in it.

While this is a biography of Herbert V. Wiley, it is, simultaneously, a seamless history of the Navy's great airship program. Not all of the prominent personalities in the program survived it. The much admired Zachary Lansdowne died in the crash of the *Shenandoah*, and the driving force for the LTA program, Adm. William Moffett, was killed in the crash of the *Akron*. As for Wiley, because of his length of service, he and the LTA program became inextricably linked— an understanding of one is not possible without an understanding of the other. Wiley was among the first group of volunteers selected for LTA and rose to command the Navy's last great airship—the *Macon*. With the crash of the *Macon*, Wiley realized, the LTA program had reached its end. He was reassigned to duties with the surface fleet; and when the Japanese attacked Pearl Harbor, Wiley was in command of Destroyer Squadron 29 in the Asiatic Fleet.

During the prewar years, it was common for Navy officers to request reassignments to new kinds of duties. In this way they improved their professional credentials and young officers learned early in their careers that promotion was linked intimately with time and service with the fleet. Wiley was keenly aware of this long-standing practice and made frequent requests for change of duty, often in response to events he saw unfolding ahead of him. Wiley was grooming himself for his career, and as a result he was a good candidate for fleet command when he left the LTA service, unlike the Lakehurst officers who had preferred to spend most of their time there, with the airships. Wiley rose to become executive officer on a battleship and gained intimate practical knowledge of the workings of the surface fleet, and it was there that he was assigned until the end of World War II. Wiley's name had been written into the history of manned flight by his contributions to lighter-than-air aviation, and it would be inscribed forever in the annals of naval warfare by his performance during the Battle of Surigao Strait.

1

Wiley

The Early Years

People in small towns, much more than in cities, share a destiny.
—*Richard Russo*[1]

On May 16, 1891, Herbert Victor Wiley was born into the small midwestern town of Wheeling, Missouri, to Joel and Minnie Wiley. This town of less than five hundred people was only eight miles from the Livingston County seat of Chillicothe, which boasted a population of nearly six thousand. Located in northern Missouri, these two small, agrarian towns both received support from three railroad lines. Since 1860, the *Chillicothe Constitution* had been the newspaper serving both towns, and, by coincidence, on the day Herbert was born it published a lengthy description of Chillicothe to attract people and businesses. The town boasted "fine schools, magnificent churches, three daily and weekly newspapers, good hotels, an opera house with a seating capacity of eight hundred people, and a public spirited people." Chillicothe, the article claimed, was the "most thrifty, progressive town in North Missouri," its ministry "represented by some very eloquent pulpit orators whose churches have a large attendance. The resident medical profession is fully up with the times, and in the matter of surgery its physicians are among the best in the west." As for the people of Chillicothe, they were "cultured and progressive, and fully up with our modern civilization, are courteous to strangers; and as neighbors and friends no better are to be found."[2]

Herbert's father, Joel, was one of nine children. While most of his siblings pursued farming as a trade, Joel, as the youngest male, did not inherit land that would allow him to follow his family into farming. At nineteen he found work in a dry-goods store, but he later pursued with his uncle a series of business ventures that included a grocery and drug store. In 1880, at age twenty-four, he married Minnie Alice Carey, who two years later gave birth to daughter Zulah May, who would be followed two years by son Floyd. In the early 1880s things began to unravel for Joel, and in 1883, after selling his interest in the store, he moved his family to Chillicothe, where he worked in a dry-goods store. After three years of this, he moved his family back to Wheeling and started his own dry-goods business. For about ten years he enjoyed a measure of success and served as a trustee of the local Baptist church, while Minnie was a trustee of the Wheeling cemetery and active in a number of women's clubs.

The pleasantness of life in Wheeling and Chillicothe did not provide immunity from tragedy. In 1895, Zulah succumbed at age thirteen to a chronic, unspecified cardiac condition from which she had suffered for a number of years. She was buried in the Wheeling cemetery, to be joined years later by her parents and her brother, Floyd. Herbert was three years old when his sister died.

In 1896 the family moved again, this time to the small community of Mountain Grove, in south-central Missouri. Sticking with what he knew, Joel opened Wiley's Department Store, on the north side of the town square. Things went well enough at first to relocate to a larger commercial space on the west side of the square in 1898. Tragedy struck again on March 11, 1899, in the form of "the most disastrous fire in the history of Mountain Grove."[3] Eight brick business buildings were destroyed with their contents.[4] The list of businesses destroyed included "J. A. Wiley & Co., general merchants."[5] The aggregate loss of stock was estimated to be about $100,000 and the loss to buildings around $50,000. The resilient Joel tried to rebound by reopening his business, but it failed and closed in 1907.

Throughout this series of personal and business tragedies, Joel continued his public and civic service, on the city council and the school board. Herbert learned during his formative years much about hard work, duty, and public service from his parents, and these lessons became part of the core of values that would define him. In 1904 Herbert's sister Minnie Fay was born. Despite the thirteen years that separated them, the two developed a close relationship that lasted their lives. The Wiley children enjoyed healthy and happy childhoods.

They were very popular, among peers and elders equally. Herbert developed a penchant for photography; he was fond of capturing images of friends and family, local landscapes, and familiar buildings.

The Wiley children enjoyed the usual privileges of small-town life, including swimming, outdoor games, and ice skating during the winter freezes. Photographs from Herbert's teen years in Mountain Grove and Chillicothe give the impression of a highly social, amiable young man with many friends. He used his camera liberally to document outings and picnics, images of young people having a grand time. For the rest of his life he would carry with him a small photograph album of these pictures.

In 1908, while Herbert was in his junior year of high school, his father moved the family again, back to Chillicothe. Herbert, one of twenty-four seniors at the small Chillicothe High School, excelled academically. At eighteen he already displayed a military bearing for which any military academy would love to claim credit—broad shoulders, puffed-out chest, strong jaw, and ramrod-straight spine. The school's yearbook, *The Cresset*, printed an appropriate literary passage beside the photograph of each student. Beside Herbert's image was a line from Shakespeare's *Julius Caesar*: "He thinks too much, such men are dangerous."[6] Four days prior to commencement, a large crowd came out to enjoy the graduating-class play, *At Yale*, with Herbert playing the lead role.[7] Herbert graduated with honors with the class of 1909 on May 24 and received a "degree of excellence" award in physics.[8]

In spite of his family's frequent moves, Herbert maintained strong emotional ties to his relatives and friends. His parents had given him a safe, comfortable, loving home environment, but he was keenly aware of his parents' financial struggles. He would always appreciate what his parents had done for him, and his gratitude created within him a determination to obtain steady employment by which he could help support his family.

Herbert was unable to afford a college education and instead went to work in his father's store. In the spring of 1910, however, an unexpected opportunity presented itself. Chillicothe's mayor, John H. Taylor, received a letter from Congressman W. W. Rucker asking if he knew of a young man who might be interested in a career in the Navy. The superintendent of public schools discussed the matter with Herbert, who was receptive immediately, and the congressman submitted his name to the Navy Department for appointment to the U.S. Naval

Academy. The local newspaper was quick to pick up this developing story and, on March 17, 1910, printed the article "Wiley Appointed a Midshipman."[9]

The exuberance of the *Chillicothe Constitution* was premature: Herbert had not yet passed the Academy's rigorous entrance examination. Herbert left home on April 8 to attend one of the schools in Annapolis, Maryland, that specialized in preparing young men to pass it. These schools were informal, with rolling admissions and no structured curricula. Their focus was exclusively on teaching recent years' examinations as a means of preparing their students to pass the next one. Herbert sat for the test in June and made the front page of the *Chillicothe Constitution* on July 2 with the announcement he had failed it.[10] Until he could retake the examination, he returned home to resume his duties in his father's store.

He brought back from his brief experience at the Naval Academy a small book of photographs of Annapolis and a determination to pass the examination on his next try, which was scheduled for April 18, 1911, in Kansas City, Missouri. Prior to that date, however, the Academy changed the venue for his examination to the Civil Service Commission building in Washington. Whether by design or by accident, the change to the East Coast was fortuitous. Herbert's twentieth birthday, May 16, was approaching: should he pass the written examination, the proximity to Annapolis would allow him ample time to travel there for his physical examination and to be sworn in before he exceeded the Academy's age limit. He passed both by May 9.

The following day, he signed the oath made by all midshipmen to "serve in the Navy of the United States for eight years, unless sooner discharged by competent authority," and began the process of being molded into an officer in the U.S. Navy.

While Herbert's star was rising, his father's business was struggling again. Before Herbert returned home from Annapolis, his father ran an advertisement in the local newspaper announcing a "closing-out sale" and that he had decided to close out his entire line of dependable merchandise and retire from the dry-goods business. In later years he tried other business ventures, but none was successful. Fortunately for the family, Herbert now had a steady paying position with the U.S. Navy. A midshipman went on the payroll immediately upon taking his oath, and this financial security would help sustain the family in the years that lay ahead.

Wiley arrived at the U.S. Naval Academy in its sixty-seventh year. That year, the Academy boasted a total enrollment of 732 midshipmen. Wiley was one of 244 "plebes"—formally, Fourth Classmen—in the entering class of 1911. Classes started on October 1, but like many Fourth Classmen, Wiley arrived in July to endure a "plebe summer." During this prelude to the academic year, much was expected of plebes as they were broken into the rigors of Academy life. All duties and inspections were subject to judgment, and offenses or deficiencies were recorded and demerits assigned. Administrators, instructors, and upperclassmen could issue demerits for the slightest infractions. By the end of the summer Wiley had accumulated demerits for such common offenses as a dirty mirror, his room out of order, his locker door left open, soiled clothes, and disorderly conduct.

When the academic year began in October, life settled into a routine. Each day began at 0630 with reveille and ended with lights out at 2130. Every minute of the day was structured. The course work was a combination of traditional education—including English, foreign languages, mathematics, physics, and chemistry—and practical training specifically useful to the Navy, such as seamanship, gunnery, navigation, and engineering. The overarching aim of this education was to produce men who would be worthy naval officers. By the end of the first year, there were only 199 midshipmen in Wiley's class—a testament to the difficulty many young men had adjusting to the rigors of the Academy. Wiley ranked 109th in his class, and his total of forty-eight demerits was one of the lowest.

The annual summer cruise was an essential part of the training of future naval officers. Midshipmen learned the organization and administration of a warship and about the living conditions and duties of enlisted personnel. During these exercises, midshipmen were evaluated on their performance and progress toward becoming effective officers. Plans for the summer cruise of 1912 were complicated by the fact that the Secretary of the Navy had to provide ships from the active fleet for use by reserve fleets at Philadelphia and Puget Sound, to identify vessels for the Academy's summer cruise, and to find crews for the USS *Wyoming* (BB 32) and the USS *Arkansas* (BB 33), which were to be commissioned in September. To find places for all 522 midshipmen, the First and Second Classes were distributed among the eighteen battleships and cruisers of the Atlantic Fleet, and the rising Third Class, including Wiley, was given to the USS *Massachusetts* (BB 2). This ship, now obsolete, had been decommissioned in 1906, only to be recommissioned in 1910 for use in the Academy's annual summer cruises.

The "Massy" took the midshipmen down the Chesapeake Bay then north to Provincetown, Massachusetts. While periodic liberty ashore was fun, life on board was rigorous. Some of Wiley's classmates later recalled the experience in issues of *The Lucky Bag*, the Academy's yearbook.

> We embarked on the Massachusetts as unversed in the ways of the sea as a lover in the ways of women, and we were given no time to acquire our "legs."[11]

> We scrubbed our own clothes, presumably in saltwater. Bancroft Hall standards of cleanliness were forgotten and we adopted instead those of primeval man. We shoveled coal and hoisted ashes. . . . We were crowded and hard-worked, the food was poor, the water nauseating . . . but we had fine liberties.[12]

> The consensus of opinion is that the cruise was the making of our class, but said opinion is somewhat divided as to what it made of us. . . . [T]hankful are we all that the cruise of the "Massy" is a reminiscence of yesterday and not a reality of tomorrow.[13]

With their first summer cruise behind them, the midshipmen settled back into the routine of academic life. Wiley had acclimated well to Academy life, and his athletic prowess found an outlet in lacrosse, a sport he learned at the Academy. He performed well enough on the team to earn his yellow letter *N*. At the end of his second year, he ranked fifty-seventh overall in his class and fourth in electrical engineering, and he had no demerits.

Midshipmen maintained close contact with their families through letters. In early 1914 his mother's health was failing badly; she experienced repeated episodes of congestive heart failure, punctuated by an episode of life-threatening pneumonia. In April his father warned him his mother was so weak that he did not expect her to do well.[14] But she was at least in stable condition, so Wiley made the transatlantic summer cruise that year on board the USS *Illinois* (BB 7). Shortly after returning, he learned she was once again seriously ill; he requested and was granted special leave to visit her. The local newspaper reported, "Mrs. J. A. Wiley is seriously ill . . . and not expected to live."[15] Wiley was able to spend time with his mother during September, but he was back at the Academy when she died on November 12. He returned home for the funeral and stayed a few days with his father and sister. Herbert's relationship with his mother appears to have been a close one. Throughout his naval career he carried with him a few letters from her written during the last year of her life.

Wiley was progressing well through his classes, but he developed a medical problem that threatened his Navy career: color blindness. It had not been present when he was examined for admission to the Academy; he had scored a perfect four out of four on color perception. However, by 1914 his ability to discriminate between colors dropped to a three, and on March 15, 1915, the year of his scheduled graduation, it was zero. He learned that it was possible to "train" his eyes to pass the examination by using pieces of colored wool yarn to practice matching their perceived tonalities to their true colors, and he set about it. However, on March 16, the president of the medical examining board informed the superintendent of the Academy by memorandum that Wiley was unfit for service due to "poor chromatic perception."

At that moment, it appeared to Wiley his career as a naval officer was over before it had started. However, not wanting to lose four years' investment in a young man, the Navy Department's Bureau of Navigation, which handled personnel matters, offered him a reprieve—with the endorsement of the Bureau of Medicine and Surgery—that Wiley be allowed to graduate and be reexamined later. If he failed then, he would be dropped from the service.

Wiley had written to his father previously about this problem with color perception and, after this latest round of testing, he wrote about it again. Wiley was concerned that he might not pass the follow-up examination and would have to sacrifice his Navy career, but he had a contingency plan and would, he believed, have little problem finding employment. Thanks to the Navy, he had acquired an education as a steam engineer and also as an electrical engineer. He was skilled in chemistry, steel processes, and surveying. He knew of midshipmen who for a variety of reasons had left the Academy short of graduation and had found jobs in shipbuilding or steel companies. He also gave consideration to seeking a commission in the Marine Corps.[16] Whatever happened, he felt he had options. There is no doubt the life of a career naval officer held a strong allure for him, but at the forefront of his thinking was the determination to obtain solid, long-term employment with which he could support his family. Waiting for his reexamination, he was under a dark cloud of uncertainty going into his final months at the Academy.

He repeated the eye examination on May 27, and to his great relief the examining board reported he had slightly defective color perception but not sufficient to disqualify him for the service. It recommended that he be found physically qualified for commissioning.

At the Academy, Wiley had an active social life. It was customary for midshipmen to acquire nicknames, and somewhere along the way Wiley became "Doc." How he earned the pseudonym is unknown, and a number of other midshipmen had it too, but among his friends and family he was to be known as "Doc" for the remainder of his life.

His last year at the Academy, disrupted by the death of his mother and a short illness of his own that caused him to miss a month of class time, was difficult academically. His order of merit fell as he ranked below the class average in "Theoretical Navigation," "Electrical Engineering," "Compass Deviation & Surveying," and "Guns and Mines," yet he passed his final round of examinations required to be graduated with his class. His higher academic performance of previous years brought up his class standing to slightly below the top third. On June 1, following a fun week of dinners, dances, and ceremonies, Wiley participated in the commencement exercises with the class of 1915.

The Lucky Bag for that year devoted an entire page to each of the graduating First Classmen. Alongside a head-and-shoulder photographic cameo and a smaller, casual image of each midshipman was a lengthy summary of how his classmates regarded him. The early pages of the yearbook set the stage for understanding these commentaries:

THE FIRST CLASS
Take this book of fact and fancy,
And, though hoping for the best,
See yourself as others see you,
Both in earnest and in jest.[17]

In Wiley's case, his classmates struck right to the nature of the young man. In describing the person they had known over the previous four years, they were also elaborating on the man's character, a character that would remain unchanged for the rest of his life.

There is nothing narrow about Doc. His smile, his shoulders, and his mind are of the broadest. When you see a large and well-cultivated pompadour over a pair of rosy cheeks pushed back by a wide grin, bearing down on you, sit up and take notice, for it is the "Doctor." Herb has been known during his four years as a square and reliable man. These qualities together with the fact that he does his best, and a very good best it is, have given him success at whatever he has turned his hand to. On the lacrosse field, he has been a consistent, hard-working defense man. In the classroom he has been one of those practical fellows whom no prof would bluff. Doc has never been known to worry over missing a hop or a party with the fellows, though he thoroughly enjoys himself at either—perhaps a little more at the latter, for Doc is the kind of man who likes men and whom men like; but when there is a man's work to be done, the call of pleasure does not deter him from doing his full share, and then some. Yet, gentlemen, this easy-going man has a goat. Insult the sacredness of the Missouri mule or depreciate anything from the "Show Me" state and out comes his goat to keep Lein's [unidentified] company for a while. Doc prefers actions to words, and as a consequence is not as well known as some of the noisier men in the class; but those who have gained his acquaintance will back him against all others as a steadfast, unwavering friend.[18]

The American involvement in the building of the Panama Canal spanned a decade leading to its official opening on August 15, 1914. The Panama Pacific International Exposition (PPIE), the world's fair for 1915, was created ostensibly as a celebration of the canal's opening but was actually intended largely to assist San Francisco, which was still recovering from its 1906 earthquake. Recognizing the importance of both the canal and the PPIE, Congress wanted a strong U.S. Navy presence. Four years earlier Congress had requested the president invite other nations to send their fleets on the occasion to Hampton Roads, Virginia, to sail south with U.S. ships and traverse the canal en route to San Francisco. Fourteen countries initially accepted, but by 1915, seven were at war: Austria, France, Germany, England, Japan, Russia, and Turkey. With things uncertain for the remaining participants—Italy, Greece, Argentina, Spain, Portugal, Norway, and Sweden—it seemed unlikely that many foreign warships would attend.

Also, the summer cruise for 1915 would be to San Francisco, traversing the Panama Canal to get there. The elaborate arrangements being made for this historic occasion were described in the U.S. Naval Institute *Proceedings* in an article stating that the Secretary of the Navy and Rear Adm. William F. Fullam, superintendent of the Academy, agreed the cruise would be a "splendid thing for the education of the midshipmen."[19] This was to be the first time in the history of the Academy midshipmen would visit the Pacific Ocean; previously, cruises had been restricted to the Atlantic. As it turned out, however, Fullam had been misquoted. He and several of his officers at the Academy were opposed to the plan. Fullam requested written opinions from Cdr. H. B. Price and Capt. L. H. Chandler, who had commanded the summer cruises of 1914 and 1913, respectively. Their objections to the cruise centered on the heat below decks in the aging ships with limited ventilation at the latitude of the canal, which, they claimed, would interfere with instruction, especially in electrical and engineering work, interfere with sleep, and create a health hazard for midshipmen not accustomed to such temperatures. Further, they felt, allowing the midshipmen to visit San Francisco might be "prejudicial to good discipline."[20] Fullam added a cover letter to those provided by Price and Chandler, and forwarded all to the Navy Department; but Victor Blue, chief of the Bureau of Navigation, rejected the arguments and directed Fullam to prepare an itinerary for the cruise.

In due course the Practice Cruise Committee planned for ships to leave Annapolis on June 6, 1915, and return on August 30. Initially, Secretary of the Navy Josephus Daniels made the USS *Ohio* (BB 12), USS *Illinois* (BB 7), and USS *Missouri* (BB 11) available for the cruise, but the *Illinois* developed major problems that could not be repaired in time, and the USS *Wisconsin* (BB 9) was assigned instead. Fullam designated the *Missouri* as the flagship.

In the midst of preparations, Fullam requested for himself the command of the Academy Practice Squadron and then assignment to one of the fleets, where he might be in line for promotion to its commander in chief. Fullam's request for sea duty was effectively an early resignation from his post as superintendent of the Naval Academy, the usual tenure being three years. He may have felt rebuffed by Blue's overriding of his objections to the canal cruise, but there was another major issue—an active investigation into a wide-scale cheating scandal at the Academy, a scandal that had happened on his watch. It was a high-profile affair, in newspapers across the country. Fullam postponed the cruise until the investigation was complete; the departure date was moved from June 6 to July 7.[21] This delay affected Wiley directly: he had been called to testify in the investigation, and his commissioning as an ensign would have to await its results.

The essentials of the scandal were that midshipmen had attempted to break into the offices and desks of the faculty heads of departments to obtain advance copies of upcoming examinations. Fullam believed that only one of these attempts had been successful—in the Department of Foreign Languages.[22] Six members of the class of 1915 who had already graduated were called back to the Academy because their names had been mentioned in connection with the incident. Secretary Daniels called for a court of inquiry and it opened its hearings on June 7, 1915. The court was composed of Capt. Robert L. Russell, who served as president of the court; Capt. Andrew T. Long and Cdr. Louis R. de Steiguer, members of the court; and Lt. Cdr. W. C. Watts, the judge advocate (i.e., lawyer). The seven defendants were Midshipmen R. M. Nelson Jr., L. P. Wessell, C. E. Evans, S. A. Hamilton, J. E. Moss, D. B. Duncan, and T. W. Harrison Jr.[23] Also present, as counsel for the defendants, were the Hon. C. C. Carlin, Hon. James Hay, and Mr. Robert Moss. With the permission of the court, these counselors were allowed to examine each of the midshipmen who were called to testify. The court interrogated midshipmen from each of the four classes to learn the details of the scandal, its extent, and the degree of involvement of each midshipman.

On the twentieth day of the inquiry, the court examined Wiley. He had been called as a witness by one of the defendants, Midshipman Nelson. A court of inquiry is serious business and for a young midshipman an anxiety-producing one. Wiley addressed the court with his characteristic military demeanor and answered all questions directly and unhesitatingly, neither hedging nor retreating from an issue. Counselor Hay asked Wiley directly whether he knew of any actual case of cheating during the last academic year, either during an examination or in the recitation room: Wiley replied, "No, sir."[24] The defendant, Nelson, took the opportunity to ask questions of Wiley, whose answers bore out Wiley's assertion that most of what he knew about the cheating scandal and those involved was hearsay, not the result of direct observation. The judge advocate asked Wiley if he had received any information regarding the recent annual examination in modern languages that later appeared on the actual examination. When Wiley responded he had, he was asked how much of the examination sheet he had seen, to which he replied, "About 75 percent."[25]

Midshipman J. E. Watts testified that he had received copies of the examination papers in the mail. It became clear through the questioning of numerous midshipmen that the "gouge" had circulated not as a single, complete document but in fragments; few, if any, had obtained a complete set of questions. Under questioning, he revealed the name of the midshipman who had given him the material and that, he believed, about 90 percent of the First Class had seen a substantial amount of advance test information.[26]

Among other things, these lengthy interrogations of midshipmen led to the acknowledgment that certain instructors at the Academy were known to "leak" pretest information to midshipmen on the athletic teams and, at times, to individual midshipmen who were in danger of failing a course. The investigation had been opened to inquire into a specific theft of examination papers, but it led to a broader understanding of cheating, of its scale and its various forms. This revelation was shocking to those who considered midshipmen young officers and gentlemen to be and, as such, men of high moral character. When the court of inquiry completed its fact finding it had interrogated 124 midshipmen and recently graduated ensigns—approximately 12 percent of the Academy's student body.

Wiley had received orders on May 28, 1915, but he had to wait for the smoke of the inquiry to clear before he could comply. His orders detached him from the Naval Academy and directed him to proceed, in a series of stops, to report to San Diego, California, and report to the Senior Officer Present Afloat (SOPA) for duty on board the armored cruiser USS *Colorado* (ACR 7). Wiley's orders were modified on July 12 to report instead to the commandant of the Naval Training Station, San Francisco, California, on September 5.[27] He was to travel to the West Coast on the USS *Wisconsin* (BB 9), standing engineering watch with responsibility for helping to ensure that all ran well in the ship's engineering department.

On July 7, with the court of inquiry adjourned to consider its findings and make judgment in a most difficult and highly publicized case, the summer cruise finally got under way. The *Wisconsin* went ahead as fleet scout. The squadron set a course for Guantanamo, Cuba, arriving July 12.[28] After taking on coal, it departed for Colon, on the Atlantic coast of Panama, "with a plentiful supply of cigars." The ships arrived off the Toro Lighthouse at 1600 on July 15, and the flagship was boarded by a canal pilot.[29] Without delay, the three ships went into Gatun Lake, an artificial body of water that was a major part of the Panama Canal, and anchored for the night "to rest the Engineer's Force, which is quite shorthanded for a cruise of this character in such warm weather."[30]

This was the first time in history that American warships had passed through the Panama Canal, and accordingly the Secretary of the Navy received frequent progress reports. The *Missouri* got under way at 1000 on July 16 to pass through the canal, arriving at the Pacific entrance sea buoy at 1900 the same day. From Gatun Lake to the Pacific the locks were "double-barreled," meaning that the

Ohio and *Missouri* locked through together. Fullam, in command reported to the secretary that he believed the entire battleship fleet could pass easily through the canal in one day. Fullam made the exuberant observation, "All necessary arrangements for the expeditious passage of the squadron had previously been made by the Marine superintendent, Capt. Hugh Rodman, U.S. Navy, and I have never witnessed anything more impressive than the quiet cooperation, skill, and efficiency of the personnel, and the perfect functioning of the materiel of this truly wonderful monument to the greatness of our country."[31]

The officers and crews of the three battleships did not traverse the canal alone. As the ships approached Colon, Fullam sent a message inviting Maj. Gen. George W. Goethals (the chief engineer of the project and now civil governor of the Canal Zone), Captain Rodman, and other officials on board the *Missouri* to experience the transit. As a result, about 150 people boarded the ship in Gatun Lake on the morning of the sixteenth, later disembarking at the Pedro Miguel Locks.[32] As the ships passed through the canal they flew flags at their mastheads and fired a twenty-one-gun salute at noon. The guests were served a luncheon, and William Jennings Price (the American minister) and Brig. Gen. Clarence R. Edwards (commanding the Panama Canal Department) were saluted with fifteen and eleven guns, respectively, as they left the ship. The ships then passed through the Pedro Miguel Locks and the Miraflores Locks into the Pacific Ocean, where they set a course for San Diego.

After two days at San Diego, where Wiley was detached and enjoyed nearly a month's leave, the squadron continued to San Francisco, arriving on August 1. That day Fullam sent his annual report as superintendent to the Bureau of Navigation. In this document he revived in part his objections to the West Coast cruise. While he deemed the cruise good in many respects, he felt it had not been in the best interests of the midshipmen to spend so many days in the tropics during the two months under way. He felt that the 10,500-mile cruise in the extremely hot boiler and engine rooms had placed a strain on the engineer's force that had necessitated the assignment of midshipmen to assist them. Finally, Fullam felt it important that the engineer's force be manned sufficiently to allow four-watch rotation during long passages at sea.[33]

The ships of the summer practice cruise of 1915 returned to Annapolis on September 9. The court of inquiry had concluded its proceedings on July 24, and while life would go on as usual for most of the midshipmen, Rear Admiral Fullam had to face the judgments of the court of inquiry and the Secretary of the Navy. From the evidence heard, Judge Advocate Watts concluded, the seven midshipmen originally charged with cheating were guilty. He insisted these men had seen one or more of the examination copies and recognized what they were. Five other midshipmen were also found guilty, for the same reason, and five more were deemed culpable on other grounds. One additional midshipman had been coerced into taking part in the scheme. Some midshipmen who had claimed not to have known what the papers represented beforehand must have known, the judge insisted, when they saw the actual examination. These men he found guilty of fraud for failing to report the situation and for submitting their own papers after realizing they had seen advanced copies.

The extent of this Naval Academy cheating scandal was appalling. A hundred eighteen members of the First Class (63.4 percent), Wiley among them, and 159 of the Second Class (80 percent) had received some form of advance test information.[34] The findings were submitted to Secretary of the Navy Daniels. The investigations had been detailed and exhaustive, and the findings filled several thousand pages. On August 13, 1915, the Judge Advocate General of the Navy, Rear Adm. Ridley McLean, conveyed copies of the records to the Bureau of Navigation. His covering memorandum gave a brief description of the proceedings: "The court met on Monday, June 7, 1915, and was in almost daily session, Sundays and holidays excepted, until July 24, 1915, and the record, consisting of approximately 4,300 pages, exclusive of appendices, was received in the Navy Department on July 26, 1915."[35]

Initially, Superintendent Fullam had recommended the outright dismissal of the seven midshipmen who, it had been charged, had seen mimeographed copies of the examination and realized what they were before actually taking it. This recommendation created an outrage at the Academy and within political circles. (Further, Fullam claimed that a number of congressmen had attempted to influence him to change his recommendations relating to midshipmen from their respective home states.) It was this reaction to Fullam's recommendations that had resulted in the court of inquiry.

In the end, on the recommendation of Secretary Daniels, two midshipmen were dismissed from the Academy; President Woodrow Wilson signed their dismissal orders. Another dozen midshipmen were disciplined: one was turned back to the previous class (extending his time at the Academy by a year); one was moved to the bottom of his class; the commissions of some were delayed by three months, during which they were restricted to the limits of the ships or stations where they were serving; and various midshipmen received from fifty to seventy-five demerits. The court of inquiry did not sustain Fullam's recommendation for dismissal of seven midshipmen.[36] In its summary of findings and recommendations, however, the court focused on systemic flaws at the Academy. It recommended tightening security around the production and storage of examination papers and ending the practice whereby faculty distributed "dope" sheets, "crib" sheets, or old examination papers to midshipmen.

On September 1, 1915, Secretary Daniels directed Acting Secretary of the Navy Franklin D. Roosevelt to order Fullam to command of the Pacific Reserve Fleet. It was understood he was being relieved of his office of superintendent because of the cheating scandal and the manner in which he had handled it.[37] On September 8, Secretary Daniels issued orders that detached nearly every department head at the Academy who had served there for two years or more. Fullam assumed his new duties on September 20.

Fullam's brief tenure at the Naval Academy had been a difficult time for him. He had objected strongly to the summer cruise of 1915, and his word as superintendent should have alone settled the matter. Fullam, however, had chosen to elicit letters of support from two subordinates—bespeaking a lack of confidence that his own argument would be valued and exposing the two subordinates to potential displeasure from the Secretary of the Navy that he should have borne himself. Rebuffed, he must have felt some diminution in his stature in the eyes of his superiors. The infamous cheating scandal of 1915 did occur "on his watch"; also, he exercised poor judgment in his early handling of the investigation and his recommendations. Now he was rebuffed by his entire administration. Having lost the confidence of his administration and faculty, as well as the Secretary of the Navy, Fullam had little choice but accept orders away from the Academy. In spite of the unpleasantness endured at the Academy, however, Fullam's career was far from over. He was to serve with distinction during the coming world war and be awarded the Navy Cross.

Wiley was not found guilty in the cheating incident and received no disciplinary action.

2

The Road to Lakehurst

Wiley reported on board the USS *Colorado*, where on September 3, 1915, he was administered the oath of office as an ensign by the ship's captain. His stay with the *Colorado* was brief. He was reassigned to the USS *San Diego* (ACR 6), which had suffered a boiler explosion that sent her to Mare Island Naval Ship Yard for repairs. Wiley was one of several young officers diverted from previous assignments to assist with her refitting.

Wiley was acquiring a sense of adventure that married well with his love of technology. These attributes surfaced at a fortuitous time in the history of the Navy, entering as it was a phase of rapid technologic development. Among these innovations was the torpedo. In 1916 Wiley twice requested transfer to the training ship USS *Montana* (ACR 13) to receive instruction in torpedoes to make him fit for service in submarines, another emerging technology;[1] separate requests for leave to visit his father accompanied them. Instead, after ten months on the *San Diego* he received orders to the light cruiser USS *Denver* (CL 6). Between 1913 and 1917, she operated frequently off the Mexican coast during this time of insurrection there and for this Wiley was later awarded the Mexican Service Medal.

The United States declared war on Germany on April 4, 1917, citing Germany's violation of its pledge to cease unrestricted submarine warfare in the North Atlantic and Mediterranean, as well as Germany's attempts to draw Mexico into an alliance against the United States. By then, the *Denver* was back in Atlantic waters. On April 24, Wiley received his desired transfer to the *Montana*.[2] Because of the war, however, no mention was made of a leave of absence.

In July, as he was completing his training in torpedoes, Wiley requested duty on a destroyer or, "if there is no vacancy on a destroyer, I request any duty that will take me to European waters."[3] Instead, he was ordered to report to the commandant of the Second Naval District for shore duty in connection with the training of the Naval Reserve Force.[4] Disappointed with this assignment, Wiley submitted another request, this time for the destroyer USS *Gwin*, in connection with her fitting-out and to be on board when she was commissioned.[5] The commandant held him to his previous orders, stressing that Wiley's "services are urgently needed for the duties indicated in his orders."[6]

On July 1, 1917, he received temporary promotion to lieutenant (junior grade), and five weeks later he was informed of his promotion to full lieutenant (temporary). As a brief respite from his shore duty, he was ordered to Rockland, Maine, on September 6 to assist with trials of the destroyer USS *Manley*. (After a number of delays, and after Wiley had moved on to other short-term assignments, she was commissioned on October 15, 1917).

Had Wiley's request for duty in European waters been granted, it would have carried the promise of naval combat, which could have helped advance his career. That would all have to wait, as the war was to come to an end soon.

Wiley's request for transfer to the *Montana* was the result of a genuine interest in torpedo training, but the East Coast had an added appeal—Marie Francis Scroggie, who lived in New London, Connecticut. Wiley had met Marie at one of the socials the Naval Academy periodically hosted. In the early twentieth century women came from as far as Boston for these socials, many hoping to meet "special someones" who might eventually become desirable husbands. Marie, one of three girls born to William James Scroggie and Maria Healy, was a highly social, playful, outgoing young lady. Among family and friends she was regarded as pretty, and she had frequent dates. The Scroggie family had a sizeable inheritance that allowed all three girls to further their educations beyond high school.

Herbert and Marie developed a romance that led to marriage on October 20, 1917. The wedding was held at the Scroggies' home in New London, with Marie's family and friends present. None of the Wiley family was able to make the trek from Missouri, but they placed a wedding announcement in the Chillicothe newspaper, and Herbert's father sent the couple a liberty bond as a wedding gift.

The newlyweds honeymooned in New York and, with an elegance and refinement that befit the times, Marie introduced herself to her new father-in-law in a letter written from their room in the Vanderbilt Hotel. She expressed regret that the Wiley family had been unable to attend what she called the simple wedding. She described the dresses her sisters wore and details of the flowers. She told of cutting the wedding cake with a sword and how it made her feel tall, though she only came up to Herbert's shoulder. She included a photograph so the Wileys could know what she looked like. She assured Herbert's father that she loved his son very much and intended to make him the happiest man in the universe.[7]

Letters between father and son from this time reveal strong bonds of love and respect. Joel thanked Herbert for his generous support of Fay and him by sending home part of his Navy salary. Wiley responded with great kindness and dignity that he did not deserve his kind words, because he would always be indebted to him and his mother for their sacrifices. He assured his father he would do all he could to repay them.[8] While pursuing his Navy career, he was fulfilling his desire to provide comfort and financial stability for his family. Having achieved that aim, he did not accept credit or praise for it but chose instead to elevate his father's self-esteem.

While Wiley was enjoying leave for his wedding and honeymoon, someone at the Bureau of Navigation noted there was an officer fully trained in torpedoes who had been assigned to shore duty training reservists. Consequently, on October 26, 1917, the bureau sent a letter to the commandant of the Second Naval District informing him Wiley would be detached, necessarily without relief, about December 1.[9] Slow to respond, the commandant wrote to the bureau on December 31, stating he would release Wiley for duty. The new duty station was to be the USS *Gwin*—a request Wiley had made the previous July.

However, his new orders were slow to arrive, and still ashore as 1918 arrived, Wiley requested to serve as engineering officer on one of the new destroyers, preferably based on the Pacific coast or near Boston.[10] If he was to be assigned to the West Coast, he asked for a delay of ten days to visit his home in Missouri, explaining that he had no opportunity to visit his family in more than three years.

Within days he received orders over the signature of Secretary of the Navy Josephus Daniels to consider himself detached from the Second Naval District on February 1, 1918, and to proceed to Bath, Maine, to report to the naval inspector of machinery at the Bath Iron Works for duty in connection with the fitting-out of the destroyer USS *Wickes* and on board that vessel when commissioned. He was to report also to the naval inspector for additional duty as his assistant.[11] He got his wish to serve on a destroyer but no leave of absence.

Wiley joined the *Wickes* with the rank of lieutenant, having taken his oath of office on January 11, 1918. The USS *Wickes* (DD 75) was the lead ship in her class. Between 1917 and 1919, 111 *Wickes*-class destroyers were built, designated DD 75 through DD 185. Advances in submarine warfare had created the need for high-speed antisubmarine ships of sufficiently simple design to allow mass production, and this class, capable of thirty-five knots, filled those needs. The *Wickes*-class destroyers, along with 156 of the *Clemson* class and the 6 *Caldwells*, were known collectively as "flush-deckers" or "four-stackers." Very few were to be completed in time for service in the world war. The *Wickes* was 314 feet, 4½ inches long, had a beam of 30 feet, 11¼ inches, and displaced 1,247 tons. Her main armament included four 4-inch/50-caliber guns and twelve 21-inch torpedo tubes.

Wiley's collateral duty in the Bath Iron Works yard interfered with his work on the *Wickes* until he was rescued by the ship's commanding officer. In a strongly worded letter to the Navy Department's Office of the Inspector of Machinery on June 11 he asked that Wiley be ordered immediately to the receiving ship (a commissioned but stationary vessel used for personnel and logistical functions) at Boston, where the *Wickes*' crew and stores were being assembled. He explained the duties being carried out by Wiley in Bath could be done easily by a number of other individuals.[12] The request was granted in short order.

After her commissioning on July 31, the *Wickes* made a brief shakedown cruise before departing for New York by way of Boston. She arrived at New York on August 8 and set out the same day for the British Isles, escorting a convoy of a dozen merchant ships. Her Atlantic crossing was without incident. On arrival, she was detached from the convoy to make a stop at Queenstown, Ireland, on August 19 before sailing to the Azores to take on passengers and mail to be returned to New York. After further escort duty off the northeast coast of the United States, she departed New York on October 7 for Halifax, Nova Scotia. En route, the crew was afflicted with influenza. When the ship made port, thirty men, including her commanding officer, were hospitalized ashore.

These men were victims of the influenza pandemic of 1918. The first phase of the pandemic occurred in the United States in late spring of 1918, manifesting itself as a three-day fever with a very rapid onset. There were few deaths during this time; people tended to recover spontaneously after a few days. When the second phase of the pandemic arrived in the fall of 1918, the clinical course became much more severe, some victims dying a few days after the onset of symptoms, others within hours. There was no specific treatment for this viral disease. With supportive care, people either died or survived. Young adults—such as the crew of the *Wickes*—constituted one of the hardest-hit subsets in the population, along with the elderly and young children.[13] Ships at sea, especially crowded troop carriers, became deadly incubators for the virus.[14]

After her crew recovered, the *Wickes* returned to New York and, on October 23, put to sea as escort for a convoy of merchant ships. At 2104 an unidentified ship appeared off the port bow on a collision course. The *Wickes* went immediately to general quarters, turned on all her lights to make herself more visible in the dark, and took evasive action; but none of these measures saved her from collision. The collision happened quickly, within minutes of the initial sighting of the unidentified ship, which struck the *Wickes'* port side, cut through the keel and caused extensive damage forward. The offending ship did not stop or in any way try to ascertain whether she could be of assistance. Fortunately for the *Wickes*, none of her crew was injured and the water pouring into her hull was contained; she made it back to New York Navy Yard in the early morning of October 24. She was still in the Navy Yard undergoing repairs when the armistice ending the war was signed on November 11, 1918.

The *Wickes* was ready again for sea by early December, when she served as one of ten screening destroyers for President Woodrow Wilson's voyage to Europe on board the transport SS *George Washington*. The ships set sail from New York on December 4 bound for Brest, France. The previous day, the Navy Department had forwarded to Wiley a telegram from his wife stating simply, "Brother seriously ill influenza will keep you informed."[15] Another telegram followed four days later with the terse message, "Brother Died Friday."[16] While the *Wickes* continued on her course into the Atlantic, the remains of Wiley's brother, Floyd, were transported from San Diego to Wheeling, Missouri, to be interred alongside his mother and sister.

Wiley and the *Wickes* remained at Brest until just before Christmas, when the ship left for England, Scotland, and Copenhagen, Denmark. From Copenhagen the *Wickes* went to the Baltic, where they visited all German ports in search of American prisoners of war. Spending several days in Danzig gave Wiley an appreciation of the conditions in wartime Germany.[17] The weather was good, but the *Wickes* had a number of narrow escapes from mines drifting in the water—hazardous remnants of the war.

The ship returned on January 11 to the Firth of Forth in Scotland, where she received orders for Hamburg, Germany. Before departing, the crew received mail, cigarettes, books, and newspapers delivered by the Red Cross. The *Wickes* had received mail only once in two months, but this time Wiley received a copy of the *Chillicothe Constitution*. He wrote home to Fay that, because he had been away from home for several years, he recognized few names but that he had enjoyed the hometown paper. He told Fay the lack of mail and entertainment had made Edinburgh monotonous. He had enjoyed a short stay in Copenhagen but found prices there higher than anywhere else he had visited. He reported that, in Germany, women and children suffered the most from a lack food. The people there lacked fats, and he and the men of the *Wickes* traded soap for war memorabilia, such as Iron Crosses, guns, helmets, and bayonets.

The *Wickes'* shipboard influenza epidemic and hit-and-run collision did not end her bad luck. On March 3, 1919, while moored in Hamburg, she collided with the German merchant ship *Ljusne Elf*.[18] Following repairs in Hamburg, she sailed to Brest to join the SS *George Washington* as an escort once again for President Wilson's return to the United States in June. In early July the *Wickes* set sail for the West Coast as part of the buildup of naval assets in the Pacific.

In mid-December Wiley received new orders. The *Wickes* was to be placed in reserve, at which point Wiley was to be detached to report again to a naval inspector of machinery, this time at the Bethlehem Shipbuilding Corporation, San Francisco, California, to help fit out the *Clemson*-class destroyer USS *Fuller* (DD 297) and then to become her executive officer.[19] Wiley assumed his duties as executive officer on February 28, 1920, the day the ship was commissioned. After a short cruise to the Hawaiian Islands, the *Fuller* arrived at San Diego on April 28. She and a group of destroyers then conducted training exercises along the West Coast between California and Oregon. In the crowded San Diego Destroyer Base there was little to distinguish the *Fuller* from the dozens of other ships.

On May 25, 1920, Wiley submitted another request for change of duty— this time for transfer to New London, Connecticut, to attend submarine school. The submarine had begun to emerge as a powerful weapon in the world war and further advances in this technology were on the horizon. Wiley's training in torpedoes and his experience with destroyers made a natural foundation for the submarine service. A private motive behind his request was the news that his wife was pregnant. Marie's aunt and sisters lived in New London, and if Wiley could arrange a transfer there, she would have a strong emotional and practical support base once her child was born. Wiley's request for submarine training made its way through proper channels, but only slowly, owing to a lack of enthusiastic support from his superiors. The reason had nothing to do with Wiley personally or with his performance; the fact was that there were no replacements for him in the burgeoning destroyer fleet.[20] The portal to New London closed when he received word from the Bureau of Navigation on June 15 that "Officers for Submarine Class beginning 1 July 1920 have been selected. Your request has been placed on file and will receive consideration in future assignments."[21]

In the end, Wiley never revisited this request but traveled a different path that did far more to advance his career. In the meantime, he remained with the destroyer fleet, but in September he received orders to report to Mare Island, California, to the president of a board of medical examiners and then to the president of a naval examining board for consideration for promotion to the permanent rank of lieutenant.[22] He succeeded in both levels of examination and in early October received his appointment as full lieutenant, retroactive to July 1.

During that summer, in their small home in Coronado, California, the Wileys prepared for the birth of their first child. Wiley was granted thirty days' leave. Gordon Scroggie Wiley was born on October 13, 1920.

Five days before Gordon's birth, Wiley received orders to the USS *Dent* (DD 116), a *Wickes*-class destroyer of the Pacific Fleet based at San Diego.[23] About six weeks after reporting on board the *Dent* he was given command of the USS *Radford* (DD 120).[24] Wiley thus received his first command at the age of only twenty-nine, but he was perfectly comfortable with the *Radford*, a destroyer of the *Wickes* class, with which he was familiar. His ship had a complement of 142 officers and men and was based in San Diego with numerous other destroyers.

Wiley commanded the *Radford* for nine months, gaining valuable leadership experience before he received new orders to the USS *Great Northern* for transportation from San Diego through the Panama Canal to Annapolis, Maryland, there to report to the superintendent of the U.S. Naval Academy "for such duty as may be assigned you."[25] Wiley received his orders on September 5, 1921, giving him short notice to get to the Academy in time for the academic year scheduled to begin on October 1.

Wiley was never as pleased with shore duty as he was at sea, but he and Marie were happy to be nearer to her sisters and aunt in New England. Wiley's days as a midshipman were not so far behind him that he had forgotten what they were like, but now he returned to his alma mater as faculty, an instructor of engineering and physics. Wiley befriended a fellow instructor, Lt. Cdr. Charles E. Rosendahl, Naval Academy class of 1914. They would be colleagues for more than a decade in a very exciting era of Navy history and would become lifelong friends.

The world war ended without Wiley's having a chance to contribute in a major way, and as he made his way back to the Academy he may have wondered where his Navy career would take him next. Wiley had so far played a minor role in history, serving on one of the first Navy warships to traverse the Panama Canal. However, in the next phase of his career, he would serve with a small group of men who would have a much greater impact. He expected eventually to be reassigned to the fleet, but an unusual opportunity presented itself and he grabbed it. In his lifetime, Wiley witnessed the birth of manned flight. Wartime demands often drive technological developments, and aviation made significant advances during the world war, and all the while the U.S. Navy had been observing.

Once humankind found ways to get airborne, advances in flight came in quick succession. On July 2, 1900—the year the Wright Brothers were experimenting with their glider at Kitty Hawk, North Carolina—the first zeppelin (*LZ 1*) made its maiden voyage in Germany. Named for its inventor, Count Ferdinand Adolph Heinrich Zeppelin, it was a lighter-than-air (LTA) craft made buoyant by hydrogen gas.[26] Although the flight lasted only eighteen minutes, cut short by technical problems, it established the feasibility of "rigid" LTA flight. Three years later, the Wright Brothers made their heavier-than-air (HTA) flight. Less impressive in duration than the flight of the zeppelin, the first manned, powered, controlled flight in an HTA craft lasted only twelve seconds. However, as had the zeppelin for LTA, it demonstrated the potential of HTA flight. Following these two seminal events in manned flight, both modes of flight made rapid advances. Businessmen realized the potential of manned flight for transporting people and cargo, and military thinkers saw aircraft as "platforms" for weapons and potentially long-range reconnaissance.

Germany was the undisputed leader in LTA flight. This mode of flight could be achieved with a variety of craft. One, the *dirigible*, is an LTA craft that is powered and can be steered, whereas another, the *balloon*, is merely a free-floating device that cannot be steered. There are three general types of dirigibles. The *blimp* is a pressure airship that is powered and steerable; the pressure of the gas in the envelope determines a blimp's shape. A *rigid airship* has a framework that surrounds one or more gas cells, and it is the framework, with an outer fabric covering, that gives this ship its shape. A *semirigid airship* has a partial rigid frame that provides structural integrity while maneuvering, but it is the lifting gas in the envelope that maintains its shape.

The term *zeppelin* became synonymous with "rigid airship," but not all rigid airships were zeppelins. In the early 1900s there were two main manufacturers of German rigid airships: Luftschiffbau Zeppelin (the Zeppelin Airship Company) and Luftschiffbau Schutte-Lanz. Only airships produced by Luftschiffbau Zeppelin could properly be called "zeppelins."[27] Each airship was given its manufacturer's designation—*LZ* for Luftschiffbau Zeppelin, *SL* for Schutte-Lanz—followed by a number that indicated its order of production. The zeppelin airship *LZ 2* made its first flight in 1906.[28]

In the early 1900s, England, aware of Germany's advances in airship technology, regarded that nation as a potential aggressor. In 1908 the British Committee of Imperial Defence established a subcommittee to evaluate advances in aviation as they might affect England. Following its fact finding and deliberation, the committee was less impressed with the promise of fixed-wing (HTA) craft than with that of dirigibles. The committee was convinced that future warfare would involve the use of airpower and that the German zeppelins posed a real threat in that regard. To counter it the committee decided to attempt to match the number and size of the German airships and recommended the government allocate the funds.[29]

Two pivotal events occurred in Germany in 1909: first, the zeppelin *LZ 3* was delivered to the German army for use and development;[30] second, the first commercial air service was established, using zeppelin airships.[31] Militaries, sensing a European war drawing closer, were developing more combat-related applications of flight. By mid-1910 French pilots had demonstrated that air photoreconnaissance was practicable.[32] Only months later, the U.S. Army was conducting trials that involved firing guns from an airplane.[33]

One of the great limitations of HTA craft (i.e., airplanes) was their relatively short range, determined by the amount of fuel they could carry. Lacking the buoyant lift of airships, they had to keep air flowing over their wings to remain aloft. To maximize their usefulness for reconnaissance or combat, ways had to be found to extend their range and flying time. One concept was to carry airplanes out to sea on board ships that could launch and recover them, thus extending their effective range. On November 14, 1910, Eugene B. Ely flew his Curtiss

Model D "pusher" off the deck of the light cruiser USS *Birmingham* (CL 2) near Hampton Roads, Virginia. This airplane had a maximum speed of forty-three knots (fifty miles per hour) and a flying time of approximately two and a half hours, but Ely proved that its range could be extended if carried by and launched from a seagoing ship. On January 18, 1911, Ely closed the conceptual loop by demonstrating he could land his airplane on the deck of a ship. He did so on a specially made platform installed on the after deck of the armored cruiser USS *Pennsylvania* (ACR 4) anchored in San Francisco Bay. Some historians have hailed these flights by Ely as the birth of naval aviation.

Meanwhile, advancing the commercial use of dirigibles, the civilian zeppelin *LZ 13*[34] was renamed Hansa for use by the world's first international passenger service, flying between Hamburg, Copenhagen, and Malmo, Sweden.[35] The stimulus for Britain's airship program seems to have been primarily the rapidly developing German zeppelin technology. Despite the Committee of Imperial Defence's intention to engage in an airship race of sorts, the British program got off to a sluggish start and chronically trailed in development. Periodically Britain would sense a heightened threat from the Germans and attempt to infuse new urgency into its dirigible program. Britain was building its own airships but to catch up both in technology and numbers of airships it tried to purchase them from other countries that were ahead. The British purchased an Astra-Torres airship from France and a Parseval from Germany.[36]

The day following the outbreak of the world war, Britain used its Parseval to conduct nighttime patrol along the Thames River and over the North Sea scouting for approaching German warships.[37] Deeper into the war, Britain pursued airship development with greater vigor and used the craft to patrol the English Channel and coastline and, vitally, to scout for German submarines.

It was events unfolding in Europe even before the United States entered the world war that would ultimately be responsible for launching Wiley on the next phase of his Navy career. From the outset Germany made zeppelins available to both its army and navy, which explored the possibilities of the airship as an offensive weapon. After three zeppelins were destroyed during a daytime bombing mission against French targets, the Germans concluded that daylight was not the best time to use airships in attack.[38] On the night of January 31–February 1, 1916, the *LZ 55* (given the tactical designation LZ 85 by the military) made a bombing raid on the harbor at Salonika, Greece. On this occasion, the darkness provided cover that resulted in surprise and some measure of success.[39]

With increasing experience, Germany began to see even greater potential for zeppelins in attack. In a land war, the only ways to get past an enemy force to attack the enemy homeland were to defeat it or outflank it. The zeppelins, however, could fly over the enemy on the ground, bypassing him, to attack from the air. The Germans conducted their first strategic air attack on the night of January 19–20, 1915. The zeppelins *L 3* and *L 4* flew over the battlefields of northern France to penetrate the skies above England. The British were not expecting nocturnal air attacks, and consequently there were many lights burning in populated areas, including London, that later became targets. In this bombing raid four people were killed and sixteen wounded.[40] The kaiser came under considerable pressure to allow the bombing of London specifically, and in May he gave his approval, with a number of restrictions. On the evening of May 31, the *LZ 38* lifted off from its base in Evere, Belgium, for London. The first bomb dropped on London was an incendiary that struck a house at 16 Alkham Road, in the Stoke Newington area of the city.[41] None of its occupants were harmed, and the resulting fire was extinguished promptly. The overall result of the raid, however, was seven people killed and thirty injured.[42]

The vulnerability of airships on the ground was demonstrated in April 1915, when Capt. L. G. Hawker of the Royal Flying Corps carried out a bold raid in his B.E. 2c—a British single-engine, two-seat biplane—in which he destroyed the *LZ 38*, along with the shed in which it was housed.[43] The first airship to be destroyed while in the air by an aircraft in flight was the *LZ 37*. On the night of June 6, 1915, Lt. R. A. J. Warneford of the Royal Navy Air Service was on the way to Evere to bomb the zeppelin sheds there when he encountered the *LZ 37*. Flying above the airship, he dropped his bombs onto it, igniting the highly flammable hydrogen gas and so bringing about her destruction.[44] The flaming mass fell on a convent, killing all but one of her crew members.[45]

The heaviest air raid directed at Britain during the world war occurred on the night of September 7, 1915. On this occasion, the zeppelins approached London in a staggered fashion. The first airship alerted the ground defenses to the threat, and subsequent airships reaching the city were each illuminated, at least in part, by searchlights from below. Antiaircraft fire, however, was minimally effective.[46]

Although over thirty missions were flown against Britain in 1915, they did little to diminish the morale of the people or to interrupt industrial productivity.[47] In 1916, increasingly eager to defeat the English through aerial bombing, Germany intensified its bombing campaign with a new line of "Super Zeppelins." However, as it did so, the British were developing countermeasures, and their airplanes were getting better at combatting the dirigibles. Between September and November 1916 the Germans lost the "Super Zeppelins" *L 31*, *L 32*, and *L 34* to airplanes. Considering such losses in the context of rapid improvements in airplanes, the Germans began to question the role of zeppelins. Indeed, it was in 1916 that von Zeppelin himself confided to Paul Hindenburg his sentiment that the airship was obsolete already and that the future belonged to the airplane.[48]

Both England and the Luftschiffbau Zeppelin Company survived the war. Count Zeppelin had died in March 1917, but Dr. Hugo Eckener, who had been one of the count's collaborators, managed the company in the postwar years. Both the airplane and the dirigible had been battle-tested during the war, and each had revealed its strengths and weaknesses. Everyone saw great potential for the airplane, but the age of the dirigible was not over yet. There were military and commercial developers who felt that dirigibles had their place and specific roles to play that current advances in airplane technology could not satisfy. Prior to the world war Germany had not sold zeppelins to foreign powers, but in the reparations agreement at the end of the war Germany was required to deliver a number of dirigibles to the victors. The zeppelins *LZ 114*, *LZ 120,* and *LZ 121* were handed over to France and renamed *Dixmude, Bodensee,* and *Nordstern,* respectively, and the United States received *LZ 126* (to be renamed the USS *Los Angeles* [ZR 3]).

The years following the end of the Great War were spent less in perfecting the peace than in preparing for the next war. The United States, with the war in Europe behind it, turned its attention to the east, sensing a war with Japan somewhere over the horizon. During the world war American observers in Europe had taken special notice of the zeppelins and their performance in long-range reconnaissance and bombing and had been favorably impressed. Much had been written elsewhere about the zeppelins' ability to fly over the gridlocked ground forces in the trenches to reach England and drop bombs. For the Americans, however, these feats were less promising than the manner in which zeppelins had been used during the naval battle of Jutland.

The only major naval engagement of the world war, it opened on the afternoon of May 31, 1916, off Denmark's North Sea coast. Earlier that month Adm. Reinhard Scheer, commander of the German fleet, had planned a raid on Sunderland, on the east coast of England, to draw out the British fleet to fight. Scheer's plan gave his zeppelins a key role in the operation. Previous commanders had kept the airships in proximity to the dreadnoughts for close tactical support, but Scheer wanted to use the zeppelins for long-range reconnaissance. This plan received the enthusiastic support of Peter Strasser, commander of the Naval Airship Division, who shared Scheer's belief this was the best use of the airships. The zeppelins provided effective reconnaissance support, as long as the weather was clear, informing the surface fleet where the enemy vessels were and—at times equally importantly—where they were not.

In the years following World War I, the U.S. Navy would be tasked with the difficult responsibility of detecting movements by the Japanese navy that might threaten the West Coast or other U.S. territories. Warfare in the vast Pacific Ocean presented special problems, greater than those encountered in the Atlantic. Reconnaissance of so large an area was impossible with a surface fleet or airplanes. The operational range of airplanes was too short. To some, the dirigibles, with their greater range, offered promise. The interest of the American navy, then, was in how the Germans employed their zeppelins over water. Even while the war raged, Secretary of the Navy Daniels listed what he thought to be the most important uses of airships.

1—A coast or scouting patrol that should be capable of covering a zone along our coast night and day a distance of 750 to 1,000 miles, which would give ample warning of the approach of an enemy fleet or even a single enemy warship within that zone.

2—Similar patrol in all directions from an outlying base, which would serve the same purpose of warning the fleet or the garrison of an advance base in ample time for either to prepare for the approach of the enemy.

3—Operation directly with the fleet as advance scouts with long-range vision, especially in clear weather, and long radius of action, similar to the supposed use of German zeppelins in the battle of Jutland. In the United States this use of zeppelins, of course, would not be so practical as in Germany, France or England, where distances are so much shorter.

4—The zeppelin or zeppelins could be made use of in numerous ways. They could be used at various stations along both coasts, at advance bases in the Caribbean, at the Guantanamo supply base, on the Panama Canal Zone and in the insular possessions. Zeppelins have the advantage of being able to remain aloft once they leave their hangars. They can travel at great speed or go slowly, giving them a distinct advantage over aeroplanes for certain lines of scouting work. They can travel along with the fleet, no matter what its speed.[49]

In 1919, Congress authorized the Navy to establish a base from which it could build and operate rigid airships.[50] Responsibility for developing the program was given to the Navy because it had expressed the highest level of interest. The same year, the Navy approved a rigid-airship program to be based at the Lakehurst Naval Air Station, located in the Pine Barrens of New Jersey.[51] Along with congressional approval for the airship base came an appropriation of $4 million for the acquisition of two dirigibles.[52] One airship was to be purchased from Britain, and the second, with a budget of $1.5 million, was to be built in the United States: the *ZR 1*. The Navy was pursuing a range of goals with this project. The *ZR 1* would demonstrate the military usefulness of a long-range reconnaissance platform as well as the commercial potential of large rigid airships. Some in the Navy's airship community hoped the program would stimulate a new airship industry in the United States.

Meanwhile, pursuing a separate, parallel strategy for extending the range of the airplane, Congress approved funding for the Navy's first aircraft carrier in 1919. This was not new construction but a conversion of the collier USS *Jupiter* (AC 3). Launched in 1912, she was built specifically as a collier, but following the installation of a flight deck in 1920, she was renamed the USS *Langley* (CV 1). As a carrier, her ability to carry, launch, and recover airplanes was critical to extending the effective range of reconnaissance. With time, dirigibles also acquired these capabilities, although carrying fewer airplanes than surface ships.

In 1922 the Navy decided to develop a corps of trained LTA officers to run the lighter-than-air service. On December 21 a request was issued to "All Ships and Stations" for volunteers for training in rigid airships.[53] When this call went out, Wiley was in his second year as an instructor at the Naval Academy. The usual tenure for an instructor at the Academy was three years. Wiley was now thirty-one years old and much preferred to be on sea duty—something with adventure and the potential to further his career. On January 4, 1923, Wiley requested of the Bureau of Navigation "that I be ordered to Lakehurst, N.J., and detailed for training in rigid airships of the ZR 1 type."[54] Of the forty-one volunteers, nine were selected: Cdr. Jacob H. Klein Jr., Lt. Cdr. Maurice R. Pierce, Lt. Cdr. Joseph M. Deem, Lt. Cdr. Lewis Hancock, Lt. J. C. Arnold, Lt. Earle K. Kincaid, Lt. W. O. Bailey, Lt. Charles E. Rosendahl, and Lt. Herbert V. Wiley.[55]

The superintendent of the Academy requested that he be allowed to retain Wiley for his full three-year tour, but instead the Navy provided a replacement. Wiley received orders dated April 5 from the Bureau of Navigation to regard himself as detached from his present duties at the Academy and to report "to the commanding officer of the Naval Air Station, Lakehurst, N.J., for duty in connection with the fitting out of rigid airships."[56] Days later, Frank R. McCrary, Commanding Officer, U.S. Naval Air Station, Lakehurst, reported to the chief of the Bureau of Navigation, "I have this day appointed [Lt. Herbert V. Wiley, USN] a Student Naval Aviator, and detailed him for duty involving actual flying in aircraft, including dirigibles, balloons, and airplanes."[57]

The superintendent's attempt to retain Wiley was not granted. Indeed, a memorandum had gone out from the chief of the Bureau of Aeronautics to the Bureau of Navigation on March 26 that signaled an eagerness on the part of Lakehurst to get its young officers on site for training: "It is urgently recommended that every effort be made to have [Wiley, H. V.], detailed for duty in the rigid airships, report at the Naval Air Station, Lakehurst, at the earliest practicable date."[58] The urgency resulted from the fact that the ground school there had opened on March 15.[59]

This opportunity for Wiley to enter the fledgling LTA service could not have come at a better time. It not only got him out of the classroom and back into more exciting service but relieved him of having to complete the usual three years there—time that he considered would not advance his career. The new Navy LTA program was small, likely providing opportunities for him to distinguish himself—far more easily than he could have as yet another commander of yet another destroyer in a peacetime Navy. It would allow him to stay on the cutting edge of new technologies, and it was a role with ample opportunities for original contributions to the service. Beyond all that, and not to be underestimated, especially with Wiley, was the strong sense of adventure associated with LTA flight. Man's ability to fly was still in its infancy, and any form of flight—from airplanes to dirigibles—had an aura of romance and danger. This was definitely the right stuff for Wiley.

Also not to be underestimated was the value of two practical aspects of this duty. Assignment to Lakehurst Naval Air Station (NAS) kept him on the East Coast, closer to Marie's family, and he would now receive flight pay. Flight pay was not insignificant. At that time, a lieutenant in the Navy received a monthly salary of $250; flight pay gave him an extra $125 per month. Flight pay was a form of hazardous-duty pay. Every flight carried significant risk of injury or death. The boost in income would allow Wiley to be of greater assistance to his family in Missouri.

Wiley reported to NAS Lakehurst on April 11, 1923. He and his friend Rosendahl had both submitted their requests for airship training in January, but Rosendahl managed to arrive four days ahead of Wiley.[60] Their new commander, Frank R. McCrary, was a Navy aviator who had been one of a dozen American officers ordered to France in September 1917 to be trained in LTA flight. They had flown pressure airships purchased from France on patrols over the Bay of Biscay. Further, during the world war the Navy had four seaplane bases in southern Ireland. With his headquarters in Queenstown, Ireland, McCrary had served as commander of U.S. Naval Air Stations in Ireland from February 14, 1918, until the end of the war. Because of his flight and administrative experience, Adm. William A. Moffett, chief of the Bureau of Aeronautics, had selected McCrary to command the *ZR 1*. On the opening day of the ground school McCrary addressed the assembled officers, explaining that they were there to initiate a course of instruction for prospective crews of the *ZR 1*. "We are," he acknowledged, "very much handicapped in this work in that none of the officers concerned have had sufficient experience to qualify as an authority on the subject and it may surprise some of you to find that you have been detailed to give lectures on subjects of which you have little if any previous knowledge."[61]

In a sense, the rigid-airship ground school brought itself to life. Each officer was assigned a block of material to study and so master that, subsequently, he could lecture on it to the entire group. The young officers received advisory assistance from Capt. Anton Heinen, a German LTA aviator with extensive experience handling dirigibles.[62] Heinen was assigned to an advisory rather than teaching role because there was too much material for one instructor to cover.

In addition to the land school, the officers in training were expected to experience flight in several types of lighter-than-air craft. Each man's cumulative flight time was recorded in hours and minutes; for example, Lieutenant Rosendahl made ten "hops" in a kite balloon on one day for a total of one hour and eleven minutes of flight time. Each of these early flights lasted for about five or ten minutes, but subsequent flights were more extended. On May 4, Wiley, Rosendahl, and Earle H. Kincaid shared a flight in a free balloon that lifted off from Lakehurst and landed three hours and twenty-five minutes later in Whitesville, New Jersey.[63] On July 12, 1923, Wiley received orders to take passage on a training flight with Lt. Arthur R. Houghton in a free balloon whose nonrigid buoyant sack contained 35,000 cubic feet of helium.[64] Wiley and Houghton lifted off from Lakehurst the next day at 1137 and landed about four and a quarter hours later in Bordentown, New Jersey, whereupon they took land transportation back to Lakehurst.

All of the ground training and flight time was geared to producing officers who would be capable of flying large rigid airships, but no such aircraft would be available to Lakehurst until completion of the USS *Shenandoah* (ZR 1). Wiley received orders from the Bureau of Aeronautics on October 6, 1923, to report to the commanding officer of the *Shenandoah* for duty once the ship was christened.[65]

3

The USS
Shenandoah (ZR 1)

As construction of the Naval Air Station was getting under way in September 1919, so was the design of the first U.S.-built airship. It was modeled after the German *L 49*, a hydrogen-filled airship captured by the Allies in 1917 after being forced down by severe weather.[1] The Navy established the practice of designating its airships "ZR" followed by a number that indicated its order of production. *Z* indicated "zeppelin-type," and *R* stood for "rigid." *ZR 1* was to be commissioned the USS *Shenandoah* (ZR 1). *ZR 2* was to have been purchased from Britain; designated *R 38* by the British, this airship broke in half and crashed during its final test flight, killing sixteen Americans and twenty-eight British airmen.

Initially, the *ZR 1* was designed to use hydrogen as her lifting gas, but following a number of fatal disasters associated with this flammable gas, the decision was made to use nonflammable helium. The *ZR 1* thus became the first airship to use helium. Helium was much safer, but it had some disadvantages: it was very expensive to produce, it had only about 92 percent of the lifting power of hydrogen, and it was heavier. The difference in weight relative to hydrogen resulted in a significant decrease in the cruising range of the airship.[2] To compensate for these disadvantages, a thirty-foot section was added to the body of the airship to allow it to carry more helium. By August 16, 1923, construction of the *ZR 1* was essentially completed, and her gas cells were filled to about 85 percent capacity—1,783,000 cubic feet of helium.[3] Helium improved safety from the standpoint of flammability, but it did not lessen the structural fragility of airships. On completion, the *ZR 1* was 688 feet long, had a beam of 78 feet, 9 inches, and stood

93 feet, 2 inches tall. Powered by five 300-horsepower, 8-cylinder Packard engines, she could achieve speeds of sixty knots and had a range of approximately five thousand miles. At 95 percent inflation (2,100,000 cubic feet of helium), the ship had a lifting capacity of 53,600 pounds. The ZR 1 was "launched" officially inside the hangar at Lakehurst on August 20, 1923.

In anticipation of the ZR 1's maiden voyage on September 4, approximately 15,000 people converged on NAS Lakehurst to witness the event. Among them were reporters, newsreel cameramen, dignitaries, and interested civilians. Four hundred twenty men were required to walk the airship out of her hangar, clinging tightly to her long handling lines. The first flight of a dirigible inflated by helium lasted approximately fifty-five minutes.[4]

In the afternoon of October 10, the ZR 1 was both christened and commissioned. On that occasion the airship was inside the hangar, secured to its north side with her bow to the west. At 1533 the ship was allowed to rise from her cradles, and a minute later Mrs. Edwin Denby, the wife of the Secretary of the Navy, christened her the USS Shenandoah, after her own beloved home in the Shenandoah Valley. (The accepted translation at the time of this Algonquin word was "beautiful daughter of the skies.") At 1535 with the ship once more secured on her cradles, the commandant of the Fourth Naval District, Rear Adm. Archibald H. Seales, read the commissioning orders. Cdr. Frank R. McCrary then read his orders from the Bureau of Navigation detailing him as the commanding officer of the Shenandoah and immediately assumed command.[5] Cdr. J. H. Klein Jr. reported for duty as the executive officer. At commissioning, the airship's list of officers also included Lt. Cdr. J. M. Deem, Lt. Cdr. J. P. Norfleet, Lt. C. E. Rosendahl, Lt. R. J. Miller, Lt. E. H. Kincaid, Lt. R. F. Tyler, and Lt. (jg) E. W. Sheppard.[6] Following an address by Secretary Denby, the handling lines were manned and the ship was walked out of the hangar for a short flight. With Secretary Denby and other dignitaries on board, the Shenandoah lifted off at 1630 and landed an hour and a quarter later.

A longer flight took place on October 27. At 0400 the crew was mustered to prepare the ship. She was out the hangar at 0650 and airborne at 0705. Although he had not been on board for the Shenandoah's initial flight, Wiley was for this one, as was Capt. Anton Heinen. Thirty-two minutes after liftoff, Shenandoah was over Fort Dix, New Jersey. From there it flew over Mt. Holly, then into Pennsylvania—Philadelphia, Lancaster, York, Hanover, and Gettysburg. It was over Washington, D.C., at 1049 and from there went on to Hagerstown and Winchester, Pennsylvania, before proceeding into Virginia—Harrisonburg, Staunton, Lexington, Lynchburg, and, at 1730, Richmond. Heading back north, *Shenandoah* passed over Fredericksburg, Virginia, the District of Columbia, then to Baltimore, Maryland, and Wilmington, Delaware, and back to Lakehurst, landing at 2245. This single flight lasted fifteen hours and forty-five minutes. The entire flight went without incident but back on the ground, as the logbook recorded, "In walking ship into Hangar number 1 car struck the ground damaging it slightly." Airships were gigantic but fragile.

The following months were filled with regional training flights, airship maintenance and repairs, and training in making the ship fast to the 165-foot-tall steel tower known as the "high mast." Early attempts to moor to the mast failed, but with continued practice, success was achieved on November 16, 1923.[7] The *Shenandoah* was proving herself a worthy training airship, and there was a great deal to be learned about maintaining and flying these complicated ships. Maintenance and repairs were a never-ending part of airship life, and everything done with or to these buoyant behemoths required large numbers of military and civilian workers performing to demanding levels of precision. Maneuvers as simple as removing the ship from its hangar and preparing it for flight required careful attention to detail, and an accurate accounting of lift versus the total weight on board had to be recorded.

Wiley was on duty as a watch officer on January 12, 1924, when, as the logbook detailed, the *Shenandoah* was removed from her hangar to be secured to the high mast. Preparations began at the start of the 1600 watch. At 1645, once the ship was ready inside the hangar, quarters for muster were held. An hour later the ship was walked out to the east field by the ground crew, which both secured and guided her with handling ropes. On this day the walk-out was achieved smoothly, but on days with high winds, moving the dirigible into and out of the hangar was difficult and fraught with risk of injury to personnel and damage to the ship. At 1754 the ship was stopped on the field as the ground crew prepared to take her to the mast. At 1804 the ship started to move, under the direction of the "shore pilot" and in full control of the ground crew. At 1815 the order was given "Up ship," and, in flight, she was walked by drag ropes toward the mast. At 1825 to lighten the airship, 775 pounds of water were released from frame 40, 550 pounds were released from frame 170, and the starboard emergency water ballast of 540 pounds was released at frame 30. At 1845 the *Shenandoah* was still on the field in the hands of the crew; at 1849 the mooring cable was connected. From 1908 to 1926, engines Nos. 2 and 3 idled; both were stopped, and at 1930 the ship was secured to the mast.

Every occasion on which the *Shenandoah* was handled—whether in the hangar, on the ground, anchored to the high mast, or in flight—was a learning encounter. With increased experience handling the ship came bolder designs for her future. President Calvin Coolidge had approved a plan to fly the *Shenandoah* over the Arctic.[8] Airplanes, with their limited flying range, could not do this, but there was a general confidence within the Bureau of Aeronautics that the *Shenandoah*, with her far greater range, could. Ostensibly for scientific purposes and the mapping of the polar region from the air, the expedition would also feed Admiral Moffett's insatiable appetite for publicity.[9]

Moffett's aspirations for the airship were vast and his confidence unwavering. Indeed, two years before the launch of the *Shenandoah* he had issued an eighteen-page "Exclusive Release to the U.S. Air Service" titled, *Airships and the Scientist*. With eloquent enthusiasm he opened, "The romance of the air is fast replacing the romance of the seas, so fast, in fact, that we scarcely think of the romance of the sea at all, our minds being constantly stimulated and thrilled by aerial exploits as some particularly daring and spectacular deed links up distant and little-known parts of the earth with the beaten tracks of men and ships. . . . Nevertheless, romance is still with us although science has dulled the keen edge of its mystery."[10]

He extolled the audacity and dedication of Arctic explorers who had gone before in efforts to reach the North Pole and survey the vast areas of the Arctic, only to be met with hardship, disaster, and death: "The Geography, as we know it to-day, and the Mariner's Chart, with its navigational data, have been built up, little by little, through the ages, at a tremendous cost of life and treasure with attendant difficulties so enormous that their recital stirs our sympathy as well as our admiration and respect for the iron-hearted voyagers who dared the elements for our welfare."[11]

Moffett reminded readers that human suffering was an inescapable factor "in all undertakings that carried men beyond the reach of civilization in the frozen zones." He was convinced, however, that the airship would solve all problems of polar expeditions, as well as of the exploration of other parts of the world. He believed explorers in airships—as opposed to walking on the frozen surface— would carry out their missions with safety and comfort: "A few seasons of aerial surveying and photographic mapping will yield more information than the combined efforts and sacrifices of all the polar explorers who have heretofore suffered and labored for the advancement of geographical knowledge."[12]

Moffett described in detail the advantages of an airship over airplanes, everything from greater range of flight to ability to hover over a region of interest. The comfort and safety of the dirigible was stressed repeatedly. That emphasis on safety may have been overstated. At the time of his press release, it was not known how the dirigible would perform under the extremes of Arctic and Antarctic conditions. Still, Moffett was a firm believer.

An Arctic expedition required a great deal of preparation, especially with regard to flight planning, logistics, and support. Secretary Denby had appointed Moffett to chair a study group to examine feasibility. The plan its members set forth was aggressive. The *Shenandoah* would depart NAS Lakehurst and, flying a southern route across the United States, would make San Diego and then turn north, flying along the West Coast to Alaska. From Alaska she would fly over the North Pole and, as Denby explained to Congress, photograph a million-square-mile area of great scientific interest.[13] The *Shenandoah* would then make the return trip to Alaska or take an alternate route to an island in the North Sea. As with many great adventures, logistical support was as complicated and expensive as the feat itself. Aside from the plan's complexity, there were some who expressed concern about the ability of the *Shenandoah* to withstand the strong wind forces to be encountered over the Arctic. Among these skeptics was the *Shenandoah's* commanding officer, Frank McCrary.

Congress was already concerned about the costs of the expedition. The House Appropriations Committee met on January 12, 1924, to consider the matter in detail. Only four days later, on January 16, an incident occurred that could have ended in disaster. It arose from the fact that if the Arctic expedition took place, the *Shenandoah* would not have bases like NAS Lakehurst. She would have to moor to masts, which would have to be provided, at strategic locations. In preparation for this, McCrary decided to conduct trials at Lakehurst to test the stresses to the airship of being moored to a mast. The plan was to leave the *Shenandoah* moored to her high mast for ten days, with a small crew on board to conduct tests.[14] As early as January 14, weather advisories warned of strong gales for the sixteenth and seventeenth. Gale-force winds were what McCrary needed for these tests, as they would closely match Arctic conditions.

On January 16 Wiley left the *Shenandoah* after standing the 0800–1200 watch.[15] Commander Klein had the deck during the 1200–1600 watch, and Commander McCrary came on board at 1410. At 1435 a moderate rain started to fall; by 1500 the airship was experiencing a constant rolling motion. The weather intensified rapidly, and at about 1600, with the ship still moored to the mast, the log recorded "stormy, gusty, rainy weather" with gusts up to sixty-three miles per hour. Nevertheless, Commander McCrary left the ship at 1615, and at 1800 Lieutenant Kincaid had the watch, with Captain Heinen also on board.[16] The rain continued steadily, and the wind gusted to fifty-six knots; at 1844 the mooring point to the mast broke away, taking with it the nose-plate to which it was attached, and the ship went adrift.

The United Press was to weave from firsthand accounts the tale of the nine dramatic hours that followed. The *News-Herald* of Franklin, Pennsylvania, ran the story under the headline, "*Shenandoah* Safe after Battle with Big Gale: Outrides 70-Mile-an-Hour Wind in Flight of 9 Hours."[17] A separate story on that paper's front page reported that the southeast gale had been the worst January storm in the fifty-two-year history of the New York Weather Bureau.[18] As the airship's struggle started the nose, torn off completely, flapped from the masthead at the end of the mooring chain. The missing nose section made maneuvering the ship in the storm more difficult.

Commander McCrary was at dinner, on the ground, when the ship was torn loose from the mast.

> A terrific report, loud above the tumult of the gale, brought the officers at mess to their feet.
>
> When they rushed out into the storm and looked up to where the enfeebled rays of searchlights wavered through the driving rain, marking the mooring mast top, the *Shenandoah* was gone into the night.[19]

Kincaid, as officer of the deck, had just completed an entry in the logbook. As he later told reporters, "Instinctively, Pierce, Heinen, and I dived for the levers." Reporters described Heinen as a "picturesque figure in an old overcoat over a blue sweater, rolled high under his jutting red Vandyke beard."[20] The press also claimed, mistakenly, that among the twenty-two men on board for this flight was another German-born commander, Lt. Roland G. Mayer. (Mayer was a member of the U.S. Navy Construction Corps and became a prominent figure in the airship program.) Actually, Heinen was the only "former German commander" on board.

To generate lift, the crew let go all the water ballast, including the emergency supply, and released three gasoline "slip tanks" that contained a total of 339 gallons. Slip tanks were rigged about every third or fourth fuel tank, secured in such a fashion that they could be released quickly to fall away in an emergency to increase the ship's buoyancy. After the initial shock and confusion of being torn away from the mast, discipline was restored quickly, and cool heads went about the work of saving the ship. According to Kincaid, it was the five thousand pounds of water ballast released within five seconds that allowed them to avoid crashing. Still, the ship swooped so low its airspeed meter slung seventy-five feet below the gondola, was swept away by the ground. But the ship was still losing altitude, and the crew began to throw overboard everything that could be spared—spare parts, emergency repair tools, emergency rations, anything with weight that was not needed.[21]

The two forward helium tanks had been destroyed and the tank behind those was leaking badly. The fabric of the ship's envelope had been torn for seventy-five feet back from the prow. While under way in the storm, the crew used the fabric covers of the ruined helium tanks to plug the leaking tank and to repair the hole in the nose of the envelope.

A narrow plank, nine inches wide, ran from one end of the ship's envelope to the other. Orders barked through a megaphone sent members of the crew running back and forth along the plank to keep the head and tail of the ship steady. A slip tank amidships had fallen and broken a central strut and torn a hole in the fabric of the envelope; at this point the men running the plank had nothing between them and the surface of the earth should they fall. Releasing the ballast allowed the ship to gain altitude, and gradually her engines made progress against the wind. At 2000 *Shenandoah* was over New Brunswick, New Jersey, the wind velocity exceeding the airship's speed by sixteen knots though engines 1 through 5 were at cruising speed.[22]

The main concern at this time was to keep the *Shenandoah* away from the ocean. Heinen was by far the most experienced dirigible commander present, and the American officers looked to him for guidance in this dire situation. As the airship drifted over New York Harbor and the Statue of Liberty, the storm started to abate; Heinen turned the ship into the wind and began to make progress back toward Lakehurst.[23] At 0150 the searchlights at the air station finally spotted the silver body of the airship. The storm was lessening, but gusts of wind were still catching the hole where the nose-plate had been ripped away. Under these conditions, it took three hours to bring her safely down; Heinen skillfully dropped her altitude by a few hundred feet at a time. Once on the ground, it took a force of three hundred men to walk her into the hangar. Marines, sailors, and ground crew seized the trailing ropes and cheered as they walked the dirigible a thousand feet to the hangar. Matching cheers were raised from the crewmen in the gondolas. Heinen, who had been directing the crew through a megaphone, used it to call down to those on the ground, "You sons of guns were waiting for something to happen, weren't you?" The *Shenandoah* landed safely at NAS Lakehurst at 0330 on January 17, 1924.[24]

Back on the ground, Heinen, sipping hot coffee from a thermos bottle, assumed a countenance common to aviators—that of assuredness—declaring calmly, "When the rain stopped, all was lovely."[25] Later that day he was to be more serious, commenting, "We narrowly escaped the fate of the *Dixmude*." The *Dixmude* was a German-built French naval dirigible carried away by a storm on December 20 and lost in the Mediterranean with her crew of fifty men.

Once his feet were back on the ground, Heinen was met by adoring people who proclaimed him a hero. Shunning the accolades, he proceeded straight to a telephone to call his wife. Everyone knew crashing into the ocean was the dirigible's greatest peril, and Heinen reassured his wife, "I haven't fallen into the Atlantic. We're all safe." He then turned his attention to the damage done to the ship. The wives of the other officers had spent the night at the field, sitting on coils of rope, bundled against the wind and rain, and receiving status reports from orderlies who ran back and forth between them and the wireless station.

Heinen was quick to give credit for the airship's survival to the crew. "In two collisions in my time, one on the Yangtse river in China, and one at the Panama maneuvers, I never saw a crew behave so faultlessly. They appeared to be enjoying the work. There was no loss of motion."[26] When asked about parachutes, he replied the *Shenandoah* did not carry parachutes on this journey. With more bravado, Heinen, with a grin, boasted, "The airship's the best parachute. Parachutes are dangerous. . . . No flyer ever is killed if he sticks to his airship."

Captain McCrary showered praise upon Heinen: "Every ounce of credit is due to Captain Heinen. It was a marvelous feat of seamanship and delicate jockeying against the wind." The ship's riggers also received well-deserved special credit for their dangerous work repairing the struts and fabric of the *Shenandoah* during the flight.

With continued enthusiasm for an Arctic expedition, Secretary Denby put a positive spin on this near disaster for the press.

> The midnight flight of the *Shenandoah* has demonstrated what the Navy Department has always believed: first, that the mooring facilities are adequate in most unusual weather; second, that so long as she is fueled and provisioned, the *Shenandoah* is safe in her natural element, the air. . . .
>
> From all our information, it may be asserted with positive certainty that there is hardly a possibility that this ship will encounter in her Arctic expedition any test so severe as that she has already met successfully.[27]

Denby's assessment of the *Shenandoah's* experience in the gale was overly optimistic. She had been saved by the piloting skill of Captain Heinen, the performance of the cool-headed crew, and a great deal of luck. The outcome could have been disastrously different.

The *Shenandoah's* safe return to Lakehurst was met with cheers, laughter, relief, pats on the back, and a general sharing of credit for jobs done well to keep the ship alive. In the aftermath, however, the experience served to amplify undercurrents of distrust at the air station. Discontent had been growing among officers and enlisted men over leadership. These issues loomed larger in view of an expected Arctic expedition, where the greatest of skill, experience, and judgment would be needed. There was disharmony among the officers, as well. Some of it was due to clashes of egos, but some stemmed from a lack of confidence in insufficiently experienced officers who would be in charge on the Arctic expedition. McCrary was the most notable figure in this regard.

The discord did not escape the notice of the press; stories about it circulated around the country. The *Brooklyn Daily Eagle* ran a story on January 19, 1924, under the title, "*Shenandoah* Crew Wary on [*sic*] Skipper for Trip to Pole. Probe of Runaway Flight Reveals Lack of Confidence in McCrary."[28] The article opened with a summary of the issue: "Facing a quiet rebellion over the choice of a commander for the *Shenandoah's* projected trip to the North Pole in June, the Navy Department may find itself in position of being compelled to remove Commander Frank H. McCrary and replace him with a skipper holding a secure grip on the confidence of the enlisted men."

The day this article appeared, the House Naval Affairs Committee was meeting to discuss a North Pole expedition, and its members were already aware of the leadership problems at Lakehurst. Originally it was expected the *Shenandoah* would make its Arctic flight with an all-volunteer crew, but enlisted men quite openly asserted that they would not volunteer if McCrary led the expedition. The situation became more complicated as tension developed among officers.

During the flight in the gale, problems had arisen between Kincaid and Heinen. The press report stated, "Lt. E. H. Kincaid, assistant navigation officer of the *Shenandoah*, and Capt. Heinen engaged in a controversy of such bitterness that relations between them are still strained." Heinen, a highly skilled and experienced airshipman, had been hired by the Navy to train Americans for service on dirigibles. Kincaid, on the other hand, was a Navy lieutenant who had been officially in charge of the *Shenandoah* on the night of the incident. A difference of opinion arose. Kincaid, aware that the ship's rudder had been damaged badly, chose to pilot the ship so as to minimize stress on the rudder. Heinen, he later claimed, became "indignant" that Kincaid was not piloting the ship the way he, Heinen, wanted it done. Kincaid felt that responsibility for the airship had rested with the Navy officers on board and that he had exercised his best judgment. The clash of egos was leading to dysfunction on the one hand and pettiness on the other. Kincaid claimed, "Capt. Heinen was apparently peeved over an article in one of the newspapers which attributed to me the statement that he was a consulting engineer to the Navy at a salary of $500 a week. As a matter of fact, I said no such thing."[29] The enlisted men were quick to state their confidence in Heinen as an expedition leader. Their trust was well placed, but Heinen was still a foreigner who had only recently applied for citizenship.

As for McCrary, this episode did nothing to strengthen his confidence in airships. Moffett had appointed McCrary as commanding officer of the *Shenandoah* because of his experience with LTA craft during the world war. McCrary had taken the position against his will; he was on record as favoring *flying boats* over dirigibles.[30] To complicate matters further, McCrary now committed an indiscretion that Moffett found unforgiveable. He publicly stated his belief that the

Shenandoah would be lost if sent on an Arctic expedition. In the Navy, this was an act of insubordination. The lack of a shared vision for airships, combined with the growing lack of confidence among the men in McCrary, left Moffett no choice but to act. He had McCrary relieved of his positions as commanding officer of the *Shenandoah* and Naval Air Station Lakehurst. In the shake-up Commander Klein, executive officer of the *Shenandoah,* was relieved of that duty and given command of the air station.[31] Command of the *Shenandoah* went to Lt. Cdr. Zachary Lansdowne.[32]

The gale incident occurred before the House Appropriations Committee had delivered its decision on funding the Arctic expedition. The episode, reported widely in the press and on the radio, spoke to the strength of the airship and the skill and courage of her crew but had nevertheless an adverse effect on the members of the Appropriations Committee. While all applauded the outcome, the frailty of an airship in severe weather had been made apparent. The massive logistical demands of such an expedition, combined with high costs and high risks, caused the committee to refuse funding; President Coolidge canceled the entire project on February 15.[33]

The changes in leadership at this time were to have a positive effect on the LTA program. Lansdowne was an excellent choice as a replacement for McCrary. A graduate of the Naval Academy, he had served as an aviator in the world war. In 1917 he had been sent to England to be trained in dirigibles and in 1919 had been on board the British airship *R 34* as she made her historic flight across the Atlantic to the United States. As assistant naval attaché in Germany in 1922–23, he had been involved in the negotiations leading to the construction of the *ZR 3* (later renamed the USS *Los Angeles*). At the time of his appointment as commanding officer of the *Shenandoah,* he had more dirigible flying time than anyone else in the Navy;[34] he had been working on a manual for the operation of rigid airships with recommendations for making dirigible flight safer. Included was a warning against flying near thunderstorms.[35]

On the morning of February 16, 1924, the airship was called to general quarters for the change of command. When Lansdowne took over, *Shenandoah* was scheduled for overhaul and modifications in preparation for the Arctic expedition, but now, following the incident in the gale, she was in need of additional repairs.

Wiley, for his part, continued his temporary duty assignment with the *Shenandoah* but saw little flight time during the remainder of his tour. In March, plans were begun for a large air show to be hosted by NAS Lakehurst on the last weekend of May; Wiley was placed in charge.[36] The *J 1*, a 174,880-cubic-foot nonrigid dirigible, was on hand for the show and in the weeks leading up to the event it flew around the area dropping fliers announcing the air show and its program.[37] The show opened on Sunday, May 31, with tens of thousands of eager spectators on hand to be entertained by a variety of aerial spectacles, including a flight of the *J 1*, aerial stunts by fixed-wing biplanes, and, as the crowning event of the day, a flight by the *Shenandoah*. Visitors were allowed to tour Hangar No. 1 and view the mechanical aspects of dirigible flight. Two civilians were allowed on board for the *Shenandoah's* twenty-fourth flight, a short excursion less than one week since her first test flight following repairs. The *Shenandoah* performed to perfection, and the entire air show was regarded as a huge success. Enthusiasm for the future of LTA flight ran high among airshipmen, and in Lansdowne, Moffett at last had someone in charge of the *Shenandoah* whose zeal matched his own.

Wiley had been off watch when the *Shenandoah* tore away from her mast and had left the ship hours before; thus, he was not present to become embroiled in or witness to the strife between Kincaid and Heinen. His was still a temporary-duty assignment, and he was junior to officers like Kincaid. In the coming months, Wiley's time was spent in ground duties while awaiting orders to his next assignment. In the meantime, Lansdowne was establishing himself with his men as a capable leader.

On August 8 he led the *Shenandoah* to another first in the world of airships—a successful mooring to a special mast on the tanker USS *Patoka* (AO 9).[38] In the U.S. Navy Register, the *Patoka* was officially a fleet oiler. She was 477 feet long with a beam of 60 feet, displaced 17,070 tons, and could achieve speeds of eleven knots. She carried a complement of 168 men. In 1924 the *Patoka* was selected to be a tender for the *Shenandoah*. A mooring mast approximately 125 feet high was constructed on her afterdeck, and modifications to the ship were made, such as facilities for helium, gasoline, and general supplies. On August 8 at 1400 the *Shenandoah* passed over the *Patoka* off Newport, Rhode Island, as the oiler was steaming toward her mooring buoy in Narragansett Bay. At 1600 the airship was over the bay with all hands at their landing stations. At 1730 she approached the *Patoka* and at 1910, after careful maneuvering, made up to the landing mast. Ten minutes later, the *Patoka* was steaming for her anchorage with the *Shenandoah* in tow from the mast.[39] It became obvious to the Navy that making mooring masts available around the globe could extend greatly the range of airships. Some of these would be installed at land bases, but masts on ships offered additional flexibility. The *Patoka* and additional ships fitted as she was could move about the ocean to intersect the flight paths of airships.

Wiley had been accumulating flying time on board the *Shenandoah*, and on September 12, 1924, the air station's examining board proclaimed that he had completed all the requirements for designation as a naval aviator (airship).[40] The board's report summarized Wiley's training and flight experience, in addition to passing written examinations. Wiley had flown a total of sixteen hours, two minutes in "free balloons," including one solo flight; twenty hours, forty-five minutes in "kite balloons"; fourteen hours, eleven minutes in nonrigid airships; and sixty-five hours, seven minutes in rigid airships—for a total of 116 hours and five minutes of LTA flying time. His ground instruction had included such practical subjects as rigid airships, aerostatics, aerodynamics, aerology, engineering, navigation, rules of the air, lighter-than-air construction, helium, hydrogen, and sundry associated topics. *Aerostatics* deals with gases in equilibrium, as well as the equilibrium of balloons or aircraft under changing atmospheric conditions. *Aerology*, loosely synonymous with *meteorology*, deals with the atmosphere at the highest altitudes, not just the air close to the Earth's surface.

The next challenge for the *Shenandoah* was a transcontinental flight during which she would test a number of strategically located mooring masts of the types needed for long-range exploration. In addition to the technical aspects of such a journey, the high visibility of the airship around the country would be good for public relations. On September 3, 1924, Lt. Charles Rosendahl left NAS Lakehurst on temporary duty to inspect new mooring masts at Fort Worth (Texas), San Diego (California), and Camp Lewis (Washington).[41] Wiley was not on board for this transcontinental flight, but because there would be other such flights, he and his colleagues who were left behind with ground duties at Lakehurst paid close attention to the *Shenandoah*'s trip, following her progress as newspapers around the country gave it daily coverage, taking special note of problems encountered over a variety of terrains. A small air service with a single airship had to learn from every flight, even from the ground. Wiley would take away information from this flight that would be of great importance to him on his own future flights.

The great adventure of approximately nine thousand miles began at 0535 on October 7, 1924, as the *Shenandoah* was walked out of her hangar to be made ready for flight. By 0700 she was secured to the mooring mast, where in short order she began to take on water ballast, food, fuel, and passengers. Attention was given to every detail about the ship, no matter how small. For example, as soon as the airship emerged from the hangar and became exposed to the sun, the helium gas warmed and began to expand. If it expanded too much, the precious gas would be vented through safety valves and lost. Conversely, the ship would cool under cloud cover. Also, even moored to the mast before flying free with her engines powering her, strict attention to the trim of the ship was essential. The trim, in turn, was crucially affected by weight distribution. Each of the eleven officers and fourteen crew members as he came on board went immediately to his duty station, ready to be told to shift to a location where his weight was needed.

The day before departure, orders were issued by the Bureau of Navigation that Rear Admiral Moffett would be in the ship's complement, to be transported to Camp Lewis. Under usual circumstances, Lansdowne was the next-to-last person to leave the mooring mast to enter the airship; the mooring officer was the last, closing the gangway behind him. On this day, however, the last to enter the *Shenandoah* was the renowned *National Geographic* photojournalist Junius B. Wood, who had been invited by the Navy to document the journey.[42] With all on board and all ready, the ship left the mast at 1000 and made for Fort Worth.[43] For the outward journey the *Shenandoah* headed southwest from Lakehurst on a path that took her over parts of North and South Carolina, Georgia, Mississippi, and Louisiana before reaching Fort Worth at 2015 on October 8 and mooring to the mast there. Rosendahl rejoined the *Shenandoah* at Fort Worth.[44] Thousands of spectators had turned out to see the famous airship, and the city's reception committee had planned a week of hospitality.[45] Its members were greatly disappointed to learn the *Shenandoah* would be in Fort Worth only overnight before continuing westward.

The next leg of the journey, to San Diego, was expected to be the most difficult, unpredictable, and potentially treacherous. The large dirigible was designed for low-altitude flight over coastal lands and the ocean. The plains and mountains of the American West presented the airship with quite different and unusual physical conditions, including heat and winds rising off deserts and turbulence around high mountaintops. One solution to the problem of mountains was simply to fly over them, but the altitudes required would cause the helium in the gas cells to expand 100 percent, the point above which gas would be lost from the escape valves.[46] An alternate was to fly as low as possible and negotiate the mountains by flying through their passes. The second approach was chosen.

To clear the lower passes Lansdowne navigated by following the path of the Texas and Pacific Railway.[47] The track was easily identifiable as it wound its way through mountain passes and cuts. At 1100 on October 9, the *Shenandoah* set a course for Pecos, Texas. The railroad "map" led them over the Texas towns of Cisco, Abeline, Sweetwater, Colorado, and Odessa. She passed over Pecos at 2000 and followed the tracks on to El Paso, taking advantage of the same mountain passes that the railway did. The challenges of this record-breaking trip were hugely instructive for the officers and crew. They traversed winding passes with strong wind turbulence that made the ride very bumpy and steering extremely difficult, but they continued to follow their "iron compass" to Tucson, Arizona.

On October 10, at approximately 1930, the officers in the gondola spotted the lights of Riverside and San Bernardino, California, just before running into a snow squall in the San Gregorio Pass. They quickly dropped from five thousand to three thousand feet to get under a large nimbus cloud and bring the ground into sight. The ship accumulated three to four thousand pounds of wet snow and became about six thousand pounds heavy but avoided disaster and was through the storm and in clear weather by 1945.[48] At 2010 the *Shenandoah* crossed the Pacific coastline, turned, and followed it south to San Diego and its naval air station, where she landed at 2330. The after car bumped the ground during the landing, breaking six girder joints and incurring other minor damage. Repairs required a layover of about a week. Fortunately, this would be the only accident of the entire cruise. On October 13 Rosendahl was flown from San Diego to Camp Lewis, where he inspected the mooring mast in anticipation of the next leg of the journey. With repairs made, the *Shenandoah* left her mast en route to Camp Lewis at 0915 on October 16. Sailing up the coast of California, at 1140 she flew over two divisions of the surface Battle Fleet.[49] At 1830 on October 18, the *Shenandoah* was securely moored to her mast at Camp Lewis.[50] The following morning, before the *Shenandoah* was to depart for her return trip, Rear Admiral Moffett departed, to make his return to the East Coast by rail. The airship left the mast at 1205 headed back to Fort Worth, but from there she took a more northerly course back to Lakehurst than the one she had followed outbound. Her round-trip journey ended at 2355 on October 25, 1924.

So remarkable was the odyssey of the *Shenandoah* that *National Geographic* devoted forty-seven pages and forty-one illustrations to Junius Wood's article. The final paragraphs of his text reflect an enthusiasm for this mode of flight shared by all who flew in airships.

> The cruise of the *Shenandoah* was over an uncharted world. Beacons by sea and signs by land have been built through the ages for those who voyage on the surface. A new era of transportation is coming nearer, in which the airship will have a place as a conveyance of peace as well as an instrument of war. Many lessons were learned on the *Shenandoah's* cruise.
>
> The American-built and American-manned airship in that cruise showed that mountains and distances are easily negotiable. . . .
>
> The voyage to the North Pole and the exploration of the vast unknown polar regions have been made nearer realization by the *Shenandoah's* venture in the face of a blustering autumn. With the spring-time, polar flights may come and the world's most inaccessible region will be within easy reach of man.[51]

It had now been three months since Wiley had flown on board the *Shenandoah*. On that day, July 24, the airship made a regional flight with ten officers, twenty-five crew, and fourteen passengers. Wiley was listed in the logbook as a passenger. At Lakehurst, Wiley had attended to routine duties and, along with many others, awaited the arrival of the German-built airship *LZ 126*, designated by the American navy as *ZR 3*. The *ZR 3* arrived at Lakehurst on October 15 as the *Shenandoah* was preparing to make the flight from San Diego to Camp Lewis. On her return to Lakehurst, the *Shenandoah* and the *ZR 3* shared the same hangar.

4

The USS
Los Angeles (ZR 3)

The Navy had waited two years for the construction and testing of the *ZR 3* to be completed. Because the terms of the Treaty of Versailles forbade Germany to manufacture military airships, the *ZR 3* was built as a passenger airship, so as to serve a dual role as an experimental craft. Her keel was laid down on November 7, 1922, in Friedrichshafen, Germany.

In 1924 three American officers were scheduled to make the trip from Friedrichshafen to Lakehurst on board the *ZR 3* when she was delivered. Klein, the commanding officer of NAS Lakehurst, arranged to get orders for temporary duty to make the flight as a fourth American. Klein's last-minute stunt irritated Moffett and the officers who had already been scheduled to make the flight. This offense against protocol would not be forgotten.[1]

Following a transatlantic flight under the command of Hugo Eckener, *ZR 3* arrived at Lakehurst on October 15, 1924. The American press had followed closely the flight of the *ZR 3*, and on the day of her arrival headlines read, "*ZR 3* Here after 80-Hour Flight."[2] The *ZR 3* was the second airship to cross the Atlantic and, by doing so in 80 hours, had broken the 108-hour record set five years earlier by the British *R 34*. *ZR 3* also set a new world's record for continuous flight, logging 5,006 miles.

The press wrote exuberantly of a "New Era in Transportation Opened by Flight; ZEPS May Be Common as Autos, Maybe."[3] Anton Heinen claimed enthusiastically that *ZR 3*'s flight marked the beginning of an economic revolution and predicted that much larger airships, craft with twice her capacity, would make practical flights from New York to Peking. Heinen also boasted that the flights of the *ZR 3* and *Shenandoah* would convince American capitalists and the public that there was a realistic future for airship development in transportation. Airship proponents generally, of their great conviction and enthusiasm, made bold promises not yet supported by science or technology.[4]

Once the *ZR 3* had been brought to the ground at Lakehurst and walked into the hangar, she was officially the property of the U.S. Navy. Consistent with German practice, the *ZR 3* had been inflated with hydrogen. Once she was in American hands, her hydrogen was released through valves, and preparations were made to fill her with helium from the *Shenandoah*. There was insufficient helium to fill both airships, and the shortage had been made worse by the *Shenandoah*'s loss of half a million cubic feet during her transcontinental trip.[5] In the hangar, the *Shenandoah* was suspended from the overhead at all the main frames in anticipation of her deflation.[6] At 1145 on November 13 the transfer of helium to the *ZR 3* began;[7] it was complete by 1610 on the fourteenth.

On November 25 Wiley was on board as the *ZR 3* left the ground at Lakehurst at 0903 to cruise to the Anacostia naval air station in the District of Columbia for her christening ceremony.[8] There gusty winds created challenges for crews on the ground and aloft, but the airship landed, and the First Lady of the United States, Mrs. Calvin Coolidge, christened her the USS *Los Angeles*. The commandant of the Washington Navy Yard commissioned the airship, and Capt. George W. Steele Jr. read his orders assigning him to command.[9] The *Los Angeles* was back at Lakehurst by 2100 the same day.

In coming months, the officers and crew members of the *Los Angeles* would challenge her range and versatility—specifically, her potential as a commercial carrier for passengers and cargo—but always in the mind of the military was the promise of the airship for long-range reconnaissance, especially over vast stretches of ocean. The German crew that had delivered the *Los Angeles* was under contract to remain at Lakehurst for a time to assist with the training of American crews, and Moffett was eager for the ship to get as much flying time as possible while they were available. Some suggested that the airship remain moored to the mast instead of being housed in the hangar, to save ground time and create more airtime.[10]

December 1924, however, was totally unsympathetic to Moffett's plans. The *Los Angeles* made only two flights for a total flying time of less than six hours.[11] The life of any airship was marked by constant maintenance and repair, and for the *Los Angeles* a significant amount of corrosion had been apparent at the time of delivery. The entire airship required a close inspection, followed by cleaning, repair, or replacement of anything that needed it. The winter weather at Lakehurst deterred flights on many occasions. Moffett grew increasingly impatient with the lack of activity due to weather but nothing he could do changed matters—Nature was indifferent to the longings of man.

On January 5, 1925, Wiley received orders ending his temporary duty on the *Shenandoah* and placing him in the regular ship's company of the *Los Angeles*.[12] Throughout much of January 1925, the *Shenandoah* was shored up in the hangar undergoing repair and maintenance. At times, her crew served as ground handlers for the *Los Angeles* as she was walked out to the mast and returned. At 1345 on January 19, Captain Steele assumed command of both the USS *Los Angeles* and NAS Lakehurst, relieving Commander Klein of the latter.[13]

The expectation of a total solar eclipse on January 24 provided the *Los Angeles* an opportunity to demonstrate her potential as a platform for scientific research. Arrangements were made for the airship to carry aloft a number of scientists to witness and document the eclipse. The observation party, led by Capt. Edwin T. Pollock from the U.S. Naval Observatory, arrived early in the week to stow gear on board the ship and to ready themselves for a rehearsal flight in advance of the Saturday eclipse. With them were two double, long-focus astronomical cameras, which they fitted in the passenger car, two motion-picture cameras for photographing all the phases of the eclipse, and a spectrograph for studying the corona. There was also a variety of still cameras. Officers were prepared to make manual sketches of the corona, others look out for comets. In addition to the equipment, there were forty-two people, sufficient fuel for thirty hours of cruising at full speed, and eight hundred pounds of food.

In the days leading to the eclipse, the weather became so severe that it was necessary to cancel the rehearsal flight. As a compromise, the observers drilled at their stations with the ship still in the hangar.[14] Thursday's forecast for Friday, the twenty-third, was that the weather would be calm enough to walk the *Los Angeles* out of her hangar and anchor her to the mooring mast, but the winds did not abate sufficiently. All day Friday and into the night, the ship was kept ready, her engines run intermittently to keep them warm.

The original flight plan had been for the scientific observations of the eclipse to be made in the vicinity of the Nantucket Lightship. To be in position in time it was necessary to lift ship by 0300, but at this hour on Saturday morning the winds were averaging fourteen miles per hour with gusts of twenty-two. About 0330 a lull allowed the ground crew to ready the ship. By this time, the temperature had fallen to 4° Fahrenheit. The flight crew boarded wearing fur-lined flying suits, helmets, and boots. The *Los Angeles* left her hangar at 0501 with all scientists and press on board. The late start necessitated a change in plan; it was decided to make the scientific observations in the vicinity of Block Island.

Wiley recorded the events in the ship's logbook for the 0800–1200 watch. They were cruising at an altitude of 4,500 feet at a constant airspeed of thirty-eight knots near Montauk Point, New York, when, at 0802, they saw their first glimpse of the developing eclipse. By 0830 the moon obscured about a third of the sun. Wiley noted many clouds to seaward at about 2,000 feet and logged that because the sun was about 75 percent obscured, the temperature inside the ship was dropping. As the moment of totality of eclipse approached, the sun could be observed with the naked eye. All that was visible were "Bailey's Beads"—small dots around the edge of the eclipsed sun. By 0913 the solar eclipse was total. In the logbook Wiley recorded, "Very wonderful color effects to Northward. Darkness. Stars."[15]

He was impressed sufficiently by the experience to publish a full account of it a few months later in which he offered a better sense of the excitement of the moment.

Darkness deepened. The moment of totality approached. The light of the sun could soon be endured by the naked eye. Little dots around the edge, Bailey's Beads, were all that were visible. Observers exclaimed at the beauty of the scene.

Then, out of the northwest, appeared a vast shadow slipping over the earth's surface at incredible speed. Picture if you can, a summer thunderstorm which blackens a distant area of the sky, and as it approaches, appears very threatening. The whole sky grows darker as the storm develops. The firmament takes on an ominous aspect. This scene fills you with awe. Suppose that, instead of the usual hour for the storm to develop and approach, all this happened in three seconds. Then you have an idea of how this shadow appeared over the great relief map of southern Connecticut and Long Island Sound and swept across the airship.

The land and water changed color rapidly. Gorgeous purples, blues and yellows predominated. The clouds below to southward looked like dirty snow drifts. The compass light and luminous dials of the altitude control instruments glowed. Stars appeared in the vicinity of the sun, which had disappeared, and the moon was seen as a coal-black disk surrounded by the much discussed but unimpressive corona of pale light. Corona sketchers were working busily. An officer was counting time for the observers, in seconds. Observers were clicking their cameras, moving picture operators grinding out film. Silence!

Then a beam of light appeared at the side of the black disk. The gigantic shadow was seen traveling away from the ship toward the southeast. Darkness faded. Sighs of ecstasy came from the observers. The stars disappeared. The crescent of the sun grew larger. Again the marvelous changing colors over land and water and clouds. Observers were continuing their observations, but the previous feeling of tension and suppressed excitement was lacking.[16]

The total eclipse ended at 0915. Weather continued to be a factor on the return trip to Lakehurst. In the approach to the air station, the ground warned of an area of low barometric pressure; the crew would have to make haste if the ship was to make it into the hangar. Weather conditions were not favorable for the mooring mast. Landing was made difficult by the lightness of the ship, which had burned a large amount of fuel. After two failed attempts, helium was released to bring the ship down. With the *Los Angeles* safely back in her hangar following a successful scientific adventure, Wiley concluded, "the eventful day was a never-to-be-forgotten memory."[17]

The January weather—cold temperatures, high winds, snow, and ice—kept the *Los Angeles* in her hangar. Things changed the next month, however. February 17 brought the promise of impending action when Rosendahl and two crewmen left the air station for temporary duty on board the USS *Patoka* in connection with a future mooring of the *Los Angeles* at Bermuda and San Juan.[18] Long flights over the ocean to such distant sites were promoted as a way to stimulate commercial interest in airships and to demonstrate to the military their potential for long-range oceanic reconnaissance.

On February 20 the Assistant Secretary of the Navy and party arrived at Lakehurst to join in the flight to Bermuda. In his log entry for the 1200–1600 watch Wiley listed the names of all on board, which included, besides Assistant Secretary Theodore D. Robinson, Rear Admiral Moffett, Capt. Emory S. Land,

Cdr. Robert L. Ghormley, and Lt. T. G. W. Settle (U.S. Naval Academy class of 1918).[19] They were under way at 1520 on a course for Barnegat Light, New Jersey. At 0300 on February 21, they spotted Gibbs Hill Light in Bermuda.

At 0550 the *Patoka* got under way to rendezvous with the *Los Angeles* to conduct the mooring, but, as often occurred, the weather interfered. Wiley's log entry for the 0800–1200 watch on February 21 recorded various speeds and courses over Bermuda in heavy rainsqualls. At 0955 they passed over Governor's Grounds, where they dropped eighty-five pounds of mail. Heavy rain making it impracticable to moor to the *Patoka*, the *Los Angeles* departed Bermuda at 0958 on a heading for Lakehurst.[20] In spite of the inability to moor to the *Patoka*, the over-ocean flight was deemed a success, one full of promise for the future of commercial airships. Meanwhile, in need of maintenance and repairs, the *Los Angeles* did not make another flight until mid-April.[21]

Wiley's tour of duty on the *Los Angeles* was making him a veteran airshipman. He was along for many "firsts," such as the trip to Bermuda, which, among other things, represented the first transoceanic airmail delivery for the United States. He was on board also for the next round trip to Bermuda, which began on April 21.[22] The airship arrived over Bermuda the next day and this time, with favorable weather, made a successful mooring to the *Patoka* before returning to Lakehurst on April 24. The growing experience from such flights brought additional confidence and momentum to the LTA program. Just a little over a week after returning from Bermuda, the *Los Angeles* left for Puerto Rico. She cast off from the high mast at 0958 on May 3 en route to Mayaguez. At 1040 on May 4, the watch spotted the American steamship *Delfina* heading southward. On board for this flight was Horace D. Ashton, a writer, photographer, and lecturer. Captain Steele maneuvered the *Los Angeles* to allow Ashton to photograph the *Delfina* below them. This simple act demonstrated again the potential of airships for reconnaissance over the oceans. The *Patoka* had preceded the *Los Angeles* to Puerto Rico, and by 2215 on May 4 the airship was secured to its mooring mast.[23] The airship cast off from the *Patoka* on May 8 and arrived back at Lakehurst on May 10. This trip had logged many hours for the crew and generated favorable publicity. Because of the success of these relatively long flights, plans were in the works for the *Los Angeles* to make the even longer flight to Hawaii. A regular airship service between the West Coast and Hawaii would be of great commercial value and allow opportunities for reconnaissance of the Pacific Ocean. However, no airship service to Hawaii ever developed for the *Los Angeles*.

Following her voyages to Bermuda and Puerto Rico, the *Los Angeles* conducted several demonstration flights carrying an impressive roster of dignitaries as passengers. Rear Admiral Moffett was very skilled at using publicity to advance his causes, and he employed the *Los Angeles* to promote both the commercial and military potentials of the airship.[24] Wiley was on board for the flight of May 15, 1925, and, keen observer that he was, it is unlikely that the composition of the passenger list was lost on him. In subsequent years, he was to be very comfortable in front of the press and public figures; he may have gained his confidence in part from his participation in the Moffett era of LTA flight. In a time when airplane and airship programs were competing for resources, both governmental and private, Moffett was doing all he could to impress influential people of the potential of airships.

One can understand Moffett's thinking by examining the passenger roster for the May 15 flight. Of the seventy people on board, twenty-three were dignitaries of various institutions, from media outlets to manufacturing to the military.[25] Everyone on the list was in a position to influence thinking about air travel. Amassing such a group for a single flight speaks well of Moffett's administrative abilities and ambitions. The *Los Angeles* treated her guests to a seven-hour flight around the Philadelphia area.

Captain Steele was planning further demonstration flights for the *Los Angeles* and acting as commanding officer of the air station wrote on May 13, 1925, to the Chief of Naval Operations (CNO) in Washington, D.C., concerning a scheduled trip to Minneapolis, Minnesota.[26] Airships were celebrities, and they never went unnoticed when flying over American cities. Landing in a city, however, incurred greater logistical problems than simply passing overhead. Trained ground crews were needed. Nevertheless, the memorandum suggested, for the upcoming trip to Minneapolis it would be advisable for the *Los Angeles* to land and refuel there. The distance from Lakehurst was 1,100 miles, and weather conditions could not be predicted. Steele requested that Wiley and two enlisted men be ordered to proceed on or about June 1 to Minneapolis to assemble an improvised ground crew and have it trained a few days prior to the arrival of the ship. The travel orders for Wiley and two enlisted men were issued as requested. As it turned out, the *Los Angeles* encountered mechanical difficulties on its way to Minneapolis and had to return to Lakehurst for major repairs.

5

The *Shenandoah* Disaster

With the *Los Angeles* relegated to her hangar undergoing repairs, the *Shenandoah* was dispatched to make the series of demonstration flights around the Midwest.[1] In preparation for the flights, the *Shenandoah* received a further transfusion of helium from her sister ship. The *Shenandoah* was ordered to proceed to Minneapolis as soon after July 4 as practicable. As that date passed and time dragged on, the flight was scheduled to take place during the first week of September.[2] As they had for the *Los Angeles* trip to Minneapolis, Wiley and two enlisted men traveled ahead to make preparations for a refueling landing at Fort Snelling.[3]

Wiley set out for Detroit, Michigan, on September 2. When he arrived there the next day, he learned that the *Shenandoah* had crashed. No longer needed at Detroit, he went directly to Dearborn Field, where he arranged a flight on an Army airplane to Cumberland, Ohio. He arrived there around 1600 and took an automobile to the crash site in Caldwell, Ohio.[4] Proceeding with no clear facts about the disaster, he urgently wanted to learn the fates of his friends and colleagues and to serve in any capacity he could. Because this was the first American airship crash, it is unlikely that he expected the sights that met him as he approached the crash scene on his arrival. The sight of an airship crash is unfamiliar to most people, but newspapers for the following day, September 4, offer some hint. United Press reporter Harry W. Sharpe wrote:

The wreckage of the giant ship, strewn in the cornfields and woods of two counties, has been stripped bare of everything removable.

Thousands of souvenir hunters swooped down on the tangled rigging with saws and hatchets, ripping and tearing, pilfering and wrecking.

Three companies of the state militia ordered to the scene by Governor Vic Donahey arrived to find nothing to guard except the gigantic motors.

Stationary cabin furniture had been chopped off and taken away. The silver fabric of the giant bag was cut and carried away in sections, lengths of the superstructure were sawed and hacked away and tied to dusty automobiles.[5]

Lieutenant Commander Lansdowne died in the crash.[6] Lieutenant Commander Rosendahl survived and, as ranking officer, took charge of the crash site to care for the injured and collect the dead. He told reporters they were flying at about 2,500 feet when a twister shot them up about 7,000 feet. Subsequently, the ship made two violent plunges and then broke in the middle. Only officers were in the control car, on the forward end, and when the struts supporting the cabin broke, it "dropped to the ground like a hunk of lead."[7]

The dead were removed from the field and delivered to final resting places designated by next of kin. Lansdowne's body was to be interred at Arlington National Cemetery, according to his wishes. Along with Lansdowne, Lieutenant Commander Hancock, Lt. John B. Lawrence, and Lt. E. W. Sheppard were buried in Arlington National Cemetery. Lieutenant Houghton was the only one of the officers not buried in Arlington. He was returned to Brookline, Massachusetts.

In an act of great kindness, the Kiwanis Club of Cambridge, Ohio, hosted an informal dinner for the survivors.

Extreme silence prevailed during the dinner. Hardly a word was spoken, until Lt. T. C. Hendley, a ranking officer, arose to thank the club for its hospitality.

"I cannot talk about the *Shenandoah*," he said, his voice choking.

"I want to thank you in behalf of all of us, for your hospitality. You have helped to lift a keen burden from our hearts."

Hendley sat down, tears filling his eyes.

The survivors were then escorted to their train.[8]

The eighteen survivors arrived at NAS Lakehurst at 0955 on September 4. More than a thousand people awaited them. By the end of the day on September 4, all had been taken care of, and the investigating team was on the ground doing its job. With nothing more to see or contribute, Wiley took a train back to Lakehurst on September 5.

The press had picked up on the disaster almost immediately and had spread the story throughout the country. In Wiley's Missouri hometown, the *Constitution-Tribune* was quick to assure its readers that Wiley had not been on the *Shenandoah* at the time of the crash.[9] People were quick to share their ideas about the cause of the crash. The *News-Herald* of Franklin, Pennsylvania, reported:[10]

Members of the crew were scattered over an area of ten miles as the giant airship whirled and twisted in the air, tossing them from the cabins swung beneath the gas bag.

Those who witnessed the disaster from the ground described the *Shenandoah* as "spinning like a giant revolving door," before she finally broke in two.

. . . Buffetted by storms, the giant craft was blown from its course to the southeast.

Unable to withstand the gusts, the ship crashed, cracking in two.

The aft-section, containing two cabins, flopped around, brushing trees and finally crashing at Sharon, O[hio], 12 miles distant. There were four men in the cook's cabin and 12 in the engineer's cabin.

The latter jumped near the top of a small hill and none was injured. The cook's cabin, in the meantime, had dropped and no one was hurt.

The *Shenandoah*, the sensationalistic reporter continued, fell to the ground in four pieces that were scattered over a ten-mile area. The keel, the article reported, had been the first part to break, and it fell away in two parts, one landing in a farmer's barnyard, the other about ten miles away. The second part of the keel carried with it eight crewmen who made the descent uninjured. "Without keel the airship careened in the storm beyond all control. Then a seam opened and the bag broke apart, the forward half dropping to earth nose-first and the stern drifting miles away and landing as it was almost lost to sight."[11]

Theories about the cause of the crash flew into the hands of reporters all too quickly from sources, many unnamed, who had not been at the scene. There was a report that the airship had been struck by lightning, breaking her in half. An unnamed source from Lakehurst told reporters, "Use of helium gas, instead of hydrogen, for inflation, proved its value in that it prevented an explosion."

Newspapers the day after the crash contained emotionally charged claims that would need to be addressed. A comment by Mrs. Lansdowne to a reporter during an interview at Lakehurst made its way into print: "He [Commander Lansdowne] was opposed to making the flight at this time," she said. "He knew the situation in the Ohio valley at this season, and asked officials at Washington to postpone the trip until weather conditions were more favorable."[12] Asked to address this claim, Secretary of the Navy Wilbur replied, "Lansdowne was permitted to choose his own time of making the flight at this time. I would not have permitted the flight against the judgment or protest of Commander Lansdowne."[13]

This issue would be revisited at length. Emotions ran high, not only in the press, in the wake of the airship disaster. There was great sadness over the loss of the brave officers and crew members. Notable among the stories was that of the widow of Lt. Cdr. Lewis Hancock Jr., one of the officers killed in the crash. Her previous husband, Lt. Cdr. Charles C. Little, had perished four years prior in another dirigible accident when the *R 38/ZR 2* crashed into the Humber River in England.

In addition to over a dozen men, the Navy had lost a very expensive piece of its LTA inventory. To that point, a number of irresponsible claims arose from parties who should have exhibited greater restraint. Citing no informed source for his comments, United Press staff correspondent Charles Williamson predicted the *Shenandoah* disaster would result in abandonment of the LTA program and that the *Los Angeles* would be sold and helium extraction curtailed.[14] Senator Duncan Fletcher of Florida, a ranking member of the Senate Military Affairs Committee, went on record for reporters that the Navy could not expect more money from Congress for construction of dirigibles, because they were too costly in both lives and dollars.[15] However, he predicted, appropriations for airplanes would not be affected adversely. In contrast, when he was informed of the crash, Rear Admiral Moffett told the press, "This disaster shall not be allowed to divert the navy department from its determination to continue the advancement of American aeronautics. . . . The men who died gave their lives for the advancement of aeronautic science, for the furtherance of the nation's air supremacy."[16]

The Navy convened a board, composed of Secret Service, military, and naval authorities, to inspect the crash site in an attempt to determine the cause, or causes, of the disaster. It did not help their efforts that Anton Heinen featured prominently among those making claims to the press. At the time of the crash he had been in Lakehurst, but he had quickly offered his opinions about what had gone wrong. He gave interviews in which he called the deaths of the fourteen crew members "plain murder." He told the press that eight of the eighteen safety valves in the *Shenandoah*'s gas cells had been removed and that this was the direct cause of the disaster. Heinen went into detail:

> From what Commander Klein told me, the ship was nearly filled with helium when she left here. As I figured it, at a height of 3,000 feet, which was pressure height, as we call it, the ship would have to valve off gas. In the storm which she struck, she rose too fast for the valves. Every 240 feet above 3,000 feet she should have discharged one per cent, or 21,000 cubic feet, of helium. The upward movement of the ship causes rapid expansion of the gas cells and the bags broke the shell of the ship in the middle.[17]

Heinen insisted that had the ship been filled with hydrogen, the disaster might not have happened—because, he claimed, the less expensive hydrogen would have been valved off more readily. He would not have flown on the *Shenandoah* for a million dollars, he declared because it was not safe with the valve changes.

The United Press informed readers that Lieutenant Commander Lansdowne had authorized the valve changes the previous May or June, as a result of the cross-country flight. The Navy Department announced it would investigate Heinen's claims but that Secretary Wilbur "has complete confidence in the wisdom of naval experts at Lakehurst who pass upon such matters, and feels that Heinen's charges can and should be disproved."[18]

Heinen had gone too far with this comment and the manner in which he handled himself. He would have been wiser to express himself in a more professional and technical manner. Even so, he was not done yet. "Now there will be a white wash board of inquiry and some camouflage to cover up the real story of the cause, which was the foolish action of the crew at the station in changing the valves. Already there have been things said to lay the blame on poor dead Lansdowne."[19] Newspapers reported Heinen had crossed the Atlantic Ocean on the *ZR 3* (later the *Los Angeles*) but had not been employed by the Navy since June 1924 and was regarded as an unfriendly critic. A court of inquiry would be convened, and Heinen would be held accountable for his words.

In the wake of what would be called forever the "*Shenandoah* disaster," the Navy had to react. There was much at stake; people were beginning to call for an end to the airship era and, in particular, an end to its public funding. Such irresponsible claims as those of Mrs. Lansdowne and Anton Heinen had to be addressed, and in a scientific and meticulous manner, avoiding any suspicion of a cover-up. On September 16, 1925, the Secretary of the Navy ordered Rear Adm. Hilary P. Jones to convene a court of inquiry "to inquire into all the facts and circumstances surrounding the loss of the USS *Shenandoah*."[20] The court of inquiry was to consist of Rear Admiral Jones as the president of the court, Capt. Lewis B. McBride, and Cdr. John H. Towers. Capt. Paul Foley was appointed the judge advocate, Lt. Cdr. Ralph G. Pennoyer and Lt. Cdr. Maurice R. Pierce as his counsels. The court was directed to sit at 1000 on Monday, September 21, 1925, at the Naval Air Station, Lakehurst. Great responsibility rested on the collective shoulders of the court, the first of its kind to evaluate what had caused an airship crash. It would set precedents for future airship disasters.

The proceedings were declared an open event, and Wiley and other officers likely attended when not on other duties. For obvious reasons, everyone in the LTA program had a keen interest in the cause of the crash; they would pay close attention to the proceedings, hoping to learn lessons that might be used to avoid further disasters.

The inquiry lasted ten days and deposed over fifty witnesses, including all the survivors of the crash (referred to as "Interested Parties"). Other witnesses included experts in aerology, stresses of materials, and lighter-than-air flight in general. The court began by attempting to identify the events that had led to the crash. One of the early witnesses, Col. C. G. Hall of the U.S. Army Air Service, a survivor, was asked to recount the circumstances leading to the loss as he had experienced them. Reading from a prepared statement, he gave a lucid and detailed account.

On the morning of the disaster, Colonel Hall had arisen at 0500 and gone into the control car, where he encountered Lieutenant Anderson, the aerologist, who called his attention to thunder clouds and lightning on both beams of the ship. For over half an hour, his full attention was devoted to the weather, trying to determine if the ship was moving away from the gathering storm, but it appeared to him that the ship was not distancing herself from the thunderclouds and lightning. Indeed, the storm clouds were becoming more threatening and the lightning more intense. Dead ahead, however, the sky seemed to be free of storm, and the officers in the control car thought they would run into fair weather if they maintained their present course. While keeping a constant eye on the unfolding situation, they felt no apprehension yet as to the safety of the ship. Hall had not noted the altitude at which they were flying but presumed it to be about three thousand feet above sea level. The first cause for alarm came when Chief Aviation Rigger Everett P. Allen, operating the elevators (horizontal control surfaces at the tail meant to control altitude), called out repeatedly that the ship was rising, and then, "Still rising, and I can't hold her down!" At this, Captain Lansdowne left his position at the forward starboard window of the control car and walked over to Chief Allen. He checked the altimeter and noted the rate of climb.

A couple of minutes later, Chief Allen called out that the ship was rising very rapidly. On Captain Lansdowne's order, Lieutenant Houghton opened the hand gas valves to release helium. A crewman called out each minute how long the valves had been open; when Lansdowne ordered the valves to be closed, they had been open for a total of five minutes. When the valves were closed, Hall looked at the altimeter and noted the ship was at 5,500 feet. Lansdowne then called out to everyone in the car that the ship would begin to descend and ordered Houghton to stand by the ballast controls. Almost immediately, Allen called out, "The ship is falling! She is falling fast, very fast!" Instantly Houghton pulled the ballast controls, holding as many in each hand as he could. He continued to drop ballast until the ship stopped at about 3,000 feet. All engines were at full speed, as Lansdowne had ordered when the ship had begun to rise. During the rise, Chief Allen had nosed the ship down at an angle of approximately ten degrees, and when the ship began to rise he had pulled the nose upward to the same angle.

Until this point, Hall recalled, the air had not been bumpy. He was aware, however, they were running into a strong headwind. As the ship stopped its descent, Hall left the elevatorman and altimeter and went to the after port window to look at the ground to get an idea of what the ship was doing. He noted a drift to port from the intended course of about forty-five degrees. He reported this to Lieutenant Anderson to be relayed to the captain, who might decide to change course. Hall then crossed to the other side of the car, but before he could look out the window he felt the car sinking below him. He had the impression the ship was falling and at a greater rate than the previous episode. When he got to the window and looked out, he realized the ship was turning rapidly in a circle.

Suddenly, she was caught in a violent blast of wind that threw the tail of the ship upward while simultaneously turning or twisting it to the right (looking aft). At exactly the same moment as the violent blast he heard the loud noise of rending girders. Lieutenant Lawrence called out, "She's gone!" Hall called everybody out of the car and started up the ladder from the control car into the body of the ship. He heard Lieutenant Anderson behind him call out, "Go up quickly, Colonel." It took Hall only two or three seconds to ascend the ladder, and when he stepped out onto the catwalk he started running aft to give room to those coming out of the control car behind him. He had taken only a couple of steps when the catwalk seemed to be pulled out from under him. Reaching out, he caught a girder and pulled himself up on top of the apex girder of the keel. Beneath him he saw Lieutenant Anderson hanging to the catwalk, which had broken loose and was hanging freely, suspended only at the end near where the ship had broken, forward of where the control car was attached. Now hanging by his hands, Hall noticed that the after part of the ship had fallen away and heard the control car falling loose. Lieutenant Mayer came to Anderson's aid, throwing him a line by which he was able to crawl back into the nose of the ship. Mayer instructed Hall to secure the one valve control wire that was available, and he manipulated it while Mayer and Anderson brought the nose of the ship to a safe landing, about ten or twelve miles from where the accident had occurred.

Hall assured the court that while he was in the control car, there had been "perfect order and discipline." The duties of the officers and enlisted men were performed as calmly and efficiently as if they had been in normal flight. He had high praise for Lansdowne:

> The conduct of Captain Lansdowne in encouraging the members of his crew is noteworthy. When the ship was falling rapidly, and it looked as if we would crash into the ground, Captain Lansdowne, in attempting to allay the apparent apprehension of the elevator man, Allen, said, "Allen, she's all right. We'll stop her. She's falling fast now but she'll slow up." I personally felt the effect of his assurances, and I am sure that its effect was felt by all members of the crew in the control car at the time of the disaster. I am sure that Captain Lansdowne with his officers and men in the control car went to their death attempting to keep control of the ship, which they had not lost until the actual breaking occurred.

In making this statement I do so with the desire that the bravery of these men be made a note of in the record of this court, and that their conduct be recorded as upholding the best traditions of the service.[21]

Following Colonel Hall's testimony, Lt. Roland G. Mayer too read a prepared statement. His account was consistent with Hall's but carried the tale of the dreadful day to its conclusion. At the time of Lieutenant Anderson's struggle, Mayer pointed out, the ship was very close to the ground. The men dropped two trail ropes and mooring wires hoping to snag a tree and stop the ship; they made two attempts, but both failed. The nose, traveling at a ground speed of approximately thirty miles per hour, finally caught against a hill, ripping and slashing its helium bags; enough gas escaped to make the wreckage heavy enough to land. The men tied down the nose and the windward side to prevent the wreck from rolling onto a nearby farmhouse. By around noon, they were able to remove all personal effects. They left the ship in the hands of a deputy who assured them he would guard the property.[22]

Subsequently, during the questioning of Captain Steele, the issue of "demonstration flights" arose; the large number of requests for visits by the *Shenandoah* were examined against the schedule and weather. Steele held in his hand a list of 383 requests by individuals, chambers of commerce, and others, and this was only a partial list. Among them were a number of state fairs in the Midwest: Columbus, Ohio; Des Moines, Iowa; Minneapolis, Minnesota; Milwaukee, Wisconsin; and Detroit, Michigan. Steele added that the personnel of the *Shenandoah* had had a keen desire to make this final trip and to satisfy the public's demand. The voyage "was undertaken in a very hopeful spirit of bringing the utility and desirability of this class of craft home to the country."[23]

Anton Heinen was subpoenaed to appear before the court of inquiry and was called as a witness. Asked to state his occupation, he answered, "Just now trying to commercialize lighter-than-air in this country."[24] On questioning, he acknowledged having been in the employ of the Navy Department from mid-May 1922 until July 1, 1924. Later in the proceedings, Rosendahl was allowed to question Heinen and, as if knowing something about Heinen the court did not know, asked, "Were your services with the Navy terminated at your own request, or by failure of the Navy Department to renew your contract? . . . or by any other cause?" Heinen objected to the question, on the ground it was not pertinent to the current matter, and the court sustained his objection.[25] Subsequently,

Rosendahl asked when and why Heinen's connection with airships in Germany had ceased. Once again, the court sustained Heinen's objection to this question.[26]

Heinen's interrogation was lengthy, detailed, and often contentious. Asked about specific comments he had made to newspapers, he often claimed to have been misquoted or otherwise misrepresented. When he was asked about the sources of the information on which he based his claims to the media, it surfaced that most had come from newspaper reports and hearsay around Lakehurst. He stuck to his thesis concerning the gas-release valves: "The valves would have been kept on the ship, and all those poor boys would be with us and happy today."[27]

Heinen also claimed that Lansdowne had mishandled the ship. He went as far as to say, under direct questioning, that had he been in command of the ship the accident would not have happened.[28] Under direct questioning, however, he admitted that he had not had access to primary-source information. Further, the court wanted to know why, it having been made clear from the beginning that the proceedings were to be open, Heinen had not been present, so he might benefit from the detailed firsthand reports.

Court: "Were you aware that this court was an open court, and that you could have been present throughout the whole of the hearing?"

Heinen: "I was. I was aware of this court being open, Mr. President, but I was aware, besides, of a strong feeling of hostility, very, very, well to be expected against me, and, therefore, I have avoided to be here, so that nobody would possibly say that I was snooping around to get information for my own personal ends. That puts me into the position of basing everything on hearsay or on the press, and weighing as carefully as I can possibly through experience what is now said and what was not. I wanted to do this not to embarrass the court, and to make it possible for everybody to present his testimony without fear or feeling or without something adverse sitting on his back."

Court: "I can only assure you that you would not have embarrassed the court, but the court would have been very glad to have had you present during the whole of the hearings, so that when you went on the witness stand, your conclusions and deductions would have been made from the evidence given before the court, which, of course, the court must consider also."

The record shows that Heinen made no response to the court's comments.

The survivors of the *Shenandoah*, wanting to offer the court their joint assessment of the disaster, submitted a forty-two-page document titled, "Brief Submitted by Interested Parties (Survivors) in the Case of the *Shenandoah* Court of Inquiry." In it the survivors meticulously reexamined the testimony of the witnesses and gave their own analysis of the facts, having been present during the crash. They praised Lansdowne highly for his leadership and handling of the airship. They exposed Heinen's many unsubstantiated claims so thoroughly as essentially to render him an unreliable witness.

The survivors concluded their brief with a strong, united statement that they had not lost faith in rigid airships and considered them of great value for naval and commercial purposes. They declared themselves ready to do and give their utmost toward the continuation and advancement of rigid-airship development in the Navy and urged the court to recommend its "retention, continuation and furtherance." As if confident of the results of the investigation, the survivors ended their statement, "Without a doubt, the record and proceedings of this court of inquiry will go into the Annals of Military Law, and even of the whole country, as one of the most searching, complete and comprehensive investigations, technical or otherwise, ever conducted."[29]

The court concluded that the primary cause of the destruction of the *Shenandoah* had been the physical stresses created by the storm and not "any inherent fault of design or misconceived alteration in the structure of the ship." The court recommended that no further proceedings be held in the matter. People at Lakehurst who awaited the results of the court shared the enthusiasm in the program expressed by the survivors. Wiley was not the least among them as his interest remained very high. The crash of the *Shenandoah* did not lead to the end of LTA flight as many had predicted it would.

The men of the LTA service were bold, brave, committed men who believed in what they were doing. They could lament their losses, absorb them, and move on to greater achievement. Whether they said so openly or not, there must have been some in their ranks who wondered about the future of their technology. Nevertheless, the *Shenandoah* disaster did not prevent a number of the survivors from serving on other airships, including the USS *Los Angeles*, USS *Akron*, and USS *Macon*.

As for Wiley, he, with the Navy's LTA program, would press ahead. On the basis of his performance and time in rank, Wiley was due for promotion. He duly received a memorandum from the Bureau of Navigation informing him that, as of December 17, 1925, he had been promoted to the rank of lieutenant commander.

6

Changes in Command

It was to be expected that the loss of the *Shenandoah* would bring changes in the LTA program in 1926. The year started with Captain Steele in command of the *Los Angeles*, but Moffett sensed the need for changes in the program's command structure. Steele's days in that role were numbered. On March 15 Lt. Cdr. Charles E. Rosendahl reported on board *Los Angeles* for temporary duty as her executive officer.[1] This time of transition was difficult for Moffett. He was faced with making the decision to promote a new commanding officer from within the LTA service or to bring in someone from the outside. The situation was delicate. Bringing in an outsider would block the advancement of officers who were junior but had more experience with airships. More senior appointments, however, might offer more weight within the Navy for getting things done. In any case, when Rosendahl was appointed it was with the expectation he would succeed Steele. Capt. Edward S. Jackson, an officer with no experience in the LTA service, was given command of NAS Lakehurst.[2] Moffett had deemed both Wiley and Pierce highly qualified but, in the end, passed them over in favor of Rosendahl. On May 10, 1926, Rosendahl took command of the *Los Angeles*, relieving Steele.[3] Wiley still commanded great respect from Moffett and all those around him. He had been serving as the *Los Angeles* navigator since April 1925. He and Rosendahl made a good pair and had logged hundreds of hours of flight time together. The command was made stronger when, on June 8, Lt. Thomas G. W. Settle reported for duty.[4] He was a solid officer of strong character and a very positive addition.

In August 1926 Wiley submitted to the chief of the Bureau of Navigation a request for leave followed by reassignment to duty on a unit of Battleship Division 5. He explained that it had been his original intent to remain in aviation for two years but that at the end of that time, he had been informed by his commanding officer that no suitable relief for him had been trained. He was told by Steele that he could expect a favorable endorsement from him in about six months. By the end of that time, however, the *Shenandoah* disaster had happened, making a request for transfer inadvisable. Prior to his own detachment in May 1926, Captain Steele had requested that Wiley remain on until his (Steele's) relief had acquainted himself with the qualifications of the available officers.[5]

Wiley had given as further justification for transfer that he had been on shore duty continuously since September 1921, with only about five years of sea service since his graduation from the Naval Academy and none in his present grade. He stated plainly he needed battleship duty for his professional advancement. When Wiley's request reached Rosenahl's desk, it ran into a brick wall. Rosendahl disapproved the request on the grounds that Wiley's services could not be spared at that time without detriment to the *Los Angeles* and to the rigid-airship program in general. That meant, owing to a shortage of trained personnel, at least an additional six months.[6] The chief of the Bureau of Navigation upheld Rosendahl's decision. By that time it appeared there would be a delay of at least ten months, even twelve, in granting Wiley's request.

When the NAS Lakehurst was founded and was being populated with officers, enlisted men, and civilian workers, there had been general excitement at the prospects of an LTA program for the Navy, but by 1926 things were changing. Artificial social strata developed that caused friction among the various elements. Things came together as a metaphorical "perfect storm" in 1926, but the stage was being set well before that. Klein had been a highly capable destroyer captain in the world war. Settle, who had served under his command, described him as a splendid officer and gentleman with plenty of energy, ambition, and initiative. People at Lakehurst, however, regarded Klein as abrasive. He had annoyed both Moffett and Steele by conniving orders to make the *ZR 3*'s transatlantic flight. Klein was commanding officer of the NAS until delivery of the *ZR 3*, at which time Steele took over both the *Los Angeles* and the air station. Klein felt he should have been given command of the *Shenandoah* instead of Lansdowne after McCrary's departure and found it difficult to take an administrative job. This was a particularly hard pill to swallow since Lansdowne was two years Klein's junior, by date of commission.

Klein and Lansdowne fought constantly. This rift between the air station officer and airship officer set a precedent that lasted for years at Lakehurst. The base was split into two factions—the airship officers and the base officers. The crews of both the *Shenandoah* and *Los Angeles* too considered themselves superior to the station-only men. The air station personnel were primarily members of staff corps or otherwise not on flight status and, thus, not receiving the higher flight pay. The pay differential was a source of jealousy, especially among the wives.[7] The children of Lakehurst did what children do—rode bicycles, played games, and made friends—impervious to the interpersonal and professional strife of the adults.

After the loss of the *Shenandoah* and the death of Lansdowne, things at NAS Lakehurst began to change. Rosendahl became the focal point of media interest. Relationships among some of the survivors began to deteriorate, and a number of them requested transfer or were reassigned to other posts. Klein himself was reassigned to command the minesweeper USS *Chewink* (AM 39), but in early 1926 he resigned from the Navy.[8]

Years later, Settle explained the atmosphere at Lakehurst during this period:

> The officers at Lakehurst then were a diverse lot, HTA, surface ship, submariner, and Naval Constructors [structural engineers]. The Station was relatively isolated in the "Jersey boon-docks,"—ship and station were small commands, and ordinarily-trivial personality clashes tended to be exacerbated into animosities out-of-proportion to cause.
>
> The physical isolation fostered a sense of "separateness," exacerbated personality clashes between some individuals, and aggravated jealousies, "rivalries," between groups, such as those-on-flight-status versus those-not-on-flight-status,—line [i.e., eligible for command] versus Staff Corps people, . . . uniformed versus civilian personnel—ships' crews versus Station personnel.[9]

While some officers likely requested transfer back to the fleet because of the atmosphere at Lakehurst, the reason Wiley gave in his letter appears to have been true. He knew a tour with the surface fleet was essential to his promotion and career development. As Settle would recall, "the Navy, in the '20s and '30s, was run by old-line, 'shellback' [i.e., have crossed the Equator at sea] battleship people, the 'Gun Club,' who viewed aviation (both HTA and LTA), and submarines, as interesting new-fangled things *possibly* having *some*, if meager, future value as support types for the battleship-cruiser-destroyer fleets. They favored *modest* appropriations for aviation development, but not of magnitudes to significantly divert funding from surface vessels and weaponry."[10]

A month after Wiley's request for transfer, the Bureau of Navigation asked Rosendahl when a relief for him might be available. In his response of September 22 Rosendahl claimed it was impossible to say: Wiley's services had been, and would continue to be, of very great value to the *Los Angeles* and Navy LTA program. He estimated another six months to a year would be needed, depending on the progress of the student officers.[11] Wiley, though longing for sea duty, continued to serve well in the LTA service and accumulated flight time. Under Rosendahl the *Los Angeles* flew frequently and logged more moorings to the mast of the *Patoka*. From the time Rosendahl assumed command until the end of 1926, she logged nearly three hundred hours of flight time and accomplished seven moorings to the *Patoka*.[12]

For the most part, 1927 passed in routine fashion, with repeated flights and no untoward incidents. January 1928, however, brought a new experiment for the *Los Angeles*, a collaborative effort between the airship and the aircraft carrier USS *Saratoga* (CV 3). The *Saratoga*, the sister ship of the USS *Lexington* (CV 2), was one of the earliest American aircraft carriers. Originally ordered as a battle cruiser, she was converted to an aircraft carrier while under construction at the New York Shipbuilding Corporation of Camden, New Jersey, to comply with the 1922 Washington Naval Treaty. She was to be assigned permanently to the Pacific Fleet, but in January 1928 she was still on the East Coast.

In preparation for a daring interaction between these two strikingly different ships, Wiley was dispatched on January 20 to report for temporary duty to the commanding officer of the Saratoga and, with plans set, he returned to Lakehurst four days later.[13] On the morning of Friday, January 27, with no rehearsals, the *Los Angeles* set out on her mission to land on the deck of the *Saratoga* while both ship and airship were moving. She took off at 0354 with a total of forty-seven men on board: nine officers, thirty-two crewmen, five student officers, and one passenger.[14]

By noon they were over Newport, Rhode Island, maneuvering in the vicinity of the *Saratoga*, anchored in Narragansett Bay. At 1220, the *Saratoga* got under way. *Los Angeles* dropped in altitude and at 1415 went to landing stations. With *Saratoga* steaming into the wind at approximately ten knots, *Los Angeles* took station about one hundred yards on the carrier's port beam. Winds were only about ten knots but very gusty. *Saratoga* was rolling and pitching moderately. The airship released gas from all the maneuvering valves for a minute and a half and at 1453 began the landing approach, descending to 225 feet and maneuvering at various speeds to overtake the *Saratoga*, which was now making fifteen knots.

The gusting winds combined with the pitching and rolling of the aircraft carrier made things much more difficult, unpredictable, and dangerous than they would have been on a calm day with flat seas. The airship was over the *Saratoga's* deck at 1524 when a gust of wind carried her up to four hundred feet. Gas was valved off for another forty-five seconds, and the airship returned to a 225-foot altitude. Two minutes later, the trail ropes were dropped and the crew on the deck below began to haul the airship down into position. This time, a gust drove the *Los Angeles* down and to starboard. This movement was checked by the emergency release of a thousand pounds of ballast. By 1535, with the *Saratoga* still pitching and rolling and the winds very gusty, the airship had landed, but the flight-deck crew was having a very difficult time securing the control car. Only seven minutes later, another strong upward gust of wind lifted the forward part of the car out of the hands of the crew trying to secure it.

A few moments before, Wiley had left the airship to join the crew on the deck of the *Saratoga* to assist the landing party. Now, owing to the unpredictable conditions, it was deemed best for the airship to cast off from the aircraft carrier entirely and make her way back to Lakehurst. It was necessary to leave Wiley behind.[15] After the fact, Rosendahl, in his capacity as commanding officer of the *Los Angeles*, requested that Wiley have orders retroactively to reflect the fact Rosendahl had "considered it necessary to have an experienced *Los Angeles* officer on board the *Saratoga* to assist the personnel of the latter. Upon the departure of the *Los Angeles* it was necessary to leave Lieutenant Commander Wiley on board the *Saratoga* until he could be taken ashore to return to base."[16]

It had not been an easy task to land a 653-foot-long airship on the deck of an 888-foot-long *Saratoga* on the sea, but Rosendahl deemed the experiment a success. He left its value unstated, however, and no further such attempts were made.

On February 26, 1928, the *Los Angeles* left Lakehurst en route to the Panama Canal Zone. Late the next day, she sighted Colon and by 2220 had landed at France Field.[17] On the morning of February 28, she departed France Field, crossed the Isthmus of Panama, and was at the Pacific end of the canal by 1110.[18] Seeing the Panama Canal from the *Los Angeles* must have instilled in Wiley a mixture of wonderment and nostalgia, given that he had been through the canal on the water. This was another first—the first time the canal had been traversed by an airship—but, more importantly to planners like Moffett, it demonstrated the possibility of forging new routes for the airship as long as there was support along the way in the form of land bases or ships like the *Patoka*. After circling Panama City, late in the day on the twenty-eighth the *Los Angeles* made for the *Patoka*, then in Luna Cay, Cuba; she was moored to the *Patoka* by 1030 the next day.[19]

Following what was considered a very successful tour, the airship was back at Lakehurst late on March 3. Lakehurst settled into a routine of regional flights, when the weather allowed, and constant maintenance and repair. In midsummer 1928, however, an unexpected opportunity presented itself that would do much to advance Wiley's career.

Between 1926 and 1928, the Germans at Luftschiffbau Zeppelin had built another airship patterned after *LZ 126*, designated *LZ 127*. True to previous German practice, she used the more cost-effective hydrogen gas rather than helium. She was the largest airship in the world at the time, with a length of 776 feet and a volume of 3,707,550 cubic feet. The *LZ 127* remained in German service, and in her first two years of operation was used primarily for experimental work and "demonstration" purposes with the long-range goal of making regular commercial transatlantic passenger flights. Her first long-distance flight, in fact, was to be transatlantic, ending at NAS Lakehurst. As the time drew near, Dr. Hugo Eckener, who would command the airship on this flight, invited one Lakehurst officer to travel to Friedrichshafen to make the flight. It was natural that Rosendahl would be selected for this purpose, and on July 6—two days before what would have been Count (*Graf*) Zeppelin's ninetieth birthday—he left Lakehurst on temporary duty to Friedrichshafen.[20] Two days later, on the anniversary date, Zeppelin's daughter, the Countess Hella von Brandenstein-Zeppelin, christened the airship the *Graf Zeppelin*.

In Rosendahl's absence, Wiley was given temporary command of the *Los Angeles*. By this time Wiley's LTA flying experience was impressive in terms of number of hours. He understood the airship and all the variables that could influence her flight and safety. He was fully capable of assuming command, and he did so with great energy. His first flight in command was a regional one on July 16 with Lt. Cdr. B. J. Rodgers as executive officer.[21] Wiley was very comfortable as the commander of the *Los Angeles* and set an ambitious schedule of flights—five between July 16 and July 30.

If most things had become routine, Nature presented unexpected challenges that required creative thinking. Wiley was quite good at this. On July 31, en route from Baltimore, Maryland, to Lakehurst, he encountered difficulty landing. The airship was over the landing area at 0345 and running about 250 pounds light at an altitude of four hundred feet. A fifteen-degree temperature inversion, a layer of cold air trapping warmer air beneath it, made the ship too buoyant to land. Standard procedure would have been to valve off some of the helium, but he chose to save the expensive gas by taking on more ballast. He used the ship's engines to maneuver as close to the ground as he could get and then dropped a "Jacob's ladder" to the ground crew. Seventeen of these men climbed the rope, and the ballast they represented allowed the airship to land safely.[22]

Weather permitting, he had the ship flying whenever he could. In October he took the ship on her longest flight since her transatlantic journey to the United States. The Bureau of Aeronautics, responding to a civilian request, ordered the *Los Angeles* to fly to San Antonio, Texas, on a demonstration flight that would coincide with an American Legion convention.[23] The ship took off from Lakehurst at 1825 on October 6, 1928, with eleven officers and thirty crewmen.[24] Drawing on what he had learned from the *Shenandoah's* previous overland experiences, Wiley was alert to changes in terrain and weather not encountered commonly over the ocean, and he navigated to avoid threatening storm fronts. The ship made her appearance over San Antonio on the morning of October 8, in time for the parade, during which she circled above the city to show herself off to the crowds below. By 1614 she was circling over Dallas, Texas, before steering for Fort Worth, site of the National Helium Production Plant, where she secured to a mooring mast.[25] At the time, this was the world's only helium production facility. Here helium had been extracted from natural gas since 1921, and it was a poignant moment when the *Los Angeles* arrived. While the airship was dependent on the helium produced by this facility, this was the first visit to it by any airship.

The next morning, the ship left the mast at 0858 on her return trip to Lakehurst, on a course toward Chicago. At 1800, having flown over Kansas City, Missouri, and Leavenworth, Kansas, Wiley set a course for his hometown of Chillicothe, Missouri.[26] The *Chillicothe Constitution-Tribune* for October 9 carried the headline, "Expect Dirigible to Pass over City at 10 Tonight."[27] Wiley had sent a wire ahead to Harry W. Graham, secretary of the Chamber of Commerce, so informing him. Graham responded, "Your home towns, Chillicothe and Wheeling, desire to do honors as you pass over on your return trip. National Guard radio ten-mile limit will signal you from here if we can learn when you will pass over. City will decorate with national colors from streets, federal and civic buildings if in day time. Suggestions will be appreciated by wire."[28]

The Chamber of Commerce had arranged to have the National Guard's radio transmitter installed on the roof of the Strand Theater and to have Wiley's sister, Fay Oren, on hand to send a message as the airship flew over. Herbert Wiley's father had been invited to travel from Wheeling to take part in the event, but he and Herbert had made separate plans to communicate by lights as he flew over Wheeling. During a luncheon meeting of the Chamber of Commerce, a fireworks committee reported having arranged for flares and rockets to be on hand for the celebration; the newspaper encouraged the people of Chillicothe to bring Roman candles, sky-rockets, and colored lights to "set them off as the *Los Angeles* passes over in recognition of the great honor bestowed upon this city and vicinity by a noble son."

The next day's edition of the newspaper reported that hundreds of his old friends were turning out for the flyover.[29] At the earliest sighting, moments before 10 p.m., the cluster of lights on the ship resembled the numerous stars visible that night, but as the huge airship got closer, the spectators in the streets and on rooftops could make out its shape. The National Guard radio operators turned out not to know the frequency needed to get messages to the ship. As a backup, the Guardsmen used "blinker lights" to signal the *Los Angeles*. After just a few flashes of light, the airship acknowledged receipt of the message. Fay was able to communicate with her brother through signal lights, as were members of Wiley's high school class. Wiley had the *Los Angeles* make a "complete circle of the city, letting the home folks take in as much of the ship as the starry though moonless night would allow." He then headed the airship eastward toward Wheeling, where his father waited on the ground to signal him by lights in a prearranged fashion. As the *Los Angeles* flew overhead, Wiley's father, crying, pointed to the big airship and proclaimed with pride, "That's my boy!"[30]

The flyover of his hometowns was a deeply moving event for both Wiley and the people of Chillicothe and Wheeling. The Chillicothe newspaper for October 11 ran the headline, "Wiley Wires Appreciation to Livingston County Folk."[31] The article reported, "His first act on arriving at Lakehurst was to wire the *Constitution-Tribune* his appreciation." His message to the newspaper read: "Arrived, thirty-five hours from Fort Worth traversing in four days, 4,000 miles and 22 states. . . . Proud to bring the navy ship to the middle west. Deeply touched by reception in Livingston county. Sorry I could not pass during daylight and stay longer. Hard to be so near and not shake hands with friends. Please thank people for reception."[32]

The anonymous author of the article could not conceal his own emotions in his concluding paragraphs:

> The big ship and its commander have been the center of attention throughout the 22 states traversed the past few days and Commander Wiley has received the plaudits of thousands during the cruise. But cheering crowds in San Antonio or Fort Worth can never be as touching as the love and best wishes of a father or a sister.
>
> It is easy to image [*sic*] the feeling of the commander as he soared over Livingston county, perhaps able to see the crowds in the streets and saying to himself:
>
> "There's a crowd down there that used to play marbles, hunt hickory nuts and go swimming with me in the old swimmin' hole a few years ago."
>
> Those are the people you know intimately and never forget and they are the people who take a real pride in your accomplishments.

For three consecutive days, the *Chillicothe Constitution-Tribune* had covered the flight of the *Los Angeles* until her return to Lakehurst. On the last day, however, a new story was unfolding, involving another airship: under the command of Hugo Eckener, the *Graf Zeppelin* left Friedrichshafen on October 11, 1928. The same day, Wiley demonstrated a deeply personal side of his leadership style when he drafted a memorandum to the ten *Los Angeles* officers who were, at that time, serving under him.

> Memo for All Officers.
> As it is expected that our Skipper will return before the ship flies again, I take this means of expressing to all officers my appreciation of their work during the time I have been in temporary command. First I want to thank you for your loyalty. I recognize that loyalty works both ways and I have tried to be loyal to you and I am satisfied that there has been more loyalty and cooperation lately than ever before. I appreciate it. I do not like for people to work for me—rather to work with me.
>
> Although, we did not operate to any great extent, I am satisfied with the work done, and particularly gratified by the cheerful manner in which you did your work and jumped in to make as much of a success as possible and I particularly congratulate you on the success of the Fort Worth trip, and am sorry that it

was necessary to leave some behind. I have felt all the time that it was shipmate or team spirit that made us get along so well in all of our operations.

If I remain as Executive Officer I hope that the same spirit will continue to give us a better and more easily earned success and we'll show the skipper some real team work.

H. V. Wiley

Lieutenant Commander, U.S. Navy Commanding.[33]

The *Graf Zeppelin* arrived at Lakehurst on October 15, following a flight of 111 hours and 44 minutes. In addition to a crew of forty men she carried twenty passengers, including Charles Rosendahl and a Hearst newspaper reporter. While successful, the journey had not been uneventful. On the morning of October 13 the ship entered a strong squall line that battered her much as had the storm that had caused the crash of the *Shenandoah*. Eckener and his men were able to regain control of the airship, and she emerged from the storm safely, though with some damage. The lower covering of the port fin had been torn away; further damage here would have left the airship uncontrollable. A four-man team was dispatched to make repairs while still in flight. Sensing the potential for disaster, Eckener sent out a distress call that was picked up by news media around the globe, giving the impression that the *Graf Zeppelin* was in such trouble that she might crash before landing. The emergency repairs appeared to save the zeppelin for the moment, but she encountered a second storm near Bermuda. The airship weathered this storm without further damage and made her successful landing at Lakehurst at 1738. She finally made it into the hangar at about 0300 on October 16.

Later the same night, a makeshift platform was constructed from chairs in one of the rooms of the hangar, and from it Eckener spoke freely to the press about the journey.[34] He said that very bad weather in the Atlantic had caused him to fly by way of Gibraltar, adding 1,200 miles to his journey. He talked about the fabric being torn away from the fin but emphasized nothing like this had been seen ever in the history of zeppelins. Safely on the ground, airshipmen were an extremely confident lot who saw things one of two ways—either a total disaster or a generally good flight in spite of difficulties. A safe landing after a near disaster was, to them, merely proof of the safety of LTA flight. With great confidence, Eckener told reporters how they had effected repairs over the midocean and how a happy outcome spoke to the safety of dirigibles for transoceanic flight. Commander Rosendahl said the ship had "taken a good beating and stood it well."

The *Graf Zeppelin* made a ground landing at Lakehurst. Eckener had a strong preference for ground handlers and a hangar; consequently, the *Graf Zeppelin* never attempted to moor to the high mast.[35] As the fatigued crew did its part to get the dirigible settled for the night so that they might get some much-needed sleep, Dr. Eckener continued to be the center of attention for the press.

Dr. Eckener was strolling across the space of the landing field which lay between the grounded Zeppelin and the hangar. The impudent nose of the *Los Angeles* was to be seen through the open doors.

"Ah!" said the Doctor expressively. He stopped still. A look of proud admiration was on his face. The pride of the father. He had brought this dirigible across four years ago.

"Yes, sir," he repeated in German, "that's my baby!"[36]

New York City feted Eckener and his crew. Millions attended a parade in their honor that was said to rival the parade afforded Col. Charles Lindbergh.[37] With the arrival of the *Graf Zeppelin*, airships had been promoted from celebrity to high celebrity, and the brave crews who brought the ship across the Atlantic Ocean safely were regarded as heroes as flight by dirigibles was not yet regarded as routine.

Wiley's stock was rising; he was becoming a key personality in the world of LTA flight. One bit of evidence of this came in the form of an invitation sent by wireless dispatch to Wiley by the Assistant Secretary of the Navy for Aeronautics on October 17, 1928. The note explained that three assistant secretaries for aeronautics were giving a luncheon in honor of Dr. Eckener and members of the zeppelin party at the Mayflower Hotel and that Wiley was cordially invited to join them.[38] Wiley's inclusion was definitely recognition from those within the world of aeronautics, but he was winning over the public as well. Following his Fort Worth round-trip flight, he received numerous letters of gratitude from mayors, city councils, and businessmen over whose cities the *Los Angeles* had flown. Exhibiting another attribute of a developing leader, he always acknowledged such letters with heartfelt replies. Harry W. Graham of the Chillicothe Chamber of Commerce wrote the most meaningful of these letters, on October

16, addressing Wiley as a dear friend. Graham told Wiley the town rejoiced in his achievements and was proud to call him their "Native Son."[39] Wiley responded thanking the town for its kind sentiments. He told Graham he had many requests from important people to fly over their cities, but that it was very gratifying for him to bring the Navy's airship to his hometown to give his own people a glimpse of her.[40]

After writing to Graham, Wiley wrote to Fay to share his feelings about the flyover of Chillicothe and to tell her of the arrival of the *Graf Zeppelin*. He told her they were swamped at Lakehurst with people wanting to see the German airship. He estimated from 100,000 to 400,000 people came out on Sundays.[41]

It took two weeks to repair the *Graf Zeppelin* for her homeward journey, but prior to her transatlantic departure she made regional demonstration flights in the United States with Wiley on board for some of them. Much like Moffett, Eckener selected passengers for the *Graf Zeppelin*'s trip who were in a position to advance his cause, such as representatives of the Hearst publishing empire.[42] The press fed the thirst of the American and European populations for news regarding developments in flight, and it piqued the interest of industrialists and investors. While in the United States, Eckener took advantage of his celebrity to meet with American bankers and financiers to gather support and financial backing for the establishment of a regular transcontinental passenger service.

It was, accordingly, no accident that Eckener was drawn to Wiley. By the time the *Graf Zeppelin* arrived in the United States, Wiley was already a well-known figure. His temporary duty as commander of the *Los Angeles*, capping his long tour as executive officer and navigator, had catapulted him to fame in the consciousness of the Navy and the public. He had captured also the respect of Hugo Eckener himself, who had requested that Wiley join the *Graf Zeppelin* on its U.S. flights; Moffett had issued the orders for Wiley to comply.[43] This personal attention from Eckener was an honor that spoke to Wiley's status.

The *Graf Zeppelin* departed Lakehurst in the afternoon of October 29 en route to Friedrichshafen, with Lt. T. G. W. Settle and Lt. C. E. Bauch on board on temporary duty.[44] The same day, Rosendahl resumed command of the *Los Angeles*, and Wiley returned to his duties as executive officer. November weather at the air station prevented the *Los Angeles* from making any flights that month, but there was plenty of activity inside her hangar. In addition to the never-ending maintenance and repairs, the ship was being used as an experimental platform for innovations to be incorporated into the next two dirigibles to be built for the Navy. These would be the products of a joint venture between the Goodyear and Zeppelin companies in Akron, Ohio.

The Navy's original interest in dirigibles was as aircraft with a longer range of operation over the ocean than airplanes had. The aircraft carriers USS *Langley* (CV 1), *Lexington*, and *Saratoga* had demonstrated the feasibility of extending the range of airplanes by carrying them far into the ocean on board surface vessels that could launch and recover them. This concept was not lost on the proponents of dirigibles. The new dirigibles were being designed to carry, launch, and recover airplanes too, though with some limitations. One of the innovations with which the *Los Angeles* was being outfitted was a hooking device for capturing airplanes in flight.

In the first week of January 1929, the weather cooperated for a training flight to Florida, where the *Los Angeles* moored to the *Patoka* in St. Joseph Bay. She returned to Lakehurst on the fifteenth after a useful but uneventful round trip. For those on board, the flight was a welcome break from hangar life but, on return, there was more, and prolonged, hangar time due both to prohibitive weather and the need for vital repairs.

The Lakehurst lull provided Wiley the opportunity to repeat his request for transfer to battleship duty. He requested specifically to be detached from his present duty about June 30 and ordered to one of the battleships of the Battle Fleet, preferably in Division 5.[45] He had been on aviation duty for six years with no fleet experience since 1921. The specific language of his request reflected a well-considered plan. He wanted "to round out [his] professional experience with a cruise in the fleet before completion of the new Scouting Airships under construction." He fully intended to return to aviation.

As before, Wiley's request found its way to Rosendahl's desk where it received a denial, this time even firmer than its predecessor. Among the reasons for denial were strong statements of the high regard in which Wiley was held within the LTA program. It was clear that Rosendahl had plans for Wiley within aviation. In his adverse endorsement forwarded to Admiral Moffett, Rosendahl stated that while it was laudable Wiley wanted to round out his professional experience, it was not then possible to make the requested change. He pointed out that a number of personnel shifts requested by the commanding officer had not been effected, including the assignment of Wiley to command of the *Los Angeles* from

February 1, 1929, to June 30, 1929—and a month of that time had already transpired. Further, there had been delays in the delivery of materials essential for airship developmental research. People of Wiley's experience would be needed in these programs before they could be handed over to others. There was a scarcity of experienced personnel of suitable rank, many of whom had to be used in training roles. While Rosendahl was sympathetic with Wiley's request, he felt he could not endorse it until September 1, 1929.[46]

Rosendahl was in the difficult position of protecting his mission—growth of the LTA program—and supporting a talented and deserving officer under his command. Admiral Moffett supported Rosendahl's decision, sharing the belief it was important to the program to have Wiley serve as commander of the *Los Angeles* for a period of six months. He reminded Wiley that his detail to the *Los Angeles* counted as sea duty, but that was little consolation to someone who wanted to actually be at sea.

Wiley's Navy career had started in the interwar years. Advancement in the military can be slow in peacetime. His reasons for volunteering for the LTA service had included a chance for recognition and advancement. He was a solid officer who did his job in a highly professional manner, avoiding political intrigue, and finding ways to contribute to the service. The denial for transfer to the surface fleet was a tacit statement he had made himself nearly indispensable to the naval air service. What appeared on the surface to be a rejection was in fact a testimonial to his worth—he had made it—but he was far from being done. Greater achievements lay ahead of him.

During 1929 the *Los Angeles* was presented with other opportunities for demonstrations that would put her in the eyes of the public. She departed Lakehurst on Monday, March 4, for Washington to participate in the inauguration parade for the newly elected president, Herbert Hoover.[47] The trip was marked by bad weather and poor visibility, but she made it on time to join the procession of airships that formed an aerial parade down Pennsylvania Avenue. After providing the crowds an impressive spectacle, the airship was released to return to Lakehurst, where she settled into her routine of training, maintenance, repair, and experimentation with new equipment, such as the hook-on device. With a number of research-and-development projects under way or on the drawing board at Lakehurst, Rosendahl was promoted to the position of Commander Rigid Airship Training and Experimental Squadron (ComRATES).[48] With two more dirigibles building, Rosendahl's new position assumed great significance. The use of the *Los Angeles* as an experimental platform at Lakehurst would be translated into the design of the new ships.

At 1440 on May 9, 1929, the crew of the *Los Angeles* was mustered, and Lt. Cdr. C. E. Rosendahl read his orders detaching him from command of the airship and ordering him to duty as ComRATES. Lt. Cdr. H. V. Wiley assumed command of the *Los Angeles* immediately, with Lt. Jack G. Richardson as his executive officer.[49] Moments after the ceremony ended, the ship was walked out of the hangar and taken aloft. In the days that followed, Wiley set an aggressive flight schedule.

7

Commanding
the *Los Angeles*

A mong the experimental projects Wiley inherited with his new command was the airplane hook-on device. This was a retractable trapeze-like structure that could be lowered from and withdrawn into the airship. When it was in its lowered position, a biplane equipped with a hook on its superior wing could maneuver into position to achieve "hook-on," or "landing." Once secure, the aircraft could be withdrawn into the body of the airship to be stored until made airborne again by lowering it from the hangar and releasing the hook. It was a simple concept that required development.

The first in-flight tests of the hook-on device were conducted on July 3. Wiley was in command of the airship as she maneuvered over Lakehurst. The biplane to be tested was a Vought UO-1 with a hook on the upper wing. At 0415 the *Los Angeles* headed into the wind, and the pilot, Lt. A. W. "Jake" Gorton, made his approach. At 0421 the plane touched the trapeze but did not hook. The approaches continued, and at 0427 the plane touched the trapeze again and remained on briefly before falling away. Minutes later, Wiley interrupted the trials briefly to adjust the airship's altitude. He dropped to 1,500 feet before climbing to 2,500 feet to start the trials again. At 0451 the plane was on the hook for about five seconds but slipped off. The tests were discontinued after a total of fifteen approaches.[1] While the results were not as good as desired, the tests were deemed successful. Following modifications, more trials would be needed to perfect the maneuver.

In the interval the airship underwent numerous repairs, maintenance actions, and modifications that preempted hook-on flight testing. The next opportunity did not come until August 20. At 1838, altitude 2,200 feet, and airspeed of fifty knots, Gorton made a successful landing and took off again about ten minutes later.[2] The landing procedure was practiced numerous times with variable, but improving, results. The feasibility of the maneuver was established solidly.

On July 22 Wiley left for Cleveland, Ohio, on temporary duty to confer with the organizers of the National Air Races regarding participation of the *Los Angeles*.[3] The races, held annually since 1920, were designed to showcase the rapid development of manned flight, focusing both on technology and the skills of the pilots. Events included cross-country races with finish lines in Cleveland, landing contests, parachute-jumping contests, dirigibles, and glider demonstrations. The 1929 races were to be held in Cleveland between August 24 and September 2. The best fliers in the country were drawn to this event every year, including such notables as James Doolittle, Wiley Post, Roscoe Turner, and Charles Lindbergh, among others. It was a fertile mixing of the best aviation minds in the country.

At the event, while Eckener and the *Graf Zeppelin* grabbed most of the attention of the press, Wiley and the *Los Angeles* impressed the crowds with a feat they had not seen previously. The *Los Angeles* had been cruising on various courses in the vicinity of Cleveland around 1530 on August 28 at an altitude of approximately 2,500 feet. At 1657 she dropped to 2,000 feet and at an airspeed of forty-seven knots prepared for Jake Gorton to land his plane hook on in full view of the crowd below. Gorton made three unsuccessful approaches, missing the landing each time, but at 1735 he made a successful hookup and ten minutes later the airplane was hoisted close to the airship. That was not all: the crowd was in for an extra treat. While the biplane was hoisted, Lt. C. M. Bolster boarded it from the airship as a passenger. At 1750 the landing device was lowered and the airplane took off with its new passenger. The *Los Angeles* herself then landed at a temporary mast that had been sent from Lakehurst for the occasion.[4] The next morning, Col. and Mrs. Charles Lindbergh expressed to Wiley an interest in a short flight on board the *Los Angeles*, but they had to be denied, because Wiley could not muster a new ground crew to land the airship once she took flight again.[5]

The successes of the *Los Angeles* with the hook-on device stimulated a larger developmental effort to evaluate the feasibility of airships that could carry scout and fighter planes great distances then release them for reconnaissance or combat.

The *Los Angeles* had not been designed to carry airplanes, and her trapeze device was merely experimental. Lessons learned from these trials, however, would be incorporated into the next two dirigibles—the USS *Akron* and *Macon*.

The aviation leaders at the Cleveland Air Races discussed among themselves the future of manned flight and the comparative advantages and disadvantages of lighter-than-air and heavier-than-air craft. Homer H. Metz of the International News Service captured some of the commentary in an article.[6] This was still a formative time in aviation, and the future of LTA flight was uncertain. Metz asked a number of the aviation experts the simple question, "Which of the two modes of air travel—lighter-than-air craft or heavier-than-air craft—offers the most in practicability and efficiency?"

Metz set the stage for his readers:

> Resurrected by the remarkable globe-circling flight of the *Graf Zeppelin* and the astounding feats being performed daily by airplanes at the national air races here, this old, but highly important question is once again a storm center between outstanding leaders in aeronautics and aviation.
>
> The successful ocean flights of the Zeppelin as contrasted to the large number of airplane pilots and passengers who have lost their lives in attempted sea flights, particularly the westward crossing of the Atlantic, has led many of the flying notables assembled here to conclude that the airplane will never be the equal of the dirigible, especially in the matter of dangerous long distance flights. This belief is by no means a unanimous one, however. For every advocate of the dirigible as the best means of air travel another person can be found who favors the airplane.

The comments of "five outstanding figures in aviation" were reproduced in the article. Metz caught up to Lindbergh just before he was about to take off to amaze the crowd with "a series of loops and spins" in a Navy fighter plane. Even that pioneer was somewhat uncertain what direction future aviation would take. "Airplanes and airships . . . are both of inestimable value as a means of transportation. There is much to be said in behalf of each of them. At the present time, however, I should say that the airship, such as the *Graf Zeppelin* for instance, is the most practical machine for over-sea travel and the airplane the best for overland travel. I look for the airplane to be developed to such an extent in the future that it will become the best medium for flying everywhere and under all conditions."[7]

Capt. Eddie Rickenbacker, the great "ace" of the world war, when asked the same question, surprised the reporter with his answer. He proclaimed the dirigible to be the most practical vehicle yet invented for traveling long distances and pointed to the flight of the *Graf Zeppelin* as proof, deeming this as "one of the greatest feats" yet accomplished by man in flight. Not all of the experts were of the same mind. The famous builder of airplanes Anthony H. G. Fokker felt the airship had reached the limits of its development while the airplane was still in its infancy. Capt. Lewis A. Yancey and Capt. Roger Q. Williams, "heroes of the Maine to Rome flight" of July 11, weighed in in favor of the airplane.

The *Los Angeles* performed well at the air races. She held the interest of believers in LTA flight and likely won over others. Wiley rose even higher in esteem as he was welcomed into the company of the world-famous aviators who had gathered at Cleveland. His stature was growing also in the mind of Hugo Eckener, who was thoroughly familiar with Wiley's experience as an airship commander. It was with a mixture of emotions that Wiley flew his airship back to Lakehurst. He was aware of his growing role in the development of LTA flight, and he knew that two new and better airships were under construction. He expected to be assigned to one of them, yet he still felt the need for battleship duty to advance his career. At a practical level, he needed to know for family reasons what the Navy had in store for him. He had sent another memorandum to the chief of the Bureau of Navigation on August 19, 1929, asking for an update on his request. He explained he needed to plan for his family, especially the schooling of his children. It was his desire to make a change during the next month, September, so his children could start school at the beginning of the academic year, and then to serve at sea for two years while the fleet of new airships was being completed. Changing his original request slightly, if there was no billet available on a battleship, his next choice would be assignment as navigator on a light cruiser, if possible.[8] It was, after all, sea duty that he needed.

Wiley's response came from M. R. Pierce, commanding officer of the air station, on August 22, 1929. Again, his request for reassignment was denied. When Wiley was given full command of the *Los Angeles*, Lt. Cdr. V. A. Clarke had been identified as his eventual successor, but first Clarke needed training and experience in LTA flight and the running of airships. Pierce's letter to Wiley reinforced this point and emphasized that both Wiley and his predecessor had several years' active experience in rigid airships and positions of responsibility in them before assuming command. Clarke's training, designed to take six months, had begun on July 5; consequently, he would not be ready to relieve Wiley until the end of December.[9] Wiley was learning that being indispensable was a two-edged sword. On the one hand, it spoke to his value to the Navy in the eyes of his superiors, but on the other it limited his mobility within the service. Still, Wiley's most recent request showed, yet again, that he was a man who preferred to make a plan rather than passively await his fate.

Meanwhile, there was plenty of publicity to go around, and the always-high-profile Hugo Eckener was not to be left out. Eckener had brought the *Graf Zeppelin* to Lakehurst on August 5, and there he would begin an around-the-world flight. William Randolph Hearst sponsored the flight to the tune of $100,000, with the requirement it begin at the Statue of Liberty in New York Harbor.[10] That made Lakehurst the logical base for operations and preflight refueling. More favorable weather had allowed Eckener to better his previous transatlantic flight time by seventeen hours and twenty-six minutes.[11] The zeppelin's cargo was an unusual collection of items. She carried a chimpanzee, a gorilla, a grand piano, six hundred canaries, and one unexpected guest—a stowaway. The stowaway was seventeen-year-old Albert Bruschkla, a baker's apprentice. He had ridden his bicycle from his home in Dusseldorf, in Westphalia, to Friedrichshafen. After scouting the layout, he used a coil of rope to reach and hide on the roof of the airship's housing until she was ready to depart. He then half-slid and half-jumped onto the upper surface of the dirigible. Fortunately, he landed on a strut instead of falling through the fabric envelope. His discovery angered the passengers, who realized he had endangered the airship. Not only would the flight have been canceled had he fallen through the outer fabric, but—as he did not understand—the weight of everything on an airship has to be accounted for and distributed. When addressing the matter with newspaper reporters, Eckener maintained the calm control of an airship commander, referring to the stowaway as a "foolish youth with romantic ideas." The stowaway was locked in a room to be punished on the airship's return to Germany.[12]

Two days after her arrival, on August 7, Lt. C. E. Rosendahl and Lt. J. C. Richardson reported on board the *Graf Zeppelin* to make the flight around the world as naval observers. Shortly before the ship's departure, President Herbert Hoover sent a bon voyage to Dr. Eckener. Eckener thanked the president for the welcome received from the American people and the splendid cooperation he had enjoyed with the Navy Department.[13]

Another stowaway incident with the *Graf Zeppelin* occurred on August 8, shortly before her scheduled departure. At a changing of the guard in the hangar, Morris Roth, an eighteen-year-old from Trenton, New Jersey, wearing a red sweater, was spotted on a catwalk sixty feet above the airship. He was captured and taken to the air station brig (prison). The German officers were not amused; in fact, they were furious. They ordered the entrances to the hangar closed while they conducted a thorough search.[14]

The zeppelin departed the NAS on August 8 and completed her global circuit when she returned to Lakehurst on August 29, boasting she had flown "around the world in twenty-one days and seven hours."[15] On August 27 the National Air Race Committee had announced receiving a wireless message from Eckener stating the airship would pass over the Cleveland airport about noon, August 28, en route to Lakehurst.[16] Subsequently, *Graf Zeppelin* landed smoothly at the air station at 8:07 a.m., having "conquered heat and cold, fog and typhoon. It had arched over two great oceans, the barren wastes of Siberia upon part of which man had never even gazed before."[17] Lyle C. Wilson, a United Press staff correspondent, reported the German zeppelin's return under the headline, "*Graf* Is Safe at Lakehurst: Great Record Set; Encircles the Globe in 21 Days, 7 Hours."[18] A large crowd awaited the airship at Lakehurst. Once the zeppelin touched down and customs agents started to board, the throngs pressed toward the ship. State police and Marines held the crowd back so the ship could be maneuvered into the hangar. Wilson claimed that fully ten thousand people were on hand to see the end of the historic flight.

The first passengers to step out of the gondola were Rosendahl and Richardson. Richardson echoed Rosendahl's simple on-the-spot assessment of the journey: "It was great." The press elaborated that the zeppelin's "feat was further glorified in that it was only in the air about 11½ days. It has spent almost an equal period of inactivity being refueled at Friedrichshafen, Tokyo and Los Angeles." By August 30 both the *Los Angeles* and the *Graf Zeppelin* were at Lakehurst. Because the *Graf Zeppelin* had flown over Cleveland and the air races without touching down, she made it back to Lakehurst a day ahead of the *Los Angeles*. Rosendahl and Richardson ended their temporary assignments and returned to duty at the air station.

Many in the crowd were aware of rumors that Eckener planned to retire after his record-breaking flight. He emerged from the airship appearing "tired but enthusiastic," and his first words were a firm denial of those rumors: "I have no thought of retiring and when the *Graf* makes future important trips I will be in command." However, he informed the crowd, because of other commitments in the United States he would not be in command of the ship on her return flight to Friedrichshafen; that duty would fall to Capt. Ernst Lehmann. Those "other commitments" began at noon the same day, when Eckener, accompanied by Rear Admiral Moffett and William A. MacCracken, former assistant secretary of commerce, boarded the *Los Angeles* to fly from Lakehurst to NAS Anacostia in time to be received by President Hoover at 3 p.m. From there, he hurried to New York City to be greeted by crowds and to be honored by a ticker-tape parade that ended at City Hall, where Mayor James J. Walker hailed Eckener as an "Ambassador of Good Will who has not only drawn Europe and America closer together but has made the far east a near neighbor to the United States."[19]

The press noted, "Overhead the navy dirigible *Los Angeles*, cruised about lazily, adding a fitting touch to the celebration in honor of the commander of a sister ship." While the *Los Angeles* was still in the air on its return flight, Hugo Eckener sent a wireless communication to Charles Francis Adams, Secretary of the Navy, extending an invitation for three U.S. Navy officers to accompany the *Graf Zeppelin* to Friedrichshafen; the Hamburg America Line offered them complimentary return passage by steamer. On August 30 the Bureau of Navigation sent a priority message to the *Los Angeles*, still in the air, authorizing Lt. Cdr. Herbert V. Wiley and Lt. Roland G. Mayer to make the flight. The third officer selected was Lt. Cdr. J. M. Shoemaker, an expert on aeronautical engines who would be sent out from Washington. They were granted ten days' delay in Europe that was to count as leave time. In Wiley's absence, the freshly returned Rosendahl was placed on temporary duty as commanding officer of the *Los Angeles*.

After landing the airship in the rain and getting her into the hangar, Wiley dashed off by train to Washington to obtain a passport. He returned to Lakehurst with twelve hours to spare before the *Graf Zeppelin* left on her homeward journey on September 1. Wiley, Mayer, and Shoemaker were in for something special in the world of LTA flight. The *Graf Zeppelin* had become the most famous airship ever built, and it was a title she would never surrender. She was modeled, somewhat, after the *Los Angeles*, with significant differences. The hull of the *Graf Zeppelin* was 775 feet long and 100 feet in diameter. Her overall height was 110 feet, including the gondola bumpers. This height brought the ship within two feet of the hangar arches when she was walked into it. "With a length/diameter ratio of 7.8/1, and a passenger gondola far forward to decrease overall height, the

Graf's appearance was not as esthetically attractive as that of the perfectly stream-lined *Los Angeles*, of which the *Graf* was a stretched version."[20] The zeppelin had a gas volume of 3,707,550 cubic feet, making her the largest airship in the world at the time. For fuel she used "Blau gas." Named for its inventor, Herman Blau, this gas had essentially the same weight as air, and hence changes in its weight due to consumption while in flight did not affect the overall weight of the ship.

For buoyancy, however, the *Graf Zeppelin* used the highly explosive hydrogen, and accordingly there was a firm rule against smoking on board the airship or around her on the ground. On the trip to Friedrichshafen an American passenger, Frederick Hogg, violated the rule and was discovered. Fortunately, no harm resulted from his actions, but the other passengers were incensed. The zeppelin officers took no action except to give a stern warning against repeating the offense.[21]

The reports caused unwanted remarks from judgmental friends. Hogg decided to rewrite this episode in his personal history by invoking Wiley's help. He wrote to Wiley requesting him to reply by stating that he had no knowledge of Hogg's having smoked on board the zeppelin.[22] Wiley wrote Hogg instead that it was impossible to comply with his request to deny, for his friends' sake, that he had smoked on the airship. He pointed to Hogg's presence in a locked room with cigar smoke and a cigar wrapper as conclusive evidence that he had smoked there.[23]

The nonstop flight to Friedrichshafen lasted sixty-seven hours and was uneventful, with good weather the entire way. They had departed Lakehurst at 0718 on Sunday, September 1, and landed in Friedrichshafen on Wednesday, September 4, at 0850 (0250 Lakehurst time), ending a journey of 5,200 miles.[24] As always, the press was on hand as the *Graf Zeppelin* set down in Friedrichshafen. American newspapers carried the headline, "*Graf Zeppelin* Reaches Home Hangar: Beat Round World Record from Home to Home by a Day."[25] In a letter to his father Wiley stated that there had been quite a reception when they landed, but that, according to the press, was a huge understatement. The atmosphere in Friedrichshafen resembled that of a major international sporting event. One of the largest crowds in the city's history greeted the airship as church bells pealed and cannons boomed salutes. Thousands of people were camped on the grounds around the aerodrome, and thousands more had simply walked through the streets, because there were no hotel vacancies. Count Zeppelin's only daughter, with her husband and family, made an appearance.

Wiley, Mayer, and Shoemaker were in the celebratory parade that ensued. The streets were flooded with people, and their open car was filled with flowers thrown by the crowd. Just before lunch, they were paying their respects to the American ambassador when the German minister of communications approached and offered them a ride in the Dornier Do X Flying Ship along with fifty other passengers. Designed by Dr. Claudius Dornier, the Do X was the largest and heaviest flying boat in the world. Following his flight in the Do X, Wiley boasted to his father that on the same day he had flown in the world's two largest aircraft—the largest airplane and the largest airship.[26]

The day was capped off by dinner with the Count and Countess Brandenstein-Zeppelin. Wiley and Mayer managed some sightseeing as they made their way to Paris and London, where they arranged a tour of the British commercial airship *R 101* before boarding the SS *Albert Ballin* for their voyage home.[27] Wiley and Mayer, good friends, stuck together throughout the trip, but Shoemaker had a separate interest. Because of his expertise in aeronautical engines, he was particularly attentive to the mechanical details of the zeppelin's flight. On his return to the States he composed a fifteen-page report, the first page of which listed what he thought the most noteworthy features of the trip: drawing weather maps twice daily, choosing courses that would have the winds always following, avoiding local storms, using drift determination, using an echo altimeter, and not using a radio compass.[28]

As the *Graf Zeppelin* passed over the United States en route to Friedrichshafen, she left in her wake heightened interest among Americans in LTA flight. While Wiley, Mayer, and Shoemaker were in Europe, American newspapers wrote of new airships to be built. Almost boastfully, newspapers predicted that "America is about to assume unquestioned leadership in the lighter-than-air field of aviation."[29] The Goodyear Zeppelin plant in Akron, Ohio, was moving forward with plans to build two dirigibles larger than the *Graf Zeppelin* for the Navy and then two commercial dirigibles. The Navy's airships, moreover, would have hangars capable of holding five scouting planes.

Wiley was back at Lakehurst on September 23 and resumed command of the *Los Angeles* the following day.[30] While he had been enjoying his time with the *Graf Zeppelin*, his repeated requests for sea duty on a battleship or light cruiser had been given further consideration. Rear Admiral Moffett, as chief of the Bureau of Aeronautics, had reiterated to the chief of the Bureau of Navigation on September 4, 1929, that the "safe and efficient operation" of the *Los Angeles* required that Wiley remain in command for several more months, until Lieutenant Commander Clarke could acquire more experience—that is, until June 1930.[31] The LTA service was small, and Wiley knew how it ran. At the moment he was irreplaceable, and his plans would have to wait.

Wiley, back in command, was quick to have the airship flying again, rehearsing the landing procedures for airplanes and testing various designs of the airplane hook and trapeze. He understood that opportunity brought with it added pressure. Moffett was always hungry for publicity for LTA and had made it clear from the beginning that he wanted the airship flying as often as possible. In any case, the Navy was bombarded with requests from cities for the *Los Angeles* to fly over or land. Sometimes civilians were allowed to take short flights on the ship at the request of mayors, prominent businessmen, and others in positions of influence. Moffett knew manned flight was in an era of competition for attention and funding between HTA and LTA craft. Public opinion was a powerful force, one that could affect government spending and private investment, and it was vital to keep the airship in the public eye. For those reasons, he wanted to accommodate as many requests as possible.

Wiley tried to satisfy such requests, but they were too numerous to fulfill them all, and some were unreasonable. Conflicting concerns for his career path, his family situation, and his command produced significant pressure at times. Such stresses can make one oversensitive, especially when one's superior is chief of the Bureau of Aeronautics who keeps a close watch on the activities of the airship. Admiral Moffett battled critics of the program constantly. On October 18, Wiley had a telephone conversation with Lt. Cdr. Ralph E. Davison of the Office of Naval Operations. Apparently, Davison called Wiley to inquire about a complaint from a prominent citizen of East Orange, New Jersey, who claimed the Navy had promised the *Los Angeles* on a particular date only to postpone the visit. Davison asked if this postponement was due to Wiley having a "disinclination" to make the requested flight.

There is neither a recording nor transcription of Davison's call to Wiley, and its "tone" cannot be known. Davison may have simply been seeking an explanation to pass along to the citizen, but Wiley apparently interpreted the query, coming as it did from the Office of Naval Operations, as a "complaint" from above. Wiley fired off a vehement written response that spoke to the level of stress of airship command. Wiley insisted he was doing his best to fulfill the wishes of the Navy: "If at any time you think you are not getting full cooperation please let me know frankly as cooperation is my middle name. This is not written in any spirit of resentment but is simply a statement of our assurance of cooperation."[32] Davison replied to Wiley in terms meant to reassure him that the matter had been no more than poor communication and that the Navy was fully aware of his accomplishments.

Wiley, may have left one unhappy complainer—Mr. Jahncke of East Orange, New Jersey—in his wake, but this was a rare event. Wiley had become nearly as recognizable as the *Los Angeles* herself and was increasingly called upon to speak to the press or civic groups on the future of manned flight. Making himself available to such requests was part of the public-relations scheme, and Wiley found time to satisfy the demand. On October 31, 1929, he spoke to approximately a hundred members and guests of the Hartford (Connecticut) Engineering Club—all keenly interested in LTA flight from a technological standpoint. Not surprisingly, newspapers covered the event. The *Hartford Courant* carried the title, "Wiley Tells of Plans for Giant Airship: Navy Dirigible, '*ZRS 4*,' Going into Construction Today Will Carry Six Scouting Planes."[33] Wiley told his attentive audience that the Navy's new airship would be the largest in the world, its dimensions and performance dwarfing those of the *Los Angeles*. He informed them the *ZRS 5* was in the construction pipeline but, as of that moment, existed only on paper. He assured his audience of the safety of airships and spoke of the "folly of fear with regard to the safety of the present dirigibles."

Much had been learned since airships had first taken to the skies, he emphasized: helium was safer than hydrogen gas, and newer ships were less vulnerable to breaking apart in the air thanks to stronger materials and reversible engines, which gave greater flexibility in maneuvering in high winds. "Not a few in the audience were surprised to hear of the invulnerability of the dirigible, which, according to Lieutenant Commander Wiley, can withstand hundreds of bullet holes in its silver skin without losing an appreciable amount of gas in 24 hours." Manned flight still carried an aura of romance, and such proclamations by Wiley fired imaginations, certainly that of an unnamed reporter who referred to the new *ZRS 4* as "a giant war-bird that will carry within its own breast a brood of darting fledglings."

In his Hartford presentation Wiley enjoyed the opportunity, after discussing the role of airships in the Navy, to speak to a group of engineers about their civilian and commercial possibilities. He always emphasized in this connection the increased safety of airships; the facts that they were faster than surface vessels and had longer range; and their comforts for passengers. He always made an enthusiastic case for this mode of travel and likely inspired and excited every audience. He was, after all, one of the greatest authorities on the subject at the time.

Moffett and Wiley were showered frequently with letters of gratitude for visits by the *Los Angeles* or, especially, for rides. On December 16, 1929, following a flurry of such letters, Admiral Moffett wrote to Wiley expressing his appreciation for what Wiley was doing for the service:

My dear Wiley:

I received the letters from Mr. George T. Fielding and the others who took the flight on the *Los Angeles* recently, and congratulate you on the fine impression which was made by you and the officers under your command upon all the passengers. You are doing fine work and accomplishing much for the project.

I meant to write to tell you how much I enjoyed my flight with you, but have been extremely busy. My duties as advisor to the Limitation of Armaments Conference are keeping me busier than ever. Please accept my apologies and at the same time my sincere thanks and appreciation for all your hospitality and that of the officers of the *Los Angeles*.

With kindest regards,

Sincerely yours,

W. A. Moffett [signed].[34]

Nothing could be a greater stress reliever than certainty of the respect, admiration, and gratitude of Rear Admiral Moffett. Not that Wiley needed the personal validation, but such praise from Moffett was supreme reassurance he was doing an outstanding job. Moffett had indeed, as he said, written to Wiley during a very busy time. On December 4 Moffett had received orders to report to the Secretary of the Navy for temporary duty related to preparations for the London Naval Conference; on December 31 he was to be formally appointed a technical advisor to the American delegation.[35] The conference would open on January 21, 1930.

As 1930 began, Wiley intended, as always, to keep the *Los Angeles* flying as often as possible. The winters at Lakehurst could be severe and if the weather did not prevent flying altogether, it could make it very uncomfortable due to the cold temperatures at the altitudes at which the airship flew. It required only a little experience with cold-weather flying to teach crewmen the need for extra layers of warm clothing during winter months. H. N. Coulter, an officer on the *Los Angeles*, recalled that in the winter of 1929–30, a period of "rigid economy" for the Navy, there was no money for cold-weather flight clothing. Consequently, he wore a raccoon coat, which gave him the appearance of a "collegiate playboy."[36]

Coulter wrote of how the ship's cook—who was exceptional—sought to stave off both hunger and cold by providing the crew large quantities of good food. Following a standard breakfast of steak and eggs, the crew was treated to large roast beef or ham sandwiches and hot coffee. Wiley, accustomed to adverse conditions, prepared himself properly for them and kept the airship flying. In late January 1930 the *Los Angeles* and her crew had a brief respite from the New Jersey weather as they flew south to Parris Island, South Carolina, where they moored on the twenty-fifth to a new stub mast that had been erected.[37] The following day they took to the air again, gaining experience and logging flight hours cruising down the coast of Florida as far as Daytona before returning to Lakehurst.[38]

Always looking for ways to expand the versatility of airships, Moffett had the idea of launching a glider from the *Los Angeles*. The usefulness of such a capability seemed limited, but Moffett thought it might serve to transport landing officers to fields where there were no crews familiar with the handling of an airship. The proposition was put to Lt. Ralph S. Barnaby, a certified glider pilot. He thought the idea feasible, and his glider was sent to Lakehurst, where Barnaby and Lt. Cal Bolster, responsible for technical gear on the airship, worked out the details.[39] On January 31 Wiley took the *Los Angeles* aloft to attempt the feat. At Barnaby's request, he took the ship to three thousand feet and stopped his Nos. 1 and 2 engines. Minutes later, Barnaby, wearing a sweater, leather flight jacket, helmet, fleece-lined boots, and a seat-pack parachute, climbed down an aluminum ladder into the cockpit of the glider. Wiley increased speed to a predetermined forty knots, and the glider was released. It fell away quickly; Barnaby leveled off about a hundred feet below the airship, dropped his speed to the normal gliding speed of thirty miles per hour, and landed safely on a snow-covered field.[40] Moffett's glider experiment was a success but indeed of little value. A glider flight from airship to ground was a one-way affair. It had been demonstrated already that powered airplanes could make round trips. A second glider experiment was conducted on May 31, with Settle as the pilot, but with the same inconsequential results. Whatever the utility of the glider experiments, this was one of Wiley's last flights in command of the *Los Angeles*. His repeated requests for assignment to battleship duty were about to be granted.

Wiley's decision to join the Navy's fledgling dirigible service had proved to be a good one. His desire to leave did not reflect a lessening of interest in LTA flight; to the contrary, he was devoted to it more than ever. His request for transfer, as noted, was based purely on his perceived need for fleet experience if he was to advance in the service, and it was timed to make him available again when the Navy's new airships were ready. Admiral Moffett would decide who would command them, but he considered himself a strong candidate.

Wiley's reputation extended deep into the civilian world. With Admiral Moffett's hearty approval, he served as an unpaid consultant to anyone in the private sector who expressed an interest in developing LTA flight for commercial uses. In Moffett's mind, the currently expanding nonmilitary use of dirigibles was a compelling justification for the Navy's experimental programs. Wiley was sought out for advice on a wide range of issues, such as the recruitment and training of commercial airship crews. One of the more bizarre commercial projects involved the Empire State Building in New York City. The building's architects and Mayor Al Smith wanted to add a mooring mast to its top, on the 102nd floor. A waiting room with a gangplank would permit passengers to board or disembark from a dirigible moored to the mast. As the Empire State Building was being erected, Wiley was consulted about this idea. He conducted a written dialogue about the matter with Dr. J. C. Hunsaker, a former Navy airship technical officer who had become vice president of the Goodyear Zeppelin Corporation. Hunsaker was more than a businessman: he was very much an insider. He was an alumnus of the Naval Academy and had been an instructor of aeronautics at the Massachusetts Institute of Technology. When a man of his background and stature asks for feedback, he expects the most detailed technical advice available, and Wiley provided it. Wiley recognized two advantages of a mooring mast atop this building: a central passenger terminal and valuable publicity. Nevertheless, he offered a long list of disadvantages.

The biggest drawback was the gustiness of the wind over the city. Wiley did not pass judgment on the proposal, but the tenor of his letter led to the eventual consensus: for solid technical and safety reasons, that the idea was not tenable.[41] Lieutenant Commander Clarke, Wiley's successor in command of the *Los Angeles*, was requested to make a simulated mooring to the top of the building. The request was made by representatives of the Paramount Sound News Company and appeared to be nothing more than a publicity stunt. Clarke rejected the idea.[42] In the end, the economic crash of the Great Depression prevented the building of any commercial airships.

8

The USS
Tennessee (BB 43)

On March 8, 1930, orders were issued relieving Wiley of command of the *Los Angeles* and assigning him to the battleship USS *Tennessee* (BB 43).[1] On March 12 he wrote his sister Fay Wiley Oren to bring her up to date. He began with news of his family: Marie was suffering from a flu-like illness and a painful dental problem, and the boys Gordon and David, ages nine and five, respectively, were battling chicken pox. All of this was keeping him busy in what he called his "hospital." He expected to be relieved of command on March 31 and to report on board the *Tennessee* in New York on May 10. He reminded Fay that he had been kept on at the air station longer than the expected six months but in that time there had been more flying than in any year they had ever had, and being "extended" meant he had had good success there.[2] He wanted to visit Fay before he went to sea, but, he told her, it would take so much money to move his family across the country that he did not have the means. Aware that Fay was soon to deliver her second child, Wiley shared the good news that he and Marie too were expecting another child, around October 1. He asked Fay about his father, having heard from him frequently but never about himself.

At 0755 on March 31, 1930, at NAS Lakehurst, the crew of the *Los Angeles* was mustered at quarters for the standard change-of-command ceremony.[3] Wiley had become a fixture at Lakehurst. He was well liked, respected, and adored by large numbers of people around the air station. He was appreciated for his frequent flyovers of nearby cities and occasional landings. Those few privileged to fly on the *Los Angeles* never forgot the experience and were forever grateful to Wiley and the Navy. There were many who wanted to thank him, honor him, and wish him well with his next assignment. It was only fitting that first among these would be the officers of the *Los Angeles*. He had treated them well, and they held him in high esteem. They threw a party for Wiley and his wife at a hotel in Asbury Park, New Jersey.[4] The Masons honored them with another party in April, as did friends in Allentown, Pennsylvania, where he had taken the airship on numerous occasions. He kept speaking engagements in Reading, Pennsylvania, and in New Jersey even in his closing days in the area.

He wrote of all these things to his father on April 8, expressing, as he had to Fay, his desire to visit. This letter reflects the closeness he felt for his father and family but also a pervasive undertone of sadness and frustration. While the casual observer would be struck by the glamour of flying to distant sites in a dirigible, life in the Navy was complicated. It was difficult to balance professional duties with those of family, and, even with the added flight pay, money was always an issue; finances generally, and particularly moving expenses, were preventing him from making a visit home. He also wrote of the difficulties he expected his family to have making the transition to the West Coast and of how he was trying to get Marie stronger following her recent illness. He planned for her to make the shortest and quickest trip across the country. He ended his letter promising to write more often.

As Marie began to feel better and get stronger, she prepared her household for the impending move. They left Lakehurst on May 1 for New London, Connecticut, where they would remain until the tenth, when Wiley was to report to the *Tennessee*.[5] In mid-May, Marie was able to travel from New London to New York without the boys, so she and Herbert could have some quality private time. They were a very close couple. As is often the case, it was their individual differences and strengths that made them so. They were both intelligent and well educated, but Marie brought to the relationship an outgoing, fun-loving personality. Life in the Navy was not easy in those years, and closeness as a couple was probably necessary to happiness.

If the Wileys were at peace in 1930, the rest of the world was not. At the London Naval Conference countries feuded while trying to reach an agreement on "parity" with regard to size and types of warships, and in the United States, congressmen argued over the same matters. Reaching an agreement among the five nations involved (United States, Great Britain, France, Italy, and Japan) was beginning to seem impossible. The conference had opened on January 1. By March 1 the press was reporting that another six to eight weeks would be needed. At that point, however, the United States and Japan could not reach a settlement on the ratio of the numbers of cruisers each was to have, and it was predicted the negotiations would break down in a matter of a few days.[6] The issues were complicated, and not every nation involved had the same goal.

> The British government cannot involve itself in any more political pacts implying or containing military commitments to preserve the peace; in reaching this conclusion Great Britain has denied France the guarantee of security which she asked as the price of reducing her unexpectedly large naval program.
>
> The statement, observers commented, left the conference just where it was until a week ago, when on the verge of breakdown as a five-power parley, the American delegation issued a statement declaring their willingness to consider "with an entirely open mind" proposals that America enter as a consultative pact, if prior to the proposals French security demands had been satisfied.
>
> The situation was summed up briefly: Great Britain, even with this offer as inducement, has not been able to satisfy France on security; the French naval demands therefore remain up; Italy's demands for parity remain unsolved, and Great Britain, whose policy has been to be as strong on the sea as the two principal European powers, may have to build up to the projected French-Italian navies.[7]

There is no record of Wiley's opinions about the London Naval Conference, but as a prominent officer in the U.S. Navy and with his superior, Admiral Moffett, in the American delegation, it is certain he kept abreast of developments. He remained focused on the work ahead of him as he prepared to go to sea. He needed to get his family across the country by land, and he would not be able to accompany them. With a loving concern for his family, and given their recent illnesses, he wanted to make their journey as comfortable as possible, and the best way seemed to be by train. Marie and the boys left New York City on the afternoon of May 18 headed for Chicago's Union Station. Arrangements had been made for transportation across town to meet the connecting train that would carry them to Los Angeles. Marie used the layover as an opportunity to send a telegram to the *Tennessee* to let Wiley know they had reached Chicago safely. They left at 2000 the same day to begin the longest, 2,300-mile, leg of their trip. This was a relatively comfortable mode of travel, but the Wiley family was making its journey in a time before trains had air conditioning.

They pulled into Los Angeles' Central Station about 0900 on the fifth day and made their way to Long Beach, twenty-four miles south. Marie was nearly exhausted. In a letter to Fay she reported the boys had been good but that the heat and excitement had "floored" her.[8] She sent another telegram to "Doc" (Wiley's nickname since the Academy days) to let him know they had arrived safely at their final destination. Her next challenge was to house-hunt for a rental property, made difficult by having the boys in tow. Her search was very successful, however, and they settled into a fine home in a good location. Marie told Fay it was the first really nice place they had ever had.

Wiley's travel to the West Coast would not be as arduous as Marie's. On May 19, 1930, he left New York on board the *Tennessee* and the following day the ship took part in a large review of the fleet by President Herbert Hoover. This was the first time in history the U.S. fleet had passed in review before the commander in chief while conducting war maneuvers.[9] President Hoover and his entourage traveled by special train that morning from Washington to Old Point Comfort, Virginia. Arriving at 0745, they immediately boarded the heavy cruiser USS *Salt Lake City* (CA 25), from which the president would review the sixty-five ships and their exercises.[10]

Such an awe-inspiring display of naval power, in front of the president, was rich material for journalists. The press covered the event from the deck of the *Saratoga*.

Fleet Is Mobilized for Hoover Review:
Mimic Warfare to Be Waged after Warships Steam Past the President—
New *Salt Lake City* with Eight-Inch Guns Plays Part

Over the blue waters of the Atlantic the massed naval power of the Nation mobilized today to steam in parade under the eyes of the commander in chief, President Hoover, and then deploy in battle maneuvers of sea and air far off shore.

Ships of the surface, from ponderous battleships to slender destroyers; giants of the underseas forces, the fleet of submarines, *V-2* and *V-3*; ships of the air, from the vast silvery bulk of the Noncombatant Zeppelin, *Los Angeles,* to the tiny one-man fighting planes and the thronging air squadrons on board the great carriers *Saratoga* and *Lexington,* were included in the great sea muster.

The combined fleet was under the command of Adm. William V. Pratt, whose flag flew from the battleship USS *Texas* (BB 35). Ten other warships were under the command of Adm. Louis M. Nulton, on board the USS *California* (BB 44). The Navy had staged the event ambitiously, "sending the great armada by the reviewing ship under conditions rarely witnessed by civilians."[11] Among the battleships taking part were the *California,* the *Texas,* the *Tennessee,* the USS *Florida* (BB 30), and the USS *Utah* (BB 31). Reporters noted the absence of three active battleships: the USS *Wyoming* (BB 32), the USS *Arkansas* (BB 33), and the USS *New York* (BB 34) had been assigned to the Naval Academy for the midshipmen's summer cruise. It was suggested that this could be the "last muster with the great fleet" for the *Florida* and the *Utah* if the London naval pact became effective; in such a case these two ships would "go to the scrap heap before another annual mobilization is held."

The review itself was carefully choreographed. Two divisions of light cruisers and two squadrons of destroyers dashed past the review ship at twenty-five knots, then swung away to make a ten-mile run to assigned positions for the simulated battle to follow. The battleships then passed by at fifteen knots. The two submarines approached the *Salt Lake City* on the surface, dove simultaneously, and after ten minutes resurfaced. The last of the surface vessels to pass were the aircraft carriers *Lexington* and *Saratoga,* "with their scores of planes crowding the vast open flying decks, under orders to sweep into the air soon after the *Salt Lake City* had been passed abeam."

Admiral Moffett was not one to miss press coverage, and the *Los Angeles* flew over the entire surface fleet. She had left Lakehurst early that morning under the command of Lieutenant Commander Clarke to join the naval review. On board were ten officers, thirty-one crew members, two student officers, and seven passengers who had been approved by the Navy Department. At 0920 she sighted the *Salt Lake City* standing out from the Chesapeake Bay flying the flag of the president of the United States. At 1034 the airship made contact with the fleet itself. At 1048, from an altitude of 1,800 feet, they sighted the submarines *V-2* and *V-3* submerging. Within minutes she was over the cruisers and then two minutes later the destroyers. At 1118 she flew over the battleships as they passed in review, and her crew witnessed them firing a twenty one-gun salute in honor of the president. At 1125 the aircraft carriers passed in review, also firing a salute to the president. At 1145 and 1148, respectively, the *Lexington* and *Saratoga* began launching their airplanes.[12]

Newspapers declared that the program included a "feat never before attempted over water and accomplished but once on land. This called for a plane to take off from one of the aircraft carriers and attach itself to the *Los Angeles*, and then, after an interval, disengage itself and return to the carrier."[13] This was a variation of the demonstration made by the *Los Angeles* at the Cleveland Air Races while under Wiley's command. At 1210 the *Los Angeles* took up a position approximately five miles to the leeward of the *Salt Lake City*, clear of the other air operations. At 1322 she began to move into position for a Vought UO-1's approach. At 1341 the airship was over the *Salt Lake City*, and a minute later the plane was hooked on; its pilot, Lt. Cdr. C. A. Nicholson, engaged the trapeze successfully. Eleven minutes later, the plane was detached from the trapeze, and the *Los Angeles* turned for Lakehurst.[14]

Wiley was *Tennessee*'s tactical officer. This duty was new to him, and it kept him busy, but he settled into the role in good order. During the fleet exercises he may have felt a touch of nostalgia seeing the *Los Angeles* overhead, but he had no desire to be back in command of her. He had planned his career, and at that moment he was where he wanted to be—on board a battleship. Wiley knew the *Los Angeles*' contributions to LTA flight were coming to an end, that she was soon to be replaced by larger, stronger, and more versatile airships. He could wait for them.

May 20, 1930, the day of the fleet review, was full of emotions for all present. The sight of so many powerful warships, moving at high speed, airplanes and a dirigible overhead, and submarines submerging and resurfacing produced waves of adrenaline-fueled excitement and pride for civilians and sailors alike. But there were other emotions as well. Admiral Pratt had served as a technical advisor during the negotiations leading to the Washington Naval Limitations Treaty in 1922, and in January 1930 he had been sent to England as head of the American technical staff at the London Naval Conference, which would attempt to limit further the size of the world's major navies. He had returned to the States in May, in time for the fleet maneuvers. He may have wondered as he watched his mighty warships pass by whether he was looking at the Navy of the past or the Navy of the future: it depended on how the international negotiations ended.

The potential outcomes of the London Naval Conference, in fact, weighed heavily on many people around the globe. On the same day as the presidential fleet review, American newspapers carried a story from Japan.

Tokyo, May 20 (AP). In the tense atmosphere surrounding the return of Admiral Kotora Takarabe, Minister of Marine, from the London Conference and his first conferences with the cabinet and senior naval officers, a sensation was created today by the suicide of a naval officer, which the press is exploiting as an echo of the Navy's bitter opposition to the London pact.

Lieutenant-Commander Eiji Kusakari, attached to the naval general staff, slashed his abdomen with a sword on board a train between Kobe and Tokyo. He died at a hospital at Numazu, where he was removed from the train. Although Kusakari's comrades declined to comment on his act, it was said he recently expressed bitterness and despondency over the future of the Navy as the result of the London treaty.[15]

After a week in port in Norfolk, Virginia, the *Tennessee* sailed south, engaging in training on the way. While at sea, en route to Colon in the Canal Zone, Wiley wrote to Admiral Moffett. Wiley's letter began, "As you probably know, I am now on the *Tennessee*," then explained how he viewed this experience as valuable to his future return to the LTA program. He was confident that the battleship experience would afford him a working knowledge of the fleet that would be valuable if he were later to operate a fleet airship. The tone of Wiley's letter and of Moffett's reply was that of mutual admiration and respect. "I can not leave the aeronautical organization without expressing my appreciation of your personal support and interest, and my admiration for your square dealing and ability as a pioneering leader. I feel sure that progress in the L.T.A. field soon will demonstrate that the fight you have made for it was worth while."[16] Wiley also put in a strong word for a fellow officer: "I do not know whether a 'makee learn' [prospective commanding officer, now under instruction] has been designated for the *Los Angeles*, or not, but I would like to put in a word for [Cdr. Frank Carey] McCord. I think he is well fitted and rates a trial at it." Moffett's reply, equally warm, reflected Moffett's understanding of why Wiley had left the LTA program: "I was very sorry to see you leave the *Los Angeles* but think it was a wise move in view of what some [promotion] Selection Board may do at some future time. As you know, I had the greatest confidence in you, in your ability and decision, while at Lakehurst, and I hope that you will be back when your cruise is up. I will keep in mind what you say about McCord."[17]

On May 30, 1930, when the *Tennessee* was south of Cuba, Wiley wrote his father, describing events since he left Lakehurst. He commented he had expected on this day to pass close to the *Graf Zeppelin*;[18] the zeppelin, nearing the end of a 13,400-mile voyage, was on a northwesterly course headed for NAS Lakehurst.[19] He had not seen her and speculated that by now the *Tennessee* and the *Graf Zeppelin* were on opposite sides of Cuba and thus beyond sight of each other. (Eckener and his famous zeppelin would make Lakehurst on May 31.) Wiley told his father he expected to arrive on June 1 in Panama, where he could send his letter and where he hoped to receive mail from Marie. His ship was scheduled to transit the canal on the second, sail for San Pedro, California, on the seventh, and arrive on about the twentieth. This journey would take longer than usual, because the *Tennessee* would engage in more exercises in the Pacific Ocean along the way.

Wiley was happy to be reunited with his family when he arrived at San Pedro on June 17 and was delighted with the small bungalow Marie had found for them in Long Beach, nearby. The location was perfect for the family—an easy walk to a magnificent beach that was a playground for the boys. Wiley wrote Fay the boys went to the beach twice a day to swim and were well tanned.[20] The *Tennessee*—now part of the United States Fleet, Battle Fleet, Battleship Division 5—was now in the Pacific to stay, for the rest of her life. For the time being, she operated up and down the West Coast; Wiley's letter to Fay was written in Seattle, Washington. While his letter contained comforting news about the family, there was also an element of concern about Marie's health during the last six to seven weeks of her pregnancy. Marie had been doing well, but now she was writing "Doc" that she was feeling uncomfortable. The *Tennessee* had been in Seattle for a week and, after another week in San Francisco, she would be back in Long Beach until early January.

About a week after Wiley's letter, Fay received one from Marie herself with further signs of a brewing health issue. She told Fay she had been meaning to write for a long time but that time was flying by and she was not feeling well. She felt she had not accomplished anything.[21] Marie said, reassuringly, that she had a splendid doctor who was very young but seemed up-to-date, and she felt she was in competent hands.

Near the end of her letter, there was a crescendo of emotion as she spoke lovingly of her husband. Her words, so positive, were veiled by sadness. She would be glad when "Doc" returned from his cruise north. She missed him very much when he was away. She said he was wonderful and very understanding. Everyone spoke very highly of him, Marie wrote, but he had been under a tremendous strain for seven years, and that had kept him from writing more often.

It is unknown how Marie's letters were interpreted at the time but, in retrospect, they contained warning signs things were soon to get worse. Wiley wrote to his father on September 28, 1930, about the great tragedy that unfolded. It was emotionally difficult for him to write very much, and he asked his father to pass the word on to Fay. Marie had caught a cold, and her doctor sent her to the hospital about September 10 to monitor her. Four days later, the doctors said they would have to take the baby because the situation was dangerous for Marie and the baby's chances of survival were slim. "Doc" said Marie was very brave but he was not. The baby was delivered around 7:30 p.m. on September 14, and everything seemed fine for the baby and Marie. "Doc" stayed with her until 11 p.m. when she was given medication to help her sleep. He returned to the hospital the next morning to find five physicians in Marie's room—and she was unconscious. She had developed kidney failure and her physicians did not expect her to survive the day, but she regained consciousness later that night and seemed to be improving slightly. "Doc" left the hospital at midnight to go home for some rest. Although he had been told there were signs of improvement, he did not go away with that impression, because she had been exhibiting delirium much of the time. He was summoned back to the hospital at 3 a.m., and he found her fading rapidly. She died at 9:30 a.m. on September 17.[22] Marie's death certificate listed the cause of death as "Nephritis—Toxemia of Pregnancy. Eclampsia."

With the consent of Marie's family in New London, Wiley made funeral arrangements in California at the church they had been attending. Ranking officers from Wiley's ship served as pallbearers and the ship's chaplain assisted. Wiley told his father he had been able to pay 75 percent of the funeral costs and had arranged terms for the rest. Little Marie Elinor was expected to remain in the hospital for at least another month, but she was progressing favorably. She was expected to live and to do well in the long term. Wiley received offers for adoption of the baby but did not want to give her up.[23]

This was the most difficult time in Wiley's life to date. He had lost the woman who was, for him, the perfect life partner. They had been the best of companions, and their mutual love and affection was deep and abiding. Unfortunately for Wiley, there was little time for mournful reverie. Decisions had to be made fairly quickly. His Navy career made demands of him that often interfered with personal life, yet he was a devoted family man. Family and friends made sincere offers to take in his children and care for them, but Wiley wanted to remain near them and to keep the family unit together as much as he could. He loved the Navy, and he was building a very successful career there. He did not want to leave it. It was what he knew best, and if he left the Navy finding employment could prove difficult, especially in the tough economic times that were already beginning. In the Navy Wiley had a job and a steady income that his entire family needed.

Staying with the Navy was the right thing to do, but it meant tough decisions for the best interests of his sons and new daughter. The Bureau of Navigation granted Wiley twenty days' leave, and, in short order, he made decisions that showed great strength of character. Wiley enrolled his boys in military school, and they quickly came to like it.[24] That the boys made the transition into life in military school so easily brought a measure of peace to him, but the baby's struggles continued a while longer.

While dealing with his great loss internally, he focused his attention outwardly on his children and his career. Wiley reported back to the *Tennessee* on September 30. Fortunately for his family in this difficult time, the ship remained in port until the end of the year, allowing him to spend time with his children as they adjusted to the death of their mother. Gordon and David were doing quite well in the Southern California Military Academy, in Long Beach, and little Marie Elinor Wiley went into the home and care of a local nurse. Wiley visited the children as often as he could to play with them and photograph them. He had family and career on an even keel for the moment, but he knew that life in the Navy could make new demands of him at any time, that he could be sent to other duty in distant places. His battleship "tour" was temporary, and he expected to return to the Naval Air Service, specifically to one of the new airships soon to be completed in Akron. When this happened, he and the children would have to move again. It was impossible to predict how much time a family would need to adjust to the loss of a wife and mother, but the exigencies of the naval service fairly soon made this factor moot.

The call back to naval aviation came in the form of orders issued on April 18, 1931, for Wiley to return to the LTA service, reporting first to the air station at Lakehurst and then, when directed by its commanding officer, to proceed to

Akron, there to report to the prospective commanding officer of the USS *Akron*. When the *Akron* was commissioned he would become the airship's executive officer.[25] Wiley's tenure with the *Tennessee* had been relatively short, approximately a year, but it had served his purpose. His Navy record would forever reflect his service on board a battleship in the rank of lieutenant commander.

The Chillicothe, Missouri, newspaper created local excitement when it reported Wiley's change of duty and alerted the population to a visit en route to his new assignment.[26] As usual, it took time for orders to make their way through channels, but in early June, Wiley made plans to move his family. He and his sons would travel to Lakehurst by train, but Marie was to be left behind for a short while with her nurse in Long Beach. Wiley left the *Tennessee* on the twelfth, and he and the boys boarded a train bound for Kansas City, Missouri, where they arrived two days later. After a short layover, they boarded another train for Chillicothe and Wheeling, where they had another stopover and a bittersweet reunion with his father and Fay. The citizens welcomed their hero with open arms, and the newspaper proudly announced, "Herbert V. Wiley, once a Livingston county school boy and now one of the leading aviators of the U.S. Navy, is home this week, visiting the folks who knew him before he gained his fame as an air man."[27] As a way of maintaining ties with the people of his hometown, he gave a brief talk in the office of the newspaper. He described the new *Akron* as having a cruising radius of nine thousand miles, which meant it could fly over the north pole and return to Lakehurst, New Jersey, without any stops for refueling.

Following their brief visit, Wiley and sons continued by train to New York, arriving there on June 19. Wiley reported to the commanding officer of Naval Air Station Lakehurst on June 22 to resume his duties with the LTA service.[28] He was not at Lakehurst long before receiving new, but expected (and personally welcome), orders sending him on the next leg of his career. Even a brief stay at Lakehurst brought a host of emotions. There was familiarity, because this had been his home previously, and nostalgia, as he recalled good times with his family and friends there, especially the Roland Mayer family. Most assuredly he felt a deep sadness, because when last at Lakehurst his beloved wife had been alive and with him. There were memories of earlier days learning the business of flying dirigibles and of absent friends who had perished with the *Shenandoah*. His prevailing sentiment, however, was eagerness to join the Navy's newest dirigible. On July 20 he was detached from the air station to report in Akron. Wiley contracted a couple traveling from California to Ohio to bring his daughter Marie with them. With family reunited, he could give full attention to flying the new airship.

Wiley reported on July 27, and it was Lt. Cdr. Charles E. Rosendahl who endorsed his orders.[29] Rosendahl had been named prospective commanding officer of the *Akron*, and it was no accident that he and Wiley were to serve together again, because they had proven to be a very effective pair in the *Los Angeles*. They were the two most experienced and capable airship officers in the Navy. Lt. Cdr. Roland G. Mayer joined them, and the Wiley and Mayer families resumed the warm relationship they had enjoyed at Lakehurst. For years the Mayers would be surrogate parents for the motherless children, to whom Mabel Mayer was "Aunt Nan." The bond between the two families was very important to Wiley during this time in his life.

9

The USS
Akron (ZRS 4)

T he Navy's newest airship had been anticipated by the entire airship industry, domestic and foreign. As was its custom, the Navy kept the public informed of airship developments every step of the way. On April 14, 1928, newspapers had announced the Navy would begin a construction program to produce a fleet of giant rigid airships for war purposes.[1] The House of Representatives had passed the Navy appropriation bill, and the Senate was expected to follow suit. The bill authorized an initial two million dollars to start work on two of the new dirigibles. Secretary of the Navy Wilbur had put out a call for bids for their construction, and of the three firms to show interest only one seemed well positioned for the task, the Goodyear Tire & Rubber Company of Ohio. This company had a long track record of building balloons and in 1923 it had formed an alliance with the German Zeppelin firm to strengthen its position as a builder of large dirigibles for the Navy. On October 6 Goodyear signed a contract with the U.S. Navy to build two airships, to be designated the USS *Akron* and the USS *Macon*.[2] The government appropriated four million dollars for each.

Newspapers carried every detail of the project. They reminded the public that the *Los Angeles* had been built under the terms of the Treaty of Versailles, which forbade her to be used as a warship, even in a time of emergency. The new airships, however, were being built specifically for military use, and they would dwarf the *Los Angeles*. Much had been learned from the *Shenandoah* disaster and experiments with the *Los Angeles*, and it was being incorporated into the new ships. Design changes were also being made that would strengthen the airships.

As a result, the new airships would be increased in girth rather than length; they would be more round and fat than long and thin. Aeronautical engineers had discovered that doing so added significantly to their longitudinal stability and would prevent the "midship" stress that caused the midair fracture of the more slender *Shenandoah*. Consequently, while the new ships would be much larger than the *Shenandoah*, they would be only about a hundred feet longer. The control car would be enclosed within the framework of the ship instead of slung from the belly on struts, making the airship more streamlined. Similarly, the power units would be concealed within the ship, with only the propellers outside. The new airships were designed to be flying aircraft carriers, with fighter planes stored within their bellies, from which they could be launched and into which they could be recovered, all in the air. Finally, the airships would be capable of self-defense: they would each have machine guns and light artillery on board.

These big rigid airships were conceived as long-range naval scouts that could accompany the surface fleet, conduct reconnaissance of vast stretches of ocean, serve as flying aircraft carriers, and, potentially, serve as aerial command-and-control "platforms" for naval forces. Alterations were made to the early models of the trapeze for capturing planes in flight, and a T-shaped cutout in the underside of the airship allowed them to be hoisted into the hangar. As an airplane made its approach for a "landing," it had to match its airspeed to that of the airship, position itself under the belly, and then fly upward to hook itself onto the trapeze, which extended downward from the vessel's hull.[3]

The crash of the *Shenandoah* had resulted in determination within the Navy and the Goodyear/Zeppelin coalition to build "two peerless vessels of Herculean strength." They achieved this, in part, with triple keels, one at the top of the hull giving access to top gas valves and the other two along the port and starboard sides, respectively, of the lower hull. The keels supported eight Maybach engines and spaces for the crew. The hull was constructed of thirty-six longitudinal girders and stiff rings eight feet deep. The scale of the new ships was to be surpassed only by the *Hindenburg* in 1936.

The use of helium instead of the highly flammable hydrogen as the lifting gas allowed the Maybach engines to be housed within the hull of the ship, but this placement caused other problems. In previous designs, engines were situated at different heights on the hull, which allowed each of them to operate in undisturbed air. In the new design, with the eight engines in parallel along the bottom of the ship, the forward engines produced a wash of air that disturbed those aft of them. This produced extreme vibration that, according to stories, was so bad it could dislodge teeth.[4]

The Navy's transparency about the airship program did not prevent potentially damaging publicity. While the ZRS 4 (future Akron) was under construction, reports in the press suggested she might be a doomed ship. In March 1931 the Associated Press published the discovery of a sabotage attempt against the Akron that had come to light during an investigation of a widespread plot against aircraft in the United States. The investigation had resulted from the crash of a Navy bomber near San Diego in September 1930 in which one of its pilots had died. Someone had weakened the plane's wings so they would fail under the stress of flight; inspections revealed two other planes made defective in a similar fashion. Investigation led to the factory where the planes were manufactured and ultimately focused on Paul F. Kassay, a thirty-seven-year-old who had worked on the Akron. After arrest, Kassay admitted that he had planned to weaken the airship's metal skeleton by omitting rivets and that he had planned to sabotage the control room before the ship was launched. Indeed, two rivets had been left out of one of the ship's fins. Lieutenant Settle, at the time the Navy's on-site inspector, reassured the press that the areas of the ship on which Kassay had worked had been inspected and no other weaknesses had been found. He proclaimed confidently that "the Akron was not harmed" and that every part of the airship would be inspected, including the 6,500,000 rivets.[5]

Kassay was charged with "criminal syndicalism," which, at the time, was punishable as a felony. Under questioning, he admitted to being a communist; he had participated in communist uprisings and had been arrested in Hungary after the world war. When arraigned, Kassay pleaded not guilty, and when he went to trial, Judge Walter Wanamaker declared the Ohio criminal syndicalism law to be unconstitutional, because it abridged the right of free speech.[6] Subsequently, Kassay denied having admitted to the plot against the dirigible and claimed to be an innocent victim of a "frame-up."

Close on the heels of the Kassay business came an unrelated incident in which two civilians working on the Akron made claims to the Navy Department that the airship was "a victim of inferior materials and shoddy workmanship."[7] Cdr. Ralph D. Weyerbacher and Lt. Karl Schmidt conducted an investigation, and following extensive interrogation of the two men, concluded they did not possess the knowledge to make their claims credible. The two officers also spent five days conducting their own close inspection of the ship and found no deficiencies. "His investigation concluded, Weyerbacher had the informers sign a statement which declared that they were not engineers, were not competent to judge airship design, and accepted the results of his investigation."[8]

The press, long enamored with airships and their exploits, was unaccustomed to printing such negative stories about them. The Navy and Goodyear Zeppelin pressed on, and they gave the public remarkable access to the first, partially built, airship. Just twenty days prior to her launch, newspapers reported that thousands of people each week—and more than 60,000 on Sundays—were showing up to inspect progress. On September 3, 1931, visitors were informed that nearly half of the fabric cover was in place, seven of the eight engines installed, and the nose covered with aluminum "dope"—a lacquer applied to the outer fabric of the airship to make it tighter, stiffer, and weatherproof. Goodyear Zeppelin provided space for the visitors at one end of the dock and along one side. There was a sense of wonderment among those who visited the site, and nothing seems to have gone unnoticed or unreported by the press. The massive hangar itself was as fascinating to the press as the airship. Its mammoth roof, a semiparabola, was 1,175 feet long, 325 feet wide, and 311 feet high. The floor area was 364,000 square feet and, with no pillars or posts, the hangar was the largest structure in the world without interior support. It was estimated that the Woolworth Building in Manhattan and the Washington Monument both could be laid inside.

The *ZRS 4* herself was indeed a behemoth, at 785 feet long with a beam of 137.5 feet. Carrying 20,000 gallons of gasoline, she had a range of 10,500 miles and could cruise at 58 miles per hour. She carried nearly 7,000,000 cubic feet of helium.[9] Although an impressive sight, the eagerly awaited airship was being born into a hostile world. In addition to the false rumors about the quality of her materials and construction, the airship faced political and economic stresses. Many in the military and civilian sectors thought the expenditure was unwise, especially with the country entering unsettled economic times. There was heated competition between those lobbying for funding for dirigibles and those wanting the same funds for airplanes. Critics thought the large airship too vulnerable to enemy gunfire, either from the surface or from airplanes. Proponents responded that the small aircraft and machine guns that the dirigible carried offered protection, but this argument seemed inadequate. These arguments surrounding the vulnerability of the large airships had been long-standing and would resurface numerous times in the future.

When Wiley arrived in Akron, Ohio, in late July, he was put to work overseeing the final touches on the airship's construction and the training of her crew. Surviving the storms of controversy, the *Akron* finally was launched on August 8, 1931—for the citizens of Akron a joyous day. The mayor had declared it a holiday, and the press proclaimed it one of the greatest days in the history of the city.[10] Over 250,000 people converged on Akron for the event. The actual launching was surrounded by impressive aviation demonstrations and celebrations that included famous aviation pioneers. As a prelude, Lt. Col. Henry H. "Hap" Arnold led a squadron of twenty-four Army fighters from Wright Field in a flyover. Thirty-eight fighters from Selfridge, Michigan, led by Maj. George H. Brett followed Arnold, and the Navy sent a flight of scout bombers from the USS *Langley* to put on an aerial demonstration.

At two o'clock, celebrities and visitors crowded the hangar to observe the christening and launching. Rosendahl, Wiley, and the officers and crew of the ship stood in formation in front of the control car while tributes were made to some of the pioneers of lighter-than-air flight, including Lansdowne. There followed Admiral Moffett's address, in which he proclaimed that the United States now led the world in airship development. The First Lady of the United States, Mrs. Herbert Hoover, performed the christening, after which the ship was allowed to float off the hangar floor, thus completing a successful launch.

Ceremonies over, the officers and crew got about the business of preparing the *Akron* for flight. Following reveille each morning the crew was mustered at the local YMCA, where Wiley conducted classroom instruction. However, instructing the flight crew was not enough; the ground crew needed to be trained as well. Wiley, Lt. Rodney Dennett, and Goodyear's Art Sewall prepared 250 inexperienced civilians for that role. The giant airship made her maiden voyage on September 23, 1931, around the Cleveland area with Rosendahl in command, Wiley as executive officer, and 113 passengers, among them Admiral Moffett. This moment was particularly gratifying, of course, for Moffett, who enjoyed a private celebration. Three decades later the historian R. K. Smith eloquently captured the feeling on board the *Akron* that day:

> To the slack-jawed spectators on the ground the *Akron* was a phenomenon; but to the 113 men riding inside her hull she was the object of a personal pride which defies definition. She was the product of their thousands of hours of thought, speculation, argument, and labor, which they had wrought

in spite of those dire moments which occurred in the wake of disaster; the *Akron* was the instrument with which they expected to prove the efficacy of their vision, which would prove the rigid airship to be an effective means of navigating the air, and gain for lighter-than-air aeronautics an assured place in the future. Their hearts, their hopes, indeed, were all with her.[11]

The *Akron* set out on the last of her precommissioning test flights on October 16. This forty-eight-hour endurance flight was also the last before she headed to her new home at Lakehurst.[12] Wiley had sent a telegram to his cousin, Ada Kester, telling her he would try to have the *Akron* fly over Chillicothe. She shared the news with the *Chillicothe Constitution-Tribune*, which quickly printed the headline, "Herbert Wiley Expects to Fly over City Tonight in New Naval Air Giant, *Akron*." The newspaper said Wiley had sent the telegram to Miss Kester on the evening of October 15 that if the ship could be brought over Chillicothe, it would happen about 10 or 11 p.m.: "Please ask Fay to come down if I wire you. Plans are not definite. Please note, plans are subject to change."

Chillicothe rushed to make plans to receive the giant visitor. Floodlights atop city hall and the courthouse would illuminate the ship. The district manager for the Southwestern Telephone Company arranged with telephone offices along the route of the ship to send word to Chillicothe as the *Akron* passed over their cities. The message would be relayed to the Chillicothe Music Company, where an amplifier had been installed. Signalmen of the National Guard were planning to install equipment to send flash signals to the ship. These preparations, elaborate for a small town, were made in short order, and word was broadcast throughout the county of the ship's prospective arrival. Crowds were expected from every direction and the roads from the Trenton part of the county to be filled that night with cars.

As it turned out, the night was filled only with disappointment. Many expectant citizens spent the entire night waiting for the *Akron*, which never came. It was learned the next morning that Wiley had sent a follow-up telegram the previous night about 10 p.m. informing his cousin that the *Akron* would not arrive and asking her to inform his father.[13] The telegram had not been delivered until the following morning, not in time to advise the public.

On October 21 the *Akron* headed for NAS Lakehurst, leaving behind her an empty hangar and eight hundred workers of the Goodyear Zeppelin Company who were eager to begin construction of *ZRS 5*.[14] The *Akron* landed at Lakehurst at 0634 the next day, a flight of eight hours and twenty-five minutes. Approaching Lakehurst, a dozen Navy airplanes joined the airship and escorted her to the field, skirting away near the end to give the big dirigible plenty of room to land. The *Akron* hovered over her hangar for four hours before landing. Below her were seventy-five sailor-handlers waiting for sunrise to illuminate the ship, along with an additional sixty-three men from the *Los Angeles* who served as emergency crew.[15] When ready, Rosendahl had three handling lines thrown from the airship to the land crew and smoke bombs were released to give the crew the direction of the wind. At 0635 the nose of the *Akron* rode into a mobile mooring mast that had been invented by Rosendahl. Minutes later, the tail settled onto a mobile cradle, and two tractor-like machines drew the giant airship into the hangar. She was docked finally at 0835, though her huge fin grazed the top of the hangar entrance as she entered. Hugo Eckener was present to witness the *Akron*'s arrival, and he chatted with Rosendahl from the floor as the ship was being docked.

On the same day the *Akron* arrived at Lakehurst, the Associated Press published an exclusive interview that Dr. Karl Arnstein, designer of the *Akron*, had given to its staff reporter, R. A. Bruner. In it Arnstein spoke in detail about the elaborate testing that had gone into the construction of the airship to ensure its strength.

> When the tests for strength were made in the docks before the trial flights, the ship was loaded down with tons of weight, until it seemed as though we were deliberately trying to break its back. In the air it was made to dive and climb at speeds deemed dangerous in former practice.
>
> Some forty men were on duty during the tests for any sign of strain, or snapping wires, or loosening rivets. The ship met the test magnificently.
>
> No airship was ever tested out with such scientific precision. From stem to stern, top side to keel, the interior of the ship was literally dotted with curious gauges and recording instruments. Even the seismograph, used for detecting earthquakes, was utilized to measure vibration.[16]

At 2000 on October 27 the crew was mustered at quarters for the airship's commissioning.[17] The ceremony, broadcast on the radio in New York City, featured the John Phillip Sousa Band, which played "Anchors Aweigh." Following speeches from the president of the Goodyear Zeppelin Company, David S. Ingalls, the Assistant Secretary of the Navy, and Secretary of the Navy

Charles F. Adams, the usual process of commissioning was followed. H. E. Shoemaker, now a captain, read his orders from the Chief of Naval Operations accepting the *Akron* on behalf of the Navy and then placed her in full commission. The ensign and commissioning pennant were broken, and the air station band played the national anthem before the ship was delivered to her commanding officer, Lieutenant Commander Rosendahl, who ceremoniously read his orders from the Bureau of Navigation. After assuming command, he ordered Lieutenant Commander Wiley to set the watch and to pipe down (dismiss) the crew. Both were done at 2055.

With a roster of officers that included C. E. Rosendahl, H. V. Wiley, B. J. Rodgers, R. G. Mayer, S. E. Peck, R. R. Dennett, and others, the *Akron* was in the best of hands, but negative press seemed to hover over her. During her trial runs, she had failed to achieve her contract speed of seventy-two knots (eighty miles per hour). While this was a minor failing (as it turned out, the result of inadequate propellers), it did not escape the attention of the press.[18] The *Akron* was caught between two camps, one of strong admirers and the other of strong detractors. The smallest of problems or mishaps would come to the public's attention.

On November 2 the *Akron* made her first flight since her commissioning. General assembly was sounded at 0430, and the ship was prepared for flight. At 0605, Admiral Moffett arrived with an entourage to make the trip. The *Akron* was to take 109 men aloft including 10 officers, 49 crew, 31 members of the press, representatives from the National Broadcasting Company, engineers from Goodyear Zeppelin, photographers, and several visitors and observers.[19] The *Los Angeles* was in company, with *Akron* in the lead. Wiley was on board the *Akron* as her executive officer. The ships set a course for Washington, where they were seen over the city around 1000 before changing course toward Atlantic City, Philadelphia, and New York City before heading back to Lakehurst.[20]

It was no coincidence that so many media personnel were on board. This was Moffett's ongoing strategy to keep the press believing in the potential of the dirigible and generating favorable publicity.[21] Nothing that had transpired to this point threatened fatal consequences for the ship or the program, just as the *Akron* was about to be handed opportunities to prove her worth to the Navy, more bad press was on its way.

Rosendahl and Wiley kept the *Akron* flying as often as possible, getting to know the ship, experimenting with and gaining confidence in her. When the airship had transferred to Lakehurst, Wiley's children had made the move too. They were still under the maternal care of Roland Mayer's wife, Mabel, but in late fall of that year a change was made. Wiley's older son, Gordon, went to New London, Connecticut, to live with his aunt and attend school there; David, now seven, was also sent to Connecticut but to live with another aunt and uncle and attend the private Warham School in Windsor. Wiley made David a local celebrity there in November: on the twenty-fifth the Hartford newspaper carried a story, "*Akron* Note Received by Wiley Boy."[22] During one of the *Akron*'s flights over New England Wiley "had attached an envelope to a small handbag with a red cloth streamer, carefully addressed to his son." The entire Warham School was at recess when the airship flew over, and the students and teachers all saw the message with its streamer falling. They watched with excitement as a gust of wind blew it into a nearby cemetery. Someone found the message the following day and delivered it to David, who was both excited and bursting with boyish pride. He was particularly happy to read the message from his father that he would be on leave and visiting David over the Thanksgiving holiday.

By the end of 1931 the *Akron* had logged over three hundred hours of flight time, including a forty-six-hour endurance run through the southern United States. Still, although demonstration flights, publicity flights, training flights, and flights for the conduct of experiments were fine, many in the Navy were eager to get the airship involved with the surface fleet to prove its worth. On January 9, 1932, the *Akron* received orders from Vice Adm. Arthur Lee Willard, who had been commander of the Scouting Force (ComScoFor) since 1930. He had been in command of a number of fleet exercises that demonstrated, with increasing force, the value of launching attacks on surface ships from ranges beyond the reach of battleship guns, through the use of aircraft carriers. Willard ordered the *Akron* to take part in such an exercise in a scouting role with the Scouting Force. At first consideration, this was the perfect task for the airship, the fruition of the tactical and design-related thinking that had gone into her construction—but the *Akron* was not ready. She had been called on too early.

Admiral Willard's operations order called for the *Akron* to be off Cape Lookout, North Carolina, by daylight on January 10, 1932. From there, she was to begin scouting for a group of destroyers that were en route from Charleston, South Carolina, to Guantanamo Bay, Cuba. She was to locate the "enemy" fleet and follow its progress, keeping ComScoFor informed of its position, course, speed, and disposition. Just before 1600 on January 9 the *Akron*, with fifteen officers and fifty-four crewmen on board, emerged from her hangar into fourteen-mile-per-hour crosswinds, a light rain, and a low ceiling.[23] She took flight on a course for Philadelphia. At 1734, she was over Wilmington, Delaware, at 1,100 feet with zero visibility. Ice began to form on her bow, and twenty minutes later, over Aberdeen, Maryland, on the horizontal fins. At 1837, over Baltimore, it began to snow. The airship passed over Washington on a course for Richmond, Virginia, where she again encountered zero visibility. The ship turned and by 2210, over Crewe, Virginia, she was into clear weather that continued over Greensboro and Raleigh, North Carolina. Having escaped the more challenging weather, the ship made Cape Lookout in the early morning of January 10, crossing the North Carolina coastline at 0720. Battle lookouts were stationed at 0700, and the ship started her search for the U.S. Navy ships playing the role of "enemy."

At 0820 flying on a southerly course toward the Bahamas, the lookouts sighted a steamer to their starboard about fifteen miles distant; at 0844 they spotted a light cruiser off the port bow at thirty miles. Neither of these was part of the "enemy" fleet. At 1140 Rosendahl changed course to the west, largely for navigational calibrations;[24] the ship was back on her original southward course by 1240, when the radio room picked up a strong signal from one of the "enemy" destroyers, a report that a ship in company was having engine problems. Because the *Akron* was not yet equipped with a radio direction finder, the crew was unable to determine the bearing of the ship that had transmitted. Consequently, the *Akron* continued on her southerly course. Meanwhile, unfortunately, though the *Akron* had not spotted any of the "enemy's" vessels, two of their destroyers had seen her. At 1350 the USS *Dickerson* (DD 157) had spotted the airship ten miles to the northwest, and minutes later the USS *Leary* (DD 158) caught sight of her. At 1701, having reached the southern limits of her planned track, the *Akron* turned toward the northwest and at 1918 spotted two cruisers, but again not "enemy." She made another course change at 2202, putting her on a southeasterly heading. At 0708 on the eleventh she reached the limit of her search area in that direction and turned to the northeast.

At 0910 the lookouts finally sighted the "enemy" ships: a squadron of destroyers and one cruiser off the starboard bow, range fifteen miles. The radiomen sent the contact report to ComScoFor, and the airship began to track the destroyers. At 0952 the lookouts spotted another squadron of destroyers, twenty miles off their starboard bow. The crew could see the two destroyer squadrons converging on the cruiser leader and continued to follow the "enemy" vessels until the scouting problem was completed at 1103. The *Akron* then set out on her way back to Lakehurst.

In the aftermath of this fleet exercise, the issue was whether it had been a success for the *Akron*. By comparison, a division of cruisers on the surface had not been able to locate the "enemy" fleet on the first day, but Admiral Willard believed the *Akron* should have. Critics saw a failure of airships to contribute to the mission of the surface Navy; proponents of the *Akron* claimed the ship had been sent on this mission prematurely. Had her radio direction finding equipment been installed, she would have located the "enemy" fleet on the first day by running down the bearing of the radio message she intercepted. More important, perhaps, the *Akron's* trapeze and airplanes had not been installed yet; use of these planes would have increased greatly the effective scouting range of the airship. Indeed, that had been a basic element of the concept of dirigibles as long-range reconnaissance vessels—to be airborne aircraft carriers.

This fleet exercise, then, was not a fair test. Had the *Akron* spotted the "enemy" fleet on the first day, it is very likely this experiment would have helped to cement the future of airships in the role of reconnaissance, but that she did not should not have led to the conclusion the experiment was a failure—although some opponents of airships would argue that. At the least, it was a poorly designed experiment, one that sent an airship on a mission without all the assets that she would be expected to have. Rosendahl and Wiley understood all of this and saw things clearly, but they were not politicians with obscure agendas; they were officers in the U.S. Navy who would continue undeterred on their path. They knew also that Admiral Moffett, though a Navy officer too, was also a skillful politician when he needed to be and would do all in his power to safeguard the airship program.

The *Akron's* troubles were far from over. As early as January 5, 1932, Representative James McClintic, a Democrat from Oklahoma and member of the House Committee on Naval Affairs, had called for an investigation. He told the committee he had reports that the airship was overweight, had not met her contract speed requirements, and suffered from faulty construction. As "evidence" he presented a letter from a man who had been employed in the construction of the *Akron* and claimed to know the ship's defects, but would not reveal the man's name.[25] Of course, McClintic was reviving claims that had been addressed and dismissed previously by the experts, but once in the public eye the committee had little choice but to approve an investigation. In response, Moffett invited members of the committee to take a flight on the *Akron* to satisfy themselves as to her safety and durability of the craft—a good idea that would turn bad. A six-hour inspection flight for visiting congressmen, including McClintic, was scheduled for February 22, to begin at Lakehurst.[26]

Patrick J. Boland, a Democrat from Pennsylvania, arrived at Lakehurst the evening before, with McClintic, to observe the entire flight-preparation process firsthand.[27] At 0855 the airship was moored to the rail mast, and at 0923 the lower fin was connected to the stern beam. Minutes later, the flight crew embarked. The rail mast began towing the ship out of the hangar, stern first, at 0938. The ship's logbook recorded that on the 0800–1200 watch the aerological truck had measured wind velocities ranging from eight to sixteen knots. When the ship was about halfway out of the hangar the rail mast slowed sharply.[28] The flight crew was already on board the ship, but Rosendahl and Wiley were on the ground, walking alongside the control car so they could communicate effectively with the crews on the mast and stern beam and also in the car.[29] At 0945 orders were received from aft to put the rudder full right. As this was taking place, an order came from aft to bring the rudder amidships.

At this point, things began to unravel quickly and in full view of the congressmen. Suddenly a "very sharp report was heard in the control car sounding like the snapping of a cable."[30] Word came from aft that a major control had broken. At 0946 when the bow crossed the sill of the hangar, the ship was listing six degrees to starboard. Subsequently, the download on the bow was estimated to be between four and seven thousand pounds and the side load between three and five thousand to starboard. The wind at this time was from the north-northwest at fourteen miles an hour. Around 0952 came the report, "She is loose!" The lower fin had carried away from the stern beam, and the stern was swinging rapidly to starboard. The crew reacted by dropping ballast from aft to create lift, but the stern did not respond quickly enough: the lower fin struck the ground with a great deal of force. When the ship was heading into the wind the swinging decreased greatly, but she was left with a hole about six feet long in the after head of the No. 2 gas cell, and within five minutes it was enlarging.

Men were dispatched to make emergency repairs to the cell, while handling lines were attached to the ship at all main frames on both sides, manned by both Navy personnel and civilians. At 1142 the lower fin was placed on a flatcar, and the stern was hauled to port into position on the docking rails. The wind continued to gust widely, between eight and sixteen knots, but by 1209 the rail mast was towing the ship back into the hangar stern first. The log recorded, "Members of the Naval Affairs Committee inspected the ship" around 1226, after she was secure in the hangar. The worst damage was to the lower fin with very little to the ship's main structure. There were only two injuries, both minor: an officer sustained a broken wrist and a facial cut, and a machinist's mate suffered contusions to a thigh.[31]

All the committee members present had witnessed the same things, but only two, McClintic and Boland, went away with strongly negative opinions of the *Akron*. The accident fueled McClintic's apparent cynicism and he shared his feelings openly with the press. He told reporters he feared that the damage sustained by the *Akron* would be permanent; he himself would not ride on board. He ventured to predict a more careful inspection of the *ZRS 5*, the future USS *Macon*, and added he *would* ride on that airship.[32] Fortunately, McClintic was not able to inflict severe political damage on the *Akron* and the Committee on Naval Affairs agreed with Dr. Hugo Eckener that she was "a masterpiece of engineering and workmanship."[33]

A greater concern to some was that the damage and the time needed to repair it would cause to the *Akron* to miss Fleet Problem XIII in March. When these naval exercises took place the *Akron* was indeed still laid up in her hangar at Lakehurst undergoing repairs to her lower fin and the installation of her trapeze and airplane-handling equipment. She did not fly again until April 28, and when she did, Rosendahl and Wiley found themselves in the usual company of Navy brass, including Secretary of the Navy C. F. Adams, Admiral Moffett, Captain Shoemaker, Commander Fulton, and representatives of Goodyear Zeppelin. When these dignitaries had joined the normal complement of officers and crew, the *Akron* lifted off with ninety-one people on board for what proved a very successful flight.[34]

With May 1932 approaching, Rosendahl and Wiley were getting the *Akron* ready to fly again on a frequent schedule and to prove herself. On May 3 she was scheduled to make a flight to determine if she was ready to resume service. Her trapeze apparatus and airplane-handling equipment were tested inside the hangar the day before the big test. The ship's bow was elevated approximately twenty-five feet, and a training biplane was hooked to the trapeze and hoisted into the hangar.[35] All went well with this static test. On the morning of May 3, the *Akron* was unmoored from the rail mast at 0831 with ninety-nine people on board: Rear Adm. G. C. Day, president of the Board of Inspection and Survey; Captain Shoemaker, Commander Rigid Airship Training and Experimental Squadron; Cdr. S. M. Kraus, Cdr. K. L. Hill, Commander Fulton, Mr. C. P. Burgess; and her twelve officers and fifty-three crewmen. There were also ten representatives from the Goodyear Zeppelin Company, three members of the Board of Inspection and Survey, three student officers, two civilian passengers, seven officer passengers, and three enlisted passengers.[36]

By 0903 the ship was crossing the New Jersey coastline at 2,500 feet preparing for the airplane hook-on tests. The trapeze was lowered at 0913, and six minutes later Lt. D. W. Harrigan approached and successfully hooked his small biplane onto the trapeze; three minutes later there was a successful hook-on by Lt. H. L. Young. Rosendahl and Wiley were pleased. All was going smoothly, as choreographed, but things were about to get better. By 1004 Lieutenant Young and Lieutenant Harrigan had achieved twelve trapeze hook-ons each. The next step was to demonstrate the airship's onboard hangar and airplane-handling equipment. At 1009 Lieutenant Harrigan again successfully hooked his biplane to the trapeze, but this time, nine minutes later, he and his plane were hoisted into the *Akron*'s hangar and secured. The airship continued to cruise on various courses and at 1255 climbed to 2,500 feet, where, at 1324, Lieutenant Harrigan left the ship in his N2Y biplane toward Lakehurst, where he landed safely. At 1859 Lieutenant Young accomplished another trapeze hook-on in his small N2Y airplane, followed just three minutes later by Lieutenant Harrigan, who was airborne again, this time in a Curtiss F9C. Less than twenty minutes after his hook-on, he and his plane were stowed safely within the airship; this time, the *Akron* demonstrated her ability to land with an airplane still in her hangar. The F9C was removed from the airship back on the ground. Meanwhile, the crew had done the work of calibrating the airship's radio direction finder.

This could not have been a better day for the *Akron*. Everything had gone very smoothly, and all on board, military and civilian, were impressed highly by the airship's performance. Wiley was one of three officers to receive written recognition from the chief of the Bureau of Navigation for his performance on this day. In the document, Admiral Upham stated the Board of Inspection and Survey had been very favorably impressed with the efficiency with which the *Akron* was handled during the trials and that special credit attached to Rosendahl, Wiley, and Rodgers.[37] The following day, May 4, the *Akron* was flying again, but this time with twelve members of the Committee on Naval Affairs. As previously, they gave a demonstration of the trapeze hook-on device, with three pilots making seven successful hook-on "landings." Following a successful cruise, the passengers were landed safely at the air station.

The Navy was now ready to demonstrate the *Akron* by way of a transcontinental trip that would attract favorable publicity and show her off to the American public. When the airship reached the West Coast, she would participate in fleet exercises in the Pacific Ocean. She left Lakehurst at 0500 on May 8, bound for Sunnyvale, California, where she was to be moored though the new airship base there was not yet complete. Cdr. Alger H. Dresel was on board; he had held command of the *Los Angeles* previously but in the spring of 1932 he had been ordered to the *Akron* for temporary duty and, as her prospective commanding officer, to make the West Coast flight as an observer. As usual, Rosendahl was in command with Wiley as executive officer. The airship began her flight with seventy-eight persons on board, including thirteen officers, sixty-three crewmen, and two observers, of whom Dresel was one.

While cruising in the area of the NAS at 0724, the trapeze was lowered, and, at 0738, Lt. H. L. Young hooked his F9C biplane onto the trapeze. He and his plane were hoisted in and secure by 0745. At 0701 (the ship's clock having been set back one hour for a change of time zone) the ship crossed the New Jersey coastline and ten minutes later lowered the trapeze once again. Lieutenant Harrigan then made his hook-up with his N2Y plane, which was on board and stowed by 0720. It had become standard practice to bring the airplanes on board in the air rather than load them on the ground. The planes added thousands of pounds of weight and, if loaded on the ground, stressed the airship's static lifting powers. It had been observed that the airship moving in flight created a dynamic lift that allowed her to carry more weight than she could have with her buoyant lift alone. With the two pilots, there were now eighty people on board.

The *Akron* set out on a southern route across the country, flying over parts of Virginia, North Carolina, South Carolina, Georgia, Alabama, Mississippi, Louisiana, and into Texas. The flight through Texas produced quite a bit of drama due to severe weather. The crew had encountered cloudy weather over Alabama, Mississippi, and Louisiana, but the weather began to thicken north of Houston;

they flew on various courses and at various altitudes to avoid the worst of the turbulence. Shortly after 1800 on May 9 they saw lightning and rain to the west, prompting further course and altitude changes.[38] Around 2000 thunderstorms to their south sent them to the north, and around 2100 the airshipmen changed course to follow the beacons from San Antonio to Big Springs, Texas. They were over the San Antonio airport at 2225 and four minutes later were circling San Angelo, Texas, with thunderstorms dead astern and very close aboard. Observers on the ground said the *Akron* hung over the city after circling the airport "as if uncertain whether to proceed into an electrical storm raging west of here."[39]

At 2320 the *Akron* called down for a landing crew of five hundred men. As if indicating a desperate situation, the *Akron* sent flashlight signals to operators on the ground asking the city's entire population to be assembled if necessary to ground the dirigible. The airport at San Angelo was advised that a landing crew was ready at San Antonio if the ship could make the return trip of two hundred miles, while negotiating thunderstorms all the way. At 2331 they were still over the San Angelo airport, with thunderstorms abeam to port about ten miles distant headed east. Around midnight, the airship was maneuvering at 3,500 feet at an airspeed of sixty-two knots, ground speed twelve knots in the fifty-knot winds, and with thunderstorms on both sides.

A tense situation had developed. The 0400–0800 watch found the *Akron* following the Pecos River, surrounded by lightning. At 0515 she entered a dense fog that cleared after just half an hour. Over Langtry, Texas, they set course for Dryden, running into another heavy fog at 0750. Flying for some time in the fog, they finally sighted the ground—they were over Langtry again, in fog, high winds, and rain. About 1419 the ship was in heavy fog again and lost sight of the ground. This prompted a course change back toward Pecos. They ran into a sandstorm about four miles east of El Paso with very turbulent air. Still over the El Paso area at 2040, they ran into another sandstorm, with "extremely bumpy" air.[40] At 2320 the ship climbed briefly to seven hundred feet to avoid mountains; five minutes later the crew sighted Douglas, Arizona, off the port beam, five miles distant.

Early on May 11 she was in the vicinity of Tucson, Arizona—finally back into clear weather, away from the Texas storms—following the mountain passes. The strong winds and extra maneuvering to negotiate the severe storms resulted in the ship's burning more fuel than planned. Although fuel was not dangerously low, Rosendahl felt it prudent to land at Camp Kearney, just north of San Diego,

California, to refuel prior to pressing on to Sunnyvale.[41] By 0800 the *Akron* was over San Diego, where the ground was covered by fog. The airshipmen maneuvered through the fog looking for an opening through which they could drop their airplanes. At 0837 they were able to drop Harrington piloting his N2Y airplane, with Lieutenant Peck as a passenger. The two aviators were to land at Camp Kearney to assist the ground crew with the mooring of the *Akron*. The airship dropped through the fog to make contact with the ground and begin the approach to Camp Kearney.

On the first approach at 1055, the crew dropped the trail ropes, but the ground crew failed to secure them. The ship veered away to make another approach and at 1125 dropped her main wire, and by 1131 the wire was connected to the main wire of the mooring mast—and then disaster struck. A strong updraft drove the airship skyward and broke the cable that secured it to the mast, so suddenly that three members of the ground crew failed to release the handling ropes and were carried aloft. Two of them, Robert Edfall from Elkhart, Indiana, and Nigel Fenton from Fresno, California, were unable to hold on and fell more than two hundred feet to their deaths. The third man, Charles "Bud" Cowart, was able to hang on by clamping his feet against a knot in the rope. The *Akron* tried to land to release Cowart, but it became apparent quickly that a mooring could not be achieved in time to save the man.

The nineteen-year-old Cowart hung on, dangling from the 350-foot rope for over an hour as the airship soared half a mile over the heads of ten thousand onlookers. As people on board the airship and on the ground were looking for options that might save the man, a volunteer from the *Akron* climbed, hand over hand, twenty-five feet down the rope to determine how secure Cowart was. The volunteer then climbed back up to report that Cowart was sufficiently secure to be pulled up into the ship.

As it turned out, Cowart remained calm and thinking throughout his ordeal. When he was first pulled aloft he held fast with one hand while he used the other to loop the rope around his legs, fashioning a "bosun's seat" where he hung about two hundred feet below the airship.[42] The crew was able to pull him slowly into the ship through a hatch. Once on board, he was examined by a pharmacist's mate and found to be unharmed. Without hesitation, he coolly expressed a desire to examine the great airship. Back on the ground after a successful landing, Cowart "demanded immediately, 'Gimme something to eat.' Calm and unconcerned, he washed and ate a hearty meal."[43] Charles Cowart was an apprentice seaman stationed at San Diego. Reporters wanted to hear the details of his nearly fatal experience, but he refused to say more than, "I hung on because I was ordered to hang on. I'll have to see my manager before I talk." As it turned out, Cowart was not only a sailor but also a welterweight fighter, and as such he had a manager. The manager told the newspapermen the story was for sale to the highest bidder. There were no bidders.

Having reached the West Coast, Rosendahl sent a message to the Navy's radio station in San Francisco: "After a rough and trying trip the *Akron* has reached the Pacific Coast in excellent condition in spite of the fact that, in my opinion, this ship underwent the most severe conditions ever experienced successfully by any rigid airship."[44] The *Akron* had landed at Camp Kearney with only a sixth of her fuel left. Refueled, she took flight again on the morning of May 12 and followed the Pacific coastline to her final destination at Sunnyvale, arriving on the morning of the thirteenth.

The *Akron* was scheduled to meet a surface force at San Francisco to take part in fleet exercises, but she was behind schedule and, newspapers reported, the Navy did not wait for her. The *Patoka*, the airship tender, was left behind for her. Being late for the rendezvous was one problem, but now there was another issue to be considered.

The emergency at Camp Kearney had required the valving off of significant volumes of helium. First, the sun had caused superheating of the gas and the ship quickly started to become too light. With the nose of the ship tethered to Kearney's mooring cable, the tail had begun to rise at a sharp angle. To correct for this Rosendahl valved off even more helium, but emergency ballast bags suddenly discharged themselves, making the *Akron* uncontrollably light. In response, Rosendahl ordered the ground crew to release the ship completely, and it was then that the ground crewmen clutching the cable were carried aloft. More helium was released as Rosendahl tried desperately to land. So much helium was released that by the time the airship was safely on the ground her lift had been reduced significantly. This could have been remedied if there had been a supply of helium at Camp Kearney, but there had not been. Without sufficient helium the *Akron* could not participate in the fleet exercises.[45] Even getting to the final destination in Sunnyvale had required special calculation and planning on the parts of Rosendahl and Wiley.

The ship's load had to be reduced significantly, and that was done by leaving a number of men at Camp Kearney and by sending the airplanes ahead on their own. On the morning of Thursday, May 1, Young departed Camp Kearney for Sunnyvale in his N2Y biplane and Harrigan in his F9C. Lt. S. E. Peck and Lieutenant (junior grade) Bailey, along with ten enlisted men, flew there in two Sikorsky amphibian planes provided by the naval air station.[46] Before the *Akron* could get airborne to follow the airplanes to Sunnyvale, she had to be inspected twice, by two different admirals. Rear Adm. T. J. Senn, commandant of the Eleventh Naval District, arrived with his aides Thursday morning at 0850, as the crew was beginning fueling and ballasting. At 1030 Rear Adm. H. E. Yarnell, Commander Aircraft, Battle Force, made an appearance with his own aides to conduct their own inspection.

With final preparations made and all inspections behind her, the airship unmoored at 1139 with ten officers, fifty-four crewmen, and Commander Dresel on board. Shortly after 1900 on Friday, May 13, the *Akron* was moored securely to the mast at NAS Sunnyvale. Here the ship was able to replenish her supply of helium and to keep her gas cells "topped off." Over the next few days she made flights about the region; the officers and crew were still getting to know their new dirigible and to become accustomed to her handling characteristics. On May 17 they were flying over the San Quentin area, en route to a mooring with the *Patoka*, when, at 1745, they dropped flowers over the home of the locally famous industrialist and philanthropist "Captain" Robert Dollar, who had died the previous day.[47]

The airship was now ready to participate to some extent in the Pacific fleet exercises. A reporter covering the exercise from the USS *California* (BB 44) gave readers on March 11 a detailed account of what the naval exercises entailed.

> Somewhere in the vast stretches of the Pacific two fleets of the United States Navy were conducting a major war game today with the "destruction" of each other their goal.
>
> The tremendous area involved in the battle maneuvers extended from Puget Sound to Hawaii and from Hawaii to San Diego. Within this range, the scouting fleet under Vice Admiral Arthur L. Willard is hunting the major portion of the battle fleet under Admiral Richard H. Lehigh [sic].

When they meet, a terrific "battle" will take place as the final dramatic episode in the 1932 fleet exercises.

Strict radio silence is maintained and the great armadas are darkened at night. Seaplanes are dispatched to cover all possible areas while submarines, destroyers and scout cruisers are deployed in search of the fictitious enemy.

The problem of the scouting fleet is to find the slower but stronger battle fleet. Taking part on both sides are practically all the Navy's fighting ships except those now in Asiatic waters. The battle fleet leaving Lahaina Roads, Hawaii, is attempting to reach the Pacific coast. The scouting fleet relying on its speed is trying to prevent this.

A grand maneuver does not end when the two fleets meet. It is vital that on any deployment for action, such as in the great battle of Jutland, all units are maneuvered properly and maximum concentration with flexibility be obtained by virtue of position. To attain this involves coordination of the entire fleet.

Admiral Frank H. Schofield, commander of the fleets afloat with headquarters aboard the dreadnaught *Tennessee*, is the chief umpire of the contest. He and his staff are in a position to study movements of both units.

Officers and men keep war time watches, all armament is manned and no precaution overlooked to insure that units are ready for action at a moment's notice.

The maneuver, in fact, is a gigantic game of chess with the ocean for a board and the ships for chess pieces—some powerful, others less strong but more mobile. The fleet with the best position will win.[48]

If the fleets moved stealthily in radio silence, there was little secret about the *Akron*. The giant airship was so recognizable that she merited separate news coverage. On the day before the *Akron*'s scheduled departure from Sunnyvale to join the exercise a newspaper reporter claimed, under the headline, "Naval Armada Awaits *Akron*," that "the biggest secret was if, when, and how the world's largest airship, USS *Akron*, would try to find the fleet."[49] The *Akron*'s departure date was in the newspapers. Commander Rosendahl told the press he would not determine the ship's course until departure time, but reporters, aware of the factors that influenced dirigibles, speculated the airship would fly over the San Joaquin Valley to avoid the stormy conditions then on the coast.[50] The prediction was correct.

On the morning of June 1, the *Akron* took on fuel and filled her gas cells with 140,000 cubic feet of helium. She left her mast at 1740 and headed south, down the San Joaquin Valley, en route to the exercise, off Baja California.[51]

At 0500 on June 2 the *Akron* posted her lookouts and began the search for the "enemy" fleet. On the 1200–1600 watch, the lookouts began to sight "enemy" destroyers, identifying one as the USS *Gilmer* (DD 233). Shortly thereafter they located the fleet itself, including cruisers with Vought O2U planes perched on their catapults, and the airship maneuvered to track it. There were many who believed that during the fleet exercises in the Atlantic in January the *Akron* had been "set up" to fail. Now, out over the Pacific Ocean, she was flying into something of an ambush. Knowing the airship would be looking for his "enemy" fleet, Rear Adm. William H. Standley ordered half of his cruisers to have their Vought O2U seaplanes readied on their catapults to intercept her on short notice. Initially, only two of the planes were sent aloft, but on June 3 thirteen were launched against the airship.[52]

They swarmed and dove about the *Akron* in simulated aerial combat. At 1535 her logbook proclaimed, "Enemy plane attack repelled. No casualties."[53] The premise for this claim was not stated. Had this been real combat, it is uncertain what the outcome would have been. Opponents of the dirigible felt she was a huge target that was easy to hit with machine-gun fire and artillery. Advocates insisted that because she carried helium instead of hydrogen, she would not be so easy to destroy; destruction would require damage to hard structures within the airship. As in the Atlantic exercise, the *Akron* did not have her fighter planes on board. Rosendahl had maintained that his fighters would be a strong deterrent to enemy aircraft. In reality, the two or three the airship could have released would have been overwhelmed easily by larger numbers of enemy planes.

A more cogent argument in defense of the *Akron* would be that once again she had been tested under unrealistic conditions. In the Pacific exercises she found herself in close-range combat with surface vessels and their planes. The wiser use of the airship would have been to keep her at a distance while her scout fighters searched for the enemy. Rosendahl and Wiley went away from this exercise still believing firmly in the military value of airships, while opponents such as Admiral Standley and Admiral Schofield were all the more convinced that airships, due largely to their vulnerability, had no role in combat support. The issue was not resolved here, however, as arguments raged.[54] In any case, the *Akron*'s participation in the tactical exercises was terminated at 1859, and she returned to Sunnyvale.

The *Akron* was now in need of a level of maintenance and repair that could be provided only at Lakehurst, and Rosendahl was eager to return there. Some Navy officials, however, felt the *Akron* should remain on the West Coast longer. The most prominent among these was the Assistant Secretary of the Navy, Ernest Lee Jahncke, who made his case to the press. He argued the Navy had a sufficient number of airshipmen who were familiar with weather conditions along the East Coast and now needed a similar familiarity with the Pacific coast, where a large proportion of airship operations would be.[55] If war came, everyone expected, it would be with Japan and there would be a reconnaissance role for the airship, regardless of the results of the two fleet exercises in which the *Akron* had participated.

Nevertheless, the *Akron* would return to New Jersey. She had had a rough time coming west to Sunnyvale, especially over Texas, and a glance at the weather situation now showed unfavorable conditions along the southern route she expected to travel. Consequently, her planned departure date of June 10 was delayed by a day to take on additional supplies, including helium.[56] The *Akron* unmoored from the mast at Sunnyvale at 1014 on June 11 and once airborne recovered Harrigan and Young in their scout planes.[57] Shortly into the flight, it seemed the Fates were sending the *Akron* a sign that her homeward journey was going to be something of an odyssey. At 1215 the No. 3 engine lost its propeller, leaving the ship one engine short.

Flying in an easterly direction as she was, it did not take long to encounter mountains, in the Phoenix, Arizona, area, that would require her to climb three thousand feet to clear. She had not consumed sufficient fuel to lighten the ship enough to do so; Rosendahl compensated by jettisoning fuel. At times, the ship rose above pressure height (at which the lifting gas expanded to the permissible limit) and the automatic valves on the gas cells blew off helium.[58] By 0450 on June 12 Rosendahl had ordered Harrigan and Young into their planes to be launched, thus lightening the airship by over four thousand pounds. The pilots were told the *Akron* would take them on board again around Pecos, Texas, but when they and the airship arrived there, Rosendahl refused to take on the weight again and, on June 12, told Harrington and Young to fly back to Lakehurst on their own.[59]

Negotiating the mountains had presented the *Akron* with two problems: she had jettisoned a great deal of fuel to lighten the ship, and she had lost over a million cubic feet of helium to automatic valve opening. She had enough fuel to make it back to Lakehurst if she did not encounter severe weather, but not wanting to take that chance, Rosendahl decided to lay over at Parris Island, South

Carolina. The airship moored there at 1835 on June 13. As the 2000–2400 watch began, her logbook recorded, "continues heavy rain," followed a short time later by an entry that she was swinging violently. Rainsqualls continued into the next day with winds gusting between twenty and thirty knots. She was able to take on fuel at Parris Island, but there was no helium available. The outer cover of the airship was waterlogged from the intense rains, and after taking on over 12,000 pounds of fuel and embarking her crew she was too heavy to fly. Consequently, fuel had to be pumped back off the ship.[60] Finally, at 1000 on June 15, the *Akron* unmoored from the mast at Parris Island; she was back in her familiar hangar at Lakehurst by 2031.

It had been an arduous journey both ways, battling severe weather on the outbound course to California and terrain and technical problems on the return. The journey reinforced two concerns surrounding airships: that they were dependent heavily on their huge hangars for missions of long duration and that they were far more secure flying over vast expanses of ocean than over land with highly variable terrain. Opponents of the *Akron* within the Navy felt these issues rendered the airship useless to the surface fleet, especially given the rapid development of airplanes. Moffett, Rosendahl, Wiley, and others, still believed the airship could be of great use to the Navy if deployed in the proper place, at the proper time, and in the proper manner. However, unknown to anyone at the time, the *Akron* had already flown her last scouting mission with the surface fleet.

As the *Akron* approached Lakehurst, Rosendahl, Wiley, and others were aware that changes in command were about to take place. Rosendahl's name was synonymous with lighter-than-air flight, and he preferred to remain in that service, but to advance in rank he needed time at sea. He had orders to the USS *West Virginia* (BB 48). He had strong feelings about who should take command of the *Akron*, and he traveled to Washington to meet with Admiral Moffett about the matter. Rosendahl made a very strong case that Lt. Cdr. Herbert Wiley was the best man for the position.[61] Wiley's reputation in the airship industry was international, and no one would deny he was the most knowledgeable and experienced airship officer available. Moffett himself would not have disagreed, and he had already expressed his admiration and respect for Wiley in writing. However, for political reasons, Moffett opted for rank over experience: he wanted the *Akron*'s new commanding officer to have the rank of commander, believing it would bring more prestige to the airship service and "draw more water" in Washington. Wiley was not yet a commander and was passed over in favor of Dresel, who was a full commander and a few years Wiley's senior but had a mere fraction of Wiley's airship experience.

Observers in the Navy's airship program believed Moffett had an obsession with rank that at times led him to make mistakes.[62] From the beginning, the LTA service had been volunteer duty, but now more senior officers were "invited in" to assume positions for which they were not necessarily qualified.[63] Until this time Moffett had been superb in dealing with the Navy, Congress, and private industry to keep the LTA program funded and alive. His preference for rank over experience appears to have been a departure from his earlier wisdom. There were other consequences to this decision as well. Favoring more senior officers "from outside" over people who were working their way up through the LTA program, acquiring knowledge and experience, blocked the upward movement of more qualified yet younger officers. From its earliest days, Lakehurst had been politically charged by differences in rank and pay; Moffett's new preference for rank over experience made all of these tensions worse than ever. Dresel's appointment was to prove emblematic.

At 0800 on June 22, 1932, at Lakehurst, with the crew at quarters, Lt. Cdr. Charles E. Rosendahl read his orders detaching him from command of the *Akron.* Cdr. Alger H. Dresel then read his orders and assumed command.[64] Dresel had spent most of his career in battleships and destroyers and preferred sea duty; still, he had volunteered for the LTA program in 1929. After spending a year on board the *Los Angeles,* he assumed command of her in 1931 and, in the spring of 1932 was ordered to the *Akron* as her prospective commanding officer. When Rosendahl's pleas failed, Moffett's plan unfolded as scripted.

As expected, the press reported the change of *Akron*'s command. The service preferences of Rosendahl and Dresel were well known and made their way into newspapers. It was reported that the change of command was not welcome to either Rosendahl or his successor: "For Commander Dresel is frank in admitting that he prefers the sea to the air, and everyone knows that Rosendahl's heart is in the clouds." The press speculated as to whether Rosendahl's tour of sea duty would end in time for him to assume command of the USS *Macon,* which was under construction at that time. However, as things would turn out, Rosendahl would never command an airship again.[65]

The *Akron* remained in her hangar during the most of June undergoing repairs, regular maintenance, and upgrades. This hangar time allowed Wiley to spend time with his family following his long trip to the West Coast and back. Other than the change of command, the most significant thing to occur in June 1932 was the arrival of the new Curtiss F9C-2 Sparrowhawks that were to be the *Akron*'s new scout-fighter planes.[66] Also, however, during the 0000–1200 watch on June 30 Cdr. Frank C. McCord reported to the *Akron* as her prospective commanding officer.[67] There were now two officers ahead of Wiley for command of the *Akron*, and there was no chance of his replacing either until he made commander, but as yet there was no indication when that would happen. He continued as the *Akron*'s executive officer.

The worsening Great Depression was causing significant cuts in government spending. With growing concern that the Navy's LTA program might become a target of cutbacks, the air station accelerated its testing of design improvements that had been made to the *Akron*, hoping to make as much progress as possible before they were hit with them. Many flights during July and August 1932 were made for that purpose, and the results of these tests were being integrated into the design of the *Macon*. Before the month was out, however, the *Akron* had another mishap.

On the afternoon of August 22, preparations were being made for another flight. From 1600 to 2104 the wind was steady, four to six knots with no gusts. As the mobile mast was towing the ship out of the hangar, bow first, an accident occurred that caused the flight to be canceled: at 1949 the towing was halted when the lower fin fouled the stern beam, causing structural damage to the lower fin and hull. The ship returned to the hangar until repairs could be made.[68] Dresel told the press the damage was "not very great" and speculated that the necessary repairs could be made at the air station.[69]

The Navy convened a board of inquiry to investigate the cause of the damage and assign responsibility. Because Wiley was the executive officer of the ship and had been participating in the flight preparations and movement of the airship, he was named as a defendant. The board found that the damage to the airship had occurred as a result of the mooring mast being moved before the stern handling beam had been taken from beneath the ship. Ultimately the board held three officers accountable, Wiley among them. Another was Lt. John M. Thornton, for directing that the "ready" signal, a green light, be displayed before the stern handling beam had been moved clear of the ship. His culpability was mitigated by the circumstance that he had not been instructed in the duties assigned him. However, he had been acting under the instruction of Lt. Cdr. William K. Phillips, who now bore blame for failing to correct an incorrect order given by Thornton. Wiley was held accountable because, while in charge of operations aft, he failed to remain in control of signals to the mast, which would have enabled him to prevent the premature showing of the ready signal.[70]

The board sent its findings to the convening authority, who was Rear Adm. Lucius Allen Bostwick, Commandant of the Fourth Naval District. He had the authority to approve or amend parts of the board's conclusions, and it was his responsibility to decide what, if any, disciplinary actions against the defendants were warranted. Bostwick gave the case serious attention, drawing upon previous experience as a judge advocate. In his decision Bostwick laid out fifteen carefully and precisely worded points regarding the incident and the documented opinion of the board. While he agreed with the opinions of the board generally, he made a specific exception in Wiley's case. Bostwick's thirteenth point was that he did not concur that responsibility rested with Wiley. He found the evidence was clear that Wiley had been some distance behind the signal light and that, because the light pointed forward, it was impossible for him to have seen it. Further, Wiley had not been informed that the signal to move the mast had been given and, at the time, had been acting according to procedure.

Dresel did not escape Bostwick's scrutiny so well. In his lengthy explanation, Admiral Bostwick repeatedly drew analogies between water-borne vessels and rigid airships with respect to Navy regulations governing them. Also, he cited article 1362 of the *Bureau of Aeronautics Manual* of 1927 regarding the duties of a commanding officer of an airship in mooring and unmooring. Basically, he found, the cause of the accident had been a lack of coordination between the commanding officer and the ground crew; for his part, Dresel had failed to act as prescribed in the manual.[71] Bostwick concluded, however, that no further action was required; the case of the damaged ship was over. Repairing the damage took three weeks and eight thousand dollars.[72]

With the *Akron* grounded for repairs, Wiley had extra time once again to spend with his children. His two-year old daughter, Marie, was in the complete care of "Aunt Nan" Mayer. Wiley was secure in the knowledge that his children were being cared for in the best possible manner.

On Wednesday, September 21, 1932, the *Akron* took flight for the first time following her repairs, under the command of Dresel, with Wiley as executive officer. Between September 21 and December 15 the *Akron* made eight flights, many of them extensive trips over the ocean to work on the airplane hook-on procedure.[73] With this nearly perfected, the *Akron* undertook experiments to extend her scouting range by using two F9C airplanes and a mathematically based system designed by Lt. Donald M. Lackey, a station officer. From the airship itself, the lookouts could scan a distance of only about thirty-five miles from horizon to horizon. Lackey's system called for two F9Cs, one on either side of the *Akron*, to fly parallel to her at a distance of about thirty miles. In this way the airship could cut a "visual swath" approximately a hundred miles wide. To ensure the airplanes could find their way back to the ship, their return courses were worked out in advance.

The new system was tried out initially close to shore, so that if an airplane lost its way it could land safely ashore rather than plummeting into the ocean.[74] Wiley was involved with the development of this new scouting method and set up "paper games," simulations, at the air station that involved Lackey, Dresel, Harrigan, and other officers.[75] These games suggested that with adequate radio communications and radio homing devices to guide the planes back to the airship, it could be possible to sweep a path two hundred miles wide. "At a rate of advance of sixty knots during twelve hours of daylight, this sweep would cover more than 165,000 square miles of ocean."[76] There were major obstacles to be overcome before the tactic could be operational, but if brought to reality it would fulfill the greatest hopes of airship proponents.

During the *Akron's* flight of Tuesday, November 22, one of the more interesting and colorful interactions among high-ranking naval officers took place, with Wiley at the heart of it. Rear Admiral Moffett had planned to make the flight and invited his old friend, and airship opponent, Rear Admiral Schofield to join him. Schofield had just recently completed a tour as Commander in Chief, U.S. Fleet. Near sunset, the ship lifted off with twenty-one officers, sixty-four crewmen, and one passenger. At 2010, after circling New York City, she turned south along the New Jersey coast. After dinner, Wiley went to the smoking room, where he found Moffett, Schofield, Shoemaker, and Dresel, among others. Wiley later described what took place:

[Schofield] did not believe in dirigibles. He made a few criticisms of airships, which I thought were uncalled for. No one seemed to want to take up the argument, and I felt that the other officers present didn't want to argue with Admiral Schofield, because they were too close in seniority to him. I was a Lieutenant Commander, and a junior one at that. I felt that it made no difference if Admiral Schofield got the best of me, and hence a poor opinion of me, and I took up the challenge. One of Admiral Schofield's remarks was that we had missed the fleet problem a few months before, because we didn't get to the west coast on time, and that ships that didn't get where he wanted them weren't any good to him. I replied that I was sure that during the problem he had had 3 battleships under overhaul in a Navy Yard—hence those 3 battleships weren't any good. He then said that even if we had done scouting and had got information, we would have been sunk anyhow. I replied that I noticed that in the problem he had "sacrificed" three scout cruisers getting information. We were "going it" hot and heavy and Admiral Moffett was very much pleased. I was sitting next to him, and I felt he was about to applaud every time I made a point. He would nudge me and whisper "go to it." He evidently felt it was better for someone else to tell him, rather than to work on Schofield personally.[77]

In January 1933 the New Year brought with it a new commander for the *Akron*. At 1300 on January 3, Commander Dresel was detached, and Commander McCord relieved him. Wiley had known the change was coming and had fully expected to be passed over again. Wiley recalled having recommended McCord to Moffett and suggested he be considered for command of the *Los Angeles*. Once again, he remained executive officer of the *Akron*. McCord was capable and brought a unique mix of experience to the game: he had served for two years on the aircraft carriers *Langley* and *Saratoga* and had been the executive officer of the *Los Angeles*.[78]

Within hours of taking command of the airship, McCord had her airborne en route to Opa-locka, Florida, with Admiral Moffett on board. Moored to the stub mast at Opa-locka, she spent a couple of days in maintenance and resupply before taking to the air again, this time to Cuba. While the *Akron* circled over Guantanamo Bay, several officers and an engineer were ferried from the airship to the ground to inspect potential sites for future moorings. Wiley had been one of the most experienced mooring officers in the Navy for nearly ten years, and it was fitting he should be one of the inspectors. He climbed into the front seat of the small Curtiss F9C Sparrowhawk biplane with the pilot, Lieutenant Harrigan, seated behind him.[79] The airplane was cranked out over an opening in the floor of the ship's hangar and lowered into the slipstream beneath. Harrigan started the airplane's engine, unhooked from the trapeze, and, after a moment's free fall, spiraled away from the *Akron* in his descent to the landing field below. Harrigan carried several officers from the airship to the ground, one at a time, and then, when their work was completed, back to the *Akron*. On his last run from the ground he brought a front cockpit full of lobsters for the ship's mess.[80] The airship spent the night moored at Opa-locka, refueling and resupplying, before starting the return trip to Lakehurst. On the evening of January 11, the *Akron* was moored safely back at the air station.

Much of the flying time for the remainder of January and February consisted of local flights, and as usual, the winter weather was a factor. There were signs that the *Macon* was soon to be ready for service. Lt. A. L. Davis and Lt. S. E. Peck were detached for temporary duty fitting out the new airship on January 14.[81] Wiley was to be assigned to the Board of Inspection and Survey for temporary duty in connection with the *Macon*'s trials.[82] First, however, there was a flight south to Florida and then to the Canal Zone.

The *Akron* left Lakehurst on Saturday, March 11, headed south. Because the severe winters at Lakehurst often prevented flying, the Navy was interested in a southern base from which to operate in winter, and Opa-locka was a good candidate. As before, the airshipmen used the mooring mast at Opa-locka as a temporary base from which to fly over Cuba and the Panama Canal Zone. On Wednesday, March 15, a number of officers, including Wiley, were taxied from the *Akron* to the ground at Coco Solo Naval Air Station. Coco Solo, on the Atlantic side of the Panama Canal near Colón, had been established in 1918 as a naval air station and submarine base. It too seemed a possibility as a mooring base for airships. After completing their inspection of Coco Solo, the *Akron* cruised over the Canal Zone, Cuba, and around Florida for several days, practicing the skills of landing and takeoff, navigation, and gunnery before heading back to Lakehurst. They arrived at the air station on the evening of March 23.

Things had been going well for the *Akron*. She was receiving her full complement of airplanes, with pilots trained in landing and takeoff with the trapeze apparatus; her radio direction-finding equipment had been installed; and now plans were afoot to create a southern base of operations. There remained a need for improvement in the use of the *Akron's* airplanes for long-range reconnaissance, but developments to date had been very promising. Better radio equipment for the airplanes would improve greatly the search procedures, and plans were under way to remedy that shortcoming. On July 1, 1932, the Chief of Naval Operations distributed to "All Bureaus and Offices, Fleets, Forces, Aviation Units and Stations Concerned" the "Naval Aeronautical Organization" for fiscal year 1933. It stated that when the *Macon* was ready for service, the *Akron* would be transferred to the Battle Force. The Chief of Naval Operations followed up, on February 14, 1933, with modifications to that organization: Commander Aircraft, Scouting Force had been discontinued; the USS *Lexington* was to be transferred to Commander Aircraft, Battle Force; and the *Akron* would go to the Commander Scouting Force. On April 1, 1933, the *Akron* became a part of the Scouting Force.

Meanwhile, on March 2, 1933, Wiley had been informed that he would be dispatched to Akron, Ohio, for the inspection and trials of the new *Macon.* On the twenty-eighth he received orders to proceed to Akron on or about April 3 to report to the senior member present of the Board of Inspection and Survey. As a practical matter, his orders authorized him to travel by his personal automobile, because it would be more economical and advantageous to the United States, but his drive to Ohio would be delayed until the *Akron* made a flight on April 3.

10

The Crash
of the *Akron*

Commander McCord planned to have the *Akron* depart Lakehurst around sunset on April 3 to be in the vicinity of Newport, Rhode Island, an hour after sunrise on the fourth. The primary mission of the flight was assisting in the calibration of the radio direction-finding stations in the First Naval District. The skies were overcast that morning, and there was some question about the ability to make the flight. In the LTA service, the weather was everything. It dictated whether flights could be made at all, and it governed the flight path of the ship once airborne. As the executive officer of the *Akron*, it was Wiley's responsibility to be aware constantly of weather conditions and to keep Commander McCord informed. However, aside from his official responsibility to do so, Wiley, as the most experienced airship officer on board, knew the wisdom of frequent updates on weather.

Admiral Moffett was a frequent figure at the air station, and he never missed an opportunity to fly with the *Akron*. In his capacity, he was aware of the ship's flight schedule, and around 1100 on April 3, he telephoned Commander McCord from Washington to learn if the flight planned for that day was still going to happen. Hearing McCord still planned to make the flight, Moffett informed him it was his desire to join the flight and that he would arrive at Lakehurst in time. While Moffett and McCord were conversing, Wiley called the ship's aerological officer to ask for a quick estimate of the probability the flight could take place. The aerologist believed that it would be possible to take the *Akron* from the hangar but doubted that conditions would be suitable for the radio compass work planned for the area around Newport, Rhode Island, the next morning. Wiley delivered the news to McCord, who repeated it to Moffett. At around 1130 McCord and Wiley together visited the station's aerological officer to examine the morning's weather map. After doing so, McCord announced that 1800, around sunset, would be "zero hour"—the time at which all hands would be mustered. Well accustomed to weather maps, Wiley formed a quick visual and mental assessment of the map. He noted an area of low barometric pressure in northern Michigan and a wind-shift line that extended from there southward to the vicinity of Cincinnati. This low-pressure area appeared to be moving to the northeast, outside the *Akron*'s scheduled area of operations, and did not appear to be a threat. There was a flat high-pressure area off the Delaware Capes, giving an area between the two highs from Sandy Hook to Nantucket where unsettled conditions with poor visibility might be expected. The pressure was also flat through the middle-Atlantic states, meaning the pressure did not change much.[1]

The aerological officer gave McCord a written forecast that predicted light winds at sunset with fog along the New Jersey coast and extending inland during the night. It was predicted the fog would continue in the Newport area until noon the next day. In view of this, McCord planned to remain in the New Jersey area during the night until the unsettled weather moved off the coast. Once the plan was decided, he ordered Wiley to be prepared to exercise airplane hook-ups immediately after takeoff, after which he was to take on board a training plane.

Around 1600 McCord and Wiley visited the aerological officer once again, to inspect the partial weather map which was being updated. Realizing visibility would be poor at sunset, McCord told Wiley to cancel the hook-on drills but to be ready to take on board the training plane if visibility was good enough. As Wiley studied the partial weather map constructed around 1600, he noted considerable change from the 0800 map. An isobar that was present on the morning map had taken a southeast direction from the vicinity of Lake Erie but now curved inland to the south from Lakehurst to Washington and back to the north along the coast. Wiley met McCord back at the aerological office around 1745. Wiley noted that the wind was light from north to northeast, and the data board indicated that at 1715 the winds had been light from the north and northeast up to 1,500 feet. Above that altitude, the winds were moderate and from the south and southeast.

By 1745 the temperature at the air station had fallen by about twenty degrees since 2 p.m. Wiley, aware the temperature of the gas in the ship would be at hangar temperature and that the colder air outside would give the airship additional buoyancy, directed the officer of the deck to load 3,500 pounds of ballast. Wiley then went to the hangar personally and discovered the temperature there was even higher than he had expected and he ordered more ballast to be added. At that time, the difference between the outside temperature and that inside was sixteen degrees. As the *Akron* left her hangar at approximately 1830 the wind on the field was from the northeast at six miles per hour. Fog was rolling in rapidly, and by the time of takeoff at 1930 the ceiling was about three hundred feet. The ship unmoored and rose through the fog. The top of the fog layer was at about 1,200 feet.

From the ship the air station could be located by the glow of lights through the fog. After circling the station, the *Akron* departed to the west, for Philadelphia, with McCord at the controls. Because the fog extended out over the Atlantic Ocean, McCord decided to sail inland, where the ground could be seen, until such time as departure had to be taken to arrive at Newport by 0700. About twenty miles west of Lakehurst the ground became visible, and visibility was fairly good in the vicinity of Philadelphia around 2010. McCord directed the officer of the deck to follow the Delaware River southward to the Delaware Capes. After the *Akron* passed Philadelphia, Wiley left the control car and went to the officers' smoking room, which was located in the gun room in the after part of the car. As he left the control car, six of the ship's eight engines were in use.[2] He was in the smoking room for fifteen or twenty minutes when he felt the engines speed up. He returned to the control car to see if conditions had changed and found all eight engines running at standard speed, and the course had been changed to the east. The navigator informed Wiley their present course would take them to the coast at Atlantic City. As McCord and Wiley were conferring they saw lightning just about abeam to the south, twenty-five to thirty miles away. Wiley suggested conditions might be better to the westward, but McCord said he had seen two flashes of lightning in that direction. The two kept a keen eye on the lightning, and McCord made several course changes during the next forty-five to sixty minutes, turning to port when the lightning appeared closer and back to the right when it seemed farther away. They dropped altitude from 2,000 to 1,600 feet, and soon after leaving the Delaware River, the ground became obscured by fog, but it was felt they had a fairly accurate idea of their track over the ground. Occasionally, they could see lights through breaks in the fog that indicated towns—a good navigational aid.

After leaving the Delaware River, they flew on a northeasterly course for approximately thirty minutes before changing it again to a more easterly course. McCord told Wiley he had ordered a fifteen-degree course change but that the order was misunderstood and the course had been changed fifty degrees to the left. Wiley was aware they had been on a course of about forty-five degrees compass for about thirty minutes. At this time, the ship was in good flying condition, but the lightning to the south became more extensive and was coming closer to the ship.[3] After Wiley saw lightning also to the west, he and McCord took turns at the starboard and port windows, observing the changing weather conditions. With every position change, Wiley would report his observations to McCord.[4]

At about 2200 they were in the vicinity of the coast near Asbury Park, New Jersey, about forty miles north of Atlantic City. The fog had risen to the *Akron*'s flying altitude. She flew along the top of it but occasionally was immersed in it, and she had become surrounded by lightning that was both horizontal and vertical. When the crew heard thunder quickly following a flash of lightning, they knew they were entirely surrounded by thunderstorms. They had hauled in their radio antenna, preventing them from receiving further weather information, and severe static kept them from sending out messages. Wiley felt that the ship had not been struck by lightning thus far.[5]

At around 2245 or 2300 McCord instructed Wiley to go look at their weather plot. Wiley went to the weather chart and asked the ship's aerological officer how much of a map he had received before radio communications were lost. After being told about two thirds of the signals had been received, Wiley took a quick glance at what they had. He was in the room with the weather map for no more than two minutes, but his quick survey of the map indicated to him that the map was not complete. The map did, however, indicate a low centered in the vicinity of Washington.[6] McCord decided to ride out the weather at sea and headed the ship due east.

After staying on that heading for about an hour, they again found themselves surrounded completely by lightning. In that situation, Wiley felt there was no way to know which would be the correct direction to turn, but McCord decided to reverse course.[7] On the reverse course, Wiley was in the navigator's room when the ship crossed the coast again, about midnight. The navigator told him they had reached the coast much sooner than expected because he had made a false assumption about the direction of the wind. Based upon his last observation in the vicinity of Philadelphia, the navigator had believed the wind was from the south-east, but now thought it was from the northeast at about twenty knots. McCord now made another course change. Wiley was aware that somewhere along the way, some of the engine telegraph wires had carried away.[8]

The ship had been flying through remarkably stable atmosphere, and for the first few minutes after midnight she was engulfed in fog. Things were about to change. At about 0030 on the April 4, the *Akron* struck turbulence. When the elevatorman reported the ship was falling rapidly, Wiley rushed to his side of the control car to give assistance. The altimeter read 1,100 feet but they were going down rapidly. The ship was almost on an even keel with the bow inclined downward. Wiley made a quick assessment of the situation and asked McCord if he should drop ballast. Without hesitation, McCord instructed him to do so. Wiley started releasing ballast from the service bags, but the ship was falling so rapidly that at 800 feet he decided to drop 1,600 pounds of ballast from the forward emergency bags. This action checked the ship's descent at about 700 feet, and she began to rise rapidly. Wiley next worked with the elevatorman to reduce the rate of rise and seemed to have regained good control when the ship was at 1,300 feet. He was then able to approach gradually the cruising altitude of 1,600 feet and level off there.[9] The *Akron's* airspeed was fifty-eight knots, and after a full assessment of the ship's static condition, Wiley concluded she was in approximate trim. Only a couple of minutes later, however, the atmosphere became violently turbulent. Wiley believed this meant they were near the center of the storm, and he had the signal sounded for landing stations to get all the men out of their bunks and available for action if needed.

The signal for landing stations sent everyone, including officers, to their usual stations for landing or maneuvering the ship. Wiley's post was by the starboard window where he could give orders for control of the rudder and McCord was at the port window. The engineering officer took his position at the engine tele-graphs. The first lieutenant, George Calnan, had responsibility for the trim and loading of the airship at landing stations, and when he arrived Wiley informed him where he had dropped ballast and instructed him to stand by the ballast board. Suddenly, the ship was struck hard by a very strong gust. Wiley thought this gust seemed far more severe than any he had ever experienced, because it had been exerted so suddenly. An ordinary gust would strike the airship with the same force and take about thirty seconds to pass whereas this one seemed to exert its maximum force in two or three seconds. Things were unfolding rapidly and Wiley noticed that the lower-rudder control rope had carried away. He released that rudder, and tried to steer with the upper one. He reported the situation to McCord, who was watching the altimeters. While the elevatorman was reporting the ship was falling, Wiley's other rudder control broke. The sound made by the sheaves being carried away in the ship caused Wiley to think the ship's structure had been damaged somewhere. The ship came up by the bow several degrees and McCord ordered the engines to full speed, but she continued to fall.

Wiley heard the report, "Eight hundred feet." The angle of the bow continued to increase, and he could feel that they were falling very rapidly. With both rudder controls broken, Wiley could steer no longer and he clung to the girder next to the window. Trying to see the water below, he called for the altitude, and the response of "three hundred feet" was called back. During the emergency there was no noise or confusion at any time in the control car. All orders were given in low, controlled voices and were carried out efficiently. Discipline was maintained perfectly at all times. Wiley then sighted the waves and unhesitatingly gave the order, "Stand by for a crash." Following this, there was no further conversation in the control car. Wiley estimated their rate of descent to be about fourteen feet per second, but when the ship hit the water, it seemed to him that she had struck much harder than he had expected.

Water surged into the control car, submerged Wiley, and carried him out the port side of the ship. Wiley had been a powerful swimmer since his youth, and that likely saved his life on this occasion. When he came to the surface, he could see the *Akron* illuminated by flashes of lightning, and he began to swim toward her only to realize she was drifting away from him rapidly and was already about five hundred yards distant. The sea was stormy and choppy, with waves ten to twelve feet from crest to trough. The water was cold, it was raining heavily, and winds of thirty to thirty-five miles per hour were blowing. Lightning flashes were the only sources of light. Wiley could see that the ship was broken in two or three places and that about a third of her diameter was submerged. About two hundred feet of her bow was inclined up into the air, at about a thirty-degree angle. Compelled to abandon his efforts to swim to the airship, he looked around him and saw lights that appeared to be from a surface vessel, and he sighted a lighthouse. He could see men in the water, and he could hear their cries, but no one was near enough for him to be of help. He decided to swim in the direction of the surface vessel. After approximately ten minutes he found a board about three feet square floating on the water and he clung to it until he was rescued.

Boatswain's Mate Second Class Richard E. Deal saw the ship's lights go out about five or ten seconds before she hit the water. In the darkness, he felt water rising around his feet and his right leg was entangled in a wire. He was able to free himself, get out of the ship, and make his way to the surface. In the aftermath, he would be unable to recall how he had gotten out of the ship. When he broke the surface, he had already taken on several mouthfuls of water mixed with gasoline. In the lightning flashes, he saw the broken *Akron* moving away from him about a hundred yards off. He momentarily considered swimming toward the ship, but after fifteen or twenty minutes in the cold water, he saw a large gasoline tank floating on the surface and swam for it instead. Climbing atop the tank, he saw three other men already on it. He asked their names. Chief Radioman Robert Copeland and Aviation Metalsmith Second Class Moody Erwin answered for themselves, but the third man did not respond. Erwin told him it was Chief Machinist's Mate Lucius Rutan. Erwin had dived into the water at the moment of impact but had quickly become aware that the airship was rolling down on top of him. He could feel it against his back. He doubled over, placed his feet against the structure, and pushed himself deeper into the water. From there he was able to swim away from or around anything that could entangle or trap him.

When Erwin emerged from under the wreckage, he, like Deal, had spotted the floating gasoline tank.[10] However, clinging to the gasoline tank was difficult, as waves repeatedly hit it causing it to roll and toss them back into the water.[11] Recovering from one such episode, Deal noticed the tank had a feed pipe that had been connected to the main gas line but had broken off in the crash. He warned the others that they had to keep the feed pipe above the water or the tank would fill and sink.

They had been in the water for what felt like a long time when Deal saw, from the crest of a wave, the running lights of a ship. He passed the news to the other men and encouraged them to hang on. The ship appeared to be moving away from them, but Deal sensed that they were drifting toward the ship faster. Partly swimming and partly supporting themselves on the gasoline tank, they pushed it ahead of them. When they got within hailing distance of the ship, Erwin and Deal started yelling continuously to get someone's attention. Finally, from on board the vessel a whistle blew, acknowledging they had been spotted. When they reached the vessel, amidships, ring lifebuoys were lowered to them. Deal saw the crew of the ship lowering the lifeboat but having difficulty with it; once hauled into the lifeboat he lost consciousness, not reviving until inside the warm ship.

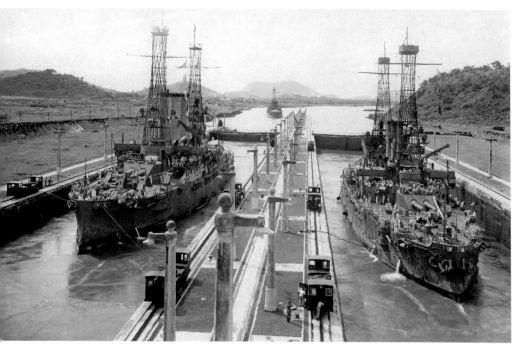

The battleships of the Naval Academy's summer practice fleet were the first warships to traverse the Panama Canal. The USS *Missouri* (BB 11) (*left*) and USS *Ohio* (BB 12) (*right*) are shown in the lower chambers of the Miraflores Locks going through "double-barreled," August 31, 1915. The USS *Wisconsin* (BB 9) is seen in the distance. *NH 82788*

The USS *Shenandoah* (ZR 1) inside her hangar at Lakehurst Naval Air Station on November 8, 1923. *NH 44092*

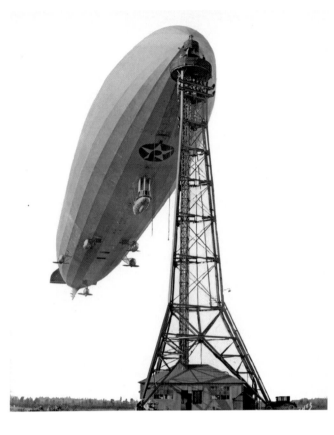

The *Shenandoah* moored to the high mast at Lakehurst Naval Air Station. *UA Archives Goodyear A6396_25*

The *Shenandoah* is shown safely back in her hangar at the naval air station, damage to her nose caused by being torn away from the mooring mast during the gale of January 16, 1924. *NH 92612*

Aerial view of the crash of the *Shenandoah* in southern Ohio on September 3, 1925; numerous sightseers converged on the site. *NH 98997*

The *Shenandoah*'s bow section shortly after crashing on a farm in southern Ohio. *NH 98998*

LZ 126 (ZR 3) on arrival at Lakehurst Naval Air Station following her transatlantic flight from Friedrichshafen, Germany, on October 15, 1924. She would be christened the USS *Los Angeles*. Note the absence of markings on the airship. *NH 42024*

The *Los Angeles* moored to the USS *Patoka* (AO 9). *NH 65301*

The *Los Angeles* approaching the USS *Saratoga* (CV 3) in preparation for landing. Handling lines have been dropped to the ground crew on the deck of the ship. *NH 44097*

The *Los Angeles* (*left*), built in Germany as *LZ 126*, shares her hangar at Lakehurst Naval Air Station with the hydrogen-filled *Graf Zeppelin* (LZ 127), August 7, 1929. *NH 69168*

Aerial view of the USS *Akron* over Akron, Ohio, during her maiden voyage. *UA Archives Goodyear, 1106x_29*

View from aft of the *Akron* moored at Lakehurst Naval Air Station, June 15, 1932. *UA Archives Goodyear, 657*

On February 22, 1932, congressmen waited to board the *Akron* for a demonstration flight. As she was being removed from the hangar, her tail carried away from the railcar used for maneuvering the airship on the ground and was seriously damaged. This photograph, taken immediately after the accident, shows Rear Adm. William A. Moffett, chief of the Bureau of Aeronautics, in the left center of the image, facing the camera. *NH 42160*

On May 11, 1932, as the *Akron* was attempting to land at Camp Kearney, California, a sudden gust of wind took her suddenly aloft. Three men were unable to let go of a handling line before they were more than two hundred feet in the air. Charles Cowart was able to hold on with one hand and with the other fashion a "bosun's chair" by wrapping the line around his legs. He was pulled into the airship and survived the experience. The other two sailors fell to their deaths. Cowart is shown in the frame to the right. *NH 84169*

Lt. Cdr. H. V. Wiley, executive officer of the USS *Akron* (ZRS 4), clothed against the cold temperatures encountered at altitude. *NH 86117*

Lt. Cdr. H. V. Wiley,
May 9, 1932. *NH AN-35990*

Rear Adm. William A. Moffett
a few days before his death
in the crash of the *Akron* off
Barnegat Light on the coast
of New Jersey, April 4, 1933.
NH 1208

On April 4, 1933, the survivors of the crash of the *Akron* receive commendations from the Secretary of the Navy in his Navy Department office. Present (*left to right*) are: Assistant Secretary of the Navy Henry A. Roosevelt; Secretary of the Navy Claude Swanson; Adm. William V. Pratt, Chief of Naval Operations; Lt. Cdr. Herbert V. Wiley, the only officer survivor; survivors Boatswain's Mate Second Class Richard E. Deal and Aviation Metalsmith Second Class Moody Erwin. Erwin apparently is wearing a borrowed uniform, as its insignia denotes a Hospital Corpsman Third Class. *NH 55468*

Macon in flight with two Curtiss F9C-2 Sparrowhawk airplanes below her awaiting hook-on and landing on board the airship. Note the hook device on the superior wings of the airplanes and the hook-on trapeze lowered from the airship. *NH 80-G-441983*

Lt. D. Ward Harrigan piloting his Curtiss F9C-2 Sparrowhawk. The airplane is shown here hanging by its hook from the trapeze of the *Macon* following a successful hook-on landing (1933). *NH 80-G-441979*

The USS *Macon* in the new airship hangar at the Naval Air Station, Moffett Field, Sunnyvale, California, October 15, 1933. This photograph was taken just after the *Macon* had arrived from her flight across the country from Lakehurst Naval Air Station. A small blimp is seen at the far end of the hangar. *NH 85743*

The USS *Houston* (CA 30) passing through the Gatun Locks of the Panama Canal on July 11, 1934, en route to the Pacific Ocean with President Franklin Roosevelt on board. (Note the ramp on the side of the superstructure below the No. 2 turret, installed for the convenience of the president.) Unknown to the president, the *Houston* would be intercepted by the *Macon* on July 18 as a demonstration of the value of airships for scouting the Pacific Ocean. The *Macon*'s airplanes would drop bags of mail and news to the *Houston* as part of the demonstration. *NH 80-G-455963*

The USS *Black Hawk* (AD 9) ca. 1934 with six destroyers alongside. After assuming command of Destroyer Squadron 29, Wiley established his administrative headquarters on board the *Black Hawk*. *NHHC 80G-1025120*

The USS *West Virginia* (BB 48) following refitting and modernization at Bremerton, Washington. This photo was taken in June 1944 just before the ship sailed for Long Beach, California, on a shakedown cruise. *Official Navy photograph taken from the personal album of Lt. Robert O. Baumrucker, USN, the* West Virginia's *gunnery and intelligence officer.*

The USS *West Virginia* shelling Leyte in the Philippine Islands, October 19, 1944. *Official Navy photograph from the records of Lt. Thomas Lombardi. Courtesy of Lombardi family.*

Battle of Leyte Gulf: the Japanese battleship *Yamashiro* is under attack in the Sulu Sea by American carrier-based planes. *NH 80-G-281763*

The landings on Okinawa began on April 1, 1945, the same day
a kamikaze crashed into the 02 deck of the *West Virginia*, killing
four sailors, although the bomb it carried did not detonate. The
West Virginia is shown here to the left, behind *LCI 14, LCI 15*,
and *LCI 16. NH 96606*

Rutan had been lost to the sea. Deal presumed he had been tossed off the gas tank and drowned before he could swim back. Copeland, like Deal and Erwin, had been taken on board the ship.

The vessel was the German tanker *Phoebus*, which had been sailing to Tampico, Mexico, from New York in the petroleum trade, under the command of Capt. Carl Dalldorf. On the morning of the disaster, the *Phoebus* was the only vessel in the area and thus was the first to arrive on the scene, twenty miles off Barnegat Light. Captain Dalldorf sent a telegram that at 12:30 on the morning of April 4, during a thunderstorm with heavy rains, he had seen aircraft lights flashing. He changed course to approach the lights, found the *Akron* crash site, and heard men hailing his ship from the water. He stopped the ship, turned on all her deck lights, and lowered lifeboats. He saw mattresses and all manner of other debris on the water, and he saw men sink below the surface before his own men could get to them.[12]

In the early moments following the crash, Wiley heard voices and, by the lightning flashes, he could see a few men swimming. In the first five minutes, he saw approximately five men twenty to fifty yards away from him. About three minutes later, no one was to be seen. He heard voices for a few more minutes but could see no one. Finally, the voices were silenced. Wiley estimated he was in the water for thirty minutes to an hour before the rescue boat hauled him out. When he boarded the *Phoebus* he was so cold and weak that he could not stand. He was put into bed to get warm and rest a bit. After about an hour, beginning to regain some strength, he rose and went in search of any other members of the *Akron*'s crew. He learned that only four men had been pulled from the sea alive but one was near death. Erwin and Deal asked Wiley what time they had been picked up. When he told them it had been around 0200, they formed the impression they had been in the water for about an hour and forty minutes. Wiley located Copeland around 0230, unconscious. He was given artificial resuscitation measures until around 0530, but Wiley believed Copeland was already dead when he first found him. Consequently, there would be only three survivors of the *Akron* crash, and Wiley would be the only officer among them.[13] The other two were Moody Erwin and Richard Deal. Seventy-four men—officers, crew, and passengers—had perished.

Gathering strength, Wiley conferred with Captain Dalldorf and learned he was doing everything he could to rescue any survivors and that he did not intend to leave the scene. In his original telegram, Dalldorf stated reassuringly he was still searching and would continue until after daylight or until relieved by the

Coast Guard.[14] Wiley found Dalldorf to be a fully capable captain and he cooperated with him in the rescue efforts and had messages broadcast requesting assistance. They got a prompt response. The heavy cruiser USS *Portland* (CA 33) was the first to arrive on the scene, followed closely by the destroyer USS *Tucker* (DD 57). The cruiser, commissioned in February, had not had a formal shakedown cruise. She had left Boston two days earlier en route to New York City when she received orders from Washington to respond to the *Akron*'s emergency.[15] Within hours of the call for assistance, a dozen warships were speeding to the Barnegat Light area, and by dawn a fleet of destroyers, the heavy cruiser, and numerous small boats and airplanes were searching for survivors. Shortly after daylight, as the *Tucker* came close aboard the *Phoebus*, Wiley requested her to send over a pharmacist's mate to treat the survivors. Subsequently, Wiley, Deal, Erwin, and the body of Copeland were transferred to the *Tucker*, which in due course delivered them to the naval hospital at the Brooklyn Navy Yard.[16] As the *Tucker* slipped out of the fog on her northerly path into New York Harbor, her flag drooped at half-mast. Wiley had recovered from the ordeal sufficiently to walk off the *Tucker* without assistance. A reporter described his appearance: "His jaw was firm and his step steady, but there was weariness and perhaps something of despair in his face."[17] Reporters crowded around Wiley wanting to know the details of what had happened, but he answered simply, "I cannot say."

As is often the case in the first hours following a disaster, confusion reigned. Newspapers were quicker to get their stories into print than to check facts. Shortly after 0200, the Bureau of Naval Communications reported, "The airship, according to all its advices, still was afloat and no lives had been lost." Naval officers at NAS Lakehurst, none of whom would allow themselves to be named, were quick to offer opinions that the *Akron* had been struck by lightning.[18] There was as yet no evidence to support it, yet the lightning story made it to press as one headline read, "Airship Fell in Flames as Lightning Hit."[19]

At about 0230 on the night of the crash, the Navy Department called the home of Admiral Moffett in Washington. When Moffett's wife answered the telephone, the spokesman announced the *Akron* had crashed and asked her to notify the admiral, to which she responded, "The Admiral is on the *Akron*."[20] As daylight broke on April 4, Mrs. Moffett tried to maintain hope that her husband had survived somehow. "Friends dropped in to see her as the day wore on. She greeted them cordially. Dry-eyed, befitting a naval officer's wife, she refused to despair."[21] A pall fell over the small Lakehurst community, where wives and families waited for news of their loved ones and Navy personnel went quietly about their daily duties. News came slowly, in dribbles, amplifying anxieties. In Washington, Mrs. Moffett gave the press an interview in which she reached out to the wives waiting in Lakehurst.

"I have every belief that Admiral Moffett is all right and I shall hear from him," she said in an interview.

"I shall not believe otherwise until I have definite word from the navy that he is really lost.

"So many little boats not equipped with radio are on those waters that there is every chance that many of the men may have saved.

"The Admiral had a way of coming out of things safely and I expect to get word from him.

"That is my message to the press, and that is my message to all the wives, who, like me, are waiting word from their husbands."

Mrs. Moffett[,] standing erect at the head of the entrance stairway in her beautiful Massachusetts Ave. home, spoke in a clear voice with no trace of faltering.

Her manner was contained, serene, except when—with an outburst of almost patriotic fervor—she expressed that faith in "my man" that Navy wives have as their creed.[22]

In Wheeling, Missouri, Wiley's father spent a nightlong vigil for news of his son. When it arrived, "Tears came to the eyes of a grey haired man of seventy here today even as they did in 1928 when he looked above the little northern Missouri village at a dirigible soaring over. But as then the tears were tears of joy."[23]

At the crash site, Capt. Herbert F. Leary of the *Portland* was SOPA and took control of the search operation, coordinating the efforts of the numerous Navy, Coast Guard, and civilian vessels and aircraft. As ships arrived, Leary assigned them areas to search and patrol. He anchored the *Portland* near the Barnegat Lightship, about ten miles south of Toms River. When it became clear that no more survivors were going to be found, the search vessels began collecting debris of the *Akron* and delivering it to the *Portland* for examination and salvage. An ugly element of humanity surfaced during the search that may have resulted from the economic realities of the Depression. Fishing vessels appeared periodically out of the fog, coming alongside the *Portland* and, to some degree, interfering with the search. Their crews yelled that they knew where the *Akron* had crashed and asked how much the reward was for revealing it. When Captain Leary replied that it was their duty to tell him what they knew, the fishing boats simply faded back into the mist.[24] The *Portland* remained on station for another two weeks until finally relieved on April 19, taking with her the mere scraps of wreckage that had been recovered.[25]

President Franklin D. Roosevelt followed the story of the disaster very closely and issued a statement from Washington that the loss of the *Akron* and her men was a national disaster, that he grieved with the nation and with the wives and families of the men who had been lost.[26] On April 6, 1933, two days later, Roosevelt met with the three survivors at the White House. "All work ceased at the White House as the survivors Lieutenant Commander Herbert V. Wiley, Boatswain's Mate Richard E. Deal and Metalsmith M. E. Erwin walked through the lobby of the executive offices to keep their appointment with the President. . . . The clicking of typewriters ceased as stenographers and clerks left their duties to see and applaud the *Akron* men . . . . [T]hey came up to the desk at which the President was seated and shook his hand." Roosevelt remarked, "I am thankful you are here. Be seated and tell me about this."[27] After hearing Wiley's brief account, the president told an aide he wanted to do something to thank the captain and crew of the German ship that had rescued the survivors, and that he would send a personal letter. The president then told the Assistant Secretary of the Navy, Henry L. Roosevelt, that all three men deserved "anything the service could do for them" and that if any wanted a leave of absence, he had only to request it.

That day, Navy and Coast Guard ships were still searching futilely off the New Jersey coast for any survivors who might be clinging desperately to drifting wreckage. In New York, Cardinal Patrick J. Hayes, Chaplain Bishop of the U.S. Army and Navy, presided over a solemn high requiem mass for the men of the *Akron* who had been lost.[28]

11

Aftermath
of the *Akron*

efore all the facts of the *Akron*'s crash were known, former critics of the LTA program resurfaced to renew their opposition. One press writer claimed, "The accident has aroused the slumbering opposition to the expenditure of money for lighter-than-air vessels."[1] When newspapermen asked Secretary of the Navy Swanson for his opinion of the LTA ships, he responded that he had never been as enthusiastic about them as some in the Navy had. Asked about the possibility of replacing the *Akron*, he gave a quiet smile and stated that appropriating for such work was a matter for Congress, but in an afterthought he said plainly, "It seems to me we need ships more than anything else." That Rear Admiral Moffett had been on board the *Akron* for this flight gave rise to an issue that would be discussed for some time: "Asked if the Admiral had taken the trip against the advice of others, the Secretary emphatically replied that he had not." That line of thinking would be expanded very shortly to the extent of implications that Moffett had insisted on the *Akron* making its scheduled flight in spite of severe weather forecasts.

Senator Dill was a former member of the House Naval Affairs Committee who had opposed vehemently any appropriations for LTA craft, and in the wake of this disaster he launched other lines of colorful criticism claiming that the mishap was another "illustration of the awful waste of money on building great gas bags that serve only as sky shows in peace time and are worthless in war," and that "one little airplane would put them out of use in a minute."[2] While Congress and the public wanted a thorough investigation into the causes of the disaster, the Navy wanted its own answers, and it announced that Capt. Gordon W. Haines, acting commandant of the Fourth Naval District at Philadelphia, would order a court of inquiry immediately.[3]

News of the airship disaster quickly traveled the globe, and the Associated Press was able to reach Dr. Hugo Eckener in Berlin for comment. Moved deeply, he told the reporter, "I am unspeakably sorry. The news of the *Akron* stuns me. Please express my deepest sympathy to the American people. . . . The news strikes me the harder as so many of my warm personal friends, such as Rear Admiral William A. Moffett, participated in the cruise."[4]

The crash of the *Akron* with the deaths of seventy-three men was the greatest disaster in aeronautical history to date. On April 4, 1933, Secretary of the Navy Swanson sent written orders to Rear Adm. Henry V. Butler, Commandant, U.S. Navy Yard, Washington, to convene a "Court of Inquiry to inquire into all the facts and circumstances surrounding the loss of the USS *Akron*."[5] Butler, as president of the court, appointed Captain Shoemaker and Cdr. Sydney M. Kraus as additional members. He named Lt. Cdr. Ralph G. Pennoyer as the judge advocate. Pennoyer had served as counsel for the judge advocate during the court of inquiry that investigated the crash of the *Shenandoah*. The court of inquiry convened at NAS Lakehurst at 1000 on Monday, April 10, 1933. Unlike the investigation of the *Shenandoah*, there were only three eyewitnesses in the *Akron* proceedings, and Wiley was the only officer. As with the *Shenandoah*, however, much of the testimony surrounded weather conditions and forecasts and the possibility of human error.

Wiley was the first witness called. After preliminary questions, he proceeded with his narrative of the events leading to the crash, referring to the letter he had sent to the Secretary of the Navy on April 6 in which he reported and described the loss of the airship. Even as Wiley was giving his testimony before the court of inquiry on April 10, word was relayed from the Coast Guard vessel *Daphne* by way of the *Portland* that the Coast Guard had found the body of Admiral Moffett, three miles off Beach Haven, New Jersey, and had made positive identification. The *Daphne* was instructed to take the body to Atlantic City. As she approached, she requested a patrol boat to transfer the admiral ashore. Examination of his body revealed he had been struck in the head by a heavy object, probably at the moment of impact of the control car with the water. The death certificate listed the cause of death as "Intracranial Injury (Airship Crash) U.S.S. *Akron.*" A message went out the same day to the officer in charge of Arlington Cemetery to expect the bodies of Rear Admiral Moffett and Commander McCord to arrive at Washington's Union Station on American Railway the next day.

Wiley knew that he was not on trial and that the purpose of the inquiry was to discover the events and causes that had led to the crash. In the early phase of his testimony, he recounted the repeated preflight consultations with the air station aerological officer and to the best of his memory described the weather maps he had seen. To aid the court, he added an important qualifier: "I have no doubt that the Aerological Officer of the station can produce a reconstructed weather map to which I refer and the record of soundings. I have not looked at any weather data since the disaster to the *Akron*, as I wish to present to the best of my ability my correct remembrance of conditions without being influenced by any afterthought."[6]

Even before the court had convened, the press had broached the possibility that Admiral Moffett had insisted the *Akron* make its final flight in the face of the forecast for severe weather. Perhaps out of respect for the late admiral, the court approached this issue gently. Wiley made it clear that Moffett had no authority over the airship other than being the senior officer present, and that according to Navy Regulations he had nothing to do with the control of or discipline within the ship. As if nudging the envelope a little further, the court asked Wiley who had selected the time at which the ship left Lakehurst. Without hesitation, he replied, "The commanding officer."[7] Years later, Wiley expanded on the suspicion of undue influence by Moffett:

> During the investigation into the loss of the *Akron*, some yellow [i.e., sen-sationalizing] journalists tried to insinuate that we knew that conditions were unsatisfactory for the flight, but went anyway because of pressure from the Admiral. The Admiral flew with us a number of times in the *Shenan-doah*, the *Los Angeles*, and the *Akron*, and I attended many of the pre-flight conferences. I never once heard him in any way try to influence the captain concerning his decisions in regard to making the flight. Furthermore, never at any time in the air did he question any decisions. He realized that under Navy regulations and traditions, the Captain is at all times responsible for the ship, and he was always loyal to his subordinates and never used his rank or position to question the Captain's course of action.[8]

As a follow-up, Wiley was asked whether, in his opinion, the latest weather forecast was favorable for such a flight. He responded, "In my opinion, there was absolutely no feeling of danger or apprehension with regard to starting the flight at that time." Decades following the court of inquiry, Charles Rosendahl, by then a retired vice admiral, gave an oral history to lighter-than-air historian and author William F. Althoff in which he declared, "Wiley recommended that the ship not go out at that time. He was told it was not his decision. Of course, Moffett was there. Moffett loved to fly at night. It was his presence that overwhelmed McCord."[9]

The report of the crash Wiley sent to the Secretary of the Navy was an orderly account of events, to the best of his memory at the time, but under questioning from the court, doubt began to infiltrate his thinking. Wiley was the only surviving officer and the only survivor who had been in the control car, and throughout the event he had been focused intently on his job. Deal and Erwin had been elsewhere in the airship. With only three survivors, stationed at different points in a ship nearly eight hundred feet long, there was no chance of combining accounts to synthesize a complete story. A major part of Wiley's growing confusion surrounded the severe gusts he reported hitting the ship—one to the side of the ship and one downward. He had believed a strong gust to the starboard side was responsible for the main damage, but upon further consideration he became unsure.[10] He now recalled that there had been no wind blowing through the windows of the control car as would be expected. The insightful questions of the court members, and a measure of time from the accident, were actually helping Wiley to gather his thoughts and formulate a more likely scenario for the crash.

On the second day of questioning, Wiley thoughtfully corrected some of his previous testimony. A discussion with Erwin and Deal had assisted him with part of his revisions. A seminal question became the springboard for Wiley's revision.

Question: In your previous testimony you have stated that when this most violent gust struck the ship you felt no gusts of air passing through the control car. How are you able to account for this?

Answer: After mature deliberation, consultation and thought, I have come to a conclusion regarding this, which first struck me yesterday afternoon in my testimony when I was asked if I noticed a difference of temperature after this gust. At that time you may have noticed that I hesitated and thought for a considerable time before answering. If I may mention several circumstances which I have studied out since that time, I have to admit, of course, that my description yesterday of what happened was based entirely on facts which had not been thoroughly tied together by me in my mind. As I thought more about the description of the time and the actions of the ship upon what I described as a gust which shook the ship severely and lasted only for two seconds, as I believe I stated, I am now of the opinion that this was not a gust of air that shook the ship. I have been asked which direction the gust came from, and I said that my impression was that it came from starboard, but I was not at all sure of this. I stated that I did not feel any air blow through the control car. I stated that these gusts or currents were over within two seconds, and never, in my experience, had I seen one that did not last for some time and its effect felt upon the ship as a more or less gradual occurrence. I desire to suggest to the court that now I am of the opinion that the shock was the result of the stern hitting the water.[11]

Wiley then explained the basis for his new hypothesis. The first thing he discussed was the feeling of the shock. He had experienced many gusts in his airship days but never anything like this one. He found it puzzling. His second concern dealt with the report of the altitude's being eight hundred feet. He was not able to place that report accurately in the timeline, and neither did he know when the stern first hit the water. There was a great deal of confusion in his mind surrounding these events. He had thought the rudder controls breaking was an indication of the ship's breaking up. He had waited for the shock of the stern hitting the water, but it never came. That then led him to believe, at the time, that both the stern and the bow were in the air because the ship had broken in half. However, when he discussed this with Deal and Erwin, they held firm to their accounts of having seen girders breaking and a moment later becoming aware the stern was in the water. Wiley recalled that when he first saw the water during the descent, the ship had no ground speed and had actually stopped. While he was not aware of it at the time, Deal informed him the leading chief petty officer had shouted orders to the personnel on the keel, "All hands forward!" From this, Wiley concluded that the chief must have realized the stern was in the water. He also remembered that the barometer could have dropped considerably, and that would have caused the altimeter to be in error by as much as 250 feet.[12]

Having in mind the loss of so many lives to drowning, the court asked Wiley directly if the *Akron* had been outfitted with lifeboats or rafts. He informed the court that the ship had carried one inflated lifeboat with a capacity of fourteen people. Also, all of the materials of the pillows, mattresses, and sleeping bags were designed for flotation. As for life preservers, Wiley was not sure if they were carried routinely or on board for the flight in question. When the court asked what the regulations were relative to carrying life preservers on airships, Wiley said he knew of none.

The judge advocate returned to the issue of the preflight weather and why the flight had taken place when its stated mission could not be fulfilled due to foul weather. Wiley reminded the court that performing radio compass calibrations was the primary objective for the flight but that because of the expected fog, the radio compass station would not be able to see the *Akron* sufficiently far away to make the work valuable. He explained that while circling the station, she needed to take both visual and radio bearings, and the expected fog would prohibit this.[13] Asked again the reason for the flight in that case, Wiley explained that the ship always had a long list of things to achieve on every flight. "We always had several missions and if conditions were not suitable for one we carried out another. In other words, for our own training and advancement in the art we had enough projects to keep us busy wherever we might fly."[14] He explained further that McCord had decided not to take the airplane on board because it would have to ascend through the fog, adding to the danger of the maneuver.

At the end of the day's questioning, Wiley was given the opportunity to make any relevant statement he might like. He closed by declaring his belief that the captain, the aerological officer, and all officers and crew members had done their duty to the best of their ability and that if any errors were made, they "were beyond the skill and experience existing today."[15]

By the third day, Wiley became aware he had been giving some conflicting information and he openly admitted he had become confused. This is understandable since the situation that night unraveled quickly, and Wiley had an awareness only of his small portion of the airship. Had more men survived, it is uncertain whether their testimony would have clarified matters or made them more confusing.

The court called Lt. Charles J. Maguire, the aerological officer for the air station, to testify. Highly educated and well trained, he testified that the weather situation on the day of the fatal flight was exceedingly complex, so much so that even with the advantage of hindsight he found it difficult to analyze. His examination was long and grueling, full of aerological discussions of weather fronts, barometric pressures, and other detailed and technical aspects of the changing weather conditions leading up to and during the flight of the *Akron*. In the face of straightforward questions, the answers seemed speculative and full of hindsight analysis. The court asked Maguire, "In your opinion, what courses of action were open to the *Akron* which might have avoided hazardous turbulence on the occasion of her last flight?" He responded:

> Of course, any other course of action than that taken in the last few minutes might possibly have avoided turbulent areas. Using hind sight [*sic*] and the knowledge of what did happen, a continuance of the course to the westward, on which the *Akron* was prior to midnight, would as the situation turned out, have avoided the severer portions of the thunderstorm. Undoubtedly, the easterly course earlier in the evening, if continued, would have led the ship into regions of fair weather, and considerably violent turbulence would have been avoided.[16]

As Maguire neared the end of his testimony, he added, "Undoubtedly, the change in course to the southeast at midnight led the *Akron* into the center of the disturbance. However, since they were frequently flying in low clouds, and lightning was visible in all directions, there is a reasonable doubt that a course other than that to the southeast could have been established to be a correct one."[17]

In earlier testimony, Wiley had told the court that as they were entering rough weather and seeing lightning, he had recommended to McCord that the best flight path would be to the west. McCord rejected this advice, having seen lightning in that direction. This difference of opinion between the two highest-ranking officers on the ship did not go unnoticed by the court. Wiley's summary statement on this issue could be regarded as an act of loyalty, defending McCord's decision, but it was probably also accurate.

> My inclination, in my own mind, was to go to the westward, but the Captain said that he had already seen lightning to the westward, although I did not see it for perhaps 20 or 30 minutes after I went into the control car. But we undertook no discussion of the weather. I would like to invite the attention of the court to the impossibility of being right in your opinion to a high

degree of certainty. Any person of ordinary intelligence can predict weather conditions with an accuracy of 50 percent for a few hours in advance. A trained observer can have an accuracy of about 75 percent, and an expert may have around 82 percent accuracy. Understanding this, and having had so much experience in predicting a certain thing, and not having it come true, and observing others who were trained observers having the same, I hope the court will understand that one cannot absolutely say with certainty that a thing was going to happen when you had very little information on the subject. Therefore, although as I say, my own inclination was to go to the westward, I could not tell the Captain that was the best, because he had as much or more information than I had. His guess of what might develop was just as good as mine.[18]

Wiley's analysis seems to have been supported by Maguire's aerological report.

A familiar figure resurfaced in the courtroom in the form of Capt. Anton Heinen. Living in Lakewood, New Jersey, he described himself as a "consulting engineer" and testified before the court of inquiry as an expert witness. Certainly, his vast experience with dirigibles and all manner of weather was to be valued. After viewing the weather map for the day of the flight, Heinen stated unequivocally that the weather conditions should not have prevented the *Akron* from operating.[19] Approaching the issue from another direction, the court asked Heinen if he believed McCord was justified in making the flight on April 3, to which he answered, "The Commanding Officer of an airship of the size of this, the *Shenandoah*, or the *Los Angeles*, or the much larger *Akron* can fly a ship of this size under all circumstances."[20] After giving all the evidence deep consideration, Heinen stated to the court his contention "that the crash of the *Akron* was due primarily, of course, to her being crushed down by a vertical current of air, and being destroyed after first touching with the fin and then her whole body in the water."[21]

Reports from the United Press on the day of the disaster claimed that the *Akron* "fell in flames" as the result of having been struck by lightning.[22] Heinen was a colorful character, but his knowledge and experience with airships was beyond question. The court sought his opinion concerning lightning as a cause of the crash. Heinen testified that, from his own experience, he knew that lightning strikes airships but did not cause structural damage. He claimed a survey of seventeen German airships revealed surface blemishes indicative of lightning strikes but without damage. He concluded with the assertion that a rigid airship, properly constructed and maintained, "is one of the safest spots to be in the Universe against lightning."[23]

The court of inquiry had opened its proceedings at NAS Lakehurst. On April 14, following the fourth day of examinations, the court concluded it had examined everyone in the Lakehurst area and adjourned to reconvene at the Washington Navy Yard on Tuesday, April 18, at 1000. From the beginning, the court had been open to anyone who had an interest in its proceedings and that remained the case in Washington. Taking advantage of the convenient Washington location, Associated Press writer Herbert C. Plummer sat in on the proceedings. In his column, "A Washington Daybook," he gave his readers a good sense of what it was like in the courtroom.

Often it is in the little known places of Washington, or, rather in those places that the average person doesn't know how to reach, that one encounters dramatic incidents in this capital city. . . .

A naval court of inquiry always is impressive. Gold-braided admirals, captains, commanders and lieutenants abound. . . .

It was the setting for the *Akron* inquiry, however, rather than the admirals that impressed observers at this particular court.

Beyond the navy yard, in the southeast section of the city, a barn-like structure wholly out of keeping with the dignity and pomp of the participants was the setting.

Nattily dressed Marines guarded the entrances. Interested observers could get in, but first it was necessary to satisfy those Marines that you were an interested observer.

Seated behind a green-covered table, resplendent in his gold braid, was the president of the court—that affable, but stern old sea dog, Rear Admiral Henry V. Butler. At his right was Captain Harry E. Shoemaker, and at his left, the third member of the court and the lowest in rank, Commander Sidney Kraus [*sic*]. Off to one side was the judge advocate, and to the other the only surviving officer of the ill-starred *Akron,* Lt. Com. H. V. Wiley.

Wiley knows more, perhaps, than any living man about what happened the night the *Akron* went to her doom. But he sat there, apparently listening to everything, but taking no part himself.[24]

Plummer gave his readers an idea of the layout of the courtroom and ended with an account of the feeling inside the proceedings: "It was a situation tense at every moment. Everybody in the room seemed to sense it, even the marine door-keepers. That is, everybody but the court. Grim countenances of the admiral, the captain and the commander seemed never to change."

On the eleventh day, the judge advocate stated the findings and conclusions of the court. Early in his statement he declared, "It would appear that the case must ever remain in the realm of conjecture. No eye witnesses can testify to what happened and even the testimony of the three survivors is conflicting and difficult to piece together."[25] The court gave its assessment of McCord's decisions concerning the *Akron*'s course in face of the developing weather situation.

> The court is of the opinion that at about 10 p.m., when the Commanding Officer observed the weather map which showed a secondary cyclone centered in the vicinity of Washington, D.C., coupled with the previous report of a thunderstorm in that vicinity at 7 p.m., lightning had been observed to the southward and westward which lightning approached closer to the ship, the Commanding Officer committed an error in judgment in not setting such courses as would have kept him in the safe semi-circle thereby probably avoiding the severe conditions finally encountered, and that this error in judgment was a contributory cause of the loss of the *Akron*.[26]

In later passages, the court softened its language relating to McCord's error in judgment with a reasonable qualification.

> The error in judgment . . . has been made evident to the court by its study of the testimony. The court has but little direct knowledge of the considerations upon which this judgment was based. Everything within the knowledge of Commander McCord at the time his decision was made might have pointed to his plan of action being justifiable. Certainly we know that many conflicting considerations had to be set one against the other, and what subsequent events show to have been an erroneous decision does not, in the opinion of the court, justify a condemnation without more information of the considerations upon which the plan of action was based. This information was lost with the ship.[27]

In a moment of remarkable prescience, the judge advocate offered the conclusion "this disaster is part of the price which must inevitably be paid in the development of any new and hazardous art."[28] In summary, the court concluded that the ultimate cause of the crash was the tail of the ship striking the water resulting in drag, and the forward momentum of the upper structure carrying the forward portion of the ship into the water, causing its final collapse. The final recommendation of the court of inquiry was that there be no further proceedings in the matter.[29]

Wiley needed to complete the logbook for the *Akron* by providing its final pages. He began, "The rough log for Monday, 3 April, 1933, was lost in the wreck of the U.S.S. *Akron* on 4 April, 1933. The following account is prepared by the Executive Officer, the only surviving officer of the flight." He then set down an abbreviated account of the events that led to the ship's loss. Beside six of the names were notations that the body had been recovered. Those recovered were:

Cdr. Frank C. McCord, U.S. Navy
Lt. Cdr. Harold E. MacLellan, U.S. Navy
Rear Adm. William A. Moffett, U.S. Navy
Cdr. Fred T. Berry, U.S. Navy
Lt. Col. Alfred F. Masury, U.S. Army Reserve
Robert Wilbur Copeland, CRM (PA).

Wiley's log entry ended, "During the remainder of the month no log has been kept and on 30 April 1933 the airship was stricken from the Navy List by order of the Secretary of the Navy and the remaining personnel were transferred to the U.S. Naval Air Station Lakehurst, N.J. for duty with the exception of Lieutenant Commander Herbert V. Wiley, U.S. Navy, who was transferred to the Commandant, Fourth Naval District, for duty involving flying."[30] The remaining personnel included men who were attached to the *Akron* but were not on her final flight. There were seven officers, including Wiley, and forty-one enlisted men, including survivors Deal and Erwin.

On April 18 the fishing boat *Olympia* snagged her trawling nets on what appeared to be the wreckage of the *Akron*. The salvage ship USS *Falcon* was dispatched to investigate. After marking the location with a buoy, three ships used grappling hooks to fish objects from the ocean. It quickly became clear that they had in fact found the remains of the *Akron*. Among the items recovered were a large section of fabric on which was printed "Port station No. 18 forward," a mass of wires, and a thirty-five-foot section of duralumin.[31] The Navy was convinced it had located the entire wreck of the *Akron*, but to the disappointment of everyone, no bodies were found.[32] The remnants of the ship and the control car were in a hundred feet of water. While the Navy was satisfied with the effectiveness of its trawling and the explorations of its divers, some people found the absence of bodies unsettling, and briefly, there were speculations that there might have been more survivors. Glenn L. Martin, a "veteran aeronautical expert," gave an interview to the International News Service in which he stated, "There is a faint possibility a sizeable section of the ill-fated naval airship is still 'free ballooning' somewhere out of range of the steamer lanes or may have reached some distant land with many of its missing crew alive."[33] Undoubtedly, Martin was recalling how, in the crash of the *Shenandoah*, part of the ship had drifted across country until stopped by trees. He maintained that the *Akron* could not be hidden in one hundred feet of water. That the Navy had conducted a thorough search and failed to recover any bodies supported his hypothesis that the ship could have risen after the crash and floated away even as far away as Africa. He felt it possible some of the crew were still alive.

Martin's speculations were unsubstantiated, and the Navy went about the business of investigating the remains of the *Akron* for evidence that might shed light on the cause of the crash. Examination of the lower stern fin revealed that its leading edge was in good shape and that damage was confined to its rear underside. This finding supported testimony the ship, up by the bow, had struck the water tail first and had been dragged into the sea.[34] To explain this, the Navy concluded that because of faulty altimeter readings, the airship had been flying much lower than anyone on board realized.

Five years later, Cdr. Charles E. Rosendahl gave a detailed and scientific analysis of the factors that had led to the crash of the *Akron*.

> From long consideration of all the available facts and from extensive discussion of the full situation with the only surviving officer, Lieutenant Commander Wiley, my shipmate of many years' standing, I am convinced that though the *Akron*'s loss occurred during a storm, it was not directly because of the storm. The ship was lost, however, through a combination of

factors and causes, not one of which can be classed as unavoidable or insur-
mountable. They include a lack of sufficient weather information relative
to the formation, travel, and intensity of the "secondary low-pressure area"
into which the ship proceeded; inability to learn the wind direction and
velocity in her vicinity; downward air currents of moderate proportions in
the turbulent zone, giving the ship her initial impetus on the two descents
during her final three minutes of existence; a deceiving altimeter, leading to
a lack of vertical maneuvering room; atmospheric turbulence and alternate
immersion in cold and warm air masses that made it difficult for an average
elevator-man at the controls to follow such "bumps" quickly enough to keep
the ship out of steep inclinations; tail-first immersion into the sea at a steep
angle, and resultant collapse of part of the tail in the water, leading to the
sudden retardation of the forward motion of the ship and the inevitable fatal
spending or slapping of the momentum of a 200-ton mass, moving ahead
at over 100 miles per hour, against the unyielding surface of the sea.[35]

Rosendahl gave detailed attention to each of his points, but his discussion of
the altimeter was particularly enlightening.

The present-day instrument used by aircraft to tell their altitude is funda-
mentally but a form of the aneroid barometer, graduated in linear units
rather than units of pressure. For each thousand feet of altitude above sea
level, the atmospheric pressure decreases at the rate of about "one inch of
mercury." Should it remain on the ground during the passage of a low-
pressure area that reduced the barometric pressure 1 inch, the helpless altimeter, actuated as it is simply by atmospheric pressure change, would falsely
indicate 1000 feet altitude, although it had actually not been off the ground.
    Never was a "non-barometric" altimeter more desperately needed than
during the *Akron's* last journey. When the airship approached the storm
center, the lowest recorded surface pressure there was at least 32 one-
hundredths of an inch less than when she departed from Lakehurst. Hence,
the ship's altimeters indicated an altitude at least 320 feet greater than the
actual height above the surface. Furthermore, under the existent conditions
near or at the very storm center, the actual pressure may have been even two-
or three-tenths of an inch lower than any recorded value. So it is certain that
when the *Akron's* altimeters read 1600 feet during the last three minutes of

the ship's existence, her actual height over the sea could not have been more than 1280 feet and may possibly have been only 1000 feet—surely not very much maneuvering room at night for an 800 foot ship in rough air.[36]

The results of the court of inquiry were met with a mixed review both within the Navy and in the press. The Chief of Naval Operations, Adm. William V. Pratt, stated publicly that the court of inquiry report was not consistent in that "it placed a degree of blame on McCord in one place and in another section said that his actions at the time might have been justified."[37] Congress wanted its own investigation, and a joint congressional committee was selected. Henry Breckenridge of New York was chosen as counsel for the investigation scheduled to convene on Monday, May 22, 1933. While the committee was not empowered to legislate, everyone knew its findings could have a profound influence on government spending for the LTA program. As it turned out its findings were essentially the same as those of the court of inquiry. In a consensus opinion, the eight congressmen who signed the report gave the Navy's lighter-than-air program a "clean bill of health"; Senator King, a Democrat from Utah, and Senator Johnson, a Republican from California, did not sign.[38]

The committee went further, to make a series of recommendations. Navy proponents of the LTA program must have been pleased with them. The committee acknowledged the world war and recent American fleet exercises had shown that airships had a special utility as scouts. It recognized further that the use of airships was still in the developmental stage and that further experience would reveal their potential. It stated specifically that airships were of little value to the Army but their allocation to the Navy for development was a sound decision. Consequently, the committee recommended that the Navy continue to maintain, develop, and operate airships; that the air station at Lakehurst be maintained as a site for training and experimentation; that balloons and nonrigid airships be provided for training purposes; that a new training airship be built immediately to replace the *Akron*; and that until it was available, the *Los Angeles* be put back into commission. Finally, given the problems with weather forecasting and reporting that had complicated the *Akron*'s last flight, the committee recommended that four general weather maps be generated each day instead of the usual two.[39]

These were bold recommendations in support of the Navy's LTA program, but given the loss of the *Shenandoah* and the *Akron*, with so many human lives and at such great expense, the airship era was coming to an end. It might have ended here if it had not been for the fact the Navy already had its next airship ready, in the form of the *Macon*. The *Macon* represented the Navy's last chance to make the LTA program viable and of service to the surface fleet.

In Akron, the *Macon* made her third test flight on May 15, 1933, and the press gave what coverage it could with minimal information at hand. Capt. Alger Dresel withheld the airship's itinerary but let it be known that a hundred men were on board, including Adm. Ernest J. King, who had replaced Admiral Moffett as chief of the Navy Bureau of Aeronautics, and Lt. Cdr. Jesse L. Kenworthy, who relieved Commander Berry at NAS Lakehurst. Just as the words *"Shenandoah"* and "disaster" had become inexorably linked, so had Wiley's name and "only officer survivor of the *Akron*" been joined, and it was in this context that the press announced that Wiley had made his second flight on board the *Macon* on May 15.[40]

Wiley was ordered to maintain an office at Lakehurst until the records of the *Akron* were completed, on temporary duty under the president of the court of inquiry. In addition, he would be ordered to report in June to the president of the Board of Inspection and Survey for temporary duty in connection with the trials of the *Macon*. Wiley received his orders to proceed to Akron on or about June 5, 1933, for temporary additional duty in connection with the trials of the *Macon*.[41] His orders dispatching him to Akron called for him to return to his post at Lakehurst when his duties in Akron were completed. As a result, he was obliged to travel repeatedly between Lakehurst and Akron. This was a time of flux for Wiley, but he knew the ways of the Navy quite well by now. He knew he would find himself an officer on board the *Macon*, but only time would tell what paths would take him there. Following the loss of life and airship experience in the *Akron* crash, the Navy's LTA program could ill afford to lose the knowledge and expertise of someone like Wiley. Nevertheless, the Bureau of Navigation changed his orders on June 14, assigning him as the navigator of the light cruiser USS *Cincinnati* (CL 6), then at San Pedro, California. He was to report on board by June 25.[42]

Wiley was duly detached from the Fourth Naval District on June 15, to report on June 24.[43] Nothing related to the Navy's LTA program escaped the watchful eye of the press and Wiley's movements in particular did not go unnoticed. Following the crash of the *Akron*, the court of inquiry, and the congressional investigation, the press developed a keen interest, if not curiosity in, Wiley's future career. The public release of the committee's findings and Wiley's assignment to sea duty came in rapid succession. The press wanted to know why Wiley had been assigned to the surface fleet instead of the *Macon*. There was a tradition of shifting officers from the LTA service to the surface fleet, but the practice came under some criticism by the congressional committee. Charles Lindbergh was among the critics of this practice.[44] He believed Navy administration should ensure continuity of personnel and experience and that only fully trained officers of wide experience should command airships.

Secretary Swanson replied to the critics with a terse statement that Wiley had been ordered to sea at his own request and that he, Swanson, foresaw no change in the Navy's policy of rotating flyers to sea duty.[45] Wiley himself put an end to speculation, by confirming that he had requested sea duty.

Wiley's trip to the *Cincinnati*, on the West Coast, was overland. En route, he was granted leave from June 18 to June 21, and he used it to visit family in Missouri where he was able to spend three days in the home of his sister Fay in Trenton.[46] The town of Chillicothe, of course, had to celebrate the return of its most famous son and the Chamber of Commerce held a special luncheon for him at noon on June 20. Everyone knew him as a celebrity, but a number of attendees were actually old friends. All were happy to see him and eager to hear him speak about his world away from the small town. Chillicothe put on its best show for Wiley, staging the luncheon in the Leeper Hotel, which had stood since 1884 at Webster and Washington Streets—the city's most prominent corner. He gave an informal presentation to the members of the Chamber of Commerce and their invited friends in which he argued that an unfavorable economy had resulted in a deterioration of the U.S. Navy.

"We of the navy," he said, "are sorry to see the navy going down. The morale of the navy is not what it once was. We are now a poor third among nations and we feel that we should be a strong first."

Wiley compared the need for a navy to the need for a police force in a city.

"Until conditions get good enough that we know there will be no crime, we do not feel that we can afford to lose our police force," he said. "Until conditions get good enough that we don't need a navy, we feel that the navy should be kept up."[47]

Wiley was not the only speaker at the luncheon. A number of people who had known him offered kind words. A high school classmate proclaimed, "The people of Livingston County won't let the people of the world forget where Wiley's home is." Another old friend congratulated Wiley on his accomplishments and expressed his pleasure that "Livingston county's hero was spared in the *Akron* crash." Also present was John Taylor, a member of the committee that had recommended Wiley for his appointment to the Naval Academy—a nomination for which Wiley had proved beyond a doubt that he was worthy. Taylor told the audience, "No man who ever went out of Chillicothe has brought to Chillicothe more of renown than he has. He has made good as a man, as a citizen and as a follower of his country's flag." After receiving a number of such encomiums, Wiley closed with, "A career in the Navy takes one a long way from Chillicothe."[48]

Wiley's career in the Navy had certainly taken him a long way from Chillicothe and for extended periods of time. While letters kept him in touch with his family, the prolonged absences prevented him from seeing the realities of their life. Wiley's father was aging and not well. He was now seventy-seven years old and frail. Still plagued by financial problems, he had been forced reluctantly to leave his hometown of Wheeling to move in with his daughter's family. After ten years as a widower, he married a widow, Hattie Churchill. The marriage was not successful and it ended in separation after about nine years. Hattie was brutal in her treatment of Wiley's father and attempted to claim all of his assets. A sympathetic Wiley advised his father not to deal with Hattie directly but to allow his lawyer to do so and to let her have whatever she wanted of his. In the end, Wiley's father was left with very little.

The country was now in the depths of the Depression, and Wiley's sister and her husband, like many Americans, were struggling. Rex Oren had lost his job, and work was difficult to find. It is unlikely the family could have maintained its standard of living had it not been for the money Wiley sent home every month. As he always had, he felt an obligation to send his family what funds he could and he never failed them.

Following his visit home, Wiley boarded a train for California and was on board the *Cincinnati* on the twenty-fourth, as ordered.[49] On August 18 he wrote his father and Fay that the housekeeper, Mrs. Case, had written and sent photographs of the baby and assured them all was well. Again, Wiley had to get his young family quickly to the West Coast and as before, they would have to travel without him. The children were too young to make the journey alone—Gordon, David, and Marie were twelve, nine, and three years old, respectively. Mary Louise Case, their forty-five-year-old housekeeper, was accustomed to caring for the children and Wiley arranged for her to accompany them. They traveled from New Haven, Connecticut, to New York City by train, then from New York to Norfolk, Virginia on board an Eastern Steamship Lines liner. In Norfolk, on September 8, they boarded the Navy transport USS *Henderson* (AP 1) for passage to San Diego. Following two days in Haiti and three in the Panama Canal, they arrived in California on October 1. The press was waiting, and with a supporting photograph, they described three-year-old Marie as the "belle of the ship"— cheery and smiling.[50] Wiley had prepared a home for his children and house-keeper in San Diego.

The news surrounding his children was all happy but in his August 18 letter to his father and sister he shared some bad news. The Building and Loan Company of Salt Lake City had closed. Wiley had been depositing fifteen dollars a month into his account there for thirteen years. In two more years he would have saved five thousand dollars—money he had planned to use for Gordon's college education. At the time of his writing, he had no idea whether he would regain any of his assets from what was a $26,000,000 bank failure. Bank failures were occurring around the country, and Wiley could not have been surprised completely. This was a setback for the future but it did not affect his monthly finances adversely. In most of his letters to his father he enclosed a check.

Wiley loved his children deeply and was succeeding in keeping his family unit intact. Having them on the West Coast with him was the source of great comfort but the geographic proximity did not guarantee he would see them as much as he wanted. His life in the Navy called for difficult and irregular work schedules that did not always match the family routine well. He often got home late, well after the children had gone to bed, and he left for work early in the mornings.[51] When opportunities arose, however, he took full advantage to spend as much time as he could with the children. He wrote home on one occasion that the *Cincinnati* had come alongside a repair ship for a three weeks' overhaul, giving him a chance to spend more time with the family.[52] He assured his father the children were well and the family was settled in except that one boy had to go to school in the morning and the other in the afternoon, which made scheduled meals and household routine difficult. They were "Navy children" and, undoubtedly, had come to understand the ways of life for service families. In spite of the absences from their father, they loved him very much, and the family was very close.

While Wiley was doing quite well with his life there were many issues that required his constant attention. He had to continue to do the best job he could for the Navy, for that was the single source of income for his immediate and extended family. He worried continually about his father's health and encouraged him to take life easy. He was concerned that the contentious divorce proceedings were taking their toll on his health and he encouraged his father to stop thinking about it, as there was nothing to be gained in any event.[53]

Wiley's father continued to worry about money and asked for an accounting of the amount his son had sent him, as if to keep an account of what he might owe him. With kind reassurance, Wiley turned the tables, replying that he had never received an accounting for all the expense of raising him. He tried to assure his father that he was in a comfortable position financially and that he should rest and enjoy the fruits of all his hard labor over the years.[54]

In November, Wiley told his father the fleet was to leave the West Coast on April 9, returning on September 1.[55] The *Cincinnati* and the rest of the fleet were to take part in exercises and war games off the East Coast. As on a previous occasion, there would be a presidential review of the fleet, this time by President Roosevelt, who would be watching from the decks of the heavy cruiser USS *Indianapolis* (CA 35). With the battleship USS *Pennsylvania* (BB 38), the flagship of the U.S. Fleet, ninety-six ships would pass in review. This was to be the largest peacetime review in the history of the U.S. Navy.[56] Wiley told his father it would take him away from his family for a long time but such was life in the Navy.

In his last letter home of 1933, Wiley described another tough family situation. He had been made aware his ship was going to move its homeport to San Diego. He made the decision not to move the family and disrupt things in the middle of the school year. After the operations in the Atlantic, his ship would leave New York on June 18 for the navy yard near Seattle, Washington. All this meant he would not be back with his family until October.[57] From these difficult matters Wiley turned an expression of gratitude for what he *did* have in his life. He had a job, and all his family were well. He would be home on Christmas Day, though back on the ship on New Year's Day. After telling them he had enclosed a check for Christmas presents, he ended by wishing them a very merry Christmas and hoping for better times in the next year.

With the *Cincinnati* based in its homeport of San Diego in early 1934, Wiley was three hours' drive from his children in Long Beach. The children remained in the constant care of Mrs. Case with Wiley visiting as often as he could. In March he took leave to spend a week with the children and wrote his father and sister about the great time he had had with them. He and the children were the guests of the Mission Inn in Riverside, California and Wiley thought it a wonderful hotel. He had been invited to place a set of bronze aviator's wings bearing his name on the Famous Fliers' Wall in the chapel there—a testament to the fame Wiley had earned as an aviator. After the Mission Inn they spent a couple of days at a desert resort near Palm Springs, where the children swam and rode horses. The final three days of his leave they stayed at home in Long Beach because his money had run out. Navy pay had been cut. However, 5 percent of that pay cut had been restored, and, as a result, he enclosed a check.[58]

Wiley's was a life defined by devotion—to his immediate family, to his family in Missouri, and to his life in the Navy. It was far more than a job. Within that context, he was devoted to the lighter-than-air service. While caring for his children and performing his shipboard duties, he found time to write a cogent article on the value of airships. His article appeared in the May 1934 issue of the U.S. Naval Institute *Proceedings*.[59] In it he attempted to use facts to correct what he considered to be erroneous impressions. He set the stage with his opening sentence: "Among the arrows in the quiver of our national defense the rigid airship seems neglected, largely because of little knowledge of its capabilities." He argued that zeppelin-type airships were so new and unusual that any casualty related to them became a front-page story in newspapers. As an example, he recalled the *Akron*'s tail fin damage during ground handling that resulted in an $8,000 repair. He compared this "big news," page-one story to another incident that same week in which three Navy planes, each costing $60,000, had been destroyed near Washington, D.C. Only two inches of type had been devoted to the story.

Wiley addressed the issue of vulnerability of the airship. The casual thinker believed that the gigantic airships could be easily spotted in the air and that their huge sacks of gas made them easy targets for enemy gunfire. However, he pointed out, there was little pressure at the top of a gas cell and none at the bottom. Gas escaped very slowly through any hole, thus allowing time for repairs or return to home base. He illustrated this point with reference to the *Macon* and her four large (thirty-two-inch-diameter) valves in the top of each gas cell. Even with all valves open in all cells, he pointed out, several minutes would be required to make an appreciable change in lift. Thus, contrary to the common idea, no flurry of machine-gun bullets would bring down an airship. During the world war, zeppelins had been able to fly back to base so badly shot up that nearly a third of their gas cells had deflated. As for weather, improved weather information and skillful handling of the airship reduced the risk, and an airship could endure a great deal of weather-induced stresses.

Wiley conceded that the size and easy visibility of dirigibles could be problems, but only within range of hostile surface ships, where they had no business. The primary mission of an airship, he declared flatly, was long-range reconnaissance. It should remain out of range, where it could do its job effectively and safely. He acknowledged that, in war, losses are to be expected and airships, like destroyers, could be lost on scouting missions. He suggested, however, that the losses would be acceptable in return for the intelligence gathered. As a practical matter, Wiley noted that one destroyer represented more men and more dollars than an airship and in that context, it would be better to lose an airship than a destroyer. He argued the "urgent need" of more airships for training and development with production to begin immediately. His article included a strongly worded challenge: "No studious naval officer is convinced of the lack of usefulness of this arm to the fleet. The doubters all say, 'I'm willing to be convinced by demonstration.' Now is the time to have a demonstration at small cost."[60]

The opportunity for Wiley to participate in a convincing demonstration was approaching as he received new orders for a change of duty, requiring him to report to the commanding officer of the *Macon* by June 30.[61] He remained with the *Cincinnati* for her cruise to the East Coast. In New York, Wiley wrote home expressing concern as to whether his father and Fay had enough money not only to live but to enjoy life. He told them he expected to have a little more money after July, as Navy personnel got back more of their pay cut. He would then be able to help them a little more, but he could always raise more money if needed. He encouraged them to call on him any time.[62]

Back in San Diego on July 3, he found his children doing well and glad to see him. He rose early on the fourth to buy fireworks for a family holiday celebration. He had been offered command of the *Macon* as a relief for Commander Dresel but, with his children growing up, he paused to think seriously about whether to accept this new assignment, which would take him away from his family for extended periods. There was always the possibility that he would die, as had so many on the *Shenandoah* and the *Akron*. To help him decide, he put the question to his sons, who he felt were old enough to have worthwhile opinions. Newspapers carried the heartwarming story of how the family reached its decision.

To Gordon Wiley, a blue-eyed, sandy-haired boy of 13, and his brother, David, 9, fell the responsibility of choosing the new commanding officer of the USS *Macon*, the navy's latest queen of the skies. . . .

The Navy Department offered Lieut. Commander Wiley the job of the *Macon*'s skipper when Commander H. Dresel is relieved this summer. . . .

Lieut. Wiley could not decide alone. He loves his children more than anything else in the world. He had been through a terrifying experience both to them and to himself in lighter than air craft. The final decision he would leave to his sons.

So it was Gordon and his brother David who agreed that the officer should go back to airship duty. They are very proud of their father and his splendid record in the service. It will be a great moment for them when he formally takes command of the graceful, silver ship that encircled three times over Long Beach last Friday afternoon on her way to join the Fleet for maneuvers in the southern drill grounds.

Gordon is the spokesman for the motherless family which lived . . . since last September with Mrs. Mary Case, whom they affectionately call Aunt Mary.[63]

His sons' approval having eased his burden, Wiley reported for duty on July 8, 1934, and assumed command of the *Macon* on the eleventh.[64]

12

The USS
Macon (ZRS 5)

he USS *Macon* (ZRS 5) was a much-improved version of the *Akron*. Lessons learned from the *Akron* were translated into modifications to the *Macon*. The *Macon's* airplane landing trapeze apparatus installed at launching reflected design changes developed, in part, on the *Akron*.[1] The *Macon* made her debut without the dark clouds of controversy that had engulfed the *Akron*. Her officers and crew had been trained on the *Akron*, and she inherited the *Akron's* airplane pilots. The *Macon* was destined to become a happy ship. "All the big rigids in the United States Navy were 'happy' ships. The hand-picked crews, like their commanders, regarded themselves as superior to heavier-than-air fliers. It took little finesse, they believed, to fly an airplane. But an airship was actually a flying battleship, and the airshipman, in addition to facing all the problems of flight, had to be an expert mariner as well—a sailor of the sky. The new dirigible, the ZR-5, was the happiest of all the great rigids." It was her crew that made her that. "Half of the men were tough veterans who had lived through crashes, narrow escapes, and free-wheeling experimentation; the other half were young, carefree, and completely oblivious of the constant hazards of their chosen profession. This combination gave birth to a ship spirit unheard of in peacetime and rare during war."[2]

The *Macon* was the last great airship the Navy had, and the future of the LTA program rested with her—and squarely on the shoulders of Wiley, as her commander. The death of Admiral Moffett meant the airships had lost their greatest supporter, but it also heralded a new attitude toward the great ships. Moffett had wanted the dirigibles flying as much as possible, and he wanted them to be active in public relations, with frequent "hand waving" flights, appearances at county fairs around the country, and rides for dignitaries. Dresel had been less inclined to make the public relations tours, preferring to avoid the press and focus on exploring the limits of what the airship could do. When Admiral King replaced Admiral Moffett, he felt it was time for the airship to prove its worth to the surface fleet beyond any question. If Moffett had devoted too little time to developing tactics that would allow the airship to be integrated with the surface Navy, King would go the opposite way. He had to be convincing if he was to prove to the Navy and to Congress that the airship had an important role in warfare.

While Wiley was still on board the *Cincinnati*, the *Macon* was put to the test in fleet exercises in the Caribbean in 1934. She left her home base at Sunnyvale on April 20 to make a most difficult fifty-four-and-a-half-hour transcontinental flight to Opa-locka. She had to endure the same challenges the *Akron* had on a previous cross-country flight—flying over mountaintops at altitudes that were unusual for airships and navigating mountain passes with strong air currents. Yet, with full knowledge of the *Akron's* experience, the trip was extremely rough on the structure of the airship. The ship had lifted off at 0937 on the twentieth, and by 1645 she was experiencing extremely turbulent air as she traversed the San Gorgonio Pass between Capazon and Indio, California.[3] Two minutes later, she was above pressure height, with all eight engines at standard speed. Between 1820 and 1840 the crew pumped 770 pounds of fuel overboard to gain extra buoyancy. Between 2020 and 2032 they pumped more fuel overboard but ceased as they flew over Yuma, Arizona, and headed toward Phoenix. Over Phoenix at 2300, she circled until daylight on April 21 to negotiate the mountains between Phoenix and Dragoon.

Once past the mountains without trouble, they made it to Van Horn, Texas, by 1140 where they encountered turbulent air. By noon the second day there were extremely violent gusts, and the *Macon* found herself rising and falling at rates ranging from twenty-four to thirty-six feet per second.[4] At 1215 a report came to the control car that the ship had a broken girder and two others buckled, at frame 17.5.[5] Chief Boatswain's Mate Robert Davis was near that point when the gust struck and he discovered one of the broken diagonal girders. Thinking quickly, he ran forward to summon a repair crew. The damage was attributed to stresses resulting from severe gusts around 1200. Temporary repairs were completed within half an hour, but signs of buckling began to appear in other girders.[6] With this series of structural failures, the *Macon* was fortunate to make it through west Texas without crashing, and much of the credit belonged to Davis' rapid response. All went well for the remainder of the trip. The *Macon* was moored securely at Opa-locka by 1916 on April 22.[7]

The press understood the significance of the fleet exercises to the future of LTA flight: headlines proclaimed, "*Macon's* Caribbean Flight to Decide Airship Policy: Fleet Maneuver Will Determine If Government Will Construct More Dirigibles," "*Macon's* Worth to Be Studied," and "Airship's Value to Fleet Will Be Known Soon."[8] Readers were told of aeronautical experts, some within the Navy, who predicted that a ship the size of the *Macon* would be destroyed in wartime shortly after fulfilling its mission of locating the enemy.[9] The press claimed that, accordingly, the problem the naval command had to solve from the results of the fleet exercises was whether the *Macon* fulfilled its mission of discovering the "enemy" fleet and reporting its position before being "destroyed."[10] The press was convinced that a wartime scouting mission for the *Macon* would be suicidal.

After repairs, the *Macon* unmoored at 0900 on Saturday, May 5, 1934, to join the exercises. The two opposing forces were dubbed "Blue" and "Gray." The Gray force was the aggressor, the "enemy," and had "seized" Puerto Rico and the Virgin Islands. The *Macon* was part of the Blue force, and it was her job to locate the Gray fleet.[11] Her scouting course was intended to sight the "enemy" fleet while avoiding (simulated) gunfire from the surface and interception by aircraft. Course changes were made during the day to avoid rainsqualls. At 0300 on May 6, the crew sighted a fleet submarine on the surface and at 0340 four "enemy" destroyers. The lookouts had little trouble, in fact, finding a variety of surface vessels: 0504 a battleship off the starboard bow, minutes later three destroyers off the port beam. This time the airship had her airplanes on board, and she put them to use. Scouting out ahead of the airship, they sighted a heavy cruiser at 0745, and at 0802 launched an airplane to investigate it.

At 1010 the *Macon* was presented with a situation many had predicted would bring about her death in real combat: The airship was "attacked" by six "enemy" planes launched from the aircraft carrier *Lexington*. Because this was a training exercise, the outcome of the encounter in actual combat could not be known, but it is quite possible the *Macon* would have been shot out of the sky.[12] At 1011 the *Macon* sighted the *Lexington* off the port beam at twelve miles and minutes later launched two fighter planes to investigate the carrier. The airship then changed course to track the "enemy" carrier from a distance. At 1500 the airship spotted an "enemy" force—an aircraft carrier, a battleship, and a cruiser—and within ten minutes had a fighter plane on its way to investigate. By 1920 the *Macon* was flying over the friendly Blue force.

Reports now surfaced that the airship had been "destroyed" and that Secretary Swanson had declared the *Macon* a failure. The secretary's office denied these claims emphatically.[13] The exercise's umpires, however, did in fact adjudge the *Macon* to have been destroyed by "enemy" aircraft.[14] The *Macon's* performance in these exercises was the subject of much debate. It seemed to many if airships had a role with the surface fleet in war, the Navy had not yet found it.

With the airship in need of permanent girder repairs, Dresel believed it urgent to get her back to home base at Sunnyvale. It was widely sensed that time was running out for the LTA program, and the *Macon* had not yet proved her worth beyond doubt. She made the return trip to Sunnyvale without incident arriving on Friday, May 18.[15] There she was grounded for a month undergoing repairs. Going into the second half of 1934, things were about to change again.

The *Macon* had been given everything an airship needed to prove herself. She had inherited the best crew an airship could have wanted. Now she was on the West Coast, where most flights took her over the ocean and where most experts felt her future lay. Her chances for success were made even better on July 11, when Lieutenant Commander Wiley took command.[16] The Navy's LTA service now had the best ship, the best crew, and the best commanding officer. Wiley felt the pressure, but he was the most experienced airship officer available and still an aggressive believer in the future of dirigibles. Moffett's absence had made it possible for Wiley to take over the *Macon* as a lieutenant commander—his experience favored over rank.

The change of command ceremony was brief. Dresel and Wiley each read his orders. Dresel assumed command of the naval air station at Sunnyvale, renamed "Moffett Field." Wiley wasted no time. Immediately after assuming command, he inspected the crew.[17] He made it a priority to investigate the incident over Texas. Lt. Calvin Bolster, the ship's construction officer, inspected the damaged part of the ship with Wiley, and they agreed major permanent repairs were needed. The repairs at Opa-locka had been made with the help of representatives of the Goodyear Zeppelin Company. When the *Macon* returned to Sunnyvale, Dresel believed the affected members were "as strong or probably stronger" than they had been originally. No sign of movement was seen in the repaired areas in the rough air encountered on the return flight. Dresel recommended only "that the entire question of fin strength should be carefully investigated in order that any possibility of failure in this portion of the ship in the future may be prevented."[18]

In ensuing months, issues related to frame 17.5 continued to arise, with an odd mixture of reassurances the ship was sound structurally and concerns that frame 17.5 needed further attention. On July 24 Capt. Frank R. McCrary, assistant chief of the Bureau of Aeronautics, addressed Wiley by letter on the frame 17.5 problem. An analysis of the failure conducted in collaboration with Goodyear Zeppelin had found no explanation. It was suspected local damage to the girder parts in question had been the fundamental cause. Working on this premise, McCrary told Wiley, there was justification for reinforcing parts of frame 17.5 and certain parts of the fins themselves. Meanwhile, the ship's structure was considered strong enough for flights over the ocean. The work should be done "from time to time, as opportunity offers, at discretion of the commanding officer, and, therefore, will not interfere with operating schedules."[19] The repairs would be made, but they would not prevent the *Macon* from flying—her time was to be split between flying and undergoing repairs.[20]

Wiley brought attributes not seen previously in a single airship leader. He was energetic and aggressive. He was less interested in public relations than in developing the *Macon* as a military weapon to be integrated into the surface fleet. His fellow officers viewed him as particularly qualified for that task. Wiley had served in a meaningful way on board warships and understood the workings of the fleet. This was not a universal quality in the LTA ranks, Lakehurst being, it seemed to many, a self-contained community in which many of its officers acquired little working knowledge of other branches of the service. In later years, Harold B. Miller, then a lieutenant and a fighter landplane pilot assigned to the *Macon*, described the situation: "Doc now had been pretty well indoctrinated with the fleet itself. An interesting thing about lighter-than-air people, they had to have alleged duty on a blimp or on the *Los Angeles*, and they'd have shore duty at Lakehurst and then have sea duty at Lakehurst, so they never left. They never really had a feel or a touch of what the hell the fleet was doing."[21]

Wiley did not rely solely on his own creativity but was always open to the ideas of his officers. Miller was one of the most productive thinkers. He sent Wiley memoranda about things he thought should be done to improve the performance of the *Macon*, to promote the airship through her airplanes. Miller suggested that the landing gear be removed from the airplanes and that the planes fly singly instead of in pairs. Removing the landing gear allowed the airplane to carry an extra thirty gallons of fuel, extending its flying time by an hour and a half. Miller's approach was sound, at least out over the ocean, where there was no use for the landing gear. The planes would fly two or three hundred miles from the airship and on return: "When you saw the ship coming back at the end of a four-hour flight, it was a damn welcome sight—to see that blob up in the sky and have a place to go to."[22]

Miller thought sending the pilots out in pairs only burned a lot of fuel and exhausted the pilots. Flying far from the airship, alone over the ocean, was a "hell of a lonely feeling," He felt the second plane had nothing to contribute. He suggested they send out one plane on each side of the airship instead of two. They could be relieved by other pilots. Wiley listened to and then approved these suggestions. Flying alone for hours over the open ocean required the pilots to have great confidence in themselves, and Wiley's did. Miller would recall, "Old Doc Wiley was for everything. He was just an old go-getter; he was great. He approved everything I wanted."[23] Wiley's willingness to "push the envelope" with the airship was infectious among his officers and he became confident they could do almost anything.[24]

Enthusiasm for the new plan grew as other officers made contributions.

The first thing you know, the tactical officer on the *Macon* developed a plan. The ship would hold whatever the course was at a speed of 60 [knots]. We would double the speed on a 60 degree angle and go up so that the three of us were progressing on the line at all times. We always had a straight line. Any time we wanted to go back to the ship, no matter what side you were on, you'd turn 90 degrees and hold the compass and you'd intersect. That was the theory of it, and it worked pretty well. . . . You could see her compass course anyway. We had about a 400-mile front there, a tremendous scouting front.[25]

The tactic worked fine with the airship on a constant course, but adjustments were needed should the ship turn. To accommodate this, a way was developed for the airship to control the flight paths of the airplanes. The airship continuously plotted the airplanes' positions relative to herself to prevent their becoming lost. Under Wiley's energetic guidance, the method was refined rapidly and showed great promise for providing a wide scouting "front." As an additional aid, they began experimenting with a new radio homing device that could guide the planes back to the ship. The methods were developed with the *Macon* operating independently; adjustments would be needed when the movements of the fleet were added. Before then, an opportunity presented itself to test the *Macon* and her airplanes in a long-range search mission.

In early July 1934 President Franklin Roosevelt began a historic 13,000-mile cruise that constituted something of a vacation for him. He and several family members departed Annapolis, Maryland, on board the destroyer USS *Gilmer* (DD 233), which carried them down the Chesapeake Bay to meet the heavy cruiser USS *Houston* (CA 30), three miles off shore, and transferred them to her for the long voyage.[26] The press accompanying the president traveled on board the cruiser USS *New Orleans* (CA 32). The small flotilla headed south to Puerto Rico and Haiti before entering the Panama Canal; Roosevelt became the first president of the United States to traverse the canal while holding office.[27]

With the press coverage, the location of these ships was known to Wiley. He decided that locating the cruisers in the open Pacific would be a good test of the *Macon*'s scouting abilities and would make a favorable impression on the president. After exiting the Panama Canal, he knew, the cruisers sailed to Isla de Cocos and then to Clipperton Island. This project was unfolding much like a military exercise in which he would have to find an enemy fleet using minimal information and good tactical judgment. Wiley estimated the ships' speeds from their published departure and arrival times, and he knew they were scheduled to leave the area of Clipperton Island in the afternoon of July 17. The *Macon*'s navigator, Lt. "Scotty" Peck, plotted a course that would take the airship to a point a hundred miles ahead of the cruisers' estimated position by 1000 on July 19.[28]

At 0925 on July 18 the *Macon* unmoored from the mobile mast at Moffett Field. At 0950, while the airship was cruising at 1,800 feet, two fighter landplanes hooked on and were taken on board. The pilots were Lt. H. B. Miller and Lt. (jg) F. N. Kivette. As the *Macon* crossed the shoreline at South San Francisco she ran into fog that obscured the ground and out to sea, the sky was overcast for the entire day and the ship passed through rainsqualls at 2220.[29] The next day, at 1032, Kivette was launched in his airplane followed nine minutes later by Miller in his; their search mission: to locate the two cruisers. At 1145 the planes reported seeing two cruisers on their port beam, range twenty miles. They were forty miles ahead of the *Macon*. Five minutes later, they were able to identify the cruisers as the *Houston* and the *New Orleans*.[30] By 1204 the *Macon* herself sighted the cruisers.

The drama that unfolded next was not recorded in her logbook. Wiley wanted the pilots to drop certain materials to the president and his party. As Miller told the story in his memoir, decades after the event,

> We had a line about two hundred feet long with a waterproof rubber bag on the end. . . . We could drop it just about where we wanted it. So we shoved off the ship, and Doc did not report to anybody; we were just going to sea for local exercises. He didn't tell anybody what we were going to do. About eighteen hours later, the *Macon* was on the line somewhere between Pearl and Clipperton, and Knappy [Kivette] and I were launched in our planes. The weather was pretty stinky at that point, cloudy with squalls. So we went ahead to about where we thought we might find something and sure as hell, out of that mess were two cruisers steaming along at about fifteen to eighteen knots. I tell you, the reporters hadn't had anything to write about at all, as you can imagine. When these two little planes dove down on them from these cloudy skies, they should have shot us down. They had the president on board.[31]

Kivette and Miller each had one of the waterproof bags on a long line, and they intended to drop them to the president on board the *Houston*. The reporters on the *New Orleans* must have had a good view of the two small planes approaching the *Houston* trailing their long lines with the bags on the ends. The United Press reported the *Macon* had found the president's flagship 1,200 miles south of California, "despite squally weather and low hanging clouds." Reporters wrote that the two planes dropped papers for the president onto the *Houston's* deck.[32] The reality was somewhat different.

The two bags had the same items: the latest issue of *Time* magazine, San Francisco newspapers of the date the *Macon* left Sunnyvale, and a sealed envelope addressed to the *Houston's* mail clerk that contained a note of instruction, eight mail covers, and postage money for the return mail of the covers to Miller.[33] It was known widely that the president was a philatelist, and members of the *Macon's* crew had put about twenty self-addressed letters into the bags. Among these were letters to the president, Mrs. Franklin D. Roosevelt, Capt. W. B. Woodson of the *Houston*, Wiley, Harold "Min" Miller, and others.[34] The letters had cancellations placed by the *Macon's* mail clerk, "marking the first delivery of mail via airship and hook-on planes to a ship at sea."[35] Miller and Kivette had planned to deliver relatively small bags, but by the time the deed was to be done, they had gotten rather bulky. Miller made his approach toward the *Houston*, the bag's rope wrapped around his hand that was on the throttle. He tried to keep the throttle open, but the load of the bag, the rope, and the wind resistance "was just about to tear me out of the airplane. It was awful."[36]

Realizing the president of the United States was on board, Wiley had obtained permission to drop something to his ship before doing it. Miller made the first pass over the *Houston*'s forecastle and overshot the mark. Trailing Miller, Kivette did no better, his bag too ended up in the ocean. The cruisers went dead in the water and the *Houston* put over a motor whaleboat to retrieve the bags.[37] The *Macon* had not been in sight during the "bombing runs," but within another half hour the airship came into view and took on board her planes. Even as they were landing, two radio messages were received from the *Houston*: "The president compliments you and your planes on your fine performance and excellent navigation [time of transmission] 1210," and "Well done and thank you for the papers. The president 1245."[38]

Wiley had obtained permission from his own superiors for the long flight out over the Pacific but not for the "bag drop," nor had he informed them of his intentions. This became a problem very quickly, as reporters filed their stories by radio from the *New Orleans* and those stories hit the streets. In the *Macon*'s radio room around 2025 came the angry, booming voice of ComBatFor wanting to know if the stories were true—Had the airship made contact with the *Houston* and delivered mail to her, and if so, by whose authority? ComBatFor demanded a reply "Immediately!"[39] Miller later recalled, "Old Doc Wiley thought, 'Oh, Christ,' that he was fired from the Navy now. It was not a very happy trip back. We had accomplished what we had started to do, but it wasn't really very successful after all."[40] Wiley was very worried about his future. He knew he was due for consideration for promotion to full commander in 1935 and wondered if this episode would prevent him from getting it.

Otherwise, Wiley had orchestrated a very successful showing for the *Macon* since assuming command. On board the *Macon*, doing all he could to prove the value of airships was earning Wiley the particular respect of his officers and crew. They understood what he was doing and supported him fully. Years later, Miller, as a rear admiral, summed up the incident: "Doc Wiley was all for everything and had pushed this job and he had nerve and courage. He was just great." Wiley knew there could be repercussions from the Navy for his intercepting the president at sea but "We were trying to sell the airships."[41]

Indeed there *were* repercussions. W. H. Standley, the Chief of Naval Operations, promptly demanded an explanation. Wiley sent a letter of explanation from Moffett Field on July 25, subject, "Operations of U.S.S. *Macon,* 18–21 July 1934; Contact with U.S.S. *Houston."* After reciting the events of the flight, Wiley explained his reason:

> Since one of the primary missions of rigid airships is long-range scouting to obtain information and transmit it much more quickly than surface vessels can, the commanding officer has been observing published reports of ships at sea with the idea of conducting scouting operations which offer typical war-time missions. Although the problem most generally presented is one of a ship en route from Hawaii to the United States or the Panama Canal, the cruise of the *Houston* offered the same problem on a reverse course at a sufficient distance to demonstrate the ability of the rigid airship for this use. No advance publicity in any quarter was given to the operation, as it was realized that very strong head winds would be encountered during the return flight, and the commanding officer wished to be free to turn back, without any feeling of embarrassment, at any time that conditions indicated such action prudent. The reason for making the decision was therefore the presentation of a typical scouting problem, an opportunity to practice scouting with airplanes attached to the ship, and a demonstration of the ability to obtain information of a surface force a long distance at sea within twenty-four hours. The decision to make the flight was made about 16 July. . . . The Commanding Officer believes that such exercises are of inestimable value in developing the efficiency of the airship and demonstrating its worth for naval scouting.[42]

Admiral Standley received a letter from J. M. Reeves, commander in chief, U.S. Fleet, who replied that he found the actions of the *Macon* to be the result of "misapplied initiative on the part of the Commanding Officer." Reeves emphasized the absence of proper authority and the resulting embarrassment to all officers in the chain of command: "It comprised a breach of fundamental Naval indoctrination." Further, the flight had been "conducted over a large area of the Pacific Ocean in which at present there are few surface naval vessels" that would have been able to assist the *Macon* in case of an emergency. Admiral Reeves "consider[ed] the flight was ill-timed, ill-advised, and conceived with disregard for proper naval procedure." Reeves felt his written objections would be sufficient to "prevent further misapplied initiative on the part of the *Macon*" and recommended no further action be taken.[43] This communication, which fell short of a formal reprimand, ended the matter.

Reporters continued to follow the president and a headline for Thursday, August 2, 1934, read, "Roosevelt Returns Today from Vacation. Presidential Party Due to Reach Astoria This Evening: Leaves Friday."[44] The story shared the front page with another that announced, "Adolf Hitler, former Austrian housepainter, became sole dictator of the German people today on the death of President Paul von Hindenburg."[45]

Between ten and fourteen days after the *Macon* dropped the bags containing the letters for mailing from the *Houston*, they began to get delivered by the U.S. mail service. Miller would recall the mail clerk on the *Houston* had been very creative, painting figures of the airship in aluminum paint on the front of each letter. Before mailing, the letters were signed by President Roosevelt. When the letters addressed to them arrived, Miller and Wiley each signed the fronts, making them valuable collectibles.[46]

Other than the written communications among Wiley, the CNO, and CinC, which remained on file, there were no lasting consequences for Wiley's having intercepted the president's ship at sea. He returned to the business of developing the airship and experimenting with a number of new devices. One was a low-frequency radio direction-finding device that allowed the airship's planes to roam farther away from the ship and return safely, using the radio as a homing device. Also, as Miller had suggested, the planes' landing gear was removed and a belly tank containing extra fuel was installed. The Army was having some success with a "spy basket" trailed from a dirigible, and the *Macon* tried to follow suit. The idea, pioneered in the world war by the Germans, was to trail the basket with a single man on board below and behind the airship. It could be lowered through clouds from an airship hidden in the clouds above; the observer could report where they were and direct bombing. The spy, or observation, basket itself was a small airplane fuselage with no wings. "It had an empennage [tail rudder and stabilizers], and you could use a half an inch of rudder and that's all. It had kind of a tripod wire connection to the fuselage. We couldn't make a one-wire telephone system work. We wanted a telephone from the observer to the ship. They never could make it work, so we put in a little key radio set."[47]

Lt. Cdr. Jesse Kenworthy Jr., the executive officer, made the first descent in the observation basket on August 8, 1934.[48] At 1712 the basket was streamed out from the airship, attached to a one-thousand-foot reel of quarter-inch cable.[49] Early experiments with the basket were hazardous, because of oscillation, but with practice this issue was resolved. Miller described his own experience in the observation basket:

> So I went down in this thing, and let me tell you, it was really weird. As you lowered away, of course, it would begin to trail the ship and develop a kind of catenary [i.e., the cable hung in a curve, under its own weight] back there. You'd be a quarter of a mile behind the ship and a quarter of a mile below the ship with no sound at all. Absolutely no sound. It was just quiet and you were sitting there—just you and nobody else. But you had a parachute. What the hell you'd do with a parachute, I don't know. They'd never know if you were below a cloud and they lost you. At any rate, that experiment didn't last very long either, but it was sort of interesting to try.[50]

The observation basket was never put to practical use. There was no need, because of the developments with the airplane. Wiley also experimented with a way to rescue a downed pilot in the water. A circular, insulated life raft was rigged with webbing inside the safety belt. The idea was to lower it onto the water with the airship's four-thousand-foot cable and then, after the downed pilot climbed onto the raft, hoist it back on board. Wiley rehearsed the maneuver in San Francisco Bay, moving it to any position he desired. Fortunately, this new technology too was never needed.[51]

These were peripheral activities. It was of much more importance that Wiley kept the *Macon* and her airplanes actively rehearsing and perfecting her main tactical mission of scouting. Officially, Admiral King had to take notice of the breach of naval protocol in Wiley's "stunt." Notwithstanding, it did not escape his attention that aside from its having been done without permission, that the airship and her planes having located the *Houston* in the Pacific was proof that Wiley had developed a method for intercepting enemy fleets. Privately the admiral recognized the airship's finding the president's cruiser as representing a successful scouting demonstration. King realized also that Wiley was doing exactly what King himself had charged him with—pushing the airship to show what it could do tactically for the surface fleet.

Wiley kept the *Macon* flying as much as possible, along the West Coast and out over the open Pacific, at times spotting and tracking commercial ships for practice. While on a training flight on September 27, the *Macon* received an order from the commandant of the Twelfth Naval District to scout west of her location for a missing private yacht.[52] The thirty-four-foot-long *Naitamba* had left Los Angeles on July 4 as a participant in a Los Angeles–to–Honolulu yacht race. On July 20, only twelve of the fourteen participating yachts had arrived.[53] Early reports that the slower *Naitamba* and *Altair* had been spotted fifty miles from Honolulu proved erroneous, and a search by Coast Guard cutters and airplanes was under way. While the *Altair* was simply slower than the others, the *Naitamba* was considered missing. On board the missing yacht were two crew members and a fourteen-year-old screen actor named Billy Butts.[54] Wiley searched for the yacht using both his lookouts and his airplanes. They never sighted the yacht, however, and landed back at Sunnyvale the next day.[55] (The *Naitamba* sailed into the west basin of Los Angeles harbor the next day with all on board her safe. The yacht's owner explained they had become "becalmed" nine days north of San Francisco outside of steamer lanes.)[56] What was noteworthy about this episode was not the *Macon*'s failure to locate the yacht but the district commandant's recognition of the airship's usefulness for scouting.

The airship and her tiny planes became, collectively, a well-oiled machine and very good at scouting. Admiral King invited Commander Rosendahl and Anton Heinen to visit Sunnyvale to observe these advances. They were on board for one of the training exercises, to locate and track the luxury liner SS *Lurline* and the cargo-carrying transport ship SS *Manini*. They were very favorably impressed. On separate occasions, demonstrating a mixture of curiosity and courage, both Rosendahl and Heinen took rides in the observation basket.[57]

An opportunity to operate with a surface fleet came in November 1934, in the form of Fleet Exercise Z. A force was to sail up the Mexican coast from Panama while an opposing force, Orange, was to intercept it. In anticipation of the exercise, the *Macon* had been moored to the expeditionary mast at Camp Kearney, California. She unmoored from the mast at 1708 on November 7 and lifted off. Once airborne, she took her airplanes on board and cruised over the Pacific, arriving at 0335 the next morning at the initiation point assigned her for the fleet exercise. At 0445 the airship sighted the main body of the Orange force and launched two of her airplanes. Their search began at 0600, and at 0905 they sighted the

Saratoga in the vicinity of Guadalupe Island making thirty knots. She was operating alone but, having all her aircraft, would need no help bringing down the *Macon*. Wiley wanted to fly due west to escape, but he could not do this until he retrieved his airplanes. He flew to the west side of Guadalupe, hoping to land his planes concealed by the island's mountains. Once the planes were on board, he could run full speed out of the range of the aircraft carrier.[58]

Unfortunately, the *Saratoga* had spotted the *Macon*. She launched planes and, at 0944 the *Macon* came under attack by five of them.[59] Within minutes the *Macon's* planes were on board and housed. She then withdrew to the west and at 1055 launched the first of two planes that would track the *Saratoga* for the duration of the exercise. It ended at 1610, and by the evening of the ninth the airship was safely at Sunnyvale.[60] ComAirBatFor, Adm. Henry V. Butler, complimented the *Macon* and her planes for an excellent job of scouting for and tracking the aircraft carrier. All of the airship's developments and rigorous training had paid off in a smoothly run operation.

Things were going very well for the *Macon*, but Wiley decided they could be better. He had learned something from the recent fleet exercises that could benefit the *Macon* in battle conditions. Attacking fighter pilots had approached the huge airship as if under the impression that she was a "sitting duck" lacking maneuverability. The *Macon* had surprised them with some sharp turns to avoid their simulated dive-bombing. Wiley wanted to develop this tactic further. On November 21, while flying over the U.S. Battle Force, Wiley launched two of his fighter planes to simulate dive-bombing against the *Macon* while the gunners practiced their skills using camera guns and the airship herself practiced evasive action. The exercise was highly successful as the officers and crew dealt with repeated simulated attacks.[61]

The *Macon* was ready for her next test. She joined the December 1934 fleet exercises, again to locate the enemy and scout for the surface fleet. For the first time, she carried four airplanes. The exercise started at 0600 on December 6 and approximately an hour later the airship launched her four planes. At 0906 cruising in clear skies at 1,200 feet, the *Macon* sighted the "enemy" battleship abaft the port beam, twenty miles away.[62] Pilots Kivette and Lt. (jg) L. C. Simpler reported a heavy escort. The *Macon* and her small planes conducted their well-rehearsed scouting maneuvers but, at 1145 lookouts on the airship sighted an "enemy" destroyer off the port bow. Wiley changed course immediately to avoid contact but continued to scout. Around noon, in partly cloudy skies and "bumpy" air, they sighted an "enemy" battleship on the port bow, followed minutes later by a light cruiser with destroyers off the starboard beam at thirty miles. Within a half hour, things turned bad for the *Macon*; she came under attack by six "enemy" dive-bombers from the *Lexington*. Skillfully, they had maneuvered to attack out of the sun. The *Macon* was "shot down," but she continued to participate in the exercises, only to be "shot down" a second time an hour later.[63]

On the second day of exercises, the *Macon* was back in the hunt for the "enemy" fleet. At 1037 she sighted two "enemy" battleships off her starboard bow, twenty miles away, but could not locate the aircraft carriers.[64] At 1325 the fleet exercises were suspended suddenly; all ships were directed to search for two sea-planes from the cruiser *Cincinnati* that had run out of fuel and gone down.[65] In quick order, Wiley had the *Macon* in the search and at 1542 her planes reported that they had located the downed planes and dropped a smoke candle to mark the location. The airship remained on station until the *Portland* arrived, followed shortly by the *Chicago* and *Indianapolis*.[66] Seaplanes and pilots were retrieved safely. The *Macon* and her planes received a commendation from ComBatFor for the manner in which they had located the *Cincinnati*'s seaplanes.

Overall, however, in the final analysis of the fleet exercises, Admiral Reeves deemed the *Macon*'s performance a failure. He concluded the airship could not perform in the vicinity of the fleet where enemy planes could shoot her out of the sky. There was still disagreement over the potential of airships. Admiral King continued to be a strong supporter but felt the airship should be used solely for very long-range reconnaissance. Admiral Standley, Chief of Naval Operations, disagreed. He believed the airship could be used in closer proximity to battle, and he planned to use the airship in bombing experiments.[67]

The officers and crew of the *Macon* were unaware of the high-level discussions surrounding the future of airships. They knew they had shown themselves well and sensed the progress they were making under Wiley's leadership. Nearing the end of 1934, many felt things were going well for the Navy in general, and for aviation, as new boundaries in flight were being established. From December 22 to 27, Amelia Earhart traveled from Los Angeles to Honolulu on board the *Lurline* with her Lockheed Vega airplane secured to the deck. She was preparing for her record-breaking solo flight from Honolulu to Oakland, scheduled for January 1935. Headlines for December 29 announced, "American Fleet Plans Greatest Pacific Maneuvers." The press reported that the U.S. Fleet would participate in a historical event in the spring of 1935; its exercises would encompass the entire "North Pacific Island." Admiral Reeves had announced that practically every craft in the Navy would sail for several months across stretches of Pacific Ocean from the Tropic of Cancer to the Aleutian Islands, from the California coast to Midway Island, 1,200 miles west of Honolulu—an area of over 5 million square miles. A fleet of 177 ships, 577 airplanes, the *Macon*, and 55,000 officers and men would participate.[68]

That front-page article appeared below another, with a bolder headline: "Japan Abrogates Naval Treaty." The Japanese ambassador, Hiroshi Saito, had filed Japan's notice of abrogation of existing naval treaties and suggested new negotiations between the United States and Japan regarding mutual limits on naval strength. Japan was proposing a radical reduction in naval armaments capable of aggression. Specifically, they sought a total abolition of capital ships and aircraft carriers. Saito explained, "On both material and moral grounds we earnestly desire a substantial reduction that will free the nations of anxiety regarding the possibilities of war. We want the others to be free of any anxiety regarding us, and we want to be free of any regarding them." Saito delivered his message to Secretary of State Cordell Hull as a legal formality required by the terms of the Washington Treaty. The effective date for termination of the treaty was set at December 31, 1936.

The State Department was not surprised.[69] Breaking the treaty threatened fourteen years of seemingly successful efforts to establish a balance of naval strength among the major powers in the Pacific. Japan's abrogation of the treaty did not end negotiations, but it reset the diplomatic chessboard. Newspapers, of course, lay out their own front pages and stories, but the juxtaposition of the articles on the Japanese treaty abrogation and an upcoming demonstration of the might of the American fleet in the Pacific could be interpreted as a tacit threat to the Japanese, as if to remind them of what they were facing already. If that was the case, however, it did not force the hand of the Japanese at the bargaining table.

Not every task assigned the *Macon* was as monumental as scouting an "enemy" fleet. Her first assignment of the year was a "visibility test." There was concern that the huge dirigible would be seen at a distance more easily than craft on the surface or others in the air. The test was a simple one. The *Macon* rendezvoused with the *Lexington*, anchored in San Pedro Harbor, and made a series of runs on different courses and distances to determine how easily she could be seen from the carrier.[70] The results were not surprising. The visibility of the airship was related to the "sun gauge," and the ship was no more conspicuous than any other vessel.[71]

January brought a number of advances that enhanced the *Macon*'s performance. Her airplanes could now get accurate radio bearings on the airship from distances up to 185 miles, almost at the limits of their operating radius. Communications with keyed radio could be achieved easily at 140 miles, and voice transmissions were clear up to 95 miles. Wiley had his pilots practicing night hook-on landings, and he and Miller formulated a plan for the *Macon*'s fighter planes to dive-bomb the *Lexington* in a surprise nighttime attack. The pilots had no difficulty with the night landings (though the *Macon* was to run out of time before she could demonstrate this new tactic).

On February 1 she conducted a maneuver that had not been done previously by an American airship. The *Macon* had an auxiliary control station in the leading edge of the lower fin and, for the first time, Wiley shifted complete control of the ship to that position. The trial was a success and he anticipated using the idea more in the future.[72] The *Macon* was building steadily on her successes and acquiring technologies and tactics she hoped to showcase during fleet exercises in February 1935. All along, when the flight schedule allowed, workers were reinforcing girders at various frames. However, as of early February, no work had been done on the upper parts of frame 17.5 at the attachment of the upper fin.[73] Issues surrounding that frame would not disappear.

As the fleet exercises scheduled for the week of February 11 through 17 approached, Wiley had a family tragedy. On the morning of February 6, he received word that his seventy-nine-year-old father had died in Fay Oren's home in Trenton, Missouri. The Chillicothe newspaper reported that Joseph [Joel] Wiley had died of a heart attack following a lengthy period of failing health. The paper stated that Herbert Wiley was to arrive the following day for the funeral.[74] Wiley had planned to fly through Kansas City en route to Trenton, but foul weather prevented his making the flights, and consequently, Fay was left to plan the funeral. Wiley's father was interred at Wheeling Cemetery on Friday, February 8, 1935. In Wiley's absence, the Trenton American Legion post stepped up to help the family in its time of need. Wiley could not find time to thank the legion until the end of February, but when he did it was in his characteristically gracious manner. He wrote the commander of the American Legion post that his organization had performed a service for the family that could never be repaid; that they had been a friend in his time of need.[75] Had the weather allowed Wiley to make it home for the funeral, he would have had little time for grieving and consoling his family before returning to Sunnyvale for the fleet exercises.

The February 1935 exercises promised to be the *Macon*'s most important. On previous occasions, the *Akron* and the *Macon* had been inserted into such exercises unprepared or into tactical scenarios that were less than optimal for an airship. This time would be different. The *Macon* would carry four fighters rehearsed in long-range reconnaissance. The airship and her planes had homing devices to ensure safe return to the dirigible, and they were equipped with effective radios. Most important, however, was the design of the exercise. This time the airship was not to engage in the combat phase and thus was not at risk of being shot down. The *Macon* had been informed the fleet would depart the San Pedro–San Diego area on February 11 and arrive at San Francisco on the 13th. The *Macon* was ordered to stand off, out of detection range and in radio silence, using her airplanes and other assets to scout the fleet. She was to report her findings at the end of the exercise.[76] Specifically, the *Macon* was instructed to locate all of the fleet vessels, identify them, and track their movements. This was finally a mission suited to the airship—long-range reconnaissance away from "enemy" firepower— although the requirement for radio silence did remove one of her assets.

13

The End
of an Era

The giant airship spent the night in her hangar at Sunnyvale, moored to the mobile mast and stern beam with her bow to the north. Halfway through the 0400–0800 watch on Monday, February 11, 1935, the base began to spring to life in preparation for what would be the last flight of the USS *Macon*. Rolled out by the master-at-arms, the crew donned flying clothes and stepped outside into chilly morning air.[1] All eight of the ship's engines were running, warming up in preparation for flight. General assembly occurred at 0600, and the crew embarked.[2] The officer of the deck, Lieutenant Campbell, turned to a waiting Wiley and announced in an easy voice, "All departments ready for flight, Captain." Without a word, Wiley nodded to the mooring officer, who blew his whistle to alert the ground crew of two hundred men. Then, through a megaphone, the mooring officer called, "Walk the ship out!"[3] The sky was partly cloudy with a gentle wind. The ship was swung into the wind and the mechanical handling gear was disconnected as the crew prepared to ballast for takeoff. Wiley gave the commands, "Get ready aft! Get ready forward!" to which came the responses, "Heavy aft!" and "Two thousand pounds heavy forward!" Thousands of pounds of water ballast were then released from the bow and stern, after which followed the reports "Two thousand pounds light forward, sir!" and "Two thousand light aft, sir." The airship was now buoyant and ready for flight.

From his position in the control car, Wiley made a final visual inspection to be certain every man was at his proper position. The rudderman was forward at the wheel, the engineering officer was at the engine-room telegraphs, and the elevatorman was on the port side, the wheel firmly in his hand and the first lieutenant beside him. Campbell, as officer of the deck, was already focused on his log and the radioman was at his telephone. Seeing that all was proper, Wiley issued the order, "Up ship!" With this, the ground crew started releasing the airship from her restraints, and a familiar metallic click was heard as the nose of the ship jerked free from the mooring cup. The airship was unmoored at 0710 and rose slowly to a cruising altitude of two thousand feet as she headed out to sea by way of San Jose.[4]

The *Macon*'s first task was to recover and stow her four airplanes, piloted by Lieutenant Miller, Lieutenants (junior grade) Simpler and Kivette, and Lt. (jg) G. L. Huff. It was raining. The small planes approached strung out in single file, each waiting its turn to hook on. The rain was striking the pilots' exposed faces at 180 miles an hour, producing quite a sting, and they were eager to get on board.[5] The members of the airplane-handling crew were standing on a six-inch girder above the trapeze, a ferocious wind lashing their pants legs. The crew members were veterans and walked the girder confidently, but a single slip would result in a two-thousand-foot fall. As on many previous occasions, all went smoothly this morning. As each plane made its successful hook-on, the winch operator hoisted it into the hangar. In preparation for scouting, the landing gear was removed from each plane and the auxiliary fuel tanks attached. Wiley began his scouting routine at 1023; first he had Huff's plane launched, followed six minutes later by Miller's. With that, the *Macon* joined the fleet exercise.

From the time the *Macon* had crossed the coastline, she encountered areas of overcast skies, fog, and intermittent rains with thirty-knot winds. At 1835 three unidentified ships were sighted in column off the starboard bow. At 2015 the *Macon*'s lookouts located other unidentified ships off the port beam, five miles distant, and at 2025 they saw two columns of ships to starboard at five miles; as before, they could not identify them. At 2147, ten miles south of Santa Catalina Island, they were able, with help from moonlight, to sight a submarine on the surface. From the early hours of Tuesday, February 12, the airship ran darkened—running lights extinguished—in clear skies and good visibility but turbulent air. The lookouts, vigilantly watching for surface vessels, at 0415 spotted an unidentified cruiser on a westward heading and then, at 0805, two Coast Guard destroyers. The *Macon* continued her well-established, methodical procedure of launching and recovering her landplanes to search as wide an area as possible. At midmorning on the twelfth the lookouts spotted a *Dobbin*-class destroyer tender; just after noon there followed a submarine tender and a submarine on the surface, both off the port bow.

The *Macon* seemed to be doing a very good job of spotting surface vessels while remaining undetected by the "enemy." Finally, at 1430, the commander in chief of the U.S. Fleet released the *Macon* to return to base at Wiley's discretion.[6] The exercises were over, but the airship's lookouts continued to sight ships on the surface. Wiley wanted to return to base by entering the Santa Clara Valley, in which Sunnyvale lies, at Watsonville, twenty miles south, if visibility permitted.[7] To get there before the weather closed in, Wiley had the *Macon* cruising at 2,700 feet and running at standard speed—sixty-three knots.

A squall line was directly in the *Macon*'s path. Emerging out of the gathering mist, Miller's small plane made its way back to the airship and landed. Miller's reconnaissance run had carried him over the fleet, fifty miles north of the airship. Campbell encountered Miller hurrying into the smoking room for a quick post-flight cigarette. When Campbell commented on the foul weather Miller had flown through, Miller replied, "If you think this is bad, you should see what those poor battlewagon sailors are taking down below! I saw 'em all. The entire fleet is ahead. And are those ships taking a pounding!" Campbell asked what the weather looked like ahead for the *Macon*; Miller told him that the squall looked tougher than it was—he did not think it would give the airship any trouble. The two men finished their cigarettes and returned to their posts at 1555.[8]

Campbell relieved the watch as officer of the deck at 1605.[9] He dropped to an altitude of 1,600 feet, only to find considerable turbulence under the squall. Within the hour the lookouts sighted a freighter, an oil tanker, and seven cruisers. Fog banks were rolling in from the west and northwest, obliterating the coastline from view: only the tallest mountain peaks could be seen. Because the visibility ahead was closing down, Campbell summoned Wiley, and at about 1615 they encountered another rainsquall. The ship took a severe vertical rise. The elevatorman regained control quickly, but the winds got more turbulent as the squall moved in. The elevatorman reported that things were getting rough. Rains hammered the ship and added tons of water weight to her acres of fabric. A sudden blast of wind caused an elevatorman to call out for help with his wheel. The force of the gale on the elevators was so strong it took two men to control. They were out of the squall within a matter of minutes and continued on their course along the coast.

Within short order, they sighted the surface fleet en route to San Francisco, and while the *Macon* was now cruising in relatively smooth air, the surface fleet was, as Miller had told Campbell, taking a beating. From the *Macon*, the 35,000-ton battleships appeared to be bobbing like corks, waves crashing over their bows. The men on the airship could not resist comparing their lot to that of the men below. With a laugh, the *Macon*'s navigator commented, "Those lads will be taking it all night, while we'll be home in bed." A keel officer (watch officer in charge of the ship's hull and structure) made fun of how slowly the ships were moving: "Twelve knots—and we must be making seventy." The rudderman chimed in, "That'd drive me nuts. . . . Imagine goin' any place at the dizzy speed of twelve knots."[10] At 1705 the Point Sur Light was abeam to starboard, about two and a half miles away.[11] The navigator pointed out the light to Wiley, and all on board began to feel that they would be home soon, dry and in bed.

At 1705 a small rainsquall was seen on the starboard side of the airship, and Wiley gave the order for left rudder. The ceiling began to lower, and a light rain fell, but the air was smooth. Suddenly, the ship took a strong gust of wind from the side that caused papers to go flying in the control car. The nose of the airship dipped at a steep angle and heeled to starboard, heading for the ocean; sounds of the ship breaking up were heard from stern to bow. Campbell reacted quickly, reaching for the engine-room telegraphs to bring all engines to idle. Wiley wondered if the vibration was connected in some way to the elevator control wheel or cables, and he asked the elevatorman, Aviation Metalsmith Conover, if the elevator controls were broken. When Conover replied that the elevator wheel had slipped out of his hand, Wiley instructed him to move the wheel to determine if he had control; he replied that he did. The ship began to swing to starboard and the rudderman, who had started to obey Wiley's order for left rudder, eased the rudder. Wiley again ordered him to put the rudder left.

The ship responded immediately by assuming a bow-up attitude and beginning to ascend rapidly. Within moments, Wiley received a telephone report that the No. 1 gas cell was gone; he knew immediately that this was the explanation for the heaviness in the tail of the ship and the rise by the bow. He compensated for it by ordering all ballast to be dropped aft of amidships. He then ordered the engines slowed, because the airship's speed was generating dynamic lift that contributed to the upward inclination of the bow. Slowing the engines also took strain off the end of the ship, where, Wiley surmised, damage must have occurred.[12] Flying the airship was quickly becoming a struggle, and one that required all the knowledge and experience Wiley had. "I had the problem of preventing rising too high by slowing the engines and trying to regain the trim by keeping the engines going so as to get good effect on the elevators. I tried to adjust between these two conditions, that is, have enough air speed to control the ship and to try to get back on an even keel and to have not too much speed so that the ship would not rise to too great a height."[13]

Though the ballast aft was being dropped, the ship's angle of inclination increased suddenly. Chief Boatswain's Mate "Shaky" Davis called Wiley by phone to report that the top fin had carried away, along with the structure on which he had been standing;[14] Wiley received word the upper rudder controls were gone, but he believed he still had control of the lower one. Also, No. 2 gas cell had deflated. Wiley then ordered all fuel slip tanks aft of amidships to be dropped; each of the slip tanks weighed 720 pounds. The *Macon* rose to over 4,600 feet; Wiley received the report that all slip tanks and all ballast aft of amidships had been dropped.

Wiley then gave a series of orders designed to drop everything that had appreciable weight. He ordered the lower gas cells in the after part of the ship be cut away and cast overboard, the stern ballast bags be cut away, and the four fighter landplanes be prepared for dropping out of the ship. As the ship dropped, Wiley found it could not be steered by the rudder, so he decided to use the ship's engines to guide her. Wiley now had trouble reengaging them. The airship was inclined at an angle of approximately twenty-five degrees, and at that angle the engines could not get cooling water to cool them; consequently, they would run for only a few minutes at a time. When the angle decreased to about ten degrees, the engines could be cut in again, and the *Macon* rose quickly into the clouds, where they lost sight of the surface of the water. He believed the time of the ship's damage was about 1710 and that all of this had happened within four minutes.

The ship was drifting toward shore as she was tossed about by the wind. There were high mountains inland, and Wiley decided that to avoid crashing into them he would land the ship on the water near the cruisers. Wiley now sent out an "SOS" and a radio message to the commander in chief that the *Macon* was in distress ten miles southwest of Point Sur.[15] Throughout the ship, however, everyone was calm. Orders were given in controlled voices and repeated back in a similar manner—there was no panic. Wiley ordered the engines ahead on the port side and those on the starboard side idled; this maneuver got the *Macon* headed back out to sea. Reports continued to pour into the control car making it apparent that discipline throughout the ship was what it should be but that she was again drop-ping steadily.[16] At one point, the rate of descent reached about six hundred feet per minute.

After the angle of the ship was reduced a second time and the altitude had dropped to about 3,000 feet, Wiley realized it was going to be impossible the get the *Macon* on an even keel and in hand before she struck the water. He sent word to the engine rooms that they were about to receive a backing signal: they were to throw their engines in reverse and abandon their stations. Word was passed to stand by to land on the water. The water became visible at about 2,000 feet;[17] at that altitude they stopped valving off helium to try to check the fall.[18] The eleva-torman, Conover, was still at his duty station, holding tightly to the wheel with an eye on the altimeter. He had not quit his job—as long as the ship was still in the air he would remain at his wheel. At 1,500 feet it was evident that control of the ship was lost completely.

To make as soft a landing on the water as possible, Wiley ordered, "Ballast forward . . . check her fall." The order was given in the same calm voice he would have used landing back at Sunnyvale. The report came back that all ballast from frame 170 had been dropped, and the ship's descent slowed. When the *Macon* reached a thousand feet, Campbell was still ballasting as Boatswain's Mate First Class Leonard E. Schellberg entered the control car distributing life jackets. Because Campbell still needed one hand to pull the ballast toggles, Schellberg helped him get his on, one arm at a time. At eight hundred feet Wiley gave the order, "All hands stand by to abandon ship." Campbell later recalled how Wiley must have felt at that moment: "The skipper's words do not betray the feelings I know are boiling within him. The feelings of a commanding officer face-to-face with the hardest decision a captain ever has to make. His ship, his men. When must he give up trying to save her, to try to save them?"[19]

With the order to stand by to abandon ship came also the order for everyone to leave the control car. At about 500 feet, Wiley noticed the dutiful Conover still at his post, hands on the wheel. Wiley told Conover to abandon his post, get into a window, and prepare to jump just before the ship hit the water. Lt. Cdr. Jesse L. Kenworthy, the executive officer, threw flares overboard to mark the ship's location and then, as the ship got closer to the water, he passed the flares out to individual men to be used once they were in the lifeboats. Wiley leaned out the window of the control car watching the tail section. With skilled timing, Wiley gave the order to "back all engines." When the airspeed gauge registered less than ten knots, Wiley ordered, "Stop all engines." "It [was]," Campbell recalled, "the captain's last command to his beloved ship." Wiley then announced, "The tail is in the water." The impact had been felt as a jar from aft as the giant airship settled gently onto the surface. Wiley had felt it while the control car was still about 250 feet in the air.[20] The softness of the landing had been a result of the training, experience, and discipline of the officers and crew under the excellent leadership of Captain Wiley.

Finally, all the men could be released from their duty stations. Wiley ordered, "All hands pick a window and jump before she hits forward."[21] The men went into the cold water. Wiley started to perch on the window sill of the forward port window of the control car when he noticed the ship was swerving slightly to port, so he went to the other side of the car and climbed out that window. He encountered Kenworthy on the handrail just outside; they both jumped just as the control car hit the water. Wiley came to the surface quickly and swam to one of the rubber life rafts that had been thrown into the water. The first men into the rafts helped others get on board while Wiley helped assemble the rafts; everyone worked at equalizing the loads as more men reached the rafts, transferring men from one to another. At one time, Wiley had five of the rubber boats tied together for strength and mutual support, but from time to time one boat would go free to help another man in the water.

When Campbell, who had followed Wiley, hit the water, he saw the ship coming down on him and was struck by something heavy. As he reached the surface he saw two life rafts on the crest of a wave. It seemed far away. When he tried to swim toward them he found his right arm was the only limb that worked; his legs were dead. He heard Wiley call out to ask if he was all right. By then Campbell had grabbed one of the life rafts; Wiley told Campbell to take it easy—he, Wiley, would come to him. Wiley swam over, grabbed him by the nape of the neck, told him to stay on his back, and towed him to a life raft. After a short time, Campbell could feel some life coming back to his legs. Wiley and Campbell were both now too weak to climb on the raft, and the men already on board pulled them in. As other men swam to the raft, they helped each other get on board. They were all blue with cold, shivering, and many were vomiting the seawater they had ingested. Men took turns rubbing each other down to get warmth and circulation back. Wiley's raft was designed to hold seven men, but it had twelve on board, and water was pouring in over the gunwales. Campbell was the only man in the raft still wearing shoes, and they came in handy for bailing water.

They were bailing and watching the *Macon* being crushed by the waves when they spotted Coxswain Hammond swimming alone. They hailed him and pulled him on board their increasingly crowded raft. Lucky to be in the raft, Hammond had nearly lost his life on a separate quest. He was at his post in the lower fin when the ship struck the water aft. Water was closing around him as he abandoned his station. As he was leaving the airship, he remembered the ship's flag: it was being carried under with the wreckage. "Coxswains are made of stout fiber, and Hammond was not an exception. With powerful strokes he had swum under the horizontal fin. It was a hundred feet long and forty feet wide."[22] He was buffeted against the sharp edges of broken girders; he heard girders snapping and wires pinging as they let go. The fin finally gave way and fell on top of him, forcing him to abandon his attempt to rescue the flag and swim to safety.

Hammond was not the only man driven to unusual acts at risk of personal safety. Two engineers leaving their engine room were seen closing the doors behind them as if they were securing at the end of a normal workday. The cool-headed engineers climbed onto the strut that held the propeller shaft, paused for a moment, and faced each other. "S'long Pat," said one. "You been a real shipmate," to which came the reply, "Well, we didn't miss no bells, Jake"—that is, fail to respond to any engine orders. They jumped into the ice-cold water to join the many others who had gone in ahead of them.

Lieutenant Miller was with a group who had not jumped. They noticed the airship had landed softly and was floating; they decided to stay on board to wait for the fleet to arrive to rescue them. It was late in the afternoon of a short February day, and it began to rain and get colder. Miller's group saw the life rafts about half a mile from the airship, huddling in a group. They themselves were still high and dry inside the airship and thought they had made a better decision than the men in the tiny rafts. It did not take long for that feeling to disappear. Instead of remaining horizontal on the water, the ship suddenly began to rise to a vertical position. As a result, the men were soon four hundred feet above the water, not just fifty. "We were sitting there on top of a cone in this beautiful airship, the lower part of it being in the water. That didn't look as good as it did a few moments ago. By this time, those of us in the ship had gathered in the bow and were all up there around the nose cone."[23]

From the top of the ship, the men in the water below and those in rafts appeared very small. Jumping from that height would have been fatal. The men could hear gas cells bursting, and the helium gas naturally rose to collect inside the cone, where they were. Miller knew it was time to get outside the ship, and he ordered the men to break out all the lines they could locate and get outside the ship. There everyone hung onto a line. "Of course, the ship was so big that it was still practically like a haystack up there. It wasn't sharp, and you weren't in danger of slipping off or anything." It was cold, of course, raining, and getting darker. From time to time the men would hear a blast and know that another gas cell had carried away, along with another structural ring and the ship slipped deeper into the water. Most of the men were wearing life jackets, and when the airship had shrunk to about the size of a two-story building, Miller ordered the men off and into the water before the whole ship went down. They released their ropes and slid over the "haystack" into the water. As they were entering the water they saw searchlights in the distance and knew that their cruisers were looking for them. At length, all the men of the *Macon* were off the ship but one. A lone straggler did not want to get into the bitterly cold water—he wanted to stay with the airship—but the men in the water shouted and screamed at him until finally he let go and joined them. The men in the water started swimming for the rafts to await rescue by the cruisers.

During the crash, gasoline had spilled onto the water, and now the navigation flares started to ignite it. Gasoline burned on the surface but also exploded inside the envelope that had been the *Macon*. Miller witnessed the explosion inside the ship: "On the outside was the red, white, and blue Navy star and inside was a flame. The silhouette of the star was the most beautiful sight I had ever seen, if you're looking for beauty. She finally just sort of, like an old dog, lay down. Away she went and disappeared. It was quite fortunate that we got off of there before this happened."[24] Many of the men found their way into one or another of the rafts, but everyone at least had something on which to hold. It was a toss-up as to whether it was colder in a raft or in the water. Not everyone, however, even got wet. Boatswain Buckley had dropped a rope from a forward cargo hatch directly under which a raft bobbed on the surface. He sent nine men down the rope, which they entered without getting their feet wet. Wiley estimated it took about thirty to forty minutes for the *Macon* to sink completely out of sight. After she sank, Wiley tried to maintain contact with all the rafts and to herd them together, but several things made this a very difficult task. The ocean was not particularly choppy, but the swells were running high. Because the boats were overloaded, water shipped over the gunwales quite readily, increasing their weight, distorting their shape, and making it almost impossible to row them with their small paddles.

The men could see the cruisers approaching and scanning the water with their searchlights, but Wiley felt it was taking an inordinately long time for them to arrive. Some of the men tied neckerchiefs around their paddles and waved them in the air to help the cruisers locate them.[25] Finally, a motor launch from the cruiser USS *Richmond* (CL 9) arrived and began to transfer the men out of their life rafts for transport back to their ship. Wiley immediately began to control traffic, directing the launch to areas on the water where he knew men were waiting. He had kept track of two of the life rafts that had drifted far from the main group and told the coxswain in the launch to go after them before they were out of sight of the searchlights. Another launch from the *Richmond* came close to Wiley's group, but because it was already heavily loaded with men, Wiley directed it back to the ship. Wiley's raft was then located by a launch from the USS *Concord* (CL 10), which transported the men back to the cruiser. When he got on board, he asked Adm. Train to search with as many boats as possible an area within two miles of where they were and to keep the searchlights working. Miller's group, in the meantime, had been picked up by a motor launch from the *Richmond.* Shaking uncontrollably and teeth chattering, the men were taken to the cruiser's sickbay, examined, and turned in with blankets. It did not take long to get warm again, and everyone was in San Francisco by morning.

⁓

Amazingly, only two members of the crew of eighty-three officers and men were lost in the crash—Radioman First Class Ernest Edwin Dailey and Mess Attendant Florentine Edquiba were missing. Dailey had followed Coxswain William H. Clarke up frame 170 on the port side, to be clear of the ship's curvature and not trapped as she settled. Clarke had reached longitudinal No. 9, kicked a hole in the outer cover, and torn a good deal of it away to make an avenue of escape. A third man, Hooper, had joined them, and the three stood side by side assessing the situation. Clarke told Dailey he felt it was too far to the water to jump. He estimated they were standing about 175 feet above the surface but that if they waited another five or ten minutes, they would be close enough to the water to jump. Dailey did not heed the advice but jumped, without warning, feet first. He was seen to turn over in the air slowly several times before landing on his back. He disappeared immediately, never to be seen again.[26] Edquiba had last been seen still inside the airship; no one had seen him in the water. Wiley surmised he had remained in the airship and had been suffocated by the gas collecting inside it.

His assessment was supported by the account of Coxswain W. A. McDonald, who was probably the last person to see Edquiba alive. The two men were together at the time of the crash. McDonald estimated they were about a hundred feet off the water when Edquiba was seen last. McDonald made his escape, as helium gas was escaping rapidly. Edquiba climbed toward the nose of the ship and, McDonald believed had been overcome.[27]

Multiple factors were responsible for the low loss of life. Wiley continued to exert leadership throughout the experience, making decisions and giving orders in a controlled manner. His ability to steer the *Macon* away from the mountains and out to sea and then to set her down softly even though the ship was not properly controllable speaks to his experience and skill as an airship officer. Failure to accomplish either of these tasks would have resulted in a much greater loss of life. For their part, his highly trained, professional crew conducted themselves in an orderly fashion, without panic. The proximity of the cruisers and their quick responses to rescue the men in the water were also of immeasurable importance. The *Macon* had been in a much better situation at the time of her crash than the *Akron,* in that everyone knew where she was and there were Navy surface vessels already alerted and awaiting her. When the *Akron* crashed into the Atlantic Ocean, families and friends had long, agonizing waits to learn the fates of loved ones. It took time for rescue vessels to arrive and for searches to be conducted; with the *Macon,* rescue ships were on site promptly. Wiley did his best to keep the life rafts together and keep track of those that drifted away and so was able to send the motor launches to them and to men in the water. Further, men were being accounted for immediately; as Miller recalled, no one was allowed on board the *Richmond* until he gave his name and service number.[28] Wiley was prompt in ordering a formal muster of the crew; all men were quickly found present or accounted for, and the two missing identified. It was always the case with airships that word of disasters spread rapidly, but on this occasion, word about survivors reached loved ones almost as quickly.

Admiral Reeves, Commander in Chief, U.S. Fleet, on board the battleship USS *Pennsylvania,* reported to Navy headquarters in Washington that because the *Macon* had sunk in 250 fathoms he had not attempted to recover any wreckage.[29] One day following the crash, Reeves ordered Rear Adm. Orin G. Murfin to convene a court of inquiry on board the battleship USS *Tennessee* at 0930 the next day, February 14, in San Francisco. Murfin, as president of the court, appointed

Commander Gatch as the judge advocate and Capt. Wilbur R. Van Auken and Captain Shoemaker as additional members of the court. Analogously with previous airship crashes, the court was convened to inquire into "all the circumstances connected with the loss of the USS *Macon* near Point Sur, California on February 12, 1935."[30] Newspapers had high praise for the crew of the *Macon*. The commandant of the Twelfth Naval District, Admiral Senn, gave his impressions to reporters: "The rescue of all but two of the survivors from the *Macon* will probably go down in the annals and archives of the United States Navy as one of the greatest feats. I sincerely feel that in my forty-eight years as a member of the Navy, I have never seen such a feat performed under conditions which I know were anything but favorable for such a task as confronted the officers and men of the United States battle fleet."[31]

Nevertheless, once again the press was quick to predict that the crash would bring an end to the LTA program. President Roosevelt told the press he had no thought of asking Congress for funds to replace the *Macon*, and Secretary of the Navy Swanson believed the money required for construction of another airship the size of the *Macon* could be better spent in construction of surface vessels—a view shared by a considerable number of congressmen.

In the past, each time an airship crashed and critics predicted the death of the LTA program, there had been a new airship waiting in the wings. With the loss of the *Macon*, however, all of the Navy's great airships were gone—there was no replacement in any hangar waiting to make her debut. The future of the American LTA program was very much in question this time. The Germans, for their part, remained optimistic about the future of zeppelins. Hugo Eckener refused to comment on the crash of the *Macon*, but Germany answered critics of the dirigible with the announcement they would complete a new one, designated *LZ 129*, establish a North American transatlantic service, start work on a new airport near Frankfurt, and complete an airport at Rio de Janeiro—all in the current year. Newspapers heralded Eckener's *Graf Zeppelin* as "a wonder of the world today" and boasted of her accomplishments. The *Graf Zeppelin* was to start her seventh season of South Atlantic commercial flights. She had made sixty-eight crossings of the South Atlantic, seven of the North Atlantic, and one of the Pacific. She had flown over a million miles and been in the air for 9,845 hours. The press recitations of German successes with its zeppelins, however, had no effect on the American navy's plans.

The court of inquiry convened as instructed, and Lieutenant Commander Wiley was the first witness called. He was asked to relate to the court what had happened on the day of the crash. Using notes he had made in the brief interval since his rescue (the rough log having been lost when the ship sank), he gave a detailed narrative of events. The court of inquiry lasted six days, during which key witnesses were called and questioned. A problem for the inquiry into the crash of the *Akron* had been that there were only three survivors; this time there were too many survivors to call them all. The court made it clear to the assembled officers and crew that anyone who had helpful testimony to offer could step forward and be heard. None did. As in previous airship crashes, the inquiry dealt with the fitness of the airship, details of weather information, and eyewitness accounts. It was to be expected, with so many men distributed throughout the huge airship, that not everyone's impressions of the causes of certain sights and sounds would be in accord, and that proved to be the case.

The court's primary interest was the sequence of events leading to the crash. It gave much attention to the prior damage and incomplete repair at frame 17.5. In this regard, the testimony of Lt. Calvin M. Bolster was particularly enlightening. Bolster was the construction and repair officer and trim officer of the *Macon*. He had spent most of the day on February 12 walking around the ship preparing for a 1600 landing. That afternoon, he took over the keel watch, concerned today primarily with the pumping of fuel and inspecting of gas cells and controls.[32] Between 1600 and 1615 he was in the control car and noted the air was turbulent but not violent. By 1630 the air was smooth, but it was raining, and Bolster went to the top of the airship to inspect for rain coming in. He found Chief Boatswain's Mate Davis and Ordnanceman Steele already there. There was, they found, no significant amount of water coming in, and the outer cover of the ship was not slack or fluttering—everything in the top part of the ship was perfectly sound. Satisfied, Bolster returned to the control car. He was standing on the port side of the car when he felt a sharp gust strike on that side. In an emergency, Bolster was primarily responsible for the ship's attitude and trim. He saw the wheel spin through the elevatorman's hands, but the elevatorman reported that he still had control. They had restored proper trim to the ship, and Bolster thought all was well again until he received the telephone message that No. 1 gas cell had deflated.

He immediately sought and received Wiley's permission to begin dropping water ballast and gasoline from aft. He dropped all four fuel tanks, accounting for 2,800 pounds. After everything that could be dropped was gone, he still could not get the tail of the ship up. The airship began a gradual rise with a bow-up inclination that varied but reached as much as twenty-five degrees. The *Macon's* airspeed picked up, and Bolster thought that meant that the tail was coming up to some extent. As the ship reached 4,800 feet, Bolster felt he had elevator control, but there was a general doubt as to whether they had directional control of the ship. In testimony, Bolster said he got permission from Wiley to go aft, apparently (the testimony is not clear on this point) to determine if it was possible to shift control to the lower fin and to steer from there. He claimed he "proceeded aft and when almost there encountered Boatswain Buckley, my assistant, and Hammond, coxswain. I told Buckley that we wanted to try to steer directionally from aft. He said, 'Aye, aye, sir, I will shift control.'" Bolster and Buckley may have misunderstood each other—very possible under the circumstances. Bolster continued, "I then started back toward the control car in order to tell the Captain and to obtain permission to make the shift of control," unaware, if recollection was correct, that the boatswain was already about to do that. However, at that moment, any possible confusion was irrelevant because, as Bolster started back toward the control car, he passed a ringing phone and stopped to answer it and was told to pass the word to abandon ship on command. He went aft to pass the word, then forward again, but, as he passed a hatch, he noticed the ship was almost in the water. He kicked a hole in the outer cover, inflated a life raft, threw it out onto the water, and climbed into it.

Because Bolster was the construction officer, with considerable experience with and knowledge of structural issues within an airship, and was in a position to witness the events that unfolded prior to the crash, the board of inquiry put particular value on his opinion regarding its cause.

> I feel in my own mind that the cause of the loss of the *Macon* was a failure of the structure, either in the fins themselves, or at their attachment point to the hull, which must have been of a great extent and violence due to the rapidity with which gas was lost from cell No. 1, and due to the fact that cell No. 2 must have deflated shortly thereafter. The exact location of such a failure is extremely hard to be certain of, but if I were told to say where I should have expected such a failure, my guess would have been that the diagonal girders in ring seventeen and one-half would have been the first to fall under a sudden severe side load on the fin since we had a very similar failure on a previous occasion.[33]

Aware of the frame 17.5 situation, the board asked Bolster directly if he had ever felt there was any danger in operating the ship without the reinforcement having been made. His answer was unhesitating: "No, sir, I felt that the ship was perfectly safe to fly in anything but extremely violent air. I did feel that another transcontinental flight would have been extremely hazardous where the possibility of encountering violent bumps was possible. I had no idea that such a failure would occur in the weather to be encountered in ocean flight."[34]

Additional input came from an unusual source. Thomas Henderson was a forty-nine-year-old lighthouse keeper at Point Sur, California, who was on duty the night of the crash. He testified he had seen the *Macon* approaching the Point Sur station from the south about three miles off shore and that, when she was approx-imately a mile past the station, "the top fin seemed to just go all to pieces very suddenly."[35] Henderson pinpointed the time of the fin's carrying away at 1710. He had been watching the airship through very good-quality binoculars and the board tried to get as much detail as it could. Henderson had seen the material of the fin tear away, some clinging to the ship and some flying off. The tear had started at the front of the fin and worked its way back.

Forty-six-year-old Harry Russell Miller, the first assistant lighthouse keeper at Point Sur, gave testimony after Henderson. He too had observed the *Macon* through good binoculars but, asked if he could report definitely where the tear started, could not. "It looked to me like it all happened at one time. It reminded me of a paper bag that had just exploded."[36]

On the sixth and final day of the proceedings, an eloquent "argument of the judge advocate" was delivered:

May It Please the Court.—

At the outset I feel that I am quite safe in saying that this court may find as a fact that the conduct of every officer and man on board the *Macon* at the time of her loss was exemplary. It was not a mere case of bravery, it was far more than that. Bravery may still be taken for granted in the United States Navy. The conduct of the officers and men of the *Macon* evinced cool-headed action in time of danger, clear thinking under stress, and a deliberate and knowing willingness to go into places of grave danger with considered disregard of personal safety. During the last half hour of the life of the *Macon* her stern was one of the most unsafe places in the world; for not only was it filled with deadly gas, but there was danger that the unsupported tail might break away from the rest of the hull and fall like a rock. Every man on board the *Macon* knew that; and yet we see men whose duty did not require their going to the stern deliberately going aft to see if they could possibly do anything to save the ship. Everyone of those men knew exactly what he was going into. That, I submit, is the highest type of bravery—far from the enthusiastic encouragement of others, with a strong possibility that his acts would never even be known to any other person—to cold-bloodily [cold-bloodedly] walk into the place of greatest danger is true bravery. The fact that a ship foundered at sea with a loss of but two lives out of eighty-three, speaks more eloquently of the discipline of that ship than words could. The quickness with which action was taken, in many cases on intelligent initiative and without waiting for orders, bespeaks a thorough training. The *Macon* is at the bottom of the sea, but this country may still be proud of her. I submit that this court may find that, subsequent to the casualty to the *Macon*, . . . there were brave deeds done and commendation earned.[37]

From the evidence and some conflicting opinions among the witnesses, the judge concluded it was impossible to determine the cause of the *Macon's* crash. "This case is a beautiful example to show that two men can not see the same thing alike. . . . Was the *Macon* hit by a gust coincident with the first casualty, or was she not? Six officers in the control car who observed the *Macon* when the casualty occurred, if polled, would vote three yea and three nay. Saying yea are Kenworthy, Bolster and Campbell; Wiley, Danis and Peck say nay."

In his list of "findings of fact," the judge advocate concluded the *Macon* had been well handled by Wiley "immediately preceding the casualty, at the time of the casualty, and following the casualty, and that he did everything within his power to save the ship and personnel." In summary, the judge advocate determined that the first indication of any trouble to the airship was a sudden "lurch" or "jar" to the ship. The court was unable to determine if the lurch was caused by a gust of wind or by the giving way of some part of the ship's structure. Whatever caused the lurch, however, was the direct cause of the subsequent damage. It was concluded that the first damage to the *Macon* occurred to or in the vicinity of frame 17.5, in the upper part of the ship close to where the fin attached to the hull; however, the court was unable to determine just what part of the structure gave way first. Gas cells No. 1 and 2 had ruptured and deflated rapidly, followed shortly thereafter by No. 0. Either following or coincident with the deflation of the cells, the upper part of the ship's structure, including the upper fin, had progressively broken up in the area of frame 17.5. From this process resulted the loss of the *Macon*.

"The court is of the opinion that no offenses have been committed and no blame incurred." The report was endorsed by Rear Admiral Murfin and by Commander Gatch. While the results of the court were still pending in San Francisco, however, Secretary of the Navy Swanson was stating publicly in Washington he would oppose construction of a dirigible to replace the *Macon*. His statement was interpreted as the end of airships for military purposes (although Swanson offered generously that they might have a commercial role).[38]

From the earliest days of LTA flight, the celebrity of the great dirigibles had spilled over onto those who flew them. Wiley had become a high-profile personality within the Navy, for the international LTA world, and for the American public. In the wake of the crash of the *Macon* there was both public admiration of and concern for Wiley. Mr. J. G. Blaine MacDade of Marcus Hook, Pennsylvania, wrote the president expressing his concern for Wiley and proclaiming him a man without equal; having survived the crashes of both the *Akron* and the *Macon*, he should be retired immediately with full pay rather than being exposed to further life-threatening hazards.[39] Lieutenant (junior grade) Campbell sent a letter to the Secretary of the Navy commending Wiley for his "conspicuous action" in rescuing him, Campbell, when he was unable to swim to a raft.[40]

Wiley, in fact, was already adored throughout the United States. His airships had been greeted wherever they went, and he had been a treasured speaker at civic groups and local governmental functions. On February 15, 1935, as the court of inquiry was in its second day, newspaper reports from both the Associated Press and the United Press carried the news that Herbert V. Wiley was one of sixty-five lieutenant commanders who had been promoted to the rank of commander. The reports were brief and failed to explain the process through which these promotions would have to travel before they were effective; readers were left with the impression that Wiley was now a commander.[41] However, there is always someone who does not share the public's esteem for a celebrity.

On February 16, 1935, John A. Rush, a lawyer in Los Angeles—who was neither under retainer nor, as far as is known, had any connection to the *Macon* or anyone on board her—wrote Secretary Swanson railing against Wiley: "I am amazed at the promotion of Lieut. Commander Wiley in the face of his gross negligence and his reckless misconduct in handling the *Macon* that resulted in its costly loss."[42] Rush continued in the strong language that one might use if familiar with airship management.

> Wiley was among those in command of the *Shenandoah* when it was taken up in a gale and crumpled and fell. He learned no lesson from that disaster. It seems he never learns anything.
>
> Wiley was among those in command of the *Akron* when it was also taken up in a storm and crumpled and fell into the sea. He learned nothing from that disaster either.
>
> For Wiley was in command of the *Macon*, and he took it up in a gale of more than 60 miles an hour that drove his ship backward nearly to Santa Catalina, and it, too, crumpled and fell into the sea. Wiley seems to have a mania for taking dirigibles up in a storm when every man of any sense knows the danger of doing so. He now seeks to excuse his shameful inefficiency by blaming the disaster on faulty construction. After the *Shenandoah* and the *Akron* went down why did not Wiley and his associates see to it that there would be no such faulty construction in the *Macon*? Is it faulty construction or is it plain damfoolishness [*sic*] in operation of dirigibles?

Using (and perhaps embroidering on) public information from the media, or perhaps from the proceedings of the court of inquiry, Rush presumed to know more about the construction and performance of airships than the average lawyer might be expected to. Referring to Bolster's testimony that the strengthening of the top fin had not been finished, he charged that "Wiley, knowing the *Macon* was crippled in a vital part, took it up in the teeth of a tornado that uprooted trees, ripped off the roof from three sections of the new race track grand stand near here, toppled over buildings and blew [out] plate glass windows." He ended, "It is inexplicable that he should be promoted for his reckless folly. He should be dishonorably discharged, not promoted." Rush's diatribe was an irrational, amateurish, and unaccountable effort to discredit a proven airship commander. Rush had selected testimony that supported his claims and ignored countertestimony by experts that *Macon* was been safe for flight. He also failed to check his historical facts. If he had made even a superficial effort to do so, he would have known Wiley was not on board the *Shenandoah* at the time of her crash. He tried to leave the reader with the impression the airships had been launched into active gales rather than having encountered them during flight.

Rush was not done. His initial letter had received a reply from Rear Adm. William D. Leahy, the chief of the Bureau of Navigation, to the effect that the conduct of Lieutenant Commander Wiley in the loss of the *Macon* was being investigated by a Navy board of inquiry. Leahy's response provoked a particularly vehement protest to Secretary Swanson. Rush did not find it reassuring a board of inquiry was investigating the matter. He cited a list of "facts" supported, he said, by a number of newspaper clippings, which he enclosed with his letter. Prominent among them was a "confession of incompetency by Wiley that he 'did not consider' the damaged condition of the *Macon* 'important enough' to finish the work of repair before taking it up on some 'fifteen or eighteen flights' after a Texas storm had seriously weakened it nearly a year ago." Rush claimed it was the evident purpose of the board and Judge Advocate Gatch to "white-wash" Wiley.[43] Rush had broadened his attack to include the entire court of inquiry, Judge Advocate Gatch, and he ended with a stab at Roland G. Mayer, now a lieutenant commander in the Navy's Construction Corps, "who testified that the crippled *Macon* 'was 25 percent stronger at the time of its fatal accident than when it was delivered to the Navy.' Either Mayer is a monumental liar and should be prosecuted for perjury or the Navy officials who accepted the *Macon* in the first place should be court-martialed and drummed out of the service."

Leahy sent a "confidential" letter to Wiley on March 22 enclosing Rush's letters of complaint. Leahy informed him that the originals, along with the miscellaneous newspaper clippings, were on file at the bureau.[44] No response from Wiley was required or requested.

In contrast, the Navy gave serious consideration to Campbell's letter commending Wiley for having saved his life. John Willis Greenslade, senior member of the Navy Department's awards board, recommended a Secretary of the Navy letter of commendation.[45] Secretary Swanson issued such a letter to Wiley on June 22: "You are hereby commended for your heroic and prompt action which saved your brother officer's life."[46] Close on the heels of the first commendation came a more compelling "special letter of commendation," dated August 21, 1935, from Swanson's Assistant Secretary of the Navy, Henry L. Roosevelt.

It has come to my attention that you, while Commanding Officer of the U.S.S. *Macon*, showed the greatest energy in raising the efficiency of personnel and promoting the safety and operating effectiveness of the vessel. You adopted measures that greatly improved the standards of morale of your officers and men, and took steps to provide complete safety equipment for the vessel and to train personnel in its use. At the time of the loss of the *Macon*, you took immediate measures with a view to saving your vessel and crew. These measures were so effective that but two men out of a total of eighty-three were lost, this being by far the lowest percentage of loss ever known to have occurred in the case of a similar vessel. You acted with the utmost coolness during the emergency and gave the officers and men an outstanding example of courage, resourcefulness, and morale.

The Department especially commends you for your heroic conduct and extraordinary achievement while in command of the *Macon* at the time of her loss.[47]

When these letters reached Wiley, he was no longer at Sunnyvale—there was no need for him or any future there. Everyone suspected the LTA program had come to an end. On March 8, Dresel started making provision for the futures in the Navy of those under his command. He wrote the Bureau of Navigation, "As the future status of this station and the personnel contemplated by the Bureau of Navigation to remain here are not known, and as there are a number of officers now on duty here who are eligible for and desirous of sea duty, this request is being forwarded, without recommendation, for action by the Bureau."[48] On the same day, Wiley sent a letter of his own requesting a change of duty. As if he knew of a vacancy, he requested specifically to be ordered to duty as damage control officer of a heavy cruiser. He had been closing out the records and correspondence of the *Macon* and felt he could have the task completed and be available by April 15. He gave two reasons for his request. First, he had had very little duty in the fleet during the past few years and he felt he needed more "to round out [his] professional experience." Second, "My services in the aeronautical organization of the Navy are not required at the present time."[49] Wiley received a prompt response—orders to report on board the heavy cruiser USS *Pensacola* (CA 24) for duty as first lieutenant and damage control officer, with an authorized delay until June 10, 1935.[50]

14

USS *Sirius* (AK 15), *Hell Gate,* and Helium

As an administrative formality, Wiley was detached from command of the *Macon* as of February 12, 1935. His orders back to the surface fleet allowed him enough delay in reporting to spend time with his family and to consider deeply what was one of the greatest changes in his life. He had invested himself in the lighter-than-air service with deep conviction and had been with it from the early days of Naval Air Station Lakehurst. He had witnessed the making of history in manned flight, and he had forged some of it himself. He had expected to see rapid advances both in airplanes and airships; he had not expected to see the end of the airship era. He had earned the recognition and respect of the greatest personalities in aviation, and he had left behind friends who had given their lives in the endeavor. He now put behind him the "romance of the air," as Admiral Moffett had called it, and allowed his pragmatic side to come to the fore. He would move on to whatever was to come next. Some of his officer friends from the LTA program were also returning to the surface fleet, and they were destined to cross paths again on the Pacific in the war that was soon to come.

In one year, 1935, Wiley had been forced to leave behind two things that were very dear to him—his father and the airship program. These voids in his life were filled in part by his beloved children but also by the former Mrs. Charlotte Mayfield Weeden—at forty-four years of age, and five years after the death of Marie, he had fallen in love again. Charlotte was from Sacramento, California, and family and friends knew her as "Blossom." Her previous marriage (to Dr. Weeden) had produced no children. She was eleven years younger than Wiley and quite the socialite. Members of Wiley's family believed he was attracted to her because she was outgoing and sociable and reminded him of Marie—the fun-loving extrovert who had rounded out Wiley's midwestern stoicism. They were married on September 21, 1935, in the Beverly Hills home of a friend, with Wiley's daughter, Marie, as the flower girl.

Wiley reported on board the USS *Pensacola* (CA 24), then in her home port of San Diego, on June 10, 1935. She was neither a battleship nor an aircraft carrier, but she was a fighting ship. When the *Pensacola*'s home port was shifted to San Pedro, Wiley moved his family to the Long Beach neighborhood of Belmont Shores, and Mrs. Case, who had served the family for a number of years, left the Wiley household. Blossom now assumed the roles of wife and stepmother. While she had not been able to have children of her own, she applied her maternal instincts to the Wiley children and came to think of Marie as her own daughter.

Wiley was at sea for extended periods as the *Pensacola* cruised up and down the Pacific coast, ranging as far as Alaska and Hawaii. During these times, Blossom was left at home to care for the family alone. While a warm, loving relationship formed between Blossom and Marie, the same did not happen with the boys. Gordon, at age fifteen, had a difficult time accepting his new stepmother. Indeed, no warm relationship ever developed between Blossom and the boys. When Wiley was at sea, he was removed from those family tensions.

His assignment as first lieutenant and damage control officer on a heavy cruiser was a career-building one. Also, he no longer felt the pressure of commanding an airship, and the weight of the entire airship program no longer sat on his shoulders. Away from airships, he was no longer under the ever-watchful eye of the press. In October 1935, the chief of the Bureau of Navigation notified Wiley he would undergo examination for promotion to the grade of commander in the U.S. Navy.[1] On February 26, 1936, the official word went out to Wiley that, effective that date, he was a commander.[2]

In 1935 diplomatic and military circles were already concerned with the threat of war in the Pacific. Of the potential aggressor nations, only Japan had the capacity for or potential interest in a war with the United States. The fleet exercise for 1935 was designed to rehearse the protection of the fleet from invaders. An International News Service Staff correspondent, Ralph Jordan, covered the exercise from the USS *Pennsylvania*: "June 17.—Phase four of problem 16, this year's fleet war game, was the prosaic task of putting more than 165 ships into

Pearl Harbor, the navy's base adjoining Honolulu Harbor. But in many ways it was the most important business of the entire game."[3] Jordan reported that no such concentration of warships had been seen previously in Pearl Harbor, but Admiral Reeves was determined to squeeze in his entire fleet because he felt it would have to be done in time of war: "A commander couldn't leave part of his forces anchored in the open roadstead off Honolulu at the mercy of enemy submarines and air attacks. He would have to get them into the base under the close protection of mines and shore batteries."[4]

Reeves did indeed get the entire fleet into Pearl Harbor, except for the huge aircraft carriers. They were sent a hundred miles away to Lahaina Roads, between two islands in the Hawaiian group. The exercise focused primarily on the ability of Pearl Harbor to berth and service the fleet properly. Navy authorities felt strongly that the channel needed to be widened to allow the carriers to enter too and called for more dry-dock facilities: "The importance of Pearl Harbor is this—If it can adequately care for the United States fleet, a war in the Pacific would be fought 2,400 miles off the American mainland instead of perhaps along the coast, not to mention the security of the Hawaiian Islands themselves. It is a naval adage that a fleet is no stronger than its bases."[5]

Maj. Gen. Briant Wells, the retired former commandant of the Hawaiian Department, told an INS reporter that no enemy fleet could attack the United States from the west without first "sweeping the sea clear" of the American fleet. Further, such a feat would require capturing Pearl Harbor and subduing the island of Oahu in which it lay: "No enemy would go by Hawaii and leave our fleet on his flanks." The piece continued, "General Wells then said that the fixed fortifications of Oahu, the Mobile guns and the air defenses are such that the army could hold out 'any reasonable length of time' against an alien power while awaiting reinforcements from the mainland."

The reporter now referred openly to the Japanese as a potential threat.

Two government men and the chief of police of Honolulu told International News Service that the young Japanese are throwing off the yoke of the empire and it is doubtful they would raise a hand against the United States if they had an opportunity.

"I think," said General Wells, "that the Japanese loyal to our government would keep their hostile countrymen in line. Pearl Harbor is too well guarded to be seriously damaged by sabotage and it would take a well trained army to threaten the base otherwise, and trained armies don't spring up overnight. The Hawaiian Japanese aren't even armed. Our armed forces on Oahu would have no trouble handling any internal situation."

Such was the military attitude in 1935 regarding a war with Japan. That year's fleet exercise—packing the entire fleet into Pearl Harbor—was, in retrospect, naïve to the level of amateurishness, yet the Navy felt strongly about it, and especially that the long channel leading into the Pearl Harbor be widened to accept more ships, especially the aircraft carriers.

This was an engineering feat requiring specialized equipment, and Wiley's next assignment would impact that. He was detached from the *Pensacola* on January 16, 1937, and on January 20 took command of the USS *Sirius* (AK 15), then at San Pedro.[6] The *Sirius* was a cargo ship that routinely operated along the coasts of the United States transporting cargo and passengers. She was 401 feet long, had a beam of 54 feet 2 inches, and displaced 4,135 tons. She could make eleven and a half knots and boasted a crew of 189 officers and enlisted men. When Wiley assumed command, he learned he commanded not only the 189 officers and crew but also one "waddling, bow legged, one eyed Boston bull-dog."[7] The *Sirius'* mascot, "Buddy," had been given full run of the ship by Wiley's predecessor. Wiley's first command had been a destroyer when he was a lieutenant. Now, as a full commander, he was in command of a cargo ship. He learned quickly, however, this seemingly unglamorous new assignment came with a challenging nautical problem. In 1937 the dredge *Hell Gate* had been purchased from the U.S. Army for $100,000 to help remove another two million cubic yards of material from Pearl Harbor's channel. The *Hell Gate* was a dipper dredge—a barge from which a single, machine-operated bucket worked at the end of an arm. Wiley and the *Sirius* were ordered to New York to pick up the *Hell Gate* and tow it to Honolulu by way of the Panama Canal.

This was expensive equipment, vital to the effort to improve Pearl Harbor, but Wiley had no experience with towing. He had to learn fast, because his orders were to depart New York about May 1. As the *Sirius* set sail for the Panama Canal, eastbound, Wiley requested from the Navy Department information about the tow and the gear that would be needed. His letter also suggested that the *Sirius* might not be the best vessel for this assignment, because of her limited deck space and lack of winches for handling towlines. In doing so, Wiley was careful to avoid giving the impression he and his ship were not ready for any job assigned them.[8] Wiley must have realized the Navy had selected the *Sirius* because it believed she could complete the task and that his letter was unlikely to change things. Resigned to that, he and his executive officer started studying the problem while at sea. They consulted Felix Riesenberg's *Standard Seamanship for the Merchant Service* and Knight's *Modern Seamanship*—both time-honored tomes dealing with everything about safety and operating ships of all sizes. Whether it was literary license or fact, Wiley later recalled, "One day while we are streaking along a placid sea at the magnificent speed of 11 knots, the officer of the deck is trying to identify a passing steamer. In thumbing through the *Merchant Ship Register* he sees 'Vessels—U.S. Army, Corps of Engineers' and there the name *Hell Gate*. Our future trailer. . . ."[9]

Wiley's education regarding dredges and their towing intensified as he got to the Panama Canal. The Army had several dredges there, and Wiley met a most amiable major in the Army Corps of Engineers who was the assistant chief engineer of the canal. Wiley found the major to be an excellent host as well as an expert on dredges. They sat in the cool of the evening on a screened-in veranda of a government house enjoying iced refreshment while the major shared his knowledge of dredges. "So you are going to tow the *Hell Gate* to Honolulu? I know her well—in fact I built her and she was one of the best dredges we had."[10] That proclamation was followed by examples of how the *Hell Gate* was "hard luck" and a real education for Wiley. Wiley did not know if the dredge was capable of self-propulsion and could get about without a tug. "No," the major responded, she was not designed for movement but to stay in one place, protected waters, for weeks or months at a time. She was rectangular in shape with no bow or stern or sloped sides; towing her was going to be a matter of "slow and easy." The major gave Wiley and his executive officer some good advice on preparing the dredge for the sea voyage—a journey she had never been meant to make. He suggested they have the dredge walled-in above the hull with a steel or heavy wooden bulkhead to keep out the seawater. He also warned them to remove the A-frame (for lifting the bucket) and as much of the top structure as they could and stow it on the deck of the *Sirius*. The major warned them that the dredge would dive if pulled faster than six knots.[11] There was some good news, in that they were sailing in the best time of the year; but in a journey of 6,700 miles they were bound to encounter some foul weather.

The *Sirius* put in for a brief stop at Norfolk, and Wiley went to Washington, about a hundred miles north, to put in a firm request for a towing engine. One was located in the Boston Navy Yard, and there he went. All along the way, they encountered people with experience or knowledge of towing dredges, and none gave encouragement. In Philadelphia he met an Army captain who had been towing for seven years (but never cared for it) and suggested Wiley get a tugboat to accompany them for stability.

When his ship reached New York and Wiley first saw the *Hell Gate*, all her top structures had already been removed and laid out on the pier. After inspection and knowing he was in for a difficult journey, he put in orders for a long list of safety and emergency equipment: a lifeboat, life rafts, life jackets, a thousand-watt light to illuminate the towing bridle on the *Sirius*' fantail, lines, line-throwing guns, and hundreds of other small items. He learned the dredge had been idle for more than a year with little upkeep. He decided to put hundred-foot legs on the towing bridle, which would turn out to be a good idea, because they prevented any yaw during the tow.[12]

Because the Navy had great need for this dredge at Pearl Harbor, it gave Wiley everything he requested, as well as fourteen additional men. With all ready, the *Sirius* left New York Harbor on May 4. Out into open water, they were surprised at how nicely the tow handled. Still, with so many uncertainties ahead, Wily laid a course that ran close to shore so he could put in if needed. Drawing upon his airship days, he kept a close eye on the weather and all the way to Cuba had daily weather maps drawn to judge the best course to follow.[13] Progress, as anticipated, was slow. On the worst day they made 99 miles and on the best day 181 miles, averaging about six and a half knots from New York to Panama.[14] Yet the "hard luck" *Hell Gate* had behaved herself and they had experienced no misfortune. The tugs in the Panama Canal encountered some difficulty handling the unwieldy bulk of the dredge in locks, and one side of the tow bridle was cut when she was jammed against a wall. While that was being repaired, the crew spent four days of liberty and rest in port. In the Pacific Ocean the *Sirius* encountered storms, high seas, and strong winds but no problems with the tow. One of their biggest difficulties, in fact, was monotony. "Even our one-eyed bulldog, mascot of the 'Dog Star' ship, got so he would not bark at the flying fish."[15] Finally, after forty-seven days and 6,700 miles, the tow was over.

Given all the hazards associated with such a trip, it was a remarkable achievement. The entire venture was so well planned and executed that the Secretary of the Navy issued Wiley a letter of commendation: "The Department . . . congratulates you, the officers and the men under your command, upon the successful completion of this undertaking so excellently accomplished."[16] When Wiley was with the LTA program, he and his ships had been constantly in the public's consciousness due to the media, but his odyssey with the *Hell Gate* "so excellently accomplished," went without notice outside the Navy.

Two days after his departure from New York Harbor another great airship disaster occurred—the zeppelin *Hindenburg* (LZ 129) burst into flames and crashed as she was attempting to moor to the mast at Lakehurst. This disaster occurred on the anniversary of her maiden flight to the United States under the command of Hugo Eckener.

On the evening of May 6, 1937, all seemed routine as "The Queen of the Skies—German dirigible *Hindenburg*—sailed serenely into Lakehurst tonight, its silver bag gleaming despite the sodden atmosphere."[17]

> Passengers stood at the windows waving gaily.
>
> There were few spectators on the broad sandy field to wave a return greeting, for the comings and goings of the Queen of the Skies, which ten times before had dropped to earth here, were considered now of little more significance than the docking of an ocean liner.
>
> The ship's motors droned loudly. Two nose lines were dropped. In a few more minutes, the ship would be fast, the passengers departing.

At 6:23 p.m. an explosion rent the air that was so loud someone claimed to have heard it in Point Pleasant, fifteen miles distant. The stern burst into flames and the fire moved forward as the airship disintegrated. The New Jersey aviation director, Gill Robb Wilson, witnessed the disaster. He told the press there was a hydrogen explosion in the second cell from the rear:

> There was something very strange about the explosion. . . . The *Hindenburg* had stopped completely and was preparing to hitch when flame broke out from the rear.
>
> The only persons possibly saved were those who were in the engine gondolas.
>
> Those in the belly of the ship absolutely had no chance.

In all my twenty-one years of flying experience I have seen crackups, explosions, flaming airplanes but nothing measures up to the explosion of the *Hindenburg*.

I cannot be too loud in my praise of those navy boys who dove into the flames like dogs after rabbits in their rescue work. . . .

I repeat there was something strange that caused the tragedy.

There were ninety-seven people on board—sixty-one officers and crew and thirty-six passengers. Twenty-two of the crew and thirteen passengers died, and one worker on the ground was killed. Some of those on board jumped to the ground in an attempt to avoid the rapidly growing fire, while others were blown from their cabins. Capt. Ernst Lehmann was the senior officer on board for the flight from Friedrichshafen, but he was listed as a passenger on this trip; his protégé Capt. Max Pruss was in command of the zeppelin.[18] After the explosion, Lehmann stayed with the ship as long as he could before the intense flames forced him to jump twenty-five feet, his clothing on fire. Lehmann stumbled dazedly from the fiery crash site. He was hospitalized with severe burns over two-thirds of his body and died a little over twenty-two hours later. In contrast to his horrifying experience in the burning ship, his final hours were full of hope, and he exhibited great dignity:

"I hope the next time we come across we'll have [nonexplosive] helium in the bags.

"I'm going to make it, I'll be all right," he said with a feeble determination.

They placed him in an oxygen tent after that, but in a short time he was dead, this slight former skipper of the *Hindenburg* who stuck to the ship until he was forced to leap from her flaming control car with his clothing ablaze.

Although horribly burned over two-thirds of his body, the smiling Zeppelin commander—who [had] bombed London as a wartime air raider—let no complaint pass his lips, his nurses said.

Fully rational and conscious to the end and in good spirits, he didn't know he was dying. His faith in zeppelins was unshaken.

"Thank you," he said softly to a nurse when she put a glass of water to his parched lips at Paul Kimball Hospital, Lakewood, yesterday just before his burns proved fatal.[19]

Pruss was taken to the same hospital as Lehmann. His burns were so severe that he was not expected to survive and was given last rites. After a long hospitalization, however, he recovered, though for the remainder of his life extensive facial scars served as a reminder of his near-death experience. In his foreword to Thor Nielson's book, *The Zeppelin Story*, Philip Gibbs paraphrased the author's words: "Every time a Zeppelin left its moorings, in peace or in war, 'Death was a passenger without a ticket.'"[20]

Rosendahl was quick to speak in defense of the LTA phenomenon, hoping to influence public sentiment.

"In judging this disaster," he said, "it must be remembered that the *Hindenburg* was lost through fire. The ship had successfully completed her westbound crossing over the North Atlantic, was under normal control in every respect and was making a normal landing.

"Whatever may have been the origin," he continued, "the loss of the *Hindenburg* can be attributed to only one basic cause, namely, that of fire. Had this ship been inflated with the noninflammable, nonexplosive helium gas, as is used in our American airships, such a catastrophe would have been impossible."[21]

Nevertheless, just as the crashes of the *Akron* and the *Macon* had marked the end of the era of airship development in the American navy, the crash of the *Hindenburg* threatened to mark the end of commercial airships. The Germans had enjoyed a long run of safety with hydrogen. They had not experienced a peacetime airship disaster since 1913 while there had been eighteen airship disasters in the past twenty-three years—three of them in the United States.[22] In the immediate aftermath of the *Hindenburg* disaster, Germany was quick to declare that it would continue commercial airship service. Newspapers reminded readers that the crash of the *Hindenburg* left only two zeppelins: the *Los Angeles*, "long worn-out and retired," and the *Graf Zeppelin*, which Eckener had commanded on many voyages, including his trip around the world.

On the day of the disaster, NAS Lakehurst officials made it known to the press that they had long feared an explosion resulting from the ignition of hydrogen. They admitted to having "edgy nerves" whenever hydrogen-filled German airships visited. Whenever the *Graf Zeppelin* arrived at the air station, the Navy's *Los Angeles* was usually away on a training flight—either by accident or design.

Rosendahl, commanding officer of the air station, shared an exemplary anecdote. On one occasion, both airships were in their big hangar together as the Germans were delaying their departure while awaiting ideal weather. At the time, Rosendahl was commanding officer of the *Los Angeles*. When the German delay became too long, Rosendahl called an officer, a personal friend, on the *Graf Zeppelin* and told him emphatically, "[Ernst], if you don't take that ship out tomorrow, I'll take her out myself." The zeppelin departed the next day.[23]

It was to be expected that the crash of the *Hindenburg* would revive discussions surrounding LTA flight.

> An old controversy flared anew tonight with the flames that consumed the dirigible *Hindenburg*.
>
> Washington fell again to debating the value of lighter than air craft for military purposes or for commercial transportation.
>
> Three times the government has invested heavily in dirigibles for the navy. One lies in the Atlantic; another in the Pacific. The third was demolished in an Ohio windstorm.[24]

The newspaper reminded its readers that in 1934 President Roosevelt's special aviation commission had recommended the expenditure of $17 million to start a regular transatlantic airship line: "With the proposal pending before the House Naval committee, the dirigible *Macon* cracked up, and little has been heard of the suggestion since. Instead, the trend has been definitely to trans-Atlantic service by heavier-than-air craft. In fact, congress recently approved an appropriation for the promotion of such a service in carrying the mails."

There was an outpouring of sentiment against the further development of LTA flight in the United States. Senator David I. Walsh of the Senate Naval Affairs Committee believed that the *Hindenburg* catastrophe indicated "the wisdom of our naval policy in refraining from further ventures into the experimental field of lighter-than-air aircraft as the result of our own unfortunate disasters." Senator John Morris Sheppard, chairman of the Senate Military Affairs Committee, told the press the disaster would have a "decided tendency to discourage the construction of that type of craft for military purposes." Senator King, who had chaired the committee that investigated the *Akron* crash, said he felt the *Hindenburg* disaster justified the position he had taken against further expenditures by the Army or Navy for dirigibles. Senator J. Lister Hill, chairman of the

House Military Affairs Committee, expressed conviction that the crash of the *Hindenburg* would have the effect of "confirming and crystalizing" sentiment in the United States against dirigibles for military purposes. Senator Elbert D. Thomas, a member of the Military Affairs Committee, predicted that the *Hindenburg* disaster would speed passage of legislation then before the Senate to increase the available supply of helium and offer it at greatly reduced prices.

While flammable, hydrogen was much cheaper to produce than the safer helium, and accordingly the Germans did not hesitate to release hydrogen in flight when they needed to decrease buoyancy. When the *Shenandoah* crashed, Anton Heinen was bold enough to declare the accident would not have happened if the ship had been filled with hydrogen. He accused the American crew of trying to preserve their expensive helium at a time when they should have been valving off gas. The fiery crash of the *Hindenburg* shattered German confidence in hydrogen and they set about trying to acquire helium for the *Hindenburg's* sister ship then under construction. The replacement for the *Hindenburg* was designated LZ 130 and named *Graf Zeppelin*. Because she was the second zeppelin to bear the name, she was referred to most commonly as *Graf Zeppelin II*.

Speaking to reporters from Graz, Austria, the day after the crash, Eckener declared the *Hindenburg* disaster demonstrated the criticality of using helium instead of hydrogen as a lifting gas for dirigibles: "One thing this accident appears to have shown clearly is the necessity, which I have always urged, of using helium in preference to hydrogen in airships. The difficulty has been that we in Germany have no helium supplies of our own."[25]

Eckener traveled to Lakehurst to inspect the crash site and participate in the investigation into the cause. A number of theories were voiced, including sabotage—an explanation favored by Heinen. Rosendahl argued that the cause of the crash was fire and the only mystery to be resolved was the cause of the fire. The most reliable testimony, in his opinion, came from a member of the crew who had been inside the ship when the gas ignited, who testified that the fire started inside a gas cell in the after part of the ship.[26] The conclusions of the board of inquiry were published in newspapers on July 22, 1937. The board emphasized that while it ruled out sabotage and had not settled on any single cause, its verdict was not a final one.

The exact cause of the explosion and fire on board the great craft may never be known, but the theory of an electrostatic spark most nearly explains the strange circumstances which surrounded the tragedy.

In arriving at their conclusion, the experts took into consideration the fact that the electrostatic strength of the atmosphere at the time of the accident was greater than normal. The big ship was landing in a thunderstorm and a rain squall was passing over the field as the landing ropes were lowered to the ground crew.

Briefly, the board of inquiry believes that the static charge of the Zeppelin, which was the same or very nearly the same as that of the atmosphere, was lowered considerably when the ropes touched the ground. It was pointed out that the explosion did not occur until four minutes after the ropes touched.

During this brief interval the charge on board the Zeppelin probably was dissipated so that the potential of the ship became similar to that of the ground. When this occurred, an electrostatic spark passed from the atmosphere to the framework of the ship.

This momentary discharge, it now is believed, chanced to ignite a mixture of hydrogen gas and air in the upper stern part of the ship, just ahead of the upper vertical fin. This explosive mixture was present there, it is stated in the report, probably because of a leak in No. 4 and 5 cells within the main envelope.[27]

On June 1 Eckener addressed the assembled personnel of NAS Lakehurst commending them for their actions during the crash of the *Hindenburg*. Members of the American and German governments paid tribute to those who had lost their lives. Rosendahl led the American contingent, and Lieutenant Colonel Joachin Breithaupt, the representative of the German Air Ministry on the Nazi government commission sent to investigate the crash, led the German party. Rosendahl and Breithaupt each placed a wreath against the ruins of the airship and Breithaupt offered a brief statement: "'In the names of the German commission and the survivors,' he said, 'I place this wreath in memory of our brave comrades and friends. Your living and your departure has not been in vain. You have died for the honor and greatness of Germany, and the Fatherland will never forget you. Good-bye, comrades, Heil Hitler.'"[28]

After the ceremony, the Americans and Germans drove to the memorial chapel at the air station, where Breithaupt placed a wreath at the door to honor the U.S. Navy men who had lost their lives in the Navy's three airship disasters. In a brief statement, Rosendahl accepted the German tribute.

Only days later, Eckener declared, "There must be no more flying with hydrogen. We must make an about face. We must use helium."[29] In the wake of the crash of the *Hindenburg* newspapers around the country gave significant coverage to the issues surrounding helium. The United States had a monopoly on helium. The government had purchased 50,000 acres of land in the Amarillo, Texas, area in 1929 to establish a helium plant. This plant had a production capacity of 24 million cubic feet of helium per year, but production could be stepped up beyond that amount if needed. The U.S. Bureau of Mines estimated large quantities of helium could be produced for about five dollars per thousand cubic feet. Using that estimate, it was calculated that the 7,063,000 cubic-foot gas requirement of the *Hindenburg* could have been met for approximately $35,315. Beyond being nonflammable, helium had an economic advantage over hydrogen: airships using helium required only one and a half times their capacity each year, while hydrogen had to be replaced five to ten times per year.[30]

Following on the heels of articles extolling the virtues of helium came discussions of who should have it. The law had put the production and control of the helium business in the hands of the president exclusively. In addition to the helium produced in Texas, there were sources in Kansas, Colorado, and Utah. Plans were afoot during the world war for the United States to ship helium to Europe to be tried there, but the armistice ended the fighting before the gas could be shipped. A Washington reporter, Earl Godwin, addressed the issue of this valuable asset: "How will this country regard its stewardship of this treasure, which is older than gold—older than diamonds?" It was recognized that dirigibles lifted by helium could be used either for war or for peaceful commerce. Godwin claimed to have it "on high authority" that the United States had once offered helium to Germany with the understanding it would be used solely for commercial purposes and not war but Germany was unwilling to be bound by such an agreement.[31]

Germany made an effort to produce enough helium at home to support her airship industry but without success. This left her in the position of having to work with the United States to acquire it. Hugo Eckener made appeals for assistance obtaining helium, promising ongoing German-American air cooperation.[32] Eckener received a personal assurance from President Roosevelt that helium would be made available, but only for peaceful uses, and in any case the president no longer controlled the sale of helium. In August 1937 the Senate passed a bill to create a government monopoly on helium but to allow exports for peacetime use in foreign dirigibles; all exports would have to be approved by the National

Munitions Control Board and by the secretary of the interior.[33] In spite of these apparent barriers, the Germans' confidence remained intact that they would acquire helium from the United States, and news made its way from Friedrichshafen to the United Press that engineers had started work to transform the *Graf Zeppelin II* to use helium instead of hydrogen.[34]

Wiley's tenure with the *Sirius* was relatively short. He received orders relieving him of command of the ship in July to report for duty at the U.S. Naval Academy. He was granted a delay of one month in reporting and used the time to take his family home for a visit. People were interested in Wiley's opinion regarding the sale of helium to European powers; he replied that he firmly believed the United States should sell foreign countries all the helium they desired. He saw a distinction between the United States and European nations with regard to the use of airships and, thus, the need for helium. In making his case, he was promoting once again his conviction that the United States should continue to develop LTA craft. He knew airships had no combat value to European countries, because any bases or hangars built for them could be located easily and bombed by enemy planes. In contrast, the Navy's air service could use airships to help protect thousands of miles of coastline by performing long-range reconnaissance. The airships and the airplanes they carried could warn of approaching enemy ships a thousand miles from land. The Europeans wanted helium for commercial uses exclusively but, Wiley suspected, sought through negative propaganda about the safety and limitations of airships to discourage Americans from developing them for defense purposes. In any case, Wiley believed selling helium to foreign powers posed no security risk to the United States.

On Friday, August 13, 1937, Wiley spoke to an audience of ninety-seven people who had gathered in the Chillicothe Rotary Club to hear him. He recounted the crash of the *Akron* and spoke of his encounter with President Roosevelt on his way to Honolulu. He knew these topics would be more entertaining than the production and sale of helium. He told his audience he was aware that newspapers had been publishing articles condemning airships but that he still believed the LTA program should be continued and developed. Not every country would find a use for airships, but they could be of great value to the United States. Aside from long-range reconnaissance, airships were very cost-effective. He claimed that for the cost of three torpedo boats, three airships could do a better job of scouting the American coastline.[35]

As Wiley was speaking and newspapers were printing, the Germans were planning. The day after Wiley's talk, newspapers carried updates from Fried-richshafen indicating that the new *LZ 130* would be ready for her first trial flights in April 1938. Changing to helium had caused a delay of about six months. Ger-man sources enthusiastically predicted that after a series of trial flights, the *LZ 130*, "the first German dirigible filled with American helium gas," would make its first test flight to the United States. The Germans were so confident of their ability to obtain helium that they publicized details of their plans. German dirigible engineers were giving serious consideration to the difficult task of transporting helium from Texas to Germany. Costs would be extremely high, because a fleet of tankers would have to be rebuilt and chartered for taking the gas from Hamburg to Bremen.[36]

However, German expectations would not be met so easily. If Wiley saw no military threat to the United States from the sale of helium to Germany, others, who knew less about airships, did not agree. As negotiations continued between prominent figures in the zeppelin industry and the American government, public arguments raged within the United States. The major barrier to its sale to Germany was the secretary of the interior, Harold L. Ickes. According to the latest rules, exporting helium required unanimous approval of the six cabinet members who constituted the National Munitions Control Board. In addition to Ickes, the board included the secretary of state, the secretaries of war and the Navy, the secretary of the treasury, and the secretary of commerce. Interestingly, Ickes, as secretary of the interior, sat on the board only when there were issues related to helium.[37] As negotiations drifted into 1938, things got ugly: criticisms and accusations were aired in the media. Ickes believed helium in large quantities had potential military use;[38] further, he had "found no formula to guarantee against military use of the gas."[39] Adding to the difficulty of getting proper assurances was the "disturbed political situation in Europe."[40] Ickes was the only member of the board to stand against the sale to Germany.[41]

As frustrations deepened, some of the greatest names in lighter-than-air flight involved themselves personally. These were old friends and colleagues of Wiley's from his time in the LTA service—Dr. Hugo Eckener, Cdr. Charles Rosendahl, and Anton Heinen. Eckener traveled from Berlin to Washington to implore President Roosevelt to approve the helium sale. Identified by the International News Service as "the grizzled airship commander," he told its reporter that he was risking his health by sailing to the United States. Eckener seemed to believe he could make a difference: "'I cannot believe for a moment,' Dr. Eckener said, 'that the United States will now let me down on the helium question. I am equally convinced that President Roosevelt will arrive at a fair decision in this matter, especially since I have already appealed personally to him and received a very friendly answer telling me that the matter is under consideration.'"[42]

There is no doubt Eckener's own interests were peaceful and commercial, but the changing face of Europe was making it difficult for such visionaries to achieve their goals. Headlines on March 15, 1938, carried the news that Adolf Hitler had proclaimed Austria to be part of the German *Reich*. Foreign trade was becoming more complicated for the United States in ways having nothing to do with helium.

German officials were telling reporters they believed Czechoslovakia too could be "Nazified" without military force, but the Czechoslovakian minister was telling the U.S. State Department that his country would fight if Hitler tried to annex it.[43] Against such a backdrop those in the United States who believed in the military utility of helium were even more reluctant to sell to Germany. Sources inside Ickes' office leaked the secretary's concerns about selling helium to Germany in the face of political uncertainties in Europe. A pledge from Hitler, if it were offered, that helium would be used only for peaceful endeavors would be regarded as useless.[44]

Some observers had wavered or changed sides on the helium issue, but Ickes had stood rock solid against sale. A case could be made that President Roosevelt was trying to avoid the issue. Originally, he had made what could be labeled a "soft offer" to Eckener that the Germans would get the helium, but he had to uphold Ickes. Roosevelt was not forthcoming with his own opinion on the issue. Ickes had told the press that if the president wanted the sale to be approved he would change his vote on the matter, but Roosevelt never signaled what he wanted. Both the Army and the Navy had told the president there was no reason not to sell helium to Germany, that it had no military significance. Eckener picked up these differences of opinion and drew attention to them in an address he gave at the opening of a new zeppelin museum in Friedrichshafen on the hundredth anniversary of Count Zeppelin's birth: "One cabinet member now has suddenly given the opinion that the helium promised us last year has military importance and therefore cannot be delivered. This seems like a joke, for this gentleman is the secretary of the interior, while military experts of the war and navy departments denied its military importance."[45]

Finally, the president decided that he needed to know what authority he actually had in the matter. He convened a meeting with Ickes, the solicitor general (Robert H. Jackson), the Chief of Naval Operations (Admiral Leahy), and the Chief of Staff of the Army (Gen. Malin Craig). After their meeting, White House secretary Stephen T. Early disclosed the president's position: "The four had the conference with the president with the result that a reading and study of act of the Senate 1567 regulating the sale of helium leaves the president powerless to make a decision."[46] The president may have been relieved to know the decision was not in his hands, for a wrong decision could have had profound political implications. As far as helium access was concerned, Secretary Ickes had become the most powerful man in the world. Eckener criticized Ickes for withholding the gas from Germany for political reasons yet considered the issue to be open still.[47] The president's inability to override Ickes' veto, however, left him "little hope for the future of Germany's lighter-than-air passenger travel without helium."[48]

Ickes, meanwhile, attacked Commander Rosendahl, accusing him of having changed his mind about the military value of helium after being "wined and dined" in Germany. (He had been invited to Friedrichshafen as guest of honor at Count Zeppelin's commemoration.) To build the case, Ickes threw some of Rosendahl's published words back at him: "'In his book, "What About the Airship?"'" Ickes remarked to reporters, Rosendahl recounted the experience of dirigibles in the World War and added, 'Small wonder then, at the high regard in which helium is held as a valuable military asset. I can't reconcile what he [Rosendahl] says now with what he said in his book,' Ickes said."[49]

Rosendahl's *What About the Airship?* had just been published and Ickes had been quick to read it, to learn all he could about helium as well as his opponents. Ickes and Rosendahl now engaged in verbal fisticuffs. Rosendahl argued that the airship had been an effective weapon in the world war but that times and weapons had changed since then "with the result that the big airship today does not fit into the military picture to any worthwhile extent in Europe." Rosendahl responded that Ickes too had changed his mind about selling helium to Germany—he had favored the idea just a year earlier. To prove it Rosendahl cited a letter Ickes had signed, along with the secretaries of state, war, Navy, and commerce.

> With adequate safeguards against the military use of exported helium, it would appear to be the duty of this country as a good neighbor to share any unneeded surplus it may have with other countries for the promotion of

commerce and science . . . and safeguarding the lives of passengers on airships. The army and navy can estimate the quantity of helium required for replenishment abroad after the initial filling in this country[,] . . . cutting off the supply in times of stress would ground all ships in a very short time because helium is dissipated at a rapid rate when in airship use.[50]

Notwithstanding, the Germans were dogged in their quest for helium. Entering November 1938 they developed a new strategy—wait until Ickes was no longer secretary of the interior and hope his successor would see things differently. They looked also to the highest level of administration—the presidency, in the sense that Roosevelt's second term would end in 1940.

The American Zeppelin Transport, Inc., of New York had a contract with the German Zeppelin Company that specified that the two companies would share equally in the profits of a business venture whereby the German company would lease a zeppelin to the American firm for transatlantic traffic if the Germans could obtain 20 million cubic feet of helium from the United States. That meant, as a newspaper article put it, "if and when [the German company] can shake 20 million cubic feet of helium gas from the tight clutches of Secretary of the Interior Ickes." The American firm held that its contract was still valid and would remain so until 1942, by which time it would be possible a new interior secretary would be in office.[51] Access to helium, however, was not the only barrier. There was a clause in the contract, which provided that neither the German Zeppelin Company nor the American Zeppelin Transport Company could contract for landing privileges in other countries unless both companies were afforded that privilege—that is, the American company could not arrange for landing rights in England or France unless it did the same for the German company.[52] Given the advance of European "Nazification," it was unlikely either England or France would grant such privileges to Germany.

Eckener's hopes for obtaining helium came to an end when Germany invaded Poland in September 1939: "Friedrichshafen, Germany—(Correspondence of the Associated Press)—The dream of Dr. Hugo Eckener, famed master of Zeppelins, the re-establishment of a regular, two-way airship line between the United States and Germany, has been shattered by the European war, temporarily, at least."[53] That autumn of 1938 and the next spring Eckener tried to keep the crews of his zeppelins in training by using hydrogen for the *LZ 130*'s test flights. Although these flights were successful, the lack of helium and the outbreak of war brought all construction work on the next airship, *LZ 131*, to a halt. Ironically, deposits of helium gas were now reported along the border of Germany and the Netherlands, but the war prevented any exploration. It is tempting to speculate whether a successful German commercial airship industry would have stimulated reciprocal interest in the United States or whether another American airship would have proved useful in the Pacific War, but neither came to pass.

The time of the great airships had passed. In the earliest days of manned flight it had made sense to pursue any mode of air travel. No one could see clearly how LTA and HTA flight would evolve—and whether one form would prevail over the other or separate roles would be found for each. LTA flight was plagued by too many fatal air crashes and the hazards of hydrogen. The Germans needed helium to continue their program but did not gain access to it. The airships themselves had grown structurally stronger but were still relatively fragile. There was no place for them in a modern theater of war—they could be destroyed too easily from either the air or the ground. In the end, however, it was the war that trumped all the other variables: when it broke out, advances in HTA flight were outstripping those of LTA.

Wiley reported to the Naval Academy on August 20, 1937, as an instructor in the Department of English, History, and Government. With the rank of commander, he was one of the more senior instructors at the Academy, and he and his family were assigned quarters on campus. This made it convenient for Marie to attend an elementary school on campus, while Gordon and David attended the Severn School, a private institution in Severna Park. Life in the "Yard"—the grounds of the Naval Academy—was good, almost "other-worldly." It was a serene, academic existence, so different from large inner cities, and the children were happy there. Blossom settled quite well into her role as wife of a commander and Academy instructor. As a former socialite on a larger stage, she found it easy to fit into the smaller, yet sociable, new setting. Because Wiley maintained an address in Chillicothe, his sons were eligible for nomination from Missouri to attend the Naval Academy if they could meet the admission requirements. The boys were proud of their father's Navy service, and it was not surprising that the elder, Gordon, would seek admission. Duly nominated by a Missouri congressman and meeting the requirements, Gordon was named a midshipman in June 1938.

Wiley was at the Academy this time for just over a year before requesting another assignment. He petitioned the chief of the Bureau of Navigation to attend the Naval War College, in Newport, Rhode Island, for the course beginning July 1, 1939. This would be a career-building assignment, one that could lead to a posting in the Navy Department, but the bureau found it "impracticable."[54] Instead, Wiley received new orders on December 21 to report by February 12, 1940, to the battleship USS *Mississippi* (BB 41), in the Pacific Fleet, as her executive officer.[55] Leaving Gordon behind at the Naval Academy and David in private school, he, Blossom, and Marie traveled across country to California by car.[56]

Wiley served on board the *Mississippi* for a year before again receiving new orders. His position as executive officer was very demanding but excellent experience for what lay ahead for him. His administrative role was pivotal to everything the ship did, and his performance contributed in a major way to the winning by the ship of two commendations. The first, dated August 31, 1940, was the red "C," for standing second in the divisional communication competition.[57] Capt. Raymond A. Spruance, who had commanded the ship prior to February 6, 1940, was authorized to extend the commendation to the officers whom he considered responsible for the results. Wiley was one of those officers, and a letter was entered into his personnel file. Spruance's relief, Capt. William R. Munroe, endorsed that recommendation with the following note: "Commander Wiley, as Executive Officer during the period February 7, 1940 to June 30, 1940, by his wise administration and helpful advice contributed materially to the results obtained by this vessel in the Communication Competition for the year 1939–40, and is deserving of commendation."[58]

The second commendation was the Navy gunnery "E," first prize for excellent performance in main-battery battle practice throughout the 1939–40 competitive year. Wiley was selected again for individual commendation as an officer who had contributed to the ship's success.[59] These "command excellence awards" were (and are today) cherished highly; competition for them was intense, as only a small number of ships won them. The ships were evaluated over the course of a year for battle effectiveness and readiness to carry out wartime missions. When a ship received one of these awards, it was authorized to paint the appropriate letter conspicuously on the port and starboard sides of the superstructure, where it would be visible to the officers and crews of other vessels. It took a highly effective executive officer to maintain the readiness and responsiveness needed to receive such an award, and Wiley's letter of commendation would weigh heavily in his favor in selection to higher command positions. He was soon to leave the *Mississippi*, and when he did the commanding officer added a note to his orders: "The

Commanding Officer regrets extremely your detachment, as your services on board have in his opinion contributed largely to the efficiency of the ship and the morale of the ship's company."[60]

As Commander Wiley was completing his tour as executive officer of the *Mississippi* he was at the peak of his form. He was now fifty years old and had earned the respect of both superiors and peers as a capable officer who was calm in the face of crises and able to survive disasters. Of equal importance to the Navy, he had proven himself an effective administrator. He was ready for whatever the Navy handed him next—which, as he must have known, would be somewhere in the Pacific.

___15___

War and Battleships

Not a part of the Atlantic or Pacific Fleets, the small Asiatic Fleet stood alone. Its primary mission was to protect American lives and interests in the Far East and the Philippines. When Japanese airplanes sank the river patrol boat USS *Panay* (PR 5) in the Yangtze River near Nanking, China, on December 13, 1937, some congressmen viewed it as an act of war. War was avoided when Japan agreed to pay reparations for its attack on the *Panay* and also on three Standard Oil ships, ending "the most serious Japanese-American incident of the Chinese war."[1] On February 4, 1938, Admiral Leahy, Chief of Naval Operations, told the House Naval Affairs Committee that the Navy was incapable of defending both the Atlantic and Pacific coasts at the same time. The *Panay* incident made Adm. James O. Richardson realize, when in January 1940 he became commander in chief of the U.S. Fleet, that the American navy at that time was too small to wage a war successfully against the Japanese navy. In September 1937 Admiral Yarnell, then commander in chief of the Asiatic Fleet, had requested a division of heavy cruisers to reinforce his fleet; but, Richardson, at the time Assistant Chief of Naval Operations, was unable to accommodate. Instead, he sent Marines to China and, in January 1938, a single light cruiser—the 7,500-ton USS *Marble-head* (CL 12)—to Yarnell.[2]

Adm. Thomas C. Hart became commander in chief of the Asiatic Fleet on July 25, 1939, inheriting a fleet of aging ships that were poorly armed, inadequately armored, and too few to confront the modern Japanese navy, with its capital ships. In a statement that became famous, Hart commented that his thirteen destroyers, built in 1917 and 1918, were "old enough to vote."[3] For many years, there had been a certain mystique surrounding the small Asiatic Fleet. The force was well situated to protect American holdings in East and Southeast Asia—but in peacetime.

During 1940–41 the United States began to construct new ships and develop a much-needed two-ocean navy. War Plan Orange, developed in earlier years to deal with the Japanese in the event of war, required having the entire fleet in the Pacific for an early thrust westward. Any transfers of warships from the Pacific to the Atlantic weakened the plan. Consequently, Richardson wanted all new ships placed in the Pacific Fleet and older ones sent to the Atlantic.[4] In early 1940 there was debate about the disposition of the U.S. Fleet in the Pacific—where to station it for protection of the United States and its territories, for its own safety from enemy attack, and for launching attacks into the western Pacific in the event of war. Richardson was opposed adamantly to maintaining the fleet at Pearl Harbor, believing that amassing the ships so close together in a single location would make them vulnerable to any aggressor, whether from sea or the air. That vulnerability had been shown, of course, in two fleet exercises, but for the moment the fleet remained based at Pearl Harbor, as events continued to unfold in the Pacific.

Discussions over fleet disposition were conducted at the highest level. On October 8, 1940, Admiral Richardson and Adm. William Leahy met with President Roosevelt. During their conversations, the president asked Leahy his opinion about strengthening the Asiatic Fleet. Leahy replied that whatever was sent would be lost and he recommended sending the least valuable combatant ships, the 7,500-ton cruisers, while Richardson recommended none be sent.[5] In later conversation, Richardson had the opportunity to discuss with the president the disposition of the Pacific Fleet. Richardson believed the fleet base should be returned to the coast of California but the president disagreed, holding that the fleet in the Hawaiian area exercised a "restraining influence on the actions of Japan." Richardson replied that Japan had a military government "which knew that the fleet was undermanned, unprepared for war, and had no train of auxiliary ships without which it could not undertake active operations. Therefore, the presence of the fleet in Hawaii could not exercise a restraining influence on Japanese action." The president was not persuaded and, as commander in chief, his opinion prevailed. Richardson had spoken honestly, but his strong disagreement with the president later resulted in his being relieved six months early.[6]

On January 8, 1941, Secretary of the Navy Frank Knox made momentous announcements to the press. The Navy was to be expanded; the president had authorized the Navy to increase its manpower by 42,000 to provide for that expansion and it was being reorganized into three fleets, designated the Atlantic, the Pacific, and the Asiatic.[7] All current and new ships were to be manned at 100 percent of war strength. The fleet reorganization was to become effective February 1, along with changes in command. Admiral Richardson was to be replaced as Commander in Chief U.S. Fleet by Adm. Husband E. Kimmel who also retained command of the Pacific Fleet. Adm. Ernest J. King and Adm. Thomas C. Hart were to remain in command of the Atlantic and Asiatic Fleets, respectively. When asked if the Navy intended to strengthen the Asiatic Fleet, Secretary Knox responded, "Not at the present time."[8]

Hart nevertheless received the encouraging news in mid-November 1940 that Richardson was preparing for the possible transfer of four heavy cruisers, an aircraft carrier, nine destroyers, and four fast minelayers to the Asiatic Fleet.[9] Since October 21, the headquarters of the Asiatic Fleet had been in Manila and none of its ships had operated north of the Philippines except for gunboats in China and occasional Navy transports.

On February 28, 1941, orders were "cut" for Wiley to proceed to Manila to relieve the commander of Destroyer Squadron 29.[10] He received his orders on April 15 and was detached from the *Mississippi* the same day. He reported to the commander in chief of the Asiatic Fleet on May 19 and assumed command of his squadron on May 22, replacing Capt. Howard F. Kingman.[11]

Wiley joined a fleet that had been on a constant war footing since the Japanese invasion of China in 1937 and since January 1941, had been engaged in intensive training to be prepared for war whenever it came. Training mostly in the southern Philippines, the ships were kept at sea almost constantly, making port only for repairs and resupply—and a few days of rest and recreation for the crews. The fleet had only about eight thousand officers and men, but its commander was one of the Navy's only four full admirals. A posting to the Asiatic Fleet carried great prestige within the Navy. If the ships were ancient and relatively weak, their crews were not. The men of the Asiatic Fleet were a special breed. Most were experienced when they arrived, having served in the Atlantic or Pacific Fleets or on the China Station, for one or more tours of two and a half years, and many were handpicked. They were well trained, resourceful, and highly disciplined. In many ways, the men of the Asiatic Fleet were better prepared for war than those in the Atlantic or Pacific Fleets. The Asiatic Fleet, unlike the other fleets, already had nearly full complements of trained crews, and they would be ready when war erupted. Unfortunately, the very month Wiley arrived, Hart learned that the promised ship reinforcements would not be forthcoming, but he did receive twenty-three new fleet-type submarines to add to his six old S-boats—altogether, a formidable strike force.[12]

Wiley's Destroyer Squadron 29 (DesRon 29) was composed of thirteen destroy-ers and a destroyer tender. The USS *Paul Jones* (DD 230) was his flagship, but he established his administrative headquarters on board the destroyer tender USS *Black Hawk* (AD 9). His remaining twelve destroyers were organized into three divisions.[13] Wiley quickly settled into the routine of training them for the coming war. His thirteen aging destroyers would be expected to "defend convoys, screen cruisers, hunt Japanese submarines, sink Japanese transports, and fight superior Japanese forces."[14] The flush decks and four high stacks of these old ships gave them distinctive silhouettes, resulting in their being referred to as "four-pipers" or "flush-deckers." With a top speed of thirty-two knots, they were 314 feet long and displaced on average 1,200 tons. They were armed with twelve torpedo tubes arranged in four triple mounts, four 4-inch deck guns, one 3-inch antiaircraft gun, and four machine guns. On July 1, with the war only five months away, Wiley was promoted to captain.

As Wiley prepared his destroyer squadron for war, his good friend Rosendahl remained behind at NAS Lakehurst, where he continued to promote LTA flight. While the Navy no longer had giant airships like the *Akron* and *Macon*, the gov-ernment was funding the design and production of nonrigid blimps to be used for coastal patrol and reconnaissance. The optimistic Rosendahl felt he could res-urrect the LTA program and was attempting to draw back into it some of the officers who had left to join the surface fleet. Wiley received a letter from Rosen-dahl dated July 17, 1941 that was full of enthusiasm for changes taking place at Lakehurst.

Dear Doc:
Since our airship program is really gathering momentum, we are faced with the necessity for providing the best possible personnel to carry it out. Naturally, every time I glance at the list of those qualified in LTA I see your name at the very top.

I am therefore taking this opportunity of asking you once more whether you would be interested in returning to the LTA organization in some adminis-trative job.[15]

Lakehurst, Rosendahl told Wiley, had about $2 million to expend on two new blimp hangars and buildings. Rosendahl had over a hundred officers and six hundred enlisted men and expected those numbers to rise. The program had six patrol-type nonrigid blimps on order, funding for another twenty-one was expected, and there were plans to build other air stations on both coasts. The new program was enjoying a wide circle of acceptance within the aviation community: "In other words we are actually moving along and above all, with the exception of very limited circles, the blimp program has been accepted by all hands as a departmental program and even the heavier-than-air boys in BuAer [the Bureau of Aeronautics] who were cool before are now definitely with us and giving us a hand. As a matter of fact, the program has the definite and enthusiastic approval of F.D.R.; we actually have that in writing." Rosendahl told Wiley he would appreciate hearing at Wiley's "very earliest convenience" whether he would be interested in returning to the LTA program in one of its key positions.

Wiley wrote back to Rosendahl on August 12 from the *Black Hawk*, then in TuTu Bay on the Philippine island of Jolo. He opened, "Dear Rosie."

> You are doing great work in getting LTA going again. Your success is astounding. More power to you! Sorry you haven't been able to get any big ships for I still think that changing conditions have not lessened their value to our fleets.
>
> In regard to my own desires for duty in LTA—I prefer to hold on to this job. The squadron consists of a tender, and 13 old DD[s] organized into three divisions and a leader [with space to accommodate a unit commander, i.e., himself, and staff]. This gives me command of about 2500 men. All my life I have moved ships on the game board or on charts, but it is much more fun to push them around the ocean.
>
> I have had the chance to handle the squadron in day and night attacks and in fleet screens, etc. I have a staff of five line officers, and the doctor and paymaster of the tender for additional duty. In other words it is a fine command for a junior captain, and coupled with my tour as exec of *Mississippi* ought to put me in line for a battleship after the next shore duty.
>
> A tour of duty here is two years. I don't expect to stay that long but want to hold this job until August 1942. At that time CO Sunnyvale [i.e., commanding officer of NAS Sunnyvale, California] might sound attractive, but there is no use planning that far ahead on account of the war situation. Certainly want to be at sea during war time.[16]

All this time, Japan was finding itself in an increasingly desperate situation. Its war in China had become a war of attrition, one that Japan had finally realized it could not win on the battlefield and that was placing a great strain on the military. Things had been made worse in October 1940 when President Roosevelt placed an embargo on the sale of steel and scrap iron to Japan (and all non-Western nations). Further, when Japan invaded southern Indochina in May 1941, Roosevelt embargoed oil to Japan entirely. Without a constant supply of war materiel, the Japanese military faced a real risk of grinding to a halt. Japan needed either to convince the United States to reverse its policy or seek other sources of these resources. Since November 1941 the Japanese ambassador, Admiral Kishisaburo Nomura, and special envoy Saburu Kurusu had been in Washington to negotiate with Secretary of State Cordell Hull, but things were not going Japan's way.

Since October 1941 Admiral Matome Ugaki had maintained a diary in which he recorded in great detail events unfolding in the Japanese military. His diary entry for November 23, 1941, contained very clear language:

> The long and short of it is entirely dependent upon the attitude of the United States toward us, since we will not change our minds. If she abandons the idea that, being the watchdog of the world, she can have her way in everything, she will be spared much. If she doesn't understand that, it can't be helped. Hull may have been cudgeling his brains. As he's clever, he might avoid war politely. But as for us, everything will be O.K. if our position is accepted and our demands met completely. Nothing else will do.[17]

By September 1941 Japan had decided war was inevitable but while its military made preparations the negotiations in Washington would continue. On November 1 it was decided the date to attack Pearl Harbor would be December 8, Tokyo time (December 7 in the United States).[18] Also on November 1, Hart was ordered to withdraw the Asiatic Fleet's Marines and gunboats from China. In mid-November he received intelligence reports that Japanese troop transports were moving southward along the coasts of China and Indochina. Consequently, he started deploying his surface vessels and air units to the southern Philippines and Borneo. Negotiations in Washington were going poorly, and on November 29 Adm. Harold Stark, Chief of Naval Operations, issued to the Asiatic Fleet the following, which was "to be considered a war warning." "Negotiations with Japan looking towards stabilization of conditions in the Pacific have ceased and an aggressive move by Japan is expected within the next few days. The number and equipment of Japanese troops and the organization of naval task forces indicates an amphibious expedition against either the Philippines Thai or Kra Peninsula or possibly Borneo. Execute an appropriate defense deployment preparatory to carrying out the tasks assigned in WP-46 [War Plan 46]. Inform district and army authorities. A similar warning is being sent by War Department."[19]

Wiley had told Rosendahl it was fun to push ships around the ocean, but in late November he was informed by Hart that a war would be a division commanders' war and that "it was unlikely he [Wiley] would command destroyer formations at sea."[20] Wiley's war would be spent largely in his administrative headquarters on board the *Black Hawk*. By December 6 war was clearly imminent, and the ships of the Asiatic Fleet had nearly complete complements of well-trained crews. They were ready. *Black Hawk* was ordered to Surabaja (Surabaya), on the northeastern coast of the island of Java.

On Sunday, December 7, 1941, Americans in the continental United States arose to their morning coffee and to newspaper headlines announcing, "Roosevelt Sends Note to Jap Emperor: FDR Is Believed Dissatisfied with Tojo's Explanation for Indo-China Troop Movements."[21] In a reflection of an ongoing battle of words, this headline shared the front page with another that the Japanese press was accusing Roosevelt of "insincerity." Of course, these early newspaper editions were distributed before morning had reached the Hawaiian Islands. Later in the day, American newspapers printed "extras" announcing, "Japanese Bomb Hawaii: Declare War on U.S."[22] When the attack on Pearl Harbor took place, it was already December 8 in Tokyo and in the Asiatic Fleet. Admiral Ugaki confided to his diary, "Monday, 8 December 1941. Fine, warm [weather]. X-day. The long-anticipated day has arrived at last."[23] Word of the attack reached Wiley's flagship at 0315 on December 8, 1941.[24]

The crews of the Asiatic Fleet may have been ready for war, but the fleet itself was no match for the Imperial Japanese Navy. Its ships were not only ancient in comparison to the Japanese ships but greatly outnumbered and outsized. The Asiatic Fleet had no battleships and no aircraft carriers. It could boast only one heavy cruiser, two light cruisers, thirteen destroyers, one destroyer tender, twenty-three large fleet-type submarines, six small S-type submarines, three submarine tenders, twenty-eight PBY seaplanes, ten single-engine utility seaplanes, four sea-plane tenders, two tankers, six motor torpedo boats, six minesweepers, one sub-marine rescue vessel, one fleet tug, and a collection of miscellaneous coastal and river vessels. This tiny force was expected to do battle against a Japanese fleet that had 10 battleships, 10 aircraft carriers, 18 heavy cruisers, 18 light cruisers, 113 destroyers, 63 submarines, and hundreds of land-based bombers and fighter planes.[25] Because of the devastation done to the American fleet at Pearl Harbor, no reinforcements would be coming to the Asiatic Fleet. The Japanese delivered another blow on December 10, when they destroyed the Cavite Navy Yard. This was the only major facility for maintenance and repair in the Far East, and its destruction placed the burden of supporting the ships of DesRon 29 solely on the *Black Hawk*.[26] The tender, with Wiley and his staff on board, was then far to the south, supporting destroyers in and around Java; by January, she would be in Darwin, Australia

A detailed account of the battles and movements of the ships of the Asiatic Fleet, as well as the problems of creating an American-British-Dutch-Australian Command, is beyond the scope of this biography. Throughout, Wiley's role con-tinued to be administrative and carried out on board the *Black Hawk*. It is note-worthy that one of Wiley's destroyer divisions—the destroyers *Paul Jones*, *Parrott*, *Pope*, and *John D. Ford*—carried out a bold night attack near Balikpapan against superior Japanese forces supported by cruisers and destroyers and, in doing so, won the first surface action by American ships in the new war in the Pacific. They sank four cargo-transports and a patrol craft while damaging several other ves-sels.[27] (In March 1945 Wiley would submit to the Navy Department Board of Decorations and Medals a recommendation that DesRon 29 be awarded the Navy Unit Commendation, but the Secretary of the Navy would deny the request on the grounds that the squadron's accomplishments "when compared with similar units performing same or similar duties were not sufficiently outstanding to justify the award.")[28] Among the Asiatic Fleet's losses was the cruiser *Houston*, President Roosevelt's favorite and the object of Wiley's tracking experiment and mailbag drop from the *Macon*.

For the previous nearly two years, representatives of the American, British, and Dutch navies had held informal discussions about joint action in the event of war, but no clear plan had emerged. Historian W. G. Winslow captures the state of affairs: "The Asiatic Fleet was not an integrated organization, as are the fleets of today. It was a collection of ships, submarines, and aircraft, all performing their separate missions. In fact, the only way one part of the fleet could find out what another part was doing was by illegally decoding their messages."[29] Admiral Hart, later reflecting on this time, felt the lack of preparation for joint action placed the American, British, Dutch, and Australian navies at a disadvantage, though for the Americans the most disadvantageous circumstance was lack of familiarity with the waters in which they had to fight.[30] Its losses mounting, the U.S. Asiatic Fleet was deactivated by the Navy Department on January 27, 1942, and its ships assigned to the Southwest Pacific Command.[31] On March 1 the ad hoc Allied structure was dissolved following the disastrous battles of the Java Sea and Sunda Strait; all surviving Allied ships were instructed to make for safe ports in Australia.

Serving in his second global war, Wiley once again had had a brief stint at sea but not in the thick of fighting. But it was a long war, and other opportunities lay ahead. For about a month, Wiley served as temporary commander of Destroyers Pacific Fleet before being ordered to the Naval Academy as the head of the Department of Electrical Engineering.[32] He reported on August 20.

By May 1943 Wiley had been back at the Academy for nine months, and on the nineteenth he wrote to Rosendahl, who was still at Lakehurst. This time his letter opened, "Dear Admiral, Ordinarily I would say Rosey—but it is such a pleasure to say *admiral*, I can't pass it up. Congrats and all good wishes."[33] Wiley reminded Rosendahl that he had not seen Lakehurst in years and had been out of touch with LTA, "not even having seen anyone in it." He confided that in his present job he had been busy with the administration of a large faculty but that he had not given up hope of getting a battleship. Rosendahl answered Wiley, on July 24, 1943, in part: "You mention getting a battleship. In my opinion one of the finest commands that anyone could have these days is one of the new fast BB's [the *North Carolina*, *South Dakota*, and *Iowa* classes, capable of twenty-eight knots or more] They certainly are honeys. I saw some firing by them while out in the Pacific and I tell you it really is something."[34] On December 6, 1943, Wiley received orders from the Bureau of Personnel (the former Bureau of Navigation) detaching him from the Naval Academy to report to Bremerton, Washington, for duty as the commanding officer of the USS *West Virginia*—not a "fast BB," but a battleship.[35]

The *West Virginia* (BB 48) was in Pearl Harbor, moored in berth F-6 outboard the USS *Tennessee* (BB 43), when the Japanese attacked. Struck by seven torpedoes and two bombs, she was saved from capsizing when her quick-thinking crew counterflooded the ship, allowing her to settle upright to the bottom.[36] In the aftermath of the attack, cleanup and repairs were started, and the ship was refloated in May 1942. She sailed under her own steam to Puget Sound Navy Yard, Bremerton, Washington, to undergo further repairs and modernization, a process that took fourteen months. When repairs were well under way, a new "wardroom" (officers) and crew were assembled. Wiley assumed command on January 15, 1944, simultaneously becoming senior officer present afloat for Bremerton.[37]

A month later Wiley, who had suffered hoarseness since August 1942, had it medically evaluated. Laryngoscopic examination revealed a nodule on his left vocal cord believed to be a papilloma, a benign lesion. Nevertheless, he was admitted to the U.S. Naval Hospital in Philadelphia on March 15 for excision of his left vocal cord. Pathologic evaluation revealed the lesion to be a squamous cell carcinoma—a malignant tumor. It had been excised completely, however, leaving no evidence of residual cancer.[38] The procedure left him with a slightly raspy voice that gave rise to a myth. The officers and crew of the *West Virginia*, not knowing of the surgery, believed his voice was the result of traumatic injury to his larynx during the crash of the *Akron*.

By July 1 the *West Virginia*'s extensive modernization was complete, and she emerged from Puget Sound Navy Yard significantly transformed. She was 624 feet long and displaced 33,590 tons. Her original beam of 97.3 feet had been increased to 114 feet. Because her new beam would no longer pass through the Panama Canal, her lot was cast permanently for the Pacific. Extensive changes had been made in her silhouette, and she bore a new camouflage pattern. She could make twenty-one knots. The *West Virginia*'s armament now comprised eight 16-inch guns, sixteen 5-inch guns, forty Bofors 40-mm guns, and fifty Oerlikon 20-mm cannons. After conducting shakedown cruises in the area of Bremerton, she took on ammunition and stores and headed south for San Pedro with the USS *Mississippi* and four destroyers. Operating from San Pedro, she made additional short shakedown cruises, with drills, gunnery practice, and underway inspections of the ship's performance. On September 18 Commander Battleships, U.S. Pacific Fleet received a report from the commander of Fleet Operational Training Command, Pacific proclaiming that the *West Virginia* had been brought to a high state of overall efficiency: "In his naval experience Commander, Fleet Operational Training Command, Pacific [Rear Adm. Francis C. Denebrink] has never inspected or been part of a more outstanding ship's company." Admiral Denebrink instructed Wiley to have a copy of the letter attached to his next fitness report, "showing he is deserving of credit which is well deserved."[39] The ship was duly released as fully operational and on September 8 headed for Pearl Harbor with a destroyer escort, conducting gunnery exercises on the way. At "Pearl," she found herself berthed once again at F-6.

As the flagship of Task Unit 12.5.2 (Wiley being its commander), the *West Virginia* got under way on September 24 for Manus, the largest of the Admiralty Islands, in company with the carrier USS *Hancock* (CV 19), ComDesRon 14, and the destroyers USS *Coghlan* (DD 606), USS *Caldwell* (DD 605), and USS *Edwards* (DD 612). They reached Manus and anchored in Seeadler Harbor on October 5, reporting to Rear Adm. Theodore D. Ruddock Jr., Commander Battleship Division 4. The previous day the ship had crossed the equator, and Wiley, as if ignoring the war, allowed the crew to conduct the traditional "shell-back initiation" ceremony in which "pollywogs"—those who had never crossed the equator—were converted, through a number of playful humiliations, into "shellbacks." On the sixth the *West Virginia* became the flagship of Battleship Divi-sion 4 and on the twelfth got under way with Adm. Jesse B. Oldendorf's Task Group (TG) 77.2 en route to Leyte Gulf in the Philippines as part of the Bombardment and Fire Support Group of Vice Adm. Thomas C. Kinkaid's Seventh Fleet.

At daybreak on October 18, they sighted Dinagat and Homonhon Islands at the entrance to Leyte Gulf. The *West Virginia* spent the morning outside Leyte Gulf, while minesweepers, under the cover of their cruisers, cleared channels through the minefields. The *West Virginia* then spent the night steaming inside the Leyte Gulf. At 0700 on the nineteenth, she proceeded to an assigned station in San Pedro Bay, Leyte Gulf—an ideal location for large ships—and fired bombardments against assigned targets ashore in the Tacloban area of Leyte until 1600. Tacloban, invaded and occupied by the Japanese on May 5, 1942, was about to be liberated. After a night of cruising in Leyte Gulf, the *West Virginia* was back on station on the morning of the twentieth and began shore bombardment at 0705 in preparation for landings at 1000. Subsequently, they stood by for "calls for fire" from ground forces (i.e., unscheduled firing, requested by radio, without notice, by troops encountering targets) until 1800, when she anchored about two miles north of Mariquitdaquit Island. While there, the *West Virginia* endured two attack alerts from enemy aircraft, shooting down several.

The next morning, while en route to its fire support area, the ship touched bottom during a turn to port, damaging her Nos. 1, 2, and 3 propellers. It was shown later that the blade tips of these propellers (of the ship's four) had been bent between forty-five and sixty degrees. This resulted in sufficient vibration to limit the ship's sustained speed to sixteen knots, eighteen knots in an emergency. Repairs would have to wait.

Over the previous two days, there had been numerous reported sightings of Japanese warships by American submarines and airplanes. The intelligence crystallized to reveal two heavy concentrations of warships heading toward TG 77.2, one through Surigao Strait. At 1443 on October 24, Admiral Kinkaid sent a message to Admiral Oldendorf, commanding TG 77.2, that the latter Japanese force was estimated at two battleships, four heavy cruisers, four light cruisers, and ten destroyers. This force was now in the eastern Sulu Sea and under attack by American carrier-based planes. The Japanese would arrive at Leyte Gulf this same night, and at 1215, Kinkaid issued orders to prepare for a night engagement. Only minutes later, he ordered the "maximum number" of patrol torpedo (PT) boats to be stationed in the lower end of Surigao Strait to report any enemy surface vessels entering Leyte Gulf and attack them.

Oldendorf had at his disposal six battleships, under the command of Rear Adm. George L. Weyler, and he intended to use them to seal the northern end of Surigao Strait. The ships would establish their battle line about the latitude of Hingtungan Point, on the southeastern coast of Leyte, and steam slowly in easterly and westerly courses, keeping their main batteries aimed down the strait, as they awaited the expected action.[40] The Japanese fleet would approach in column up the strait toward the American battle line. Thus, it was planned, the American battleships would have, from the outset, "crossed the T"—able to fire all their turrets and smaller guns on the engaged side at the enemy ships while the Japanese ships could use only their forward guns. The battle line was led by the *West Virginia*, followed in order by the *Maryland*, the *Mississippi*, the *Tennessee*, the *California*, and the *Pennsylvania*. Two columns of cruisers would steam in a similar pattern two and a half miles south of the battle line, closer to the oncoming enemy. On the right flank (looking down strait) was TG 77.3: the heavy cruiser HMS *Shropshire* and the two light cruisers USS *Phoenix* and *Boise*, under the command of Rear Adm. Russell S. Berkey.[41] On the left flank were the cruisers USS *Louisville*, USS *Portland*, USS *Minneapolis*, USS *Denver*, and USS *Columbia*, under Oldendorf. The *Portland* had been the first American vessel on the site of the crash of the *Akron* on April 4, 1933, and now, in Surigao Strait, she was under the command of Capt. Thomas G. W. Settle, friend and former colleague of Wiley from the LTA service at NAS Lakehurst.[42] For his actions on this day, Admiral Oldendorf would nominate Settle for the Navy Cross.[43]

Oldendorf also had the nine destroyers of DesRon 56 and the six destroyers of DesDiv 47, in addition to six screening destroyers and a host of PT boats.[44] The PT boats and destroyers presented a particular problem in the narrow strait. The radar of the battleships and cruisers could not distinguish friendly from enemy surface vessels. To prevent mistaken identity, the destroyers and PT boats were instructed to keep close to the sides of the strait during their attacks and with-drawals. Until the Japanese came within radar range, the battleships had to rely on radio reports of visual sightings from these smaller vessels, which, at the southern end of the strait, would be the first to encounter them.

A second problem was a logistical one—the battleships and cruisers were low on ammunition. The original mission of these ships had been shore bom-bardment in support of troop landings on Leyte. When the landings started, the battleships had carried 77 percent bombardment shells and only 23 percent armor-piercing shells, the type needed to sink enemy ships. Consequently, to con-serve ammunition, Weyler was now told to hold fire until the Japanese closed to within 17,000 to 20,000 yards, where the percentage of hits would be the high-est.[45] Fire control on board the *West Virginia* was in the best of hands. Two of the key officers in the coming battle were to be Lt. Thomas A. Lombardi and Lt. Robert O. Baumrucker. Lombardi was a naval reserve officer who had served on board the *West Virginia* since November 1940. He was there when she was attacked and sunk at Pearl Harbor, and he participated in the unsuccessful attempt to save the life of her captain—Mervyn S. Bennion—who was wounded mortally by shrap-nel from bombs striking the *Tennessee*, moored alongside. Lombardi remained with the ship as she was salvaged and refloated in Pearl Harbor and sailed to Bremerton for her modernization. He had an intimate knowledge of the ship and her workings. In the coming naval battle, he would get the first look at the oncoming Japanese fleet from his position high in the superstructure in Spot I.

Lieutenant Baumrucker, in Spot II, already had combat exposure. He served on the USS *Mississippi* (BB 41) and then the USS *Tennessee*, where he obtained experience with fire control in the Aleutian campaign, the bombardment of Betio in the battle for Tarawa, and Kwajalein. He had joined the *West Virginia* in Brem-erton, where he was assigned again to the gunnery department. Baumrucker was the tireless sort of officer who was constantly training his men and calibrating his equipment and when he got word of the approaching Japanese fleet, he got his men into Spot II to make ready for battle.

Wiley's action report describes the battle as it unfolded from the stand-point of the *West Virginia*.[46] At 2000 on October 25, the battle line was sailing its back-and-forth easterly–westerly courses with guns trained to the south. Wiley did not have definitive information on the enemy forces that would confront him, but reports from airplanes and PT boats suggested the Japanese force consisted of two battleships, two heavy cruisers, two light cruisers, and about ten destroyers. The enemy fleet was standing up Surigao Strait, zigzagging in column in two groups separated by three to four thousand yards. The sea was smooth and the visibility 12,000 yards. In preparation for battle, Wiley had catapulted his planes earlier that evening to clear the gun turrets' arcs of fire.

At 0026 on October 25, the *West Virginia* received a report from a patrol torpedo boat, *MTB 127*, that there were three enemy destroyers and two large ships ten miles off the southeast tip of Bohol heading north, eighty-nine miles from the *West Virginia*. The *West Virginia*'s radar was not able to detect the ships. Fifteen minutes later came a second report of a contact ten miles from Camiguin Island, eighty-five miles away. At 0130 three star shells were sighted to the northwest. Wiley speculated they were over land and may have been fired in connection with troop movements. He commented for the record that he "wished they would stop as light might silhouette us." Fourteen minutes later, DesRon 54 reported a contact ten miles southwest of Panaon Island, and at 0204 *MTB 134* had a contact abeam of Panaon Island—that is, entering Surigao Strait. Only a minute later, Wiley had a report that large enemy ships were under attack by PT boats. Six minutes later, the PT boats reported that the ship they were attacking was attempting to drive them off with gunfire. At 0232, the *West Virginia* went to general quarters; nine minutes later there came the report of a surface contact eighteen miles distant. At 0246 destroyers reported surface contacts, four in column, fifteen miles distant; fifteen minutes later the destroyers reported they had fired torpedoes at the enemy.

At 0304 just one minute after gunfire was sighted from the *West Virginia* to the south, the enemy appeared on the extreme edges of the radar-plan-position-indicator scopes of her SG-1 surface-search radar, at 44,000 yards. "Several groups of friendly pips appeared on the scopes as our DDs closed to attack from east and west. Two DDs patrolling to north of Dinagat [the island that bounded the strait on the east] and our cruisers a few thousand yards to the southwest were showing on the scopes. However, in the dark, and from CIC [Combat Information Center] reports only, it was difficult for the Captain to be certain just where our forces were." At 0307 destroyers reported two large and one small enemy vessel straddling them and at 0310 the *West Virginia*'s Main Battery Plot reported Spot II's Mark 8 radar had the target (and would continue to track it until the end of the coming battle). Three minutes later, two large and two small enemy vessels were detected in the strait, headed north at twenty knots.

Things began to unfold fairly rapidly from this point. At 0314 destroyers reported five enemy vessels, two of which had probably been hit, because they were slowing and dropping behind. A minute later, CIC reported two groups of enemy vessels at about 39,000 yards, one seen as three small pips on radar and the other as a large and a medium pip. The latter group was preceded by several smaller ones. At 0322 a destroyer reported spotting two enemy battleships, two cruisers, and a destroyer; eight minutes later CIC reported a group of enemy vessels at 36,000 yards and another at about 32,000 yards. At 0332 Wiley received orders from the commander of the Battle Line to commence firing at 26,000 yards. Simultaneously, there came the report that the destroyers had attacked. Due to technical problems, Lombardi in Spot I was unable to detect the targets coming up the strait, and control was transferred to Baumrucker in Spot II. When fire control was transferred to him he was ready with a firing solution, having been tracking the enemy for some time. At 0333 with 4,000 yards to go, the gunnery officer reported the enemy's range at 30,000 yards and announced he had a firing solution on a large target, a battleship. An explosion was seen in the target area at 0345, and Wiley discussed it with the gunnery officer to be certain his target was not among friendly destroyers. Baumrucker assured him that friendly destroyers were clear. At 0349 star shells were seen in the target area, but it was impossible to tell who was firing them. Now, at 24,000 yards, Wiley was reluctant to fire until he was certain his target was the enemy. ComBatDiv 4 directed Wiley to open fire. At 0351 as the American cruisers on the right flank were opening fire, Baumrucker assured Wiley that it was the same large target he had been tracking and it was enemy. Reassured, Wiley gave the order to open fire.

At 0352 the *West Virginia* was the first battleship to fire, sending an eight-gun salvo of 16-armor-piercing shells 22,800 yards downrange. Within a minute, the gunnery officer announced the first salvo had struck its target—Wiley could hear him chuckle. Through glasses, Wiley could see the explosions. The *West Virginia* followed up its first fire with regular salvoes every forty seconds; the other battleships opened fire after *West Virginia*'s second or third salvo. At 0358 the gunnery officer reported the target had stopped and that the pip on the radar was getting smaller. Wiley ordered "cease fire" at 0402; he was concerned about his ammunition reserves, with only 110 armor-piercing shells left. Simultaneously, CIC reported the target speed to be zero. At 0411 the target pip on the radar "bloomed" and then faded; a minute later it disappeared.

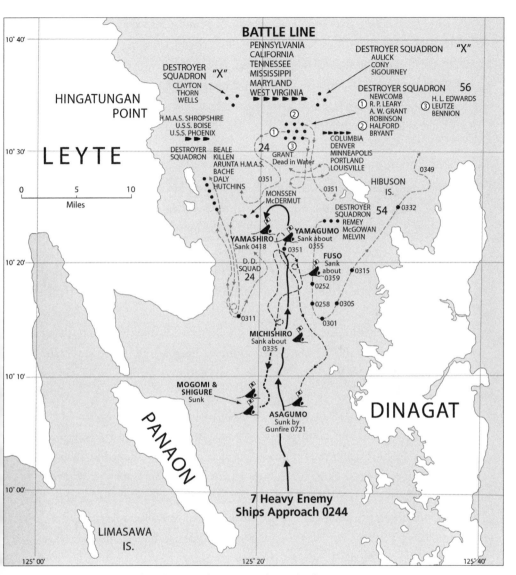

Chart depicting the events in the Battle of Surigao Strait
as they unfolded on October 25, 1944.

During this action, the *West Virginia* had fired ninety-three armor-piercing
and four high-capacity shells. Remarkably, she had hit the battleship *Yamashiro*
with her first salvo and had sunk her at approximately 0420, with Admiral Shoji
Nishimura, commander of the attacking Japanese force, on board.[47] After the *West
Virginia's* opening salvo, the *Tennessee* and *California* had opened fire with their

14-inch guns, firing sixty-nine and sixty-three rounds, respectively. The other three American battleships had had difficulty arriving at firing solutions; the *Maryland* had obtained visual ranging by using the splashes from the rounds of the other ships and got off forty-eight 16-inch rounds. The guns of the *Pennsylvania* remained silent, as she was unable to find a target. The *Mississippi* fired a single salvo of twelve 14-inch shells but did not get them off until just after the order was given to "cease fire."

The *West Virginia*, *Tennessee*, and *California* had been responsible for most of the damage done by the battle line because they had been modernized with the new Mark 8 fire-control radar. These three battleships fired 225 rounds of 16-inch and 14-inch armor-piercing shells, firing in six-gun salvoes to conserve their limited supply of ammunition. The reason the other three battleships had difficulty finding targets was that they carried the Mark 3 fire-control radar.[48]

The overall Battle of Leyte Gulf constituted four separate actions: the Battle of Sibuyan Sea on October 24; the Battle of Surigao Strait on October 24–25; the Battle off Samar on October 25; and the Battle off Cape Engano on October 25–26. Wiley on the *West Virginia* had shown himself well in Surigao Strait, having sunk an enemy battleship with no damage to his own ship or injuries to its personnel.

Admiral Nishimura had sent the battleships *Yamashiro* and *Fuso*, the heavy cruiser *Mogami*, and four destroyers into Surigao Strait. American PT boats had provided valuable intelligence on them, but their torpedoes inflicted no damage on the Japanese. However, by 0300, both Japanese battleships had been hit with torpedoes from destroyers on both flanks. The *Fuso* exploded and sank, and two of the four destroyers were sunk. *Yamashiro* continued forward, to be sunk by the ships of the battle line. By that time the Japanese force had been so disrupted that the idea of "crossing the T" was meaningless.

It had not been lost to history that all but one of the battleships of the line had been sunk or damaged at Pearl Harbor on December 7, 1941. The *West Virginia* and *California* had been sunk, settling upright to the bottom, while *Maryland*, *Tennessee*, and *Pennsylvania* had received bomb damage. The *Mississippi* was not in Pearl Harbor that day. The *West Virginia*, leading the battle line in Surigao Strait, flew the same colors she had carried to the bottom at Pearl Harbor.

Lieutenant Baumrucker, in charge of Spot II during the engagement, had collateral duty as the ship's intelligence officer. As such he was entitled to carry and use a camera on board ship. He had spent innumerable off-duty hours photo-graphing all the officers and crew of the ship, as well as the details of the shellback initiation, for a "cruise book" that he was to write and publish: *USS* West Virginia *Crosses the Equator Again.* Once the battle was over in Surigao Strait, he retired at once to his stateroom to write a detailed report of the action while it was still fresh in his mind. He titled it "That Night at Surigao" and included it in the cruise book. Once the book was finished, he would have a copy printed for every officer and crew member of the ship.[49]

For his conduct at Surigao Strait, Wiley was awarded the Silver Star with Citation. The citation read:

For distinguishing himself conspicuously by gallantry and intrepidity in action with the enemy as commanding officer of a battleship which con-tributed outstandingly to the sinking of the Japanese surface forces, includ-ing two battleships, in Surigao Strait, Philippine Islands, during the early morning of 25 October 1944. Captain Wiley directed his ship coolly and capably and, because of the previous high degree of training instilled in his officers and men, caused his ship to deliver rapid prolonged and accurate gunfire into the enemy's ships. His courage, conduct and outstanding leader-ship throughout were in keeping with the highest traditions of the naval service.[50]

16

Kamikazes and Beyond

T he first organized "kamikaze" suicide attacks had taken place on October 25 during the Battle off Samar while the *West Virginia* was in Surigao Strait.[1] By October 27 they were increasing, and several ships had been struck. Wiley's executive officer, Cdr. George J. King, distributed a bulletin with specific instructions on handling this threat. The Japanese, he wrote, had announced the creation of a corps of specially trained bomber pilots whose mission was to crash their planes into Allied ships. King pointed out that previously it had been sufficient to damage a plane enough to be certain it was going to crash, but things were different now. He told gunners the kamikaze planes had to be broken up in the air—shot at until they exploded or a wing came off. He emphasized that the expenditure of large amounts of ammunition would result: "Either we get them or they will get us." A third point dealt with safety. All hands not on exposed gunnery stations were to take cover when "Air Defense" was sounded and to wear long trousers and long sleeves to avoid flash burns. All hands were to wear life jackets for their protection should they be knocked overboard, and all exposed men were required to wear helmets as protection from shrapnel and flying debris.

On October 29, 1944, the *West Virginia* set out for Manus, then to Espiritu Santo Island in the New Hebrides group, where she moored in a floating dry dock on November 9 for repair of her propellers. Five days later, she made a successful trial run; replenished fuel, ammunition, and stores; and set sail for Leyte Gulf, again by way of Manus. While patrolling in Leyte Gulf on November 27, the

West Virginia, under attack by enemy planes, shot down a kamikaze attempting a suicide dive on the ship. It crashed close aboard the ship but did not strike it.[2]

On December 10 Wiley's ship was en route to the Sulu Sea with Task Group 77.12 to cover landings on Mindoro, the seventh-largest island in the Philippines.[3] The Battle of Mindoro took place from December 13 to 16 with no serious opposition from the Japanese army or navy except for kamikaze attacks on American ships. The Allies needed Mindoro for airfields that would be within range of Lingayen Gulf in northern Luzon, the site of the next major amphibious invasion in the Philippines. On December 15 the *West Virginia* came under air attack several times during the day, and after the amphibious forces landed on Mindoro Island, she retired. The construction of an airfield required an ongoing supply of food, clothing, building materials, and war materiel. The resupply vessels provided rich targets for the kamikaze corps, which sank three tank landing ships (LSTs) en route to Mindoro and five Liberty ships. Nonetheless, P-38 Lightning fighters were operating from the new airfield by December 24.[4]

In the predawn hours of January 1, 1945, the *West Virginia* got under way with TGs 77.2 and 77.3 for Lingayen Gulf on the northwestern side of Luzon. This gulf was to be an important logistics and marshalling base for American ground operations on Luzon. On January 3 air and kamikaze attacks intensified, and many enemy planes were shot down, principally by the U.S. force's air cover. At 1712 on January 4, a single kamikaze plane crashed into the escort carrier USS *Ommaney Bay* (CVE 79) 1,100 yards ahead of the *West Virginia*, killing a hundred men. The kamikaze struck the escort carrier amidships on the starboard side and produced horrific explosions of ammunition and fires that raged out of control. Unable to save the ship, the crew abandoned her to be scuttled by torpedoes from the destroyer USS *Burns* (DD 588).[5] Two hundred survivors were collected by the USS *Twiggs* (DD 591) and transferred to the *West Virginia*.

West Virginia came under air attack several times during the day of January 5 as she entered the China Sea. The general plan for this campaign was for the carriers to remain outside Lingayen Gulf while gunnery ships moved inside to do their work. *West Virginia* entered the gulf on the sixth with TG 77.2 to shell San Fernando Point at the northeastern limit of the gulf. The task group, penetrating about twenty miles into Lingayen Gulf, came under frequent attacks by suicide planes. The cruiser HMAS *Australia* and the battleships USS *California* and USS *New Mexico* (BB 40) were hit by kamikazes prior to retiring.[6] Each morning from January 7 until the nineth, the *West Virginia* moved deep into the gulf to fire into the San Fabian area; on the nineth, she completed the bombardment of designated targets ten minutes after the first ground forces landed on the beach at 0930.[7] The landings were largely unopposed. On the morning of January 11, TG 77.2 was divided into Task Units (TUs) 77.2.1 and 77.2.2, which joined TUs 77.4.1 and 77.4.2, respectively, to patrol together. This new group, known as the Lingayen Defense Force, had the responsibility of preventing Japanese forces from entering Lingayen Gulf. The *West Virginia*'s war diary for January 11 noted that about thirty ships of this force had been hit by kamikazes and that there was "considerable tension among exposed personnel. However, since this vessel is one of the few that has not been hit, the personnel are very alert to keep it so."[8]

The distinguished historian Samuel Eliot Morison notes that while the kamikazes had considerable success against convoys between Leyte Gulf and Mindoro in December 1944, "their full fury was unleashed against the expedition proceeding to Lingayen, and at the beachhead itself, in early January 1945."[9] He described the interval from January 6 to 9 as "three hellish days for ships present." Men serving on battleships felt generally invulnerable, but not when it came to kamikazes: "This operation in Lingayen Gulf with the constant possibility of air attack is considered extremely hazardous and we feel like ducks in a mill pond in the presence of unscrupulous hunters. However, no air attacks developed. Our air forces must be doing a good job."[10] After January 15 there were only ten Japanese planes remaining on the island of Luzon, and for "the Allies, the kamikazes now seemed but a horrible dream. Unfortunately, like other bad dreams, this one was to recur."[11]

On February 16, 1945, Wiley received orders from Commander in Chief Pacific Fleet (CINCPAC) to make all possible haste in preparing *West Virginia* for departure. He was given the highest priority for refueling and provisioning. Because provisions came on board faster than they could be stowed, they were stacked on the quarterdeck. At 0230 Wiley received orders for *West Virginia* to proceed when ready for sea to Iwo Jima, in the Volcano Islands, to report to Commander Task Force 51. His crew completed loading provisions at about 0400 but was still striking them below when the ship got under way at 0730 escorted by the destroyers USS *Izard* (DD 589) and USS *McCall* (DD 400). From a distance of thirty-two miles, they sighted Iwo Jima at 0907 on February 19. Approaching, they saw various units bombarding the island from every side: the landings were taking place. Wiley noted in his war diary, "We made the 900 mile run from Ulithi [in the Caroline group] in about fifty (50) hours at an average speed of 18 knots, which speaks well for the Engineering Department."[12] It is not known with certainty, but this fast run by the *West Virginia* may have accounted for an affectionate name given the captain by his crew: H. V. "High Velocity" Wiley.

Iwo Jima—four and a half miles long and two and a half miles wide—was uninhabited except for the Japanese garrison. Its distinctive feature was Mount Suribachi, an inactive volcano that rose 550 feet above sea level. There was only one reason for the Americans to want this tiny island—airfields. These were needed for emergency landings for bombers attacking Tokyo from the Marianas and as bases for their fighter escort planes.[13] *West Virginia* took her position and started bombarding her assigned targets at 1249, eliminating tanks, blockhouses, supply dumps, and gun emplacements. In the ship's Orders of the Day, Commander King had cautioned all hands to be "on their toes, keep their eyes open, be alert every minute on watch and saw them up [i.e., cut kamikazes into pieces] in the air." Fortunately, no enemy planes were sighted that day. Throughout the battle for Iwo Jima the major threat to the *West Virginia* was counterbattery fire. Even so, in his war diary entry for February 28, Wiley commented, "While furnishing fire support at Iwo Jima on D-Day and thereafter, this vessel observed many more near misses from 'friendly overs' [U.S. rounds fired overhead] and 'friendly ricochets' than from enemy counter battery."[14] For the *West Virginia*, the Iwo Jima campaign settled into something of a routine—arriving on station each morning, bombarding assigned targets, supplying "call fire" in support of the Marines ashore, delivering counterbattery fire, and retiring each evening

Wiley and his crew could have no greater satisfaction for the job they were doing than compliments from the Marines slugging it out with the enemy on the ground. They received repeated praise for the accuracy of their "call fire" that saved Marines' lives. Their gunnery's accuracy was seen also from the air. In the Orders of the Day for February 25, Commander King added, "The Gunners were up to their usual high standard yesterday which brought forth a remark from a carrier spotting plane to the effect that our shooting was the most accurate he has ever seen in this operation. During one phase of the firing he called it pin-point accuracy; keep up the good work. You certainly cleared the way for the Marines yesterday."[15] Not all fire was from the big guns; the *West Virginia* was often close enough to shore to hit targets with 20-mm and 40-mm guns.

Praise for the performance of the *West Virginia* came all the way from the commander in chief of the Pacific Fleet. It was only two words long, but they were a traditional phrase that was and is full of meaning for American naval personnel—"Well Done." As he had done in the LTA years, Wiley distributed the credit to every man on board. The commendation, with remarks by Wiley, was posted on all bulletin boards on the ship.

Captain's Memorandum to the Crew
The following message was received this morning:

From: Commander in Chief, Pacific Fleet
To: USS *West Virginia*
    "Well Done"
    This unusual citation is to the credit of every department of the ship and man in the crew. It was not alone for our quick preparations in Ulithi, for that was due to our previous good work.
    It was for the Engineers who turned up 36,000 miles the first six months in commission and kept us ready for full power at all times and enabled us always to report "ready for any mission now."
    It was for the Gunnery Department which has been always ready and alert so that in battle we could pitch big league every time.
    It was for the C&R [Construction and Repair] Department which has kept our gear in repair and enabled us to answer all calls. It was for the Supply Department which has delivered the goods and kept us supplied with everything we needed, and for the Communicators who kept us at the peak with orders and information. The Medical Department guarded our health so that we were physically tip-top. The Chaplain guided our mental attitude and thinking.
    This "Well Done" was therefore for a rapid shakedown, the ability quickly to take our place on the firing line, our accomplishments such as doing a 48 hour replenishment job in one night at Espirito Santo; the performances in Leyte Gulf, Surigao Straits, Sulu Sea and Lingayen.
    In other words it was a "Well Done" for every man in the crew whose cheerful cooperation and hard work contributes to the demonstration that the *West Virginia* is a smart ship and always ready for any mission.
    H. V. Wiley
    Captain, U.S. Navy
    Commanding, USS *West Virginia*

On the afternoon of February 27, spotter planes flew over the island looking for targets of opportunity but no enemy activity was noted in the *West Virginia*'s area of responsibility. The same day, a letter was sent from ComBatDiv 4 to the Secretary of the Navy recommending a Navy Unit Commendation for the *West Virginia*.[16]

Wiley's ship continued to provide fire support for ground troops and night harassing fire with secondary batteries until March 1, 1945, when she withdrew in company of other vessels to Ulithi for resupply and for rest and recreation for the crew. By the end of the first week of the month, the airfields on Iwo Jima were ready for use by bombers and fighters. At 1030 on March 5, Commander King was relieved as executive officer by Cdr. John E. Fitzgibbon.[17] This change was unwelcome but not unexpected. In a letter to his wife dated February 8, 1945, now–Lt. Cdr. Thomas Lombardi expressed the feelings of the officers and crew of the *West Virginia* about their leadership.

> The Exec's orders came in recently by despatch, detailing him as Chief of Staff to the Commander of a battleship division. He's to leave as soon as his relief arrives, whenever that may be. He was selected for Captain several months ago, but the rank is not awarded until one is ordered to a position that calls for such a rank. This is it for George [King]. We'll be sorry to see him go—the next one may not be as pleasant as G.K. has been, to have around.
>
> I suppose Captain Wiley will go in a few months. He's due to be relieved, having been aboard for a year now, which is about the length of time battleship captains hold that job. Everyone is pulling hard for him to make Admiral, and he certainly deserves to. He has won the admiration and respect of everyone aboard, and has been tops with one and all. Under the conditions we've been operating, one couldn't ask for a more ideal skipper. Calm, reasonable, never a word of censure, good ship handler, knows his business— his replacement will have to be pretty good to fill his shoes. I do hope I go before he does, for it will be hard trying to get used to a new man on the same ship, after Captain Wiley. You may gather that we all think he's o.k.—we all think they don't come any better. Hope it isn't too long before he makes Admiral.[18]

Wiley and King had been well matched for the two highest positions on a battleship. Their leadership and management styles were similar, and, as in previous assignments, Wiley contributed materially to making the *West Virginia* a happy ship. Fitzgibbon would prove not to have acquired the same leadership skills.

On March 11, 1945, the *West Virginia* was anchored at Ulithi Atoll, a base felt to be so secure it was not blacked out at night. The ship's officers and men were watching movies on the quarterdeck and forecastle when, at about 2030, a large explosion was heard from the carrier USS *Randolph* (CV 15) anchored off the *West Virginia's* starboard bow.[19] The *Randolph* had been hit by a kamikaze plane from the Azuza Special Attack Unit sent by Admiral Ugaki with the specific mission of crashing into American carriers.[20] The bomb the plane carried did no significant structural damage but killed 27 and wounded 105 men, most of whom had been watching a movie on the hangar deck. The airplane itself did not explode, because it was nearly out of gas. A second kamikaze crashed on an island, doing no harm. No other enemy planes were seen that night.

At 0805 on March 21, Wiley got the *West Virginia* under way as part of Task Unit 54.2.2 bound for Okinawa. En route, the line of ships conducted antiaircraft firing exercises using drones and sleeves for targets. It was expected that aerial attacks, including kamikazes, would intensify as the fleet got closer to the Japanese home islands. The planners for this campaign had cause for concern; they were aware that in addition to Okinawa's several airfields there were others on nearby islands, airdromes 150 miles away in the Amami Gunto and on the Sakishima Gunto about 230 miles away, as well as sixty-five airfields on Formosa and fifty-five on Kyushu. Because there were no other active operations to draw off their forces, the Japanese could concentrate two or three thousand planes on the Americans approaching Okinawa.[21] En route to Okinawa the line of ships sighted occasional enemy aircraft, but they remained out of range. At 1635 on March 25, they sighted Kerama Retto, a cluster of small islands fifteen miles west of Okinawa. Several enemy aircraft were picked up on radar, but they too remained out of range of the fleet's guns.

The next day, while the *West Virginia* was traversing a channel west of Kerama Retto, her radar began to pick up more enemy planes and at the same time received numerous radio reports from other vessels of "bogies," air contacts. The destroyer-minesweeper USS *Robert H. Smith* (DM 23) reported shooting down an enemy plane but the closest bogies to the *West Virginia* were twenty-two miles distant. At 0902 Wiley had two floatplanes launched to serve as artillery spotters and at 0910 went to general quarters in preparation for bombardment of the west coast of Okinawa. Following sightings by several ships of torpedo wakes, the sound of depth charges dropped from destroyers was heard the entire morning. Wiley had his main battery commence firing at assigned targets at 1034 and secured from general quarters at 1233.[22] About six hours later, the ship sounded Air Defense having detected an estimated nine bogeys closing from the northeast; no aircraft attacked the fleet.

From March 27 through March 31, the daily routine was essentially the same—bombarding assigned targets on Okinawa, standing by for calls for fire, detecting and tracking bogies in increasing numbers (and shooting down some), and retiring to the northwest of the island each night. The island had been "prepared" by naval and air bombardments for five days. The landing site was to be the five-to-six-mile-long stretch known as the "Hagushi beaches," selected because of their proximity to Yontan and Kadena airfields. There was a thick six-to-ten-foot-high concrete seawall behind each beach.[23] On March 30 Wiley received orders from CTF 52 to close to within a thousand yards of one of the beaches and knock at least three large holes in it. This was accomplished with a few minutes of fire from *West Virginia*'s main battery. Air Defense was sounded several times on the thirty-first, and during the night the *West Virginia* operated very close to Okinawa to support the transport groups arriving there. Wiley ended his war diary entry for March 31, "Tomorrow is the day our troops go ashore on Okinawa! Easter."[24]

H-hour for landings on Okinawa on April 1, 1945, was set for 0830. Enemy air activity had been spotted near the island as early as 0100. Wiley had the *West Virginia* sound Air Defense at 0500 and twenty-two minutes later launched two planes as artillery spotters. The ship went to general quarters at 0610 in preparation for shore bombardment; within minutes, a bogey was sighted off the port quarter fifteen miles away. The antiaircraft batteries opened fire and shot it down about two hundred yards off the port quarter. The batteries opened fire again at 0617 at four bogeys off the port quarter, sending one crashing into the sea. Wiley commenced his shore bombardment at 0630 and recorded, "Landing craft dot the ocean as far as we can see, waiting for 'H' hour."[25] At 0800 the *West Virginia* was lying about nine hundred yards off shore, being passed by landing craft moving toward the beaches. An LCI, or infantry landing craft, exploded and disintegrated, apparently having hit a mine. By 0830 the first wave of landing craft was about three hundred yards from the beach, and by 0842 troops were going ashore, then moving inland rapidly against little resistance. The *West Virginia* continued its bombardment throughout the day.

The *West Virginia's* luck with kamikazes ran out on April 1. At approximately 1907, four Oscars (Nakajima Ki-43 [Type 1] fighters) were sighted by lookouts at an altitude of two thousand feet, range approximately three thousand yards, flying directly toward the ship. When antiaircraft fire opened on the lead plane, the foursome split, two planes flying aft along the starboard side and two crossing the bow to port. The pair of planes flying aft on the starboard side received fire from the 20-mm and 40-mm batteries. One was shot down in flames; the other continued down the starboard side to crash into a transport ship about 2,500 yards away. Similarly, the other two planes were taken under fire by the 20-mm and 40-mm batteries on the port side. One of these crashed into a landing craft on the port quarter, but most of the fire was directed at the second plane. This one, carrying a 250-kg bomb, made a tight left turn and dived vertically on the *West Virginia*, crashing into the 20-mm group No. 6, just forward of 5-inch director No. 2.[26]

Fortunately, the bomb did not explode. It was a Type 92, a Japanese army general-purpose high-explosive bomb eleven and three-quarters inches in diameter with a fuse set to detonate after a short delay. The bomb initially impacted a 20-mm gun platform on the O3 deck (i.e., three levels above the main deck). Making a clean circular hole twelve inches in diameter, it continued within the ship at an angle of fifty-eight degrees from horizontal. It traveled inboard a distance of nine feet and aft a distance of eleven feet, penetrating the three thicknesses of ten-pound steel and one high-tensile steel plate of the main deck. When the bomb struck the armored second deck, it burst.[27] The suicide attack killed four enlisted men and injured twenty-three others, one seriously. The body of the Japanese pilot was still in the mangled cockpit of his plane, and a chart taken from one of his boots indicated he had come from Kyushu. The body of the kamikaze pilot was buried at sea "with dignity but no fanfare," followed a day later by more formal services for the four sailors who had been killed.[28]

Analysis of the failure to shoot down the suicide plane resulted in this conclusion: "It is considered that the poor visibility of evening twilight combined with the volume of tracers [brightly glowing pyrotechnics that reveal the path of projectiles] blinded the 20MM gunners and 40MM sight operators so [that] they experienced great difficulty in staying on targets and in some cases lost targets completely." This analysis led to the recommendation that "40MM self destructive ammunition with a dim tracer feature be supplied ships in sufficient quantity to provide for more effective night firing against suicide planes."[29]

Structural damage resulting from the suicide attack was slight. The galley and laundry were the hardest hit, but these were made operational again very quickly. At the end of a most eventful April 1, Wiley's ship provided illumination fire throughout the night for the Marines ashore. The next day, bogies were reported in the area, but none came close to the *West Virginia*.

The sense of routine once felt in supporting amphibious assaults was disrupted at Okinawa. Nearly every day for three weeks following the hit on the *West Virginia* enemy aircraft were sighted either in groups or alone, and there were numerous reports of incoming aircraft. Several were shot down by antiaircraft fire from the *West Virginia* or other ships in the area. Also, the combat air patrol, fighters from the carriers constantly overhead, did a good job of knocking down enemy aircraft. In spite of this, suicide planes managed to crash into a number of vessels in Wiley's general area. *West Virginia's* gunners were firing on a bogey just before it crashed into the USS *Maryland* (BB 46) on April 7; the USS *Gregory* (DD 802), one of the picket destroyers, was hit on April 8; USS *Tennessee* (BB 43), USS *Salt Lake City* (CA 25), USS *Zellars* (DD 777), and USS *Stanley* (DD 478) were all hit on April 12; and the USS *Isherwood* (DD 520) was struck on April 22. None of these vessels was sunk.

Officially, the battle for Okinawa spanned April 1 to June 22, 1945, but Wiley's contribution to it ended on April 24, when he was ordered to take the *West Virginia* to Ulithi as part of TU 51.29.21.[30] The same day he was informed by the Bureau of Personnel that he was to be relieved by Capt. Raymond W. Holsinger; when relieved, he was to proceed to the United States by the first available air transportation. Wiley responded with a request to travel by surface ship if one was available. Having completed a tour as captain of a battleship at war, he undoubtedly knew it was unlikely he would be assigned to sea duty again; perhaps the request was the way an old captain said "good-bye" to the sea. In any event, his request was denied. Holsinger reported on board the *West Virginia* as Wiley's relief at 1447 on April 30, 1945.[31] Wiley left the ship on May 2. Baumrucker, who had maintained an illicit diary on all three of the battleships on which he had served, confided to it on May 2, "Our fine captain since Bremerton leaves the ship, and all hands are almost instantly dubious about his successor."[32]

Lt. (jg) Robert Wilson had been communications officer on the *West Virginia* since the ship left Bremerton following her refitting. In his role, Wilson had worked closely with Wiley on a daily basis, and for him Wiley's departure was a sad event. Wilson watched from the communications bridge as a twenty-six-foot motor whaleboat, with a single sailor at the helm, carried Wiley away from the ship. Wiley sat motionless near the bow of the boat looking back at the *West Virginia*. Although Wilson could not see his face, Wiley seemed to him the loneliest man in the world.[33]

—

As the *West Virginia* returned to Okinawa under her new commanding officer to help finish the work there, Wiley returned to the continental United States and reported to the commandant of the Twelfth Naval District. There he got new orders, to report to the commander of Fleet Operational Training Command, Atlantic and to assume command of the Training Group Guantanamo Bay, in Cuba, designated Task Group 23.1 of Task Force 23. Required to hoist his broad command pennant from a vessel of that group, he would select the USS *Broome* (AG 96), a World War I–era destroyer rated as a "miscellaneous auxiliary ship" while awaiting inactivation, but he was to administer the group from an appropriate shore location in the Guantanamo Bay area. The paramount mission of his task group was to carry out the most effective possible shakedown or refresher training for ships of all types ordered to it.[34]

As Wiley made his way to his new assignment, he took time to assist the son of the late Lt. (jg) Morgan Redfield of Madison, Connecticut, who had died in the crash of the *Akron*. John Morgan Redfield was to finish high school in June and had been preparing to apply for entrance to the Naval Academy. To help this son of a former *Akron* officer, Wiley wrote to the Honorable Thomas C. Hart. Hart, the former commander of the Asiatic Fleet, had retired in July 1942 but had been recalled the next month to serve on the Navy's General Board. Hart retired a second time to assume, upon the appointment of the governor of Connecticut, the senatorial seat held by Francis T. Maloney following his death on January 16, 1945. As a senator, Hart was in a position to be of great assistance in obtaining an appointment to the Naval Academy. Wiley told Hart he had known the young man all his life and that an appointment to the Academy "would satisfy the lifetime ambition of a deserving boy, be a credit to his state, and honor the memory of a naval officer father."[35] With the assistance of Wiley and Hart, young Redfield gained admission.

At war's end, Lt. Robert Wilson communicated with Wiley to let him know he, Wilson, had thought of him when the *West Virginia* entered Tokyo Bay for the surrender ceremony. Wiley replied that he was deeply touched and wished he could have remained on board for four more months to complete the ship's mission, "On to Tokyo." Wiley said his copy of *Crossing the Line* made him homesick and recalled how, throughout the *West Virginia's* battles, Wilson had been always at his elbow.

The duties and responsibilities of Wiley's new command were heavy, and changes were unfolding that would make them weightier. In recognition of this, the commander of Fleet Operational Training Command, Atlantic, Rear Adm. Carleton F. Bryant, recommended to the commander in chief of the Atlantic Fleet that Captain Wiley receive a "spot promotion" to flag rank, effective during the time he was to hold this position: "It is considered necessary for the proper performance of duty by the officer heading this expanded organization that he hold a rank commensurate with the responsibility which will devolve upon him. In view of his continual dealing with senior captains and with officers of flag rank of interested commands, and the fact that his staff will include no less than three senior captains, it is felt that he might properly be of the rank of a Rear Admiral, and most assuredly should be at least a Commodore."[36]

On August 9, Wiley received a handwritten note from Admiral Bryant. It was addressed to "Doc" and stated, "I understand that your appointment to Commodore is on the President's desk for signature. Hope so. Sorry we didn't get Rear Admiral. We tried. Maybe later."[37]

Wiley's new duties were interrupted when, on November 26, 1945, he was hospitalized in the Naval Dispensary at Guantanamo with chest pain. He was fifty-five years old and had been on active service in the Navy for thirty-four years and eleven months. He told the medical officer he had gone out into cold air and felt a sudden, painful pressure in the middle of his chest. It had that lasted for about eighteen hours, but there had been no shortness of breath. It developed that he had been experiencing occasional chest pain, radiating down his left arm, for about eighteen months prior to this episode. These symptoms were characteristic of coronary artery disease—and he had been experiencing them throughout his participation in the Pacific campaign. Otherwise, the results of a physical examination were unremarkable, except for diminished hearing presumed to be the effect of heavy naval gunfire. However, an electrocardiogram revealed a posterior-wall myocardial infarction. He was hospitalized for three weeks, followed by another three weeks of progressive ambulation under observation, before being transferred to the United States. His medical condition made the front page of his hometown newspaper: "Capt. Herbert Wiley Is Ill in Cuba."[38]

Even before the paperwork could be generated, Wiley knew his heart attack had brought his Navy career to an end. As if clinging to the only career he had known—and loved—Wiley sought a way to stay connected to the Navy. While still in Guantanamo Bay, but expecting discharge to a medical facility in the States, Wiley requested an assignment as curator of the U.S. Naval Academy Museum. He felt he had special qualifications for this billet "because of my knowledge of Naval History, having considerable service in combat zones in both World War I and II and having taught U.S. Naval History and Modern European History at the Naval Academy."[39] His request was forwarded to the superintendent of the Naval Academy for comment and recommendation, but regrettably, the billet Wiley requested was not vacant.[40]

On June 24, 1946, Wiley's military and medical records were forwarded to the Naval Retiring Board for review;[41] after prompt consideration, the Chief of Naval Personnel issued orders relieving Wiley of all active duty.[42] Subsequent letters between Wiley and his good friend Rosendahl had the tenor of two old sailors facing the inevitabilities of advancing age. On July 3, Wiley wrote, "Dear Rosey: I saw your orders the other day and do hope you are not ill. I haven't seen anyone in L.T.A. for some time and haven't any dope on your situation." He informed Rosendahl of his own heart attack and caught him up on family affairs, reporting that Gordon was a lieutenant commander in aviation in California; David, just out of the Navy, was applying to Cornell University; and Marie, who had been in private school in Florida while Wiley was in Guantanamo, was to be a senior in high school and had become a "knockout young lady."[43]

In his reply, "Rosey" seemed eager to catch up with his old friend. He had heard only "in a vague sort of way" about Wiley's heart attack until he got definitive word from George Campbell. Rosendahl informed Wiley that he too was about to retire. He had been diagnosed with hypertension and had exacerbated a chronic back problem that would make it unsafe for him to go back to sea. A thorough medical examination had concluded, in fact, that he was not qualified for further active duty. He told Wiley he had been considering retirement on his own for some time and planned on taking a rest. "Rosey" was delighted with the news of Wiley's children but admitted that it "brings home the fact that you and I certainly are no longer spring chickens."[44] Rosendahl promised to send Wiley a copy of a booklet he had put together on blimp operations during the war.[45]

Fittingly, the news of Wiley's retirement made the front page of his hometown newspaper. The writer summarized Wiley's life and career, recalled the flyover of Chillicothe by the *Los Angeles* under Wiley's command on October 10, 1928, and reminded readers, "This was a time when news of aviation was making headlines daily."[46] On August 18 Wiley informed the Navy of a change of address to San Francisco. He had received a letter dated December 26, 1946, over the signature of Capt. C. W. Moses of the Officer Performance Division, informing him that the Naval Retiring Board had found him incapacitated for active service by reason of physical disability incurred in line of duty while serving in the rank of captain and that his retirement would be effective on January 1, 1947.[47] Accordingly, he received his Notice of Separation from U.S. Naval Service on that date.

The notice listed the medals and ribbons to which he was entitled: the Mexican Campaign Ribbon for service in 1916; the World War I Ribbon; the Philippine Liberation Ribbon; the Legion of Merit; the Navy and Marine Corps Medal; the Bronze Star; the World War II Victory Medal; and the Navy Cross.[48] Fleet Adm. Chester W. Nimitz, Commander in Chief, Pacific Ocean Areas, had presented the Navy Cross to Wiley personally. A letter dated January 20 informed Wiley of the final action of the Retiring Board. He had been placed on the retired list as of January 1, 1947. This letter was addressed not to Captain Wiley but to Rear Adm. Herbert Victor Wiley. Explanation was given in the body of the letter, signed by James Forrestal:[49]

> Having been specially commended by the head of the executive department for performance of duty in actual combat with the enemy, you were, when placed on the retired list, advanced to the rank of Rear Admiral. However, your retired pay is based on that of the rank of Captain. . . .
>
> During your career you have witnessed many advancements in the morale, strength, and efficiency of the Navy. You have contributed materially to the accomplishment of these results. I regret your retirement from active service and take this occasion to extend to you my heartiest congratulations and appreciation for your long and efficient service to our Nation. May I wish for you many years of health and happiness.
> James Forrestal

Settling into San Francisco, Wiley enjoyed spending time with old friends and golfing, but he also put his knowledge and experience to use by taking a position with the University of California as a lecturer in engineering and an assistant to the dean of the College of Engineering. Referring to a letter Wiley had written a relative in Chillicothe, the *Constitution-Tribune* reported he was doing personnel work, interviewing the 3,500 engineering students at the school. He said, "The work is very interesting as I see all kinds of persons. I have been handling young men all my life, so I feel able to do the job."[50]

It is likely that the last phase of "Doc's" life would have been richer had his first wife survived to share the retirement years with him. His marriage to Blossom was tumultuous and lacking the warmth and love he had known with Marie, though he found joy in the friendships he had established in the Navy. Wiley's career had taken him far from home and family on a frequent basis, but now he was able to be there as father of the bride when his beloved daughter was married. Young Marie Elinor Wiley had attended Stanford University but had graduated from the University of California and now was to be married to William Nisbet Ross, a graduate of Brown University, in Rhode Island. It was with great pride that Wiley walked his daughter down the aisle during a 4 p.m. wedding on Sunday, June 14, 1953, in St. Clement's Episcopal Church in Berkeley. As would be expected, Wiley's hometown newspaper reported the event.[51]

Wiley's cardiovascular disease was severe, however, and he survived a little over a year after Marie's wedding. His coronary symptoms had become manifest, but apparently had not been recognized for what they were on the *West Virginia*; the ship's steep metal "ladders" (stairs) constituted as good a cardiac stress test as any devised by modern medicine. His myocardial infarction (heart attack) was the natural extension of the angina pectoris that resulted from occlusion (blockage) of his coronary arteries, but his atherosclerotic cardiovascular disease (hardening of the arteries) was not limited to his coronary arteries. He now developed pain in his left leg on exertion, and an examining physician noted the absence of a *dorsalis pedis* pulse—a sign of diminished blood flow to the leg and foot due to atherosclerotic disease. He died on April 28, 1954; the cause of death was listed as myocardial infarction.[52] He was sixty-three years old. He was buried in the Golden Gate National Cemetery, San Bruno, California.

In his February 8 letter to his wife, Thomas Lombardi had spoken for all who had served with Herbert Victor Wiley, very succinctly summarizing the virtues that made him a solid leader. While Wiley had achieved heroic deeds in his military career, he was not one of the storied heroes about whom films are made.

He was instead a steadfast leader, of the type that populates the officer corps of America's navy—devoted to the service, dedicated to the task before them, and constantly training to be prepared for the moment Fate taps them on the shoulder and calls them to greater deeds.

Victories are won, not by greater numbers or by the possession of superior engines of war, but rather by the character and training of the men. . . . [T]he desired military virtues tend to spread from officer to men by a sort of contagion. . . . Doubts dissolve and obstacles vanish when he appears, and the impossible happens.

—*Charles M. Blakewell.*[53]

NOTES

CHAPTER 1. WILEY: THE EARLY YEARS

1. Quoted in Bruce Weber, "Richard Russo, Happily at Home in Winesburg East," *New York Times*, July 2, 2004, www.nytimes.com/.
2. *Chillicothe* (Mo.) *Constitution-Tribune*, May 16, 1891, 2.
3. "Sparks from the Wires," *Salt Lake* (Salt Lake City, Utah) *Tribune*, March 12, 1899, 15.
4. "Fire at Mountain Grove, MO," *Marietta* (Ohio) *Daily Leader*, March 12, 1899, 1.
5. "Mountain Grove Ablaze," *Kansas City* (Mo.) *Journal*, March 12, 1899, 2.
6. *The Cresset 1909: The Annual of the Chillicothe High School, Chillicothe, MO*, published by the Junior Class, 1908–1909.
7. "A Large Crowd Witnessed Play," *Chillicothe* (Mo.) *Constitution-Tribune*, May 21, 1909, 9.
8. "Holds Gladstone as Class Model," *Chillicothe* (Mo.) *Constitution-Tribune*, March 25, 1909, 9.
9. "Wiley Appointed a Midshipman," *Chillicothe* (Mo.) *Constitution-Tribune*, March 17, 1910, 8.
10. "Herbert Wiley Failed to Pass Examination," *Chillicothe* (Mo.) *Constitution Tribune,* July 2, 1910, 1.
11. Class of 1915, *The Lucky Bag*, vol. 22 (Philadelphia: Wm. H. Hoskins, 1915), 219.
12. Class of 1913, *The Lucky Bag*, vol. 20 (New York: Chas. L. Willard, 1913), 210.

13. Class of 1915, *Lucky Bag*, 223.
14. Joel Wiley to Herbert Wiley, April 13, 1914, Wiley family.
15. *Chillicothe* (Mo.) *Constitution-Tribune*, August 1, 1914, 8.
16. H. V. Wiley [hereafter Wiley] to Joel Wiley, April 7, 1915, Wiley family.
17. Class of 1915, *Lucky Bag*, 21.
18. Class of 1915, 199.
19. C. H. Woodward, "The Navy's Participation at the Panama Pacific International Exposition," U.S. Naval Institute *Proceedings* 41, no. 1 (January–February 1915), 167–72.
20. Cdr. H. B. Price, Department of Engineering and Naval Construction, U.S. Naval Academy, to Commandant of Midshipmen, January 7, 1915, 1; Capt. L. H. Chandler, Head of Department / Member of the Practice Cruise Committee, U.S. Naval Academy, to the Commandant of Midshipmen, January 7, 1915, 1; both Special Collections and Archives Department, Nimitz Library, U.S. Naval Academy, Annapolis, Md. [hereafter Nimitz Library.]
21. U.S. Naval Academy, Annapolis, Md., 3 July 1915, Notice, Subject: Corrections to N.A. Order No. 66 of 9 April 1915, Nimitz Library.
22. "Extended Cribbing Net," *Washington Post*, June 8, 1915, 2.
23. U.S. Naval Academy Court of Inquiry into 1915 Cheating Scandal, 1, Nimitz Library.
24. Court of Inquiry, 2423.
25. Court of Inquiry, 2425.
26. Court of Inquiry, 2427.
27. Orders of July 12, 1915, to Wiley, Nimitz Library.
28. Log of United States Crab Fleet, 1915, 2, Nimitz Library.
29. Report from Captain Preston, Report, Re: Passage through Canal, U.S.S. *Missouri*, 17 July 1915, Nimitz Library.
30. Preston.
31. Preston.
32. W. F. Fullam to Navy Department (Operations), At Sea, enroute to San Diego, Calif., 24 July, 1915, Nimitz Library.
33. W. F. Fullam, Annual Report of the Superintendent, August 1, 1915, Nimitz Library.
34. Records of Boards: Proceedings of the Court of Inquiry Convened at the Academy into Alleged Frauds Committed by Midshipmen in the Annual Examinations of 1915, RG 405.6.4. entry 217, 4258, Nimitz Library.

35. Department of the Navy, Office of the Judge Advocate General, Washington, August 13, 1915, 1st Indorsement [*sic*], From: Judge Advocate General, To: Bureau of Navigation, Subject: Record of Proceedings of the Court of Inquiry Which Inquired into the Alleged Fraud, Deceit, Cheating, and Other Irregularities on or in Connection with the Annual Examinations at the U.S. Naval Academy, Annapolis, Maryland, in the Year 1915, 1, Nimitz Library.

36. U.S. Naval Academy, "Examinations Inquiry," *Information Quarterly* 1 (October 1915).

37. "Naval Academy Head Is Ordered Relieved: Change Attributed to Admiral Fullam's Dissatisfaction at Result of Cribbing Inquiry," *New York Times*, September 2, 1915, 4.

CHAPTER 2. THE ROAD TO LAKEHURST

1. H. V. Wiley to U.S. Bureau of Navigation, February 12, 1916, National Archives, St. Louis, Mo.

2. Bureau of Navigation to Wiley on board USS *Denver*, April 24, 1917, National Archives, St. Louis, Mo.

3. Wiley to Secretary of the Navy, July 10, 1917. National Archives, St. Louis, Mo.

4. Letter to Herbert V. Wiley, Ensign, USS *Montana*, July 16, 1917, National Archives, St. Louis, Mo.

5. Wiley to Secretary of the Navy (Bureau of Navigation), July 30, 1917, National Archives, St. Louis, Mo.

6. Commandant Second Naval District to Bureau of Navigation, July 31, 1917, National Archives, St. Louis, Mo.

7. Marie Scroggie Wiley to Joel Wiley, October 22, 1917, Wiley family.

8. Wiley to Joel Wiley, October 18, 1917, Wiley family.

9. Bureau of Navigation to Commandant Second Naval District, Newport R. I., October 26, 1917, National Archives, St. Louis, Mo.

10. Wiley to Secretary of the Navy (Bureau of Navigation), Subject: Request for Duty, January 2, 1918, National Archives, St. Louis, Mo.

11. Josephus Daniels, Secretary of the Navy to Wiley, Second Naval District, January 7, 1918, National Archives, St. Louis, Mo.

12. Commanding Officer USS *Wickes*, Bath Iron Works, Bath, Maine, to Navy Department, Bureau of Steam Engineering, Office of the Inspector of Machinery, June 11, 1918, National Archives, St. Louis, Mo.

13. The Influenza Epidemic of 1918, National Archives and Records Administration [NARA], Washington, D.C., 304. Though the world war captured

most of the attention of the media, the influenza pandemic of 1918 killed more people than the war did. An estimated 16 million people died in the war, while the influenza pandemic claimed the lives of an estimated 50 million people worldwide; www.archives.gov/exhibits/influenza-epidemic.

14. John M. Barry, *The Great Influenza: The Story of the Deadliest Pandemic in History* (New York: Penguin Books, 2009), 304–5.

15. Navy Department, Bureau of Navigation, to USS *Wickes*, December 3, 1918, National Archives, St. Louis, Mo.

16. Navy Department, Bureau of Navigation, to USS *Wickes*, December 7, 1918, National Archives, St. Louis, Mo.

17. "Operating in European Waters," *Chillicothe* (Mo.) *Constitution-Tribune*, February 25, 1919, 2.

18. P. H. Silverstone, *The New Navy, 1883–1922*, U.S. Navy Warship Series (New York: Rutledge Taylor & Francis, 2006), 48.

19. Letter to Herbert V. Wiley, USN, USS *Wickes*, December 18, 1919, National Archives, St. Louis, Mo.

20. Commanding Officer USS *Fuller* to Bureau of Navigation, May 25, 1920; Commander Destroyer Flotilla 5 to Bureau of Navigation, Navy Department, May 27, 1920; Commander Destroyer Squadrons, U.S. Pacific Fleet, to Secretary of the Navy (Bureau of Navigation), May 29, 1920; Commander in Chief Pacific Fleet to Chief of Bureau of Navigation, June 4, 1920; all National Archives, St. Louis, Mo.

21. Bureau of Navigation to Wiley, USS *Fuller*, June 15, 1920, National Archives, St. Louis, Mo.

22. Bureau of Navigation to Wiley, USS *Fuller*, September 1, 1920, National Archives, St. Louis, Mo.

23. Bureau of Navigation, to USS *Fuller*, Commander Destroyer Force U.S. Pacific Fleet, October 8, 1920, National Archives, St. Louis, Mo.

24. Commander Destroyer Force U.S. Pacific Fleet to Wiley, December 18, 1920, National Archives, St. Louis, Mo.

25. Bureau of Navigation to Wiley, USS *Radford*, September 10, 1921, National Archives, St. Louis, Mo.

26. C. Stephenson, *Zeppelins: German Airships 1900–1940* (Oxford, U.K.: Osprey, 2004), 5.

27. Stephenson, *Zeppelins*, 3.

28. J. Winchester, *A Chronology of Aviation: The Ultimate History of a Century of Powered Flight* (New York: Metro Books, 2007), 23.

29. Stephenson, *Zeppelins*, 9.
30. Winchester, *Chronology of Aviation*, 27.
31. Winchester, *Chronology*, 29.
32. Winchester, *Chronology*.
33. Winchester, *Chronology*, 31.
34. There is much about the history of zeppelins beyond the scope of this book, but a note about the numbering of zeppelins may help avoid some confusion in the literature. The convention of adding "LZ" (Luftschiffbau Zeppelin) followed by a number indicating the order of the airship's production was the practice of the Zeppelin corporation. Once the zeppelin left the corporation's control, it assumed a designation determined by its new owner. Commercial enterprises gave zeppelins formal names. A list of zeppelins with their manufacturer's and later designations can be found in Douglas H. Robinson, *The Zeppelin in Combat: A History of the German Naval Airship Division 1912–18* (Atglen, Pa.: Schiffer Military/Aviation History, 1994), 387–94.
35. Winchester, *Chronology*.
36. Winchester, *Chronology*.
37. Winchester, *Chronology*, 15.
38. Stephenson, *Zeppelins*, 11.
39. Stephenson, *Zeppelins*.
40. Stephenson, *Zeppelins*, 15.
41. I. Castle, *London 1914–1917: The Zeppelin Menace* (Oxford, U.K.: Osprey, 2008), 19–20.
42. Stephenson, *Zeppelins*, 15.
43. Stephenson, *Zeppelins*.
44. Stephenson, *Zeppelins*, 15–16.
45. Robinson, *The Zeppelin in Combat*, 97.
46. Stephenson, *Zeppelins*, 16.
47. Stephenson, *Zeppelins*, 18.
48. Stephenson, *Zeppelins*.
49. "Secretary Daniels Discusses the Need of Zeppelins," *State Journal (Raleigh, N.C.)*, September 29, 1916, 16.
50. William F. Althoff, *Sky Ships: A History of the Airship in the United States Navy* (New York: Orion Books, 1990), 3.
51. Douglas H. Robinson and Charles L. Keller, *"Up Ship!" U.S. Navy Rigid Airships 1919–1935* (Annapolis, Md.: Naval Institute Press, 1982), 11.
52. Althoff, *Sky Ships*, 19.
53. Althoff, *Sky Ships*, 22.

54. Wiley to Bureau of Navigation, January 4, 1923, National Archives, St. Louis, Mo.

55. Robinson and Keller, *"Up Ship!"* 68–69.

56. Bureau of Navigation to Wiley, U.S. Naval Academy, Annapolis, Maryland, April 5, 1923, National Archives, St. Louis, Mo.

57. F. R. McCrary, Commanding Officer U.S. Naval Air Station Lakehurst N.J. to Chief of Bureau of Navigation, April 11, 1922, National Archives, St. Louis, Mo.

58. Chief of Bureau of Aeronautics to Bureau of the Navy, March 26, 1923, National Archives, St. Louis, Mo.

59. Robinson and Keller, *"Up Ship!"* 68.

60. Althoff, *Sky Ships,* 23.

61. Althoff, *Sky Ships,* 24.

62. Althoff, *Sky Ships.*

63. Althoff, *Sky Ships,* 26.

64. Commanding Officer Naval Air Station Lakehurst N.J. to Wiley, July 12, 1923, National Archives, St. Louis, Mo.

65. Bureau of Aeronautics, orders to Wiley, October 6, 1923, National Archives, St. Louis, Mo.

CHAPTER 3. THE USS *SHENANDOAH* (ZR 1)

1. Aaron J. Keirns, *America's Forgotten Airship Disaster: The Crash of the USS Shenandoah* (Howard, Ohio: Little River, 2010), 20.

2. Althoff, *Sky Ships,* 28.

3. Althoff, *Sky Ships,* 27.

4. Althoff, *Sky Ships,* 28.

5. Logbook, USS *Shenandoah* (ZR 1), October 10, 1923, boxes 1–2, RG 24, A-1, entry 118-G-S, NARA.

6. Logbook, USS *Shenandoah.*

7. Althoff, *Sky Ships,* 32.

8. Keirns, *America's Forgotten Airship Disaster,* 26.

9. Althoff, *Sky Ships,* 32.

10. Capt. W. A. Moffett, Director of Naval Aviation, "Airships and the Scientist," Press Release 089, June 28, 1921, 1, Nimitz Library.

11. Moffett, "Airships and the Scientist," 2.

12. Moffett, "Airships and the Scientist."

13. William F. Trimble, *Admiral William A. Moffett: Architect of Naval Aviation* (Washington, D.C.: Smithsonian Institution Press, 1994), 129–30.

14. Althoff, *Sky Ships*, 33.
15. Logbook, USS *Shenandoah*, January 1, 1924.
16. Logbook, USS *Shenandoah*.
17. "*Shenandoah* Safe after Battle with Big Gale," (Franklin, Pa.) *News-Herald*, January 17, 1924, 1.
18. "Gale Blowing 70 Miles an Hour Hits New York; Six Dead, 3 Ships in Distress," (Franklin, Pa.) *News-Herald*, January 17, 1924, 1.
19. "*Shenandoah* Safe after Battle with Big Gale," 1.
20. "*Shenandoah* Safe after Battle with Big Gale."
21. Logbook, USS *Shenandoah*, January 16, 1924; "*Shenandoah* Safe after Battle with Big Gale," 1.
22. Logbook, USS *Shenandoah*, January 16, 1924.
23. "*Shenandoah* Safe after Battle with Big Gale," 1.
24. Logbook, USS *Shenandoah*, January 17, 1924.
25. "*Shenandoah* Safe after Battle with Big Gale," 6.
26. "*Shenandoah* Safe after Battle with Big Gale."
27. "*Shenandoah* Safe after Battle with Big Gale."
28. "*Shenandoah* Crew Wary on [*sic*] Skipper for Trip to Pole," *Brooklyn (N.Y.) Daily Eagle*, January 19, 1924, 1.
29. "*Shenandoah* Crew Wary."
30. Althoff, *Sky Ships*, 23.
31. Trimble, *Admiral William A. Moffett*, 130.
32. Logbook, USS *Shenandoah*, February 15, 1924.
33. Trimble, *Admiral William A. Moffett*, 130.
34. Althoff, *Sky Ships*, 37.
35. Trimble, *Admiral William A. Moffett*, 130.
36. "In Charge of Aerial Circus," *Chillicothe* (Mo.) *Constitution*, May 8, 1924, 1.
37. Althoff, *Sky Ships*, 37–38.
38. Althoff, *Sky Ships*, 42.
39. Logbook, USS *Shenandoah*, August 8, 1924.
40. Report of Examining Board, U.S. Naval Air Station, Lakehurst, N.J., September 12, 1924, National Archives, St. Louis, MO.
41. Logbook, USS *Shenandoah*, September 3, 1924.
42. Junius B. Wood, "Seeing America from the '*Shenandoah*': An Account of the Record-Making 9,000-Mile Flight from the Atlantic to the Pacific Coast and Return in the Navy's American-Built, American-Manned Airship," *National Geographic* 67, no. 1 (January 1925), 2.
43. Logbook, USS *Shenandoah*, October 7, 1924.

44. Logbook, USS *Shenandoah*, October 8, 1924.
45. Wood, "Seeing America from the *'Shenandoah*,'" 27.
46. Althoff, *Sky Ships*, 44.
47. Logbook, USS *Shenandoah*, October 9, 1924.
48. Logbook, USS *Shenandoah*, October 10, 1924.
49. Logbook, USS *Shenandoah*, October 16, 1924.
50. Logbook, USS *Shenandoah*, October 18, 1924.
51. Wood, "Seeing America from the *'Shenandoah*,'" 47.

CHAPTER 4. THE USS *LOS ANGELES* (ZR 3)

1. William F. Althoff, *USS* Los Angeles: *The Navy's Venerable Airship and Aviation Technology* (Washington, D.C.: Potomac Books, 2004), 30.
2. "*ZR-3* Here after 80-Hour Flight," (Franklin, Pa.) *News-Herald*, October 15, 1924, 1.
3. "*ZR-3* Here after 80-Hour Flight."
4. On the front page of the same issue of this newspaper was a report of another airship disaster. A photograph showed the wreckage of the Army dirigible, *TC 2*, below the heading, "After Bomb Let Go on Army Blimp." This dirigible crashed at Langley Field, Newport News, Virginia, after a bomb on board exploded. Lt. Bruce H. Martin died in the incident; according to the newspaper, "Others of the crew owe their lives to the fact that the balloon was filled with helium instead of highly explosive hydrogen." The arrival of the *ZR 3*, with all its promise, overshadowed this front-page article.
5. Althoff, *USS* Los Angeles, 48.
6. Logbook, USS *Shenandoah*, November 12, 1924.
7. Logbook, USS *Shenandoah*, November 13, 1924.
8. Logbook, USS *Shenandoah*, November 25, 1924.
9. Althoff, *USS* Los Angeles, 51.
10. Althoff, *USS* Los Angeles, 53.
11. Althoff, *USS* Los Angeles.
12. Lt. Cdr. R. R. Paunack, USN, memorandum for the chief of Bureau of Navigation, January 5, 1925, National Archives, St. Louis, Mo.
13. Logbook, USS *Shenandoah*, January 19, 1925.
14. Wiley, "A Celestial Cruise," U.S. Naval Institute *Proceedings* 81, no. 266 (April 1925), 604.
15. Logbook, USS *Los Angeles* (ZR 3), January 24, 1925, RG 24, A1, entry 118-G-L, boxes 1–7, NARA, Washington, D.C.
16. Wiley, "Celestial Cruise," 608.

17. Wiley, "Celestial Cruise," 609.
18. Logbook, USS *Los Angeles*, February 17, 1925.
19. Logbook, USS *Los Angeles*, February 20, 1925.
20. Logbook, USS *Los Angeles*, February 21, 1925.
21. Logbook, USS *Los Angeles,* April 16, 1925.
22. Logbook, USS *Los Angeles,* April 21, 1925.
23. Logbook, USS *Los Angeles,* May 4, 1925.
24. Trimble, *Admiral William A. Moffett,* 152.
25. Logbook, USS *Los Angeles,* May 15, 1925. Among the dignitaries were Graham McNamee, a renowned, pioneering sports radio broadcaster with WEAF in New York City; a representative from Pathé News in New York City; and three flag officers, Rear Adm. C. F. Hughes, Rear Adm. C. C. Bloch, and Rear Adm. Hilary P. Jones. Jones was a senior rear admiral serving on the influential General Board of the U.S. Navy. Hughes served as president of the American Society of Naval Engineering (ASNE). Capt. J. T. Tompkins had been the president of the ASNE from 1923 to 1924. From industry were Irénée du Pont, president of the DuPont Company; Maj. K. K. V. Casey, manager of military sales, DuPont Company; J. W. Rawls, vice president and general manager of the J. G. Brill Company, a manufacturing firm specializing in transportation; a Mr. Stumble from Bethlehem Steel Corporation; Dr. William Elgin from the Franklin Institute in Philadelphia; George Horace Lorimar and Churchill Williams, editor and assistant editor, respectively, of the *Saturday Evening Post*; Eldridge Johnson, founder and president of the Victor Talking Machine Company; John C. Jones, chief of the Philadelphia District Ordnance Office; Maj. J. K. Crane from the Bureau of Ordnance and the War Department; Maj. Gen. Dennis Nolan, acting Chief of Staff of the Army, Atwater Kent, president of the Atwater Kent Company, which in 1925 was the largest maker of radios in the United States; A. C. Dinkey, president of Midvale Steel Company, Philadelphia; Dwight F. Davis, assistant secretary of war; and a few lesser military figures.
26. Commanding Officer, Naval Air Station, Lakehurst, N.J., to Chief of Naval Operations, Subject: Minneapolis: Landing of USS *Los Angeles,* May 13, 1925, NARA.

CHAPTER 5. THE *SHENANDOAH* DISASTER

1. Keirns, *America's Forgotten Airship Disaster,* 31.
2. Commanding Officer, Naval Air Station, Lakehurst, N.J., to Chief of Bureau of Navigation, August 15, 1925, National Archives, St. Louis, Mo.

3. Commanding Officer, Naval Air Station, Lakehurst, N.J., to Chief of Bureau of Navigation, memorandum, Subject: Travel Orders, June 29, 1925, National Archives, St. Louis, Mo.

4. Wiley to Chief of the Bureau of Navigation, September 10, 1925, National Archives, St. Louis, Mo.

5. H. W. Sharpe, "Survivors Return to Lakehurst while Board Visits Scene," (Franklin, Pa.) *News-Herald*, September 4, 1925, 1.

6. Keirns, *America's Forgotten Airship Disaster*, 62.

7. Keirns, *America's Forgotten Airship Disaster*.

8. Sharpe, "Survivors Return to Lakehurst."

9. "*Shenandoah* Caught in a Storm and Sent Crashing to Earth Killing Fourteen," *Chillicothe* (Mo.) *Constitution-Tribune*, September 3, 1925, 9.

10. "*Shenandoah* Crashes in Storm," (Franklin, Pa.) *News-Herald*, September 3, 1925, 1.

11. "*Shenandoah* Crashes in Storm."

12. "*Shenandoah* Crashes in Storm."

13. "Wilbur Denies That Lansdowne Balked at Flight to West," (Franklin, Pa.) *News-Herald*, September 4, 1925, 1.

14. Charles P. Williamson, "Disaster May Mean Finish of Dirigible Plans," (Franklin, Pa.) *News-Herald*, September 4, 1925, 1.

15. Williamson, "Disaster May Mean Finish of Dirigible Plans."

16. "*Shenandoah* Caught in a Storm."

17. "Begin Probe of Air Disaster, Gave Lives to Save Helium, Heinen Says," (Franklin, Pa.) *News-Herald*, September 4, 1925, 11.

18. "Begin Probe of Air Disaster, Navy Will Investigate Capt. Heinen's Charges," (Franklin, Pa.) *News-Herald*, September 4, 1925, 1.

19. "Navy Will Investigate Capt. Heinen's Charges," 11.

20. Secretary of the Navy to: Rear Adm. Hilary P. Jones, President, General Board, Washington, D.C., 16 September 1925, NARA.

21. Proceedings of the Court of Inquiry to Inquire into All the Facts and Circumstances Surrounding the Loss of the U.S.S. *Shenandoah*, September 1925, 6–11, NARA.

22. Proceedings of the Court of Inquiry, 57–66.

23. Proceedings of the Court of Inquiry, 167–68.

24. Proceedings of the Court of Inquiry, 554.

25. Proceedings of the Court of Inquiry, 596.

26. Proceedings of the Court of Inquiry, 597.

27. Proceedings of the Court of Inquiry, 560.

28. Proceedings of the Court of Inquiry, 575–77.

29. Proceedings of the Court of Inquiry, 2224.

CHAPTER 6. CHANGES IN COMMAND

1. Logbook, USS *Los Angeles*, March 15, 1926.

2. Althoff, *USS* Los Angeles, 90.

3. Logbook, USS *Los Angeles*, May 10, 1926.

4. Logbook, USS *Los Angeles*, June 8, 1926.

5. Wiley to Chief of the Bureau of Navigation, August 12, 1926, National Archives, St. Louis, Mo.

6. Commanding Officer, USS *Los Angeles* to Chief of the Bureau of Navigation, August 12, 1926, National Archives, St. Louis, Mo.

7. William F. Althoff, oral history, T. G. W. Settle, July 1976, transcript, 64.

8. Robinson and Keller, *"Up Ship!"* 147.

9. Settle, oral history, 93.

10. Settle, oral history, 9.

11. Bureau of Navigation to Commanding Officer, Naval Air Station, Lakehurst, N.J., September 13, 1926, National Archives, St. Louis, Mo.

12. Althoff, *USS* Los Angeles, 92.

13. Logbook, USS *Los Angeles*, January 20, 1928.

14. Logbook, USS *Los Angeles*, January 27, 1928.

15. Logbook, USS *Los Angeles*.

16. Commanding Officer, USS *Los Angeles*, to Chief of the Bureau of Navigation, March 15, 1928, National Archives, St. Louis, Mo.

17. Logbook, USS *Los Angeles*, February 27, 1928.

18. Logbook, USS *Los Angeles*, February 28, 1928.

19. Logbook, USS *Los Angeles*, February 29, 1928.

20. Logbook, USS *Los Angeles*, July 6, 1928.

21. Logbook, USS *Los Angeles*, July 16, 1928.

22. Logbook, USS *Los Angeles*, July 31, 1928.

23. Althoff, *USS* Los Angeles, 110.

24. Logbook, USS *Los Angeles*, October 6, 1928.

25. Logbook, USS *Los Angeles*, October 8, 1928.

26. Logbook, USS *Los Angeles*, October 9, 1928.

27. "Expect Dirigible to Pass over City at 10 Tonight," *Chillicothe* (Mo.) *Constitution-Tribune*, October 9, 1928, 1.

28. "Expect Dirigible to Pass over City at 10 Tonight."

29. "Wiley Makes His Promised Visit Here Tuesday Night," *Chillicothe* (Mo.) *Constitution-Tribune*, October 10, 1928, 1.

30. "Tears Again Come to Eyes of Wiley's Aged Father at Wheeling," (Jefferson City, Mo.) *Daily Capital News*, April 5, 1933, 1.

31. "Wiley Wires Appreciation to Livingston County Folk," *Chillicothe* (Mo.) *Constitution-Tribune*, October 11, 1928, 1.

32. "Wiley Wires Appreciation to Livingston County Folk."

33. Wiley, memorandum to All Officers, USS *Los Angeles*, October 11, 1928, National Archives, St. Louis, Mo.

34. J. L. Killgallen, "*Graf Zeppelin* Rests in Lakehurst Hangar beside *Los Angeles*," *Olean* (N.Y.) *Times*, October 16, 1928, 1.

35. Harold G. Dick, with Douglas H. Robinson, *The Golden Age of the Great Passenger Airships Graf Zeppelin and Hindenburg* (Washington, D.C.: Smithsonian Institution, 1985), 35.

36. Killgallen, "*Graf Zeppelin* Rests in Lakehurst Hangar beside *Los Angeles*," 1.

37. Killgallen, "*Graf Zeppelin* Rests in Lakehurst Hangar beside *Los Angeles*."

38. Despatch [*sic*] to Wiley, NAS Lakehurst, N.J., October 17, 1928, National Archives, St. Louis, Mo.

39. Harry W. Graham, Secretary, Chillicothe Chamber of Commerce Associates, Inc., to Wiley, October 16, 1928, Wiley family.

40. Wiley to Harry W. Graham, October 22, 1928, National Archives, St. Louis, Mo.

41. Wiley to Fay, October 23, 1928, Wiley family.

42. Dick and Robinson, *Graf Zeppelin and Hindenburg*, 37.

43. William A. Moffett, memorandum for Chief of the Bureau of Navigation, October 24, 1028, National Archives, St. Louis, Mo.

44. Logbook, USS *Los Angeles*, October 29, 1928.

45. Wiley to Chief of the Bureau of Navigation, Subject: Change of Duty: Request For, February 16, 1929, National Archives, St. Louis, Mo.

46. Commanding Officer, USS *Los Angeles*, first endorsement to Wiley to Bureau of Navigation, March 6, 1929, National Archives, St. Louis, Mo.

47. Logbook, USS *Los Angeles*, March 4, 1929.

48. Althoff, *USS* Los Angeles, 118.

49. Logbook, USS *Los Angeles*, May 9, 1929.

CHAPTER 7. COMMANDING THE *LOS ANGELES*

1. Logbook, USS *Los Angeles*, July 3, 1929.

2. Logbook, USS *Los Angeles*, August 20, 1929.

3. Chief of Naval Operations to Chief of the Bureau of Navigation; Subject: Lieutenant Commander H. V. Wiley, U.S. Navy: Authorization to Proceed to Cleveland, Ohio, July 22, 1929, National Archives, St. Louis, Mo.

4. Logbook, USS *Los Angeles*, August 28, 1929.

5. Wiley to J. A. Wiley, September 21, 1929, Wiley family.

6. H. H. Metz, "Flying Notables Differ on Efficiency of Dirigible over Airplane," (Zanesville, Ohio) *Times Recorder*, August 29, 1929, 1.

7. Metz, "Flying Notables Differ."

8. Wiley to Chief of the Bureau of Navigation, August 19, 1929, National Archives, St. Louis, Mo.

9. Commanding Officer, U.S. Naval Air Station, Lakehurst, N.J., to Chief of the Bureau of Navigation, Subject: Lieutenant Commander H. V. Wiley, U.S.N.: Change of Duty, Request For, August 22, 1929, National Archives, St. Louis, Mo.

10. Dick and Robinson, *Graf Zeppelin and Hindenburg*, 39.

11. United Press, "Refueling of Zeppelin Started at Lakehurst for Trip around the World," (Harrisburg, Pa.) *Evening News*, August 5, 1929, 1.

12. "Zeppelin Stowaway to Be Punished in Berlin," (Harrisburg, Pa.) *Evening News*, August 5, 1929, 5.

13. United Press, "Giant Airship Starting Flight around World, Far Out over Atlantic," (Harrisburg, Pa.) *Evening News*, August 8, 1929, 19.

14. "Youth Detected Trying to Board *Graf Zeppelin*," (Harrisburg, Pa.) *Evening News*, August 8, 1929, 19.

15. "*Graf Zeppelin* Ends World-Circling Flight Thursday," (Zanesville, Ohio) *Times Recorder*, August 29, 1929, 1.

16. "Due at Cleveland Today," *Scranton* (Pa.) *Republican*, August 28, 1929, 1.

17. "*Graf Zeppelin* Ends World-Circling Flight Thursday."

18. L. C. Wilson, "Graf Is Safe at Lakehurst: Great Record Set—Encircles the Globe in 21 Days, 7 Hours," (Franklin, Pa.) *News-Herald*, August 29, 1929, 1.

19. "Plaudits of N.Y. Accorded Dr. Eckener," (Franklin, Pa.) *News-Herald*, August 30, 1929, 1.

20. Dick and Robinson, *Graf Zeppelin and Hindenburg*, 32.

21. "American Smokes on Zep, Arouses Ire of Passengers," *Brooklyn* (N.Y.) *Daily Eagle*, September 4, 1929, 16.

22. Frederick S. Hogg to Wiley, n.d. (early October 1929), Wiley family.

23. Wiley to Hogg, 3 October 1929, Wiley family.

24. J. M. Shoemaker, Report of Trip to Germany and France, October 28, 1929, NARA.

25. "*Graf Zeppelin* Reaches Home Hangar: Beat Round World Record from Home to Home by a Day," *Sterling* (Ill.) *Daily Gazette*, September 4, 1929, 1.

26. "*Graf Zeppelin* Reaches Home Hangar."

27. A year after this visit by Wiley and Mayer, the *R 101* crashed in France, killing forty-eight of her fifty-four passengers and crew. This disaster effectively put an end to Great Britain's airship program.

28. Shoemaker, Report of Trip to Germany and France, 1–15, enclosure to Shoemaker to Wiley, October 28, 1929, National Archives, St. Louis, Mo.

29. "Two Great Craft Now Being Built for Navy May Be Followed by Big Trans-Pacific Liners," *Santa Cruz* (Calif.) *Evening News*, September 5, 1929, 12.

30. Logbook, USS *Los Angeles*, September 24, 1929.

31. Chief of the Bureau of Aeronautics to Chief of the Bureau of Navigation, Subject: Lieutenant Commander H. V. Wiley, U.S.N.; Change of Duty, Request For, September 4, 1929, NARA.

32. Wiley to Ralph E. Davison, Office of Naval Operations, October 18, 1929, NARA.

33. "Wiley Tells of Plans for Giant Airship: Navy Dirigible, '*ZRS-4*,' Going into Construction Today, Will Carry Six Scouting Planes," *Hartford* (Conn.) *Courant*, October 31, 1929, 17.

34. W. A. Moffett to Wiley, December 16, 1929, NARA.

35. Trimble, *Admiral William A. Moffett*, 214.

36. Althoff, *USS* Los Angeles, 86.

37. Logbook, USS *Los Angeles*, January 24, 1930.

38. Logbook, USS *Los Angeles*, January 26, 1930.

39. Althoff, *USS* Los Angeles, 131.

40. Logbook, USS *Los Angeles*, January 31, 1930.

41. Wiley to Dr. J. C. Hunsaker, January 29, 1930, National Archives, St. Louis, Mo.

42. Althoff, *USS* Los Angeles, 138.

CHAPTER 8. THE USS *TENNESSEE* (BB 43)

1. Wiley to Bureau of Navigation, March 31, 1930, Report of Compliance with Orders, National Archives, St. Louis, Mo.

2. Letter from H.V. Wiley to Fay Wiley Oren, March 12, 1930, 2, Wiley family.

3. Logbook, USS *Los Angeles*, Monday, March 31, 1930.

4. Wiley to J. A. Wiley, April 8, 1930, 4, Wiley family.

5. Wiley to Fay and Rex Oren, April 22, 1930, 2, Wiley family.

6. "Naval Parley Long Drawn Out, Will Last Two Months If the French Return," *Sterling* (Ill.) *Daily Gazette*, March 1, 1930, 1.

7. "End of Naval Parley Is Near: Breakdown of Negotiations Said Only Matter of Few Days," *Harrisburg* (Pa.) *Telegraph*, March 31, 1930, 3.

8. Marie Wiley to Fay Wiley Oren, August 14, 1930, 1, Wiley family.

9. "Fleet Is Mobilized for Hoover Review: Mimic Warfare to Be Waged after Warships Steam Past the President—New *Salt Lake City* with Eight-Inch Guns Plays Part," *Brooklyn* (N.Y.) *Daily Eagle* (Brooklyn, NY), May 20, 1930, 2.

10. "Battle Fleet Leaves for Hoover Review: Sixty-five Vessels, Led by *Texas*, Steam Out of Harbor—*Bremen* Salutes at Quarantine," *New York Times*, May 20, 1930, 25.

11. "U.S. Naval Fleet Mobilizes to Parade before Commander-In-Chief in Stately Review: President Hoover on Cruiser *Salt Lake City* Witnesses Parade and Then Sham Battle of Ships of the Air, Ships of Sea and Ships of the Underseas—Air Feats Will Complete Day's Programs," *Lebanon* (Pa.) *Daily News*, May 20, 1930, 7.

12. Logbook, USS *Los Angeles*, May 20, 1930.

13. "U.S. Naval Fleet Mobilizes."

14. Logbook, USS *Los Angeles*, May 20, 1930.

15. "Suicide of Naval Officer Laid to Naval Treaty," *Moberly* (Mo.) *Monitor-Index*, May 20, 1930, 4.

16. Wiley to W. A. Moffett, May 27, 1930, National Archives, St. Louis, Mo.

17. Moffett to Wiley, June 10, 1930, National Archives, St. Louis, Mo.

18. Wiley to J. A. Wiley, May 30, 1930, 1–3, Wiley family.

19. "Zeppelin Lands Safely, Riding Out 40-Mile Gale; Sails for Home Today," *Brooklyn Daily* (N.Y.) *Eagle*, May 31, 1930, 1.

20. Wiley to Fay Wiley Oren, August 9, 1930, 2, Wiley family.

21. Marie S. Wiley to Fay Wiley Oren, August 14, 1930, 1, Wiley family.

22. Wiley to J. A. Wiley, September 28, 1930, 1–4.

23. Wiley to J. A. Wiley. Marie S. Wiley was laid to rest at Angeles Abbey in Compton, California, on September 20, 1930. In 2012, Gordon, David, and Marie Wiley (Ross) had Marie relocated to Golden Gate National Cemetery alongside her husband.

24. Wiley to Fay Wiley Oren, September 30, 1930, 1, Wiley family.

25. Commanding Officer, Naval Air Station, Lakehurst, N.J., to Chief of the Bureau of Navigation, April 18, 1931, National Archives, St. Louis, Mo.

26. "Herbert Wiley to the *Akron* Airship," *Chillicothe* (Mo.) *Constitution-Tribune*, May 28, 1931, 1.

27. "Herbert V. Wiley, Famed Aviator, Home This Week," *Chillicothe* (Mo.) *Constitution-Tribune*, June 15, 1931, 1.

28. Wiley to Bureau of Navigation, Compliance with Orders, June 22, 1931, National Archives, St. Louis, Mo.

29. Wiley to Bureau of Navigation, Report of Compliance with Orders, October 27, 1931, National Archives, St. Louis, Mo.

CHAPTER 9. THE USS *AKRON* (ZRS 4)

1. "New Air Giants to Meet Attack with Own Planes," *Brooklyn* (N.Y.) *Daily Eagle*, April 15, 1928, 72.

2. John Swinfield, *Airship: Design, Development and Disaster* (Annapolis, Md.: Naval Institute Press, 2012), 216.

3. Swinfield, *Airship*, 217.

4. Swinfield, *Airship*, 220.

5. "Huge Sabotage Plan Seen in *Akron* Plot," *Salem* (Ohio) *News,* March 20, 1931, 1.

6. "Judge Frees Man Held in 'Akron' Plot," *Coshocton* (Ohio) *Tribune*, April 28, 1931, 1.

7. Richard K. Smith, *The Airships* Akron *&* Macon: *Flying Aircraft Carriers of the United States Navy* (Annapolis, Md.: Naval Institute Press, 1965), 35.

8. Smith, Akron *&* Macon.

9. Swinfield, *Airship*, 221–22.

10. Smith, Akron *&* Macon, 39.

11. Smith, Akron *&* Macon, 43.

12. "Herbert Wiley Expects to Fly over City Tonight in New Naval Air Giant, *Akron*," *Chillicothe* (Mo.) *Constitution-Tribune*, October 16, 1931, 1.

13. "*Akron* Disappoints Curious Crowds about Chillicothe," *Chillicothe* (Mo.) *Constitution-Tribune*, October 17, 1931, 1.

14. "*Akron* Will Leave Tonight for Lakehurst," (Franklin, Pa.) *News-Herald*, October 21, 1931, 1.

15. "*Akron* Lands at Lakehurst," (East Liverpool, Ohio) *Evening Review*, October 22, 1931, 1.

16. "*Akron* Lands at Lakehurst."

17. Logbook, USS *Akron*, October 27, 1931, RG 24 A-1 entry 118-G, box 1, NARA.

18. Smith, Akron *&* Macon, 43.

19. Logbook, USS *Akron,* November 2, 1931.

20. "*Akron* and Sister Ship over Capital," (Franklin, Pa.) *News-Herald,* November 2, 1931, 1.

21. Smith, Akron *&* Macon, 49.

22. "'Akron' Note Received by Wiley Boy," *Hartford* (Conn.) *Courant,* November 25, 1931, 10.

23. Logbook, USS *Akron,* January 9, 1932.

24. Smith, Akron *&* Macon, 49.

25. "House Naval Committee Votes Probe of Rumored Defects of U.S.S. *Akron,*" (Monongahela, Pa.) *Daily Republican,* January 5, 1932, 1.

26. "Giant Airship Damaged, U.S.S. *Akron* Breaks Loose and Fabric of Stern Torn, Leaving Wide Gap," *Rushville* (Ind.) *Republican,* February 22, 1932, 1; "'Akron' Is Rejected by Solons: Rep. McClintic of House Committee Ends Investigation of Dirigible," *Coshocton* (Ohio) *Tribune,* February 23, 1932, 1.

27. Smith, Akron *&* Macon, 53.

28. Logbook, USS *Akron,* February 22, 1932.

29. Smith, Akron *&* Macon, 53.

30. Logbook, USS *Akron,* February 22, 1932.

31. "'Akron' Is Rejected by Solons," 5.

32. "'Akron' Is Rejected by Solons," 1.

33. Smith, Akron *&* Macon, 55.

34. Logbook, USS *Akron,* April 28, 1932.

35. Logbook, USS *Akron,* May 2, 1932.

36. Logbook, USS *Akron,* May 3, 1932.

37. Chief of the Bureau of Navigation to Wiley, Subject: U.S.S. *Akron:* Excerpts from Report of Full Speed Trials, 20 June 1932, National Archives, St. Louis, Mo.

38. Logbook, USS *Akron,* May 9, 1932.

39. "'Akron' Strikes Storm: Forced to Retreat," *Santa Cruz* (Calif.) *Sentinel,* May 10, 1932, 1.

40. Logbook, USS *Akron,* May 10, 1932.

41. "Two Men Killed Attempting Moor [*sic*] Navy's Dirigible," *Corsicana* (Tex.) *Daily Sun,* May 11, 1932, 1.

42. "Air Cruiser *Akron* Kills Two Men," *Dunkirk* (N.Y.) *Evening Observer,* May 12, 1932, 1.

43. "*Akron* Ties Up after Accident: Will Go On to Sunnydale Report," *Albuquerque* (N.Mex.) *Journal,* May 12, 1932, 1.

44. "Two Men Killed."

45. Smith, Akron & Macon, 57.

46. Logbook, USS *Akron*, May 12, 1932.

47. "Capt. Robt. Dollar 'Grand Old Man of Pacific' Is Dead," *Corsicana* (Tex.) *Semi-Weekly Light*, May 17, 1932, 1.

48. "Rival American Fleets Battle," (Danville, Pa.) *Morning News*, March 12, 1932, 2.

49. "Naval Armada Awaits *Akron*," *Modesto News-Herald* (Modesto, Calif.), May 31, 1932, 1.

50. "Naval Armada Awaits *Akron*."

51. Logbook, USS *Akron*, June 1, 1932.

52. Smith, Akron & Macon, 58.

53. Logbook, USS *Akron*, June 3, 1932.

54. Robinson and Keller, *"Up Ship!"* 184; Althoff, *Sky Ships*, 99.

55. "Jahncke Wants *Akron* Retained on Pacific," *San Bernardino County* (Calif.) *Sun*, August 7, 1932, 5.

56. "*Akron* to Leave on Trip to East Early Tomorrow," *Santa Cruz* (Calif.) *Evening News*, June 10, 1932, 1.

57. Logbook, USS *Akron*, June 11, 1932.

58. Smith, Akron & Macon, 61.

59. Smith, Akron & Macon.

60. Smith, Akron & Macon, 62.

61. William F. Althoff, oral history, C. E. Rosendahl, July 13, 1975, 1.

62. Althoff, oral history, Rosendahl.

63. During his cited interview with William F. Althoff in 1976, Settle described what was happening: "Relatively senior officers—senior [lieutenant commanders, commanders, and captains]—were inducted into LTA, given ground-school, perfunctory balloon and blimp courses, carried on board rigids 'in training,' and given Head-of-Department, or Exec, or command billets without the experience of working their way up thru the more junior levels of ships' officers. Some of these senior inductees were conscientious airship 'believers' who wanted to, and tried to, qualify themselves and 'do a job.' Others were just 'riders on the line,' exerting themselves just enough to 'get by,' whose main purpose in 'volunteering' for LTA was to get flight pay and a 'soft shore billet.'" Settle added, "In the '30s I advocated abolishing flight pay for LTA because it had brought in 'dead-wood' which were no assets, rather liabilities, to LTA. But my advocacy did not succeed."

64. Logbook, USS *Akron,* June 22, 1932.

65. *"Akron's* Change of Commanders Sends Rosendahl Back to Sea," *Shamokin* (Pa.) *News-Dispatch,* June 28, 1932, 12.

66. Smith, Akron & Macon, 65.

67. Logbook, USS *Akron,* June 30, 1932.

68. Logbook, USS *Akron,* August 22, 1932.

69. "Accident Damages Fin of U.S.S. *Akron,*" *Marion* (Ohio) *Star,* August 23, 1932, 7.

70. Commandant, Fourth Naval District, to Wiley, Subject: Board of Investigation to Inquire into and Report upon Damage Done to U.S.S. *Akron* at Lakehurst, N.J., August 22, 1932, National Archives, St. Louis, Mo.

71. Commandant, Fourth Naval District, to Wiley.

72. Smith, Akron & Macon, 66.

73. Logbook, USS *Akron,* September–December 1932.

74. Smith, Akron & Macon, 67.

75. Smith, Akron & Macon, 69.

76. Smith, Akron & Macon.

77. Edward Arpee, *From Frigates to Flat-Tops* (Lake Forest, Ill.: Edward Arpee, 1953), 256.

78. Smith, Akron & Macon, 73; Robinson and Keller, *"Up Ship!"* 185.

79. Logbook, USS *Akron,* January 8, 1933.

80. Smith, Akron & Macon, 73.

81. Logbook, USS *Akron,* January 14, 1933.

82. Chief of the Bureau of Navigation to Wiley, Subject: Temporary Additional Duty, 2 March 1933, National Archives, St. Louis, Mo.

CHAPTER 10. THE CRASH OF THE *AKRON*

1. *Akron* Court of Inquiry, 9.

2. Wiley to Secretary of the Navy, Subject: Report of Loss of the U.S.S. *Akron,* April 6, 1933, 1, NARA.

3. *Akron* Court of Inquiry, 12; Wiley to Secretary of the Navy, April 6, 1933, 2.

4. *Akron* Court of Inquiry, 13.

5. Wiley to Secretary of the Navy, April 6, 1933, 2.

6. *Akron* Court of Inquiry, 14.

7. Wiley to Secretary of the Navy, April 6, 1933, 2.

8. *Akron* Court of Inquiry, 15.

9. Wiley to Secretary of the Navy, April 6, 1933, 2.

10. *Akron* Court of Inquiry, 84.

11. *Akron* Court of Inquiry, 66.

12. "Ship's Captain Saw Men Die after *Akron* Hit," *Brooklyn* (N.Y.) *Daily Eagle*, April 4, 1933, 2.

13. Wiley to Secretary of the Navy, April 6, 1933, 4.

14. "Ship's Captain Saw Men Die."

15. William T. Generous Jr, *Sweet Pea at War: A History of USS* Portland (Lexington: University Press of Kentucky, 2003), 9.

16. Wiley to Secretary of the Navy, April 6, 1933, 4.

17. "3 Survivors, Body of Copeland Reach Shore," (Franklin, Pa.) *News-Herald*, April 4, 1933, 6.

18. "Three Rescued in *Akron* Wreck," *Brooklyn* (N.Y.) *Daily Eagle*, April 4, 1933, 3.

19. "Airship Fell in Flames as Lightning Hit" (Franklin, Pa.) *News-Herald*, April 4, 1933,1.

20. Arpee, *From Frigates to Flat-Tops*, 245.

21. "Admiral Moffett's Wife Still Hopeful," (Franklin, Pa.) *News-Herald*, April 4, 1933, 1.

22. "Wives of *Akron* Crew Waiting," *Brooklyn* (N.Y.) *Daily Eagle*, April 4, 1933, 4.

23. "Tears Again Come to Eyes of Wiley's Aged Father at Wheeling," (Jefferson City, Mo.) *Daily Capital News*, April 5, 1933, 1.

24. Generous, *Sweet Pea at War*, 4.

25. Generous, *Sweet Pea at War*, 10.

26. "Roosevelt Joins Nation in Mourning Terrible Disaster," (Franklin, Pa.) *News-Herald*, April 4, 1933, 1.

27. "Survivors of *Akron* Meet Roosevelt," *Oakland* (Calif.) *Tribune*, April 6, 1933, 1.

28. "High Mass to Be Said for Lost Crew," *Oakland* (Calif.) *Tribune*, April 6, 1933, 2.

CHAPTER 11. AFTERMATH OF THE *AKRON*

1. "Will Build No More Dirigibles," *Brooklyn* (N.Y.) *Daily Eagle*, April 4, 1933, 6.

2. "Will Build No More Dirigibles."

3. "Will Build No More Dirigibles," 2.

4. "Will Build No More Dirigibles," 3.

5. Secretary of the Navy to Rear Admiral Henry V. Butler, U.S. Navy, Commandant, U.S. Navy Yard, Washington, D.C., Subject: Court of Inquiry to Inquire into All the Facts and Circumstances Surrounding the Loss of the U.S.S. *Akron*, 4 April 1933, NARA.

6. *Akron* Court of Inquiry, 11.

7. *Akron* Court of Inquiry, 16.

8. Arpee, *From Frigates to Flat-Tops*, 255.

9. Althoff, oral history, Rosendahl.

10. *Akron* Court of Inquiry, 31.

11. *Akron* Court of Inquiry, 48–49.

12. *Akron* Court of Inquiry, 50.

13. *Akron* Court of Inquiry.

14. *Akron* Court of Inquiry, 55.

15. *Akron* Court of Inquiry, 62.

16. *Akron* Court of Inquiry, 175.

17. *Akron* Court of Inquiry, 176.

18. *Akron* Court of Inquiry, 18.

19. *Akron* Court of Inquiry, 191.

20. *Akron* Court of Inquiry, 193.

21. *Akron* Court of Inquiry, 194.

22. "Airship Fell in Flames as Lightning Hit," 1.

23. *Akron* Court of Inquiry, 198.

24. H. A. Plummer, "A Washington Daybook," (Greenville, Pa.) *Record-Argus,* May 23, 1933, 4.

25. *Akron* Court of Inquiry, 456.

26. *Akron* Court of Inquiry, 470.

27. *Akron* Court of Inquiry, 471.

28. *Akron* Court of Inquiry, 459.

29. *Akron* Court of Inquiry, 472.

30. Logbook, USS *Akron,* April 3, 1933.

31. "Wreckage of *Akron* Inspected by Divers But No Bodies Found," *Statesville* (N.C.) *Record and Landmark,* April 21, 1933, 7.

32. "Entire Wreckage of Big Navy Blimp Located," *Hutchinson* (Kans.) *News,* April 27, 1933, 1.

33. "*Akron* May Still Be Sailing Skies, Aeronautical Expert's Theory," *Waco* (Tex.) *News-Tribune,* April 27, 1933, 1.

34. Smith, Akron *&* Macon, 85.

35. Charles Emery Rosendahl, *What About the Airship?* (New York: Charles Scribner's Sons, 1938), 115–16.

36. *What About the Airship?,* 123–24.

37. "*Akron* Crash Laid to 'Error In Judgment,'" *Kingsport* (Tenn.) *Times,* May 17, 1933, 1.

38. "*Akron* Probe Favors New Ship Built," *Santa Cruz* (Calif.) *News,* June 10, 1933, 1.

39. "Committee Recommends Replacement of *Akron* for Service in Navy," (Harlingen, Tex.) *Valley Morning Star,* June 16, 1933, 3.

40. "U.S.S. *Macon* on New Test Trip," (Greenville, Pa.) *Record-Argus,* May 15, 1933, 2.

41. Bureau of Navigation to Wiley, Subject: Travel Orders to Akron, Ohio, Trials of U.S.S. *Macon,* June 1, 1933, National Archives, St. Louis, Mo.

42. Bureau of Navigation to Wiley, Subject: Change of Duty, June 14, 1933, National Archives, St. Louis, Mo.

43. Wiley to Bureau of Navigation, Report of Compliance with Orders, June 27, 1933, National Archives, St. Louis, Mo.

44. "*Akron* Probe Favors New Ship Build," *Santa Cruz* (Calif.) *Evening News,* June 10, 1933, 1.

45. "Navy Expects to Continue to Give Flyers Sea Duty," *Santa Cruz* (Calif.) *Evening News,* June 16, 1933, 3.

46. NAS Lakehurst, naval message to Navy Department, 16 June 1933, National Archives, St. Louis, Mo.

47. "Wiley Shows the Need for Preparedness," *Chillicothe* (Mo.) *Constitution-Tribune,* June 20, 1933, 1.

48. "Wiley Shows the Need for Preparedness."

49. Wiley Report of Compliance with Orders, June 27, 1933.

50. "Marie Wiley Was Belle of the Ship," *Chillicothe* (Mo.) *Constitution-Tribune,* October 16, 1933.

51. Wiley to father and sister, October 29, 1933, Wiley family.

52. Wiley to father, October 23, 1933, Wiley family.

53. Wiley to father and sister, July 5, 1934, 2, Wiley family.

54. Wiley to father and sister, July 5, 1934, 3–4.

55. Wiley to father and sister, November 13, 1933, 1, Wiley family.

56. "Fleet Salutes President in Navy Review," *Mason City* (Iowa) *Globe-Gazette,* May 31, 1943, 1.

57. Wiley to father and sister, December 16, 1933, 1–2, Wiley family.

58. Wiley to father and sister, April 1, 1934, Wiley family.

59. Wiley, "Value of Airships," U.S. Naval Institute *Proceedings* (May 1934), 665–71.

60. Wiley, "Value of Airships," 671.

61. Bureau of Navigation to Wiley, Subject: Change of Duty, March 22, 1934, National Archives, St. Louis, Mo.

62. Wiley to father and sister, June 7, 1934, Wiley family.

63. "Commander-Elect Puts Decision Up to His Two Boys," *Long Beach* (Calif.) *Press-Telegram*, April 25, 1934, 1.

64. Wiley, Report of Compliance with Orders, U.S.S. *Macon*, July 11, 1934, National Archives, St. Louis, Mo.

CHAPTER 12. THE USS *MACON* (ZRS 5)

1. Smith, Akron *&* Macon, 93.

2. John Toland, *The Great Dirigibles: Their Triumphs & Disasters* (New York: Dover, 1972), 276.

3. Toland, *Great Dirigibles.*

4. Toland, *Great Dirigibles.*

5. Logbook, USS *Macon*, April 21, 1934, NARA.

6. Smith, Akron *&* Macon, 117.

7. Logbook, USS *Macon*, April 22, 1934.

8. "*Macon's* Caribbean Flight to Decide Airship Policy," *Salt Lake Tribune* (Salt Lake City, Utah), May 7, 1934, 1; "*Macon* Worth for Fleet to Be Discussed," *San Bernardino County* (Calif.) *Sun*, May 10, 1934, 1; "Airship's Value to Fleet Will Be Known Soon," *Sedalia* (Mo.) *Democrat*, May 10, 1934, 3.

9. "*Macon* Worth for Fleet," 2–3.

10. "Airship's Value to Fleet," 3.

11. Smith, Akron *&* Macon, 121.

12. Logbook, USS *Macon*, May 6, 1934.

13. "*Macon* Worth for Fleet," 2–3.

14. "Navy Chieftains Debating Giant Airships' Worth," *Scranton* (Pa.) *Republican*, May 10, 1934, 1.

15. Logbook, USS *Macon*, May 18, 1934.

16. Logbook, USS *Macon*, July 11, 1934.

17. Logbook, USS *Macon*, July 11, 1934.

18. A. H. Dresel, U.S.S. *Macon*: Damage to Structure in Flight to Opa-locka, Florida—Report of, U.S. Naval Air Station, Sunnyvale, Mountain View, Calif., June 8, 1934, NARA.

19. Capt. F. R. McCrary, Asst. Chief of Bureau of Aeronautics to Commanding Officer, U.S.S. *Macon*, Subject: U.S.S. *Macon*: Damage to Girders, July 24, 1934, NARA.

20. Toland, *Great Dirigibles*, 279–80.

21. John T. Mason Jr., "Reminiscences of Rear Admiral Harold B. Miller, U.S. Navy (Retired)," U.S. Naval Institute, Annapolis, Md., 1995, 73.

22. "Reminiscences of Rear Admiral Miller," 74.

23. "Reminiscences of Rear Admiral Miller," 75.

24. "Reminiscences of Rear Admiral Miller," 84.

25. "Reminiscences of Rear Admiral Miller," 75.

26. "President Starts On His Vacation Cruise," *Gaffney* (S.C.) *Ledger*, July 3, 1934, 6.

27. "Roosevelt to Visit Panama Wednesday," *Bismarck* (N.Dak.) *Tribune*, July 11, 1934, 1.

28. Smith, Akron & Macon, 128. At the time of this adventure, Harold B. Miller was a lieutenant. In later life, as a retired rear admiral, he gave an interview to author John T. Mason Jr. in which he claimed credit for the idea of intercepting the president: "I was a promoter type, so I got together with Doc Wiley and said, 'Gee, this is our chance. Let's go out and intercept the President. We'll drop all this new stuff on him, the newspaper published the morning before, and we'll just really let the world know he met an airship around here.' He thought that was great." "Reminiscences of Rear Admiral Miller," 77.

29. Logbook, USS *Macon*, July 18, 1934.

30. Logbook, USS *Macon*, July 19, 1934.

31. "Reminiscences of Rear Admiral Miller," 78.

32. "'Macon' Contacts the President's Cruiser and Delivers Papers," *Santa Cruz* (Calif.) *Sentinel*, July 20, 1934, 1.

33. W. O. Boss, "The *Macon* Mail Drop to FDR on the *Houston*," *Jack Knight Air Log: The Zeppelin Collector*, July 1997, 44, NARA.

34. "Reminiscences of Rear Admiral Miller," 78; Smith, Akron & Macon, 128.

35. Smith, Akron & Macon, 128.

36. "Reminiscences of Rear Admiral Miller," 78.

37. Smith, Akron & Macon, 131.

38. Smith, Akron & Macon.

39. Smith, Akron & Macon.

40. "Reminiscences of Rear Admiral Miller," 79.

41. "Reminiscences of Rear Admiral Miller."

42. "Reminiscences of Rear Admiral Miller."

43. "Reminiscences of Rear Admiral Miller."

44. "Roosevelt Returns Today from Vacation: Presidential Party Due to Reach Astoria This Evening—Leaves Friday," *Santa Ana* (Calif.) *Register,* August 2, 1934, 1.

45. "Nazism Strengthened by House Painter's Rise to Supreme High Command," *Santa Ana* (Calif.) *Register,* August 2, 1934, 1.

46. "Reminiscences of Rear Admiral Miller," 79.

47. "Reminiscences of Rear Admiral Miller," 81.

48. "Reminiscences of Rear Admiral Miller."

49. Logbook, USS *Macon,* August 8, 1934; "Reminiscences of Rear Admiral Miller."

50. "Reminiscences of Rear Admiral Miller."

51. "Reminiscences of Rear Admiral Miller," 82.

52. Logbook, USS *Macon,* 27 September 1934.

53. "Six of the Twelve Boats to Honolulu Complete Trip," *Tipton* (Ind.) *Daily Tribune,* July 20, 1934, 4.

54. "Planes to Hunt Missing Yachts," (Harrisburg, Pa.) *Evening News,* July 21, 1934, 1; "Search Started for Trio in Small Ship," *San Bernardino County* (Calif.) *Sun,* September 27, 1934, 1.

55. Logbook, USS *Macon,* September 28, 1934; "*Macon* Back Home after a Cruise of Three Days," *Santa Cruz* (Calif.) *Sentinel,* September 29, 1934, 1.

56. "Overdue Craft Reaches Harbor," *San Bernardino County* (Calif.) *Sun,* September 30, 1934, 1.

57. Logbook, USS *Macon,* October 11, 1934.

58. Logbook, USS *Macon.*

59. Logbook, USS *Macon,* November 8, 1934.

60. Logbook, USS *Macon,* November 9, 1934.

61. Logbook, USS *Macon.*

62. Logbook, USS *Macon.*

63. Logbook, USS *Macon.*

64. Logbook, USS *Macon,* 7 December 1934.

65. Smith, Akron *&* Macon, 141.

66. Logbook, USS *Macon,* December 7, 1934.

67. Smith, Akron *&* Macon, 145.

68. Smith, Akron *&* Macon.

69. "Hull Given Note Today Ending Pact," *Santa Ana* (Calif.) *Register,* December 29, 1934, 1.

70. Logbook, USS *Macon,* January 3, 1934.

71. Smith, *Akron & Macon*, 147.

72. Smith, *Akron & Macon*; logbook, USS *Macon*, February 1, 1934.

73. Smith, *Akron & Macon*, 147.

74. "Joseph A. Wiley Dies at Trenton," *Chillicothe* (Mo.) *Constitution-Tribune*, February 6, 1935, 1.

75. Wiley to Charles Kelso, February 27, 1935, Wiley family.

76. Smith, *Akron & Macon*, 151.

CHAPTER 13. THE END OF AN ERA

1. George W. Campbell, "Five O'Clock off California," *Saturday Evening Post*, May 15, 1937, 20.

2. Logbook, USS *Macon*, February 11, 1934.

3. Campbell, "Five O'Clock off California," 20.

4. Logbook, USS *Macon*, February 11, 1934.

5. Campbell, "Five O'Clock off California," 21.

6. Logbook, USS *Macon*, February 12, 1934.

7. Logbook, USS *Macon*, February 12, 1934

8. Campbell, "Five O'Clock off California," 122.

9. Lt. (jg) George W. Campbell, USN, Testimony Given during Court of Inquiry Convened by Commander-In-Chief, U.S. Fleet, to Inquire into All the Circumstances Connected with the Loss of the U.S.S. *Macon* near Point Sur, California, on 12 February 1935, 107, Case No. 18580, box 656, NARA.

10. Campbell, "Five O'Clock off California," 122.

11. Logbook, USS *Macon*, February 12, 1934.

12. Lt. Cdr. Herbert V. Wiley, USN, Testimony Given during Court of Inquiry, U.S.S. *Macon*, on 12 February 1935, 1–2.

13. Wiley, testimony.

14. Campbell, "Five O'Clock off California," 124.

15. Campbell, "Five O'Clock off California."

16. Campbell, "Five O'Clock off California."

17. Wiley, testimony, 3.

18. Campbell, "Five O'Clock off California," 125.

19. Campbell, "Five O'Clock off California."

20. Wiley, testimony, 4.

21. Campbell, "Five O'Clock Off California," 125.

22. Campbell, "Five O'Clock off California," 126.

23. Mason, "Reminiscences of Rear Admiral Miller," 87.

24. Mason, "Reminiscences of Rear Admiral Miller," 88.

25. Wiley, testimony, 4.

26. Coxswain William H. Clarke, USN, Testimony Given during Court of Inquiry, U.S.S. *Macon* on 12 February 1935, 77.

27. Coxswain W. A. McDonald, USN, Testimony Given during Court of Inquiry, U.S.S. *Macon* on 12 February 1935, 98.

28. Mason, "Reminiscences of Rear Admiral Miller," 89.

29. "2 Die as Navy Airship Falls into Sea," (Harrisburg, Pa.) *Evening News*, February 13, 1935, 9.

30. Commander in Chief, U.S. Fleet to Rear Adm. Orin G. Murfin, NARA.

31. "2 Die as Navy Airship Falls into Sea," 9.

32. Lt. Calvin M. Bolster, USN, Testimony Given during Court of Inquiry, U.S.S. *Macon* on 12 February 1935, 43–44.

33. Bolster, testimony, 45.

34. Bolster, testimony, 46.

35. Bolster, testimony, 63.

36. Bolster, testimony, 69.

37. T. L. Gatch, Argument of the Judge Advocate, Court of Inquiry, U.S.S. *Macon* on 12 February 1935, 123.

38. "Chief of Navy Will Oppose New Airship, Swanson Stand Seen as End of Dirigible Ships for U.S.," *Salt Lake* (Salt Lake City, Utah) *Tribune*, February 21, 1935, 1.

39. J. G. Blaine MacDade to Franklin D. Roosevelt, February 14, 1935, Wiley family.

40. George W. Campbell, to Secretary of the Navy, Subject: Report of Conspicuous Action of Lieutenant Commander Herbert V. Wiley, U.S. Navy, February 26, 1935, NARA.

41. "*Macon* Officer Gets Promotion to Commander," (Franklin, Pa.) *News-Herald*, February 15, 1935, 1; "Wiley Is Promoted," *North Adams* (Mass.) *Transcript*, February 15, 1935, 1

42. Law Offices of John A. Rush to Hon. Claude A. Swanson, Secretary of the Navy, February 16, 1935, 1, National Archives, St. Louis, Mo.

43. John A. Rush to Claude A. Swanson, Secretary of the Navy, March 9, 1935, 1, National Archives, St. Louis, Mo.

44. Chief of the Bureau of Navigation to Wiley, Subject: Complaint of John A. Rush, Los Angeles, California, March 22, 1935, National Archives, St. Louis, Mo.

45. Senior Member, Board for the Award of Medals of Honor, Distinguished-Service Medal, Navy Cross, Distinguished Flying Cross and Life Saving Medals, to Secretary of the Navy, June 12, 1935, National Archives, St. Louis, Mo.
46. Secretary of the Navy to Wiley, Subject: Commendation, June 22, 1935, National Archives, St. Louis, Mo.
47. Secretary of the Navy to Wiley, Subject: Special Letter of Commendation, 21 August 1935, National Archives, St. Louis, Mo.
48. Commanding Officer, Naval Air Station Sunnyvale, Mountain View, California, to Chief of the Bureau of Navigation, March 8, 1935, National Archives, St. Louis, Mo.
49. Wiley to Bureau of Navigation, Subject: Change of Duty: Request For, March 8, 1935, National Archives, St. Louis, Mo.
50. Bureau of Navigation to Wiley, Subject: Change of Duty, March 29, 1935, National Archives, St. Louis, Mo.

CHAPTER 14. USS *SIRIUS* (AK 15), *HELL GATE*, AND HELIUM

1. Bureau of Navigation to Wiley, Subject: Examination for Promotion to the Grade of Commander in the U.S. Navy, October 18,1935, National Archives, St. Louis, Mo.
2. Bureau of Navigation to Wiley, Subject: Commission, Regular, February 26, 1936, National Archives, St. Louis, Mo.
3. R. Jordan, "Widen Pearl Harbor, Navy Defense Cry," (Hammond, Ind.) *Times*, June 17, 1935, 17.
4. Jordan, "Widen Pearl Harbor."
5. Jordan, "Widen Pearl Harbor."
6. Wiley to Bureau of Navigation, Report of Compliance with Orders, January 20, 1937, National Archives, St. Louis, Mo.
7. "Bulldog Ranks as Top Sailor on War Vessel," *Indiana* (Pa.) *Democrat*, January 20, 1937, 9.
8. H. V. Wiley, "It's a Long Trail to Hawaii," U.S. Naval Institute *Proceedings* 63 (December 1937), 1737.
9. Wiley, "Long Long Trail," 1737–38.
10. Wiley, "Long Long Trail," 1738.
11. Wiley, "Long Long Trail."
12. Wiley, "Long Long Trail," 1740.
13. Wiley, "Long Long Trail," 1741.
14. Wiley, "Long Long Trail," 1742.

15. Wiley, "Long Long Trail," 1744.

16. Secretary of the Navy to Wiley, Subject: Commendation, February 23, 1938, National Archives, St. Louis, Mo.

17. "33 Die as Explosion and Fire Destroy Giant German Dirigible *Hindenburg* at Lakehurst: Few Persons Saw the *Hindenburg* Destroyed," (York, Pa.) *Gazette and Daily*, May 7, 1937, 1.

18. "Explosion and Fire Destroy *Hindenburg*."

19. "No 'Next Time' for Lehmann," (Hazelton, Pa.) *Plain Speaker*, May 8, 1937, 1.

20. Thor Nielson, *The Zeppelin Story: The Life of Hugo Eckener* (London: Allan Wingate, 1955), x.

21. "Air Disaster Probes Open as Officer Expires," *Pottstown* (Pa.) *Mercury*, May 8, 1937, 1.

22. "18 Dirigible Disasters Recorded in Past 23 Years," *Pottstown* (Pa.) *Mercury*, May 7, 1937, 14.

23. "Lakehurst Officials Long Feared the Explosion Possibility," (York, Pa.) *Gazette and Daily*, May 7, 1937, 16.

24. "Old Controversy Flares Up Anew," (York, Pa.) *Gazette and Daily*, May 7, 1937, 16.

25. "Disaster Demonstrates Need of Helium to Lift Dirigibles Says Eckener," *(York, Pa.) Gazette and Daily*, May 7, 1937, 16.

26. "Rosendahl Urges Airship Building," (York, Pa.) *Gazette and Daily*, June 18, 1937, 6.

27. "Static Spark Is Found Cause of *Hindenburg* Fire," (Hammond, Ind.) *Times*, July 22, 1937, 72.

28. "Germany, U.S. Join in Tribute," *Asbury Park* (N.J.) *Press*, June 1, 1937, 2.

29. "Why Did the *Hindenburg* Crash?" (Granbury, Tex.) *Hood County Tablet*, June 10, 1937, 7.

30. "Why Did the *Hindenburg* Crash?" 2.

31. "Why Did the *Hindenburg* Crash?"

32. "Germany Seeks Helium Source in Own Country," *Sedalia* (Mo.) *Weekly Democrat*, July 22, 1937.

33. "U.S. Senate Moves to Protect Helium: Plan Kern Tests," *Bakersfield* (Calif.) *Californian*, August 12, 1937, 13.

34. "New Zep Changed So It Will Use Helium: Will Not Be Made Larger," (Harlingen, Tex.) *Valley Morning Star*, August 1, 1937, 4.

35. "Rotarians Hear Com. Wiley Tell of *Akron*'s Crash," *Chillicothe* (Mo.) *Constitution-Tribune*, August 13, 1937, 1.

36. "Rotarians Hear Com. Wiley Tell of *Akron's* Crash."

37. "Germany Unable to Get Helium, FDR Unable to Change Ickes," *Amarillo* (Tex.) *Globe-Times*, May 11, 1938, 1.

38. P. J. Huss, "Dr. Hugo Eckener Sailing for U.S. to Plea [*sic*] for Sale of Helium Gas," (Bloomington, Ill.) *Pantagraph*, April 26, 1938, 1.

39. "Sale of Helium to Germany Delayed Pending Guarantees, Lack of Assurance That Gas Will Not Be Used for War Causes Ickes to Hold Up Shipments," *Albuquerque* (N.Mex.) *Journal*, March 24, 1938, 1.

40. "Ickes Blocks Helium Sale, German Firm Seeks Contract for Gas," *Hutchinson* (Kans.) *News*, March 24, 1938, 12.

41. "No Helium for Germany," (Fairbanks) *Alaska Miner*, May 17, 1938, 11.

42. "German Firm Seeks Contract for Gas."

43. "Britain Warns German Reich: Million Viennese Hail Hitler, Frenzied Mobs Hear Him Defy World Powers," (San Bernardino, Calif.) *San Bernardino County Sun*, March 15, 1938, 1.

44. C. P. Stewart, "Helium Causes Jabs at Hitler: Germany Needs It for Dirigibles, But Are They War Machines?," *New Castle* (Pa.) *News*, April 30, 1938, 14.

45. "Nazi Airman Raps Ickes' Helium Ban," *Kingsport* (Tenn.) *Times*, July 8, 1938, 1, 8.

46. "Secretary Ickes Blocking Helium Sale to Germany," *Pittston* (Pa.) *Gazette*, May 11, 1938, 1.

47. "Jews, Arabs and British Concerned," *Waxahachie* (Tex.) *Daily Light*, July 8, 1938, 1.

48. "Nazi Airman Raps Ickes' Helium Ban," 1.

49. "Nazi Airman Raps Ickes' Helium Ban."

50. "Nazi Airman Raps Ickes' Helium Ban."

51. P. Grover, "Watching Trends," (Mansfield, Ohio) *News-Journal*, November 10, 1938, 14.

52. Grover, "Watching Trends."

53. L. P. Lochner, "German Zeppelin Kept in Hangar: Dream of Dr. Eckener Must Wait until End of the War," (Massillon, Ohio) *Evening Independent*, December 13, 1939, 7.

54. Bureau of Navigation to Wiley, Subject: Request for Assignment to Naval War College, December 6, 1938, National Archives, St. Louis, Mo.

55. Bureau of Navigation to Wiley, Subject: Orders of 21 December 1939, Modified, National Archives, St. Louis, Mo.

56. "Com. H. V. Wiley Goes to New Post," *Chillicothe* (Mo.) *Constitution-Tribune*, January 4, 1940, 4.

57. Chief of Naval Operations to Capt. William R. Monroe, August 31, 1940, National Archives, St. Louis, Mo.

58. CNO to Monroe.

59. Letter From: The Chief of Naval Operations. To: Capt. William R. Monroe, U.S.N., Commanding Officer, U.S.S. Mississippi, September 20, 1940, National Archives, St. Louis, Mo.

60. Letter from: Commanding Officer. To: Commander Herbert V. Wiley, U.S. Navy. Subject: Change of Duty. April 13, 1941, National Archives, St. Louis, Mo.

CHAPTER 15. WAR AND BATTLESHIPS

1. "Japan Pays Bill for Bombing of *Panay*," *Mount Carmel (Pa.) Item*, April 22, 1938, 2.

2. George C. Dyer, *On the Treadmill to Pearl Harbor: The Memoirs of Admiral James O. Richardson, USN (Retired)*. Washington, D.C.: Naval History Division, Department of the Navy, 1973), 17.

3. W. G. Winslow, *The Fleet the Gods Forgot: The United States Asiatic Fleet in World War II* (Annapolis, Md.: Naval Institute Press, 1982), 37.

4. Dyer, *On the Treadmill to Pearl Harbor*, 404.

5. Dyer, *On the Treadmill to Pearl Harbor*, 425.

6. Dyer, *On the Treadmill to Pearl Harbor*, 427.

7. "Navy Organized into Three Major Fleets," *Rhinelander* (Wis.) *Daily News*, January 8, 1941, 1.

8. "U.S. Splits Navy to Make Three Complete Fleets," *Decatur* (Ill.) *Daily Review*, January 8, 1941, 1.

9. Winslow, *Fleet the Gods Forgot*, 4.

10. Commander in Chief, U.S. Asiatic Fleet to Wiley, Subject: Change of Duty: Modification of Orders, May 19, 1941, National Archives, St. Louis, Mo.

11. Wiley to Bureau of Navigation, Report of Compliance with Orders, May 29, 1941, National Archives, St. Louis, Mo.

12. Winslow, *Fleet the Gods Forgot*, 5.

13. Destroyer Division 57 was composed of the USS *Whipple* (DD 217) (flag), the USS *Alden* (DD 211), the USS *John D. Edwards* (DD 216), and the USS *Edsall* (DD 219). Destroyer Division 58 contained the USS *Stewart* (DD 224) (flag), the USS *Parrott* (DD 218), the USS *Bulmer* (DD 222), and the

USS *Barker* (DD 213). Destroyer Division 59 was made up of the USS *Peary* (DD 226) (flag), the USS *Pope* (DD 225), the USS *John D. Ford* (DD 228), and the USS *Pillsbury* (DD 227).

14. Winslow, *Fleet the Gods Forgot*, 37.

15. Charles E. Rosendahl to Wiley, July 17, 1941, 1, National Archives, St. Louis, Mo.

16. Wiley to Rosendahl, August 12, 1941, 1, National Archives, St. Louis, Mo.

17. Donald M. Goldstein and Katherine V. Dillon, eds., *Fading Victory: The Diary of Admiral Matome Ugaki, 1941–1945* (Pittsburgh, Pa.: University of Pittsburgh Press, 1991), 28.

18. Goldstein and Dillon, *Fading Victory*, 18.

19. Goldstein and Dillon, *Fading Victory*.

20. Charles Culbertson, comp., *War in the Pacific: End of the Asiatic Fleet—The Classified Report of Admiral Thomas C. Hart* (Staunton, Va.: Clarion, 2013), 42.

21. "Roosevelt Sends Note to Jap Emperor," (Allentown, Pa.) *Morning Call*, December 7, 1941, 1.

22. "Japanese Bomb Hawaii: Declare War on U.S.," *Fresno* (Calif.) *Bee*, December 7, 1941, 1.

23. Goldstein and Dillon, *Fading Victory*, 43.

24. Lt. Cdr. John J. Hourihan to Commander Destroyer Squadron 29, December 27, 1941, 1, NARA, College Park, Md.

25. Winslow, *Fleet the Gods Forgot*, 8.

26. Winslow, *Fleet the Gods Forgot*, 39.

27. Winslow, *Fleet the Gods Forgot*, 40.

28. Secretary of the Navy to Wiley, Subject: Navy Unit Commendation for Destroyer Squadron Twenty-Nine: Consideration Of, National Archives, St. Louis, Mo.

29. Winslow, *Fleet the Gods Forgot*, 12.

30. Culbertson, *War in the Pacific*, 12.

31. Winslow, *Fleet the Gods Forgot*, 11.

32. Superintendent U.S. Naval Academy to Wiley, August 20, 1942, National Archives, St. Louis, Mo.

33. Wiley to Rosendahl, May 19, 1943, National Archives, St. Louis, Mo.

34. Rosendahl to Wiley, July 24, 1943, National Archives, St. Louis, Mo.

35. Chief of Naval Personnel to Wiley, Subject: Change of Duty, December 6, 1943, National Archives, St. Louis, Mo.

36. See Ernest M. Marshall, *That Night at Surigao: Life on a Battleship at War* (Mechanicsburg, Pa.: Sunbury, 2013), 8–9.

37. War Diary, USS *West Virginia* (BB 48), BatDiv 4, January 15, 1944, NARA, College Park, Md.

38. Report of Medical Survey, U.S. Naval Hospital, Philadelphia, Pa., April 10, 1944, National Archives, St. Louis, Mo.

39. Commander Fleet Operational Training Command, Pacific to Commander Battleships, U.S. Pacific Fleet, Subject: Report on Completion of Shakedown Training of the USS *West Virginia* (BB 48), September 18, 1944, National Archives, St. Louis, Mo.

40. Logbook, USS *West Virginia*, October 24, 1944, NARA, College Park, Md.

41. USS *West Virginia* BB 48, Action in Battle of Surigao Straits 25 October 1944: USS *West Virginia*—Report of, serial 0538, November 1, 1944, 3, NARA, College Park, Md.

42. Generous, *Sweet Pea at War*, 9.

43. Generous, *Sweet Pea at War*, 176.

44. USS *West Virginia*, Action in Battle of Surigao Straits, 3.

45. Anthony P. Tully, *Battle of Surigao Strait* (Bloomington: Indiana University Press, 2009), 87.

46. USS *West Virginia*, Action in Battle of Surigao Straits, 4.

47. See Marshall, *That Night at Surigao*, 85.

48. Samuel Eliot Morison, *The Two-Ocean War: A Short History of the United States Navy in the Second World War* (New York: Galahad Books, 1963), 446.

49. Robert O. Baumrucker, ed., *USS* West Virginia *Crosses the Equator Again* (San Francisco, Calif.: Trade Pressroom, October 1944).

50. Commander Battleship 4 to Commander in Chief U.S. Pacific Fleet, Subject: Recommendation for Award (with enclosed citation), December 10, 1944, National Archives, St. Louis, Mo.

CHAPTER 16. KAMIKAZES AND BEYOND

1. Morison, *Two-Ocean War*, 480.

2. See Marshall, *That Night at Surigao*, 96.

3. War Diary, USS *West Virginia* BB 48, December 10, 1944, 2.

4. Morison, *Two-Ocean War*, 478.

5. War Diary, USS *West Virginia* BB 48, January 4, 1945, 1; and see Marshall, *That Night at Surigao*, 101.

6. War Diary, USS *West Virginia* BB 48, January 6, 1945.

7. War Diary, USS *West Virginia* BB 48, January 6, 1945.

8. War Diary, USS *West Virginia* BB 48, January 11, 1945, 3.

9. Morison, *Two-Ocean War*, 480.

10. War Diary, USS *West Virginia* BB 48, January 15, 1945, 4.

11. Morison, *Two-Ocean War*, 485.

12. War Diary, USS *West Virginia* BB 48, February 19, 1945, 5.

13. Morison, *Two-Ocean War*, 514.

14. War Diary, USS *West Virginia* BB 48, February 28, 1945, 9.

15. War Diary, USS *West Virginia* BB 48, February 25, 1945, 8.

16. Commander Battleship Division 4 to Secretary of the Navy; Subject: Recommendation of Navy Unit Commendation for USS *West Virginia*, February 27, 1945, NARA, College Park, Md.

17. War Diary, USS *West Virginia* BB 48, March 5, 1945, 2.

18. Lt. Cdr. T. A. Lombardi to Mrs. Lombardi, February 8, 1945, Lombardi family.

19. War Diary, USS *West Virginia* BB 48, March 11, 1945, 4.

20. Edwin P. Hoyt, *The Last Samurai: The Story of Admiral Matome Ugaki* (Westport, Conn.: Praeger, 1993), 168.

21. Morison, *Two-Ocean War*, 528.

22. War Diary, USS *West Virginia* BB 48, March 26, 1945, 8–9.

23. Morison, *Two-Ocean War*, 531.

24. War Diary, USS *West Virginia* BB 48, March 31, 1945, 13.

25. War Diary, USS *West Virginia* BB 48, April 1, 1945, 1–2.

26. Deck Log, USS *West Virginia* (BB 48), revised form for reporting AA action by surface ships, April 1, 1945, NARA, College Park, Md.

27. Battle Damage Report, USS West Virginia (BB 48), 27 April 1945. (NARA, College Park, Md.).

28. See Marshall, *That Night at Surigao*, 101.

29. War Diary, USS *West Virginia* BB 48, April 1, 1945

30. War Diary, USS *West Virginia* BB 48, April 24, 1945.

31. War Diary, USS *West Virginia* BB 48, April 30, 1945.

32. See Marshall, *That Night at Surigao*, 127.

33. See Marshall, *That Night at Surigao*, 128.

34. Commander Fleet Operational Training Command, Atlantic Fleet to Wiley, Subject: Orders, June 1, 1945, National Archives, St. Louis, Mo.

35. Wiley to Thomas C. Hart, June 2, 1945, National Archives, St. Louis, Mo.

36. Commander Fleet Operational Training Command, Atlantic to Commander in Chief, U.S. Atlantic Fleet, June 10, 1945, National Archives, St. Louis, Mo.

37. C. F. Bryant to "Doc," August 9, 1945, National Archives, St. Louis, Mo.

38. "Capt. Herbert Wiley Is Ill in Cuba: Suffered a Heart Attack the First of December—In Naval Hospital," *Chillicothe* (Mo.) *Constitution-Tribune*, January 10, 1946, 1.

39. Wiley to Bureau of Naval Personnel, Subject: Detail to Duty upon Release from Hospital, January 11, 1946, National Archives, St. Louis, Mo.

40. Chief of Naval Personnel to Superintendent, U.S. Naval Academy, January 16, 1946, National Archives, St. Louis, Mo.

41. John L. Sullivan, Acting Secretary of the Navy to President, Naval Retiring Board, Subject: Consideration and Report on the Record in the Cases of Certain Officers, June 24, 1946, National Archives, St. Louis, Mo.

42. Chief of Naval Personnel to Wiley, Subject: Orders Relieving You of All Active Duty, June 28,1946, National Archives, St. Louis, Mo.

43. Wiley to Rosendahl, July 3, 1946, National Archives, St. Louis, Mo.

44. Rosendahl to Wiley, July 4, 1946, National Archives, St. Louis, Mo.

45. Charles E. Rosendahl, *United States Navy Airships in World War II* (repr. n.p.: Atlantis Media Productions, 2007).

46. "Classmates of Retiring Captain Recall His Dirigible Flight Here," *Chillicothe* (Mo.) *Constitution-Tribune*, August 26, 1946, 1.

47. Capt. C. W. Moses, Officer Performance Division to Wiley, Subject: Retirement, 26 December 1946, National Archives, St. Louis, Mo.

48. Bureau of Naval Personnel to Wiley, Notice of Separation from U.S. Naval Service, January 1, 1947, National Archives, St. Louis, Mo.

49. James Forrestal to Wiley, January 20, 1947, National Archives, St. Louis, Mo.

50. "Admiral Wiley Now on University Staff: Former Chillicothean Now an Assistant Dean at California U," *Chillicothe* (Mo.) *Constitution-Tribune*, June 17, 1947, 7.

51. "Society," *Chillicothe* (Mo.) *Constitution-Tribune*, May 19, 1953, 11.

52. Commandant Twelfth Naval District to Chief of Naval Personnel, Subject: RADM Herbert Victor Wiley, USN (Ret.), Official Report of Death: Confirmation Of, May 27, 1954, National Archives, St. Louis, Mo.

53. Charles M. Blakewell, "Moral Training in Preparation for War," U.S. Naval Institute *Proceedings* 40, no. 1 (January–February 1914), 159.

BIBLIOGRAPHY

Althoff, William F. Oral History Library, Smithsonian Libraries / National Air and Space Museum, Washington, D.C.

———. *Sky Ships: A History of the Airship in the United States Navy.* New York: Orion Books, 1990.

———. *USS* Los Angeles: *The Navy's Venerable Airship and Aviation Technology.* Washington, D.C.: Potomac Books, 2004.

Arpee, Edward. *From Frigates to Flat-Tops.* Lake Forest, Ill.: Edward Arpee, 1953.

Barry, John M. *The Great Influenza: The Story of the Deadliest Pandemic in History.* New York: Penguin Books, 2009.

Baumrucker, Robert O., ed. *USS* West Virginia *Crosses the Equator Again.* San Francisco, Calif.: Trade Pressroom, October 1944.

Campbell, George W. "Five O'Clock off California." *Saturday Evening Post,* May 15, 1937, 20–127.

Castle, Ian. *British Airships 1905–30.* Oxford, U.K.: Osprey, 2009.

———. *London 1914–1917: The Zeppelin Menace.* Oxford, U.K.: Osprey, 2008.

Court of Inquiry Convened by Commander-in-Chief, U.S. Fleet, to Inquire into All the Circumstances Connected with the Loss of the USS *Macon* near Point Sur, California, on 12 February 1935, box 656 (#18580), NARA, Washington, D.C.

Court of Inquiry Convened by Order of the Secretary of the Navy, to Inquire into the Circumstances Connected with the Loss of the USS *Akron,* off Barnegat Inlet, New Jersey, on 4 April 1933, boxes 614 and 615 (#18069), National Archives and Records Administration [hereafter NARA], Washington, D.C.

Court of Inquiry No. 13965 (Shenandoah), Record Group [hereafter RG] 125, Records of the Office of the Judge Advocate General (Navy), Records of Proceedings of Courts of Inquiry and Boards of Inquiry. May 1866–Dec. 1940, boxes 407–9, NARA, Washington, D.C.

Cresset, The: The Annual of the Chillicothe High School 1909. Published by the Junior Class, 1909.

Culbertson, Charles, comp. *War in the Pacific: End of the Asiatic Fleet—The Classified Report of Admiral Thomas C. Hart.* Staunton, Va.: Clarion, 2013.

Dick, Harold G., with Douglas H. Robinson. *The Golden Age of the Great Passenger Airships Graf Zeppelin and Hindenburg.* Washington, D.C.: Smithsonian Institution, 1985.

Dyer, George C. *On the Treadmill to Pearl Harbor: The Memoirs of Admiral James O. Richardson, USN (Retired).* Washington, D.C.: Naval History Division, Department of the Navy, 1973.

Generous, William T., Jr. *Sweet Pea at War: A History of USS Portland.* Lexington: University Press of Kentucky, 2003.

Goldstein, Donald M., and Katherine V. Dillon, eds. *Fading Victory: The Diary of Admiral Matome Ugaki, 1941–1945.* Pittsburgh, Pa.: University of Pittsburgh Press, 1991.

Hoyt, Edwin P. *The Last Kamikaze: The Story of Admiral Matome Ugaki.* Westport, Conn.: Praeger, 1993.

Kehn, Donald M., Jr. *In the Highest Degree Tragic: The Sacrifice of the U.S. Asiatic Fleet in the East Indies during World War II.* Lincoln, Neb.: Potomac Books, 2017.

Keirns, Aaron J. *America's Forgotten Airship Disaster: The Crash of the USS Shenandoah.* Howard, Ohio: Little River, 2010.

Lehmann, Ernst, Captain, and Howard Mingos. *The Zeppelins.* J. H. Sears, 1927.

Lombardi, Thomas A. Military Personnel Records, National Personnel Records Center, National Archives, St. Louis, Mo.

Lucky Bag. Vol. 20, Class of 1913. New York: Chas. L. Willard, 1913.

Lucky Bag. Vol. 22, Class of 1915. Philadelphia: Wm. H. Hoskins, 1915.

Marshall, M. Ernest. *That Night at Surigao: Life on a Battleship at War.* Mechanicsburg, Pa.: Sunbury, 2013.

Mason, John T., Jr. "Reminiscences of Rear Admiral Harold B. Miller, U.S. Navy (Retired)." Annapolis, Md.: U.S. Naval Institute, 1995.

Maurer, John H., and Christopher M. Bell. *At the Crossroads between Peace and War: The London Naval Conference of 1930.* Annapolis, Md.: Naval Institute Press, 2014.

Moffett, William A. Persons of Exceptional Prominence Records, Official Military Personnel File, Archival Programs Division, National Archives, St. Louis, Mo.

Moffett, William A., Captain, Director of Naval Aviation. *Airships and the Scientist.* Exclusive Release to U.S. Air Services, Press Release 089, June 28, 1921. Nimitz Library, Department of the Navy, U.S. Naval Academy, Annapolis, Md.

Morison, Samuel Eliot. *The Two-Ocean War: A Short History of the United States Navy in the Second World War.* New York: Galahad Books, 1963.

Nielson, Thor. *The Zeppelin Story: The Life of Hugo Eckener.* London: Allan Wingate, 1955.

Pace, Kevin, Ronald Montgomery, and Rick Zitarosa. *Naval Air Station, Lakehurst.* Charleston, S.C.: Arcadia, 2003.

Records of Boards: Proceedings of the Court of Inquiry Convened at the Academy into Alleged Frauds Committed by Midshipmen in the Annual Examinations of 1915, RG 405.6.4, entry 217, Special Collections & Archives Department, Nimitz Library, United States Naval Academy, Annapolis, Md.

Robinette, Paul. "Herbert V. Wiley (1891–1954), Who Was Born for Adventure," 1960. Transcript collection, item #121 (C995) of the State Historical Society of Missouri, Columbia, Mo.

Robinson, Douglas H. *The Zeppelin in Combat: A History of the German Naval Airship Division, 1912–1918.* Atglen, Pa.: Schiffer Military/Aviation History, 1994.

——— and Charles L. Keller. *"Up Ship!" U.S. Navy Rigid Airships 1919–1935.* Annapolis, Md.: Naval Institute Press, 1982.

Rosendahl, Charles Emery. National Personnel Records Center, National Archives, St. Louis, Mo.

———. *SNAFU: The Strange Story of the American Airship.* Edgewater, Fla.: Atlantic, 2004.

———. *What About the Airship?* New York: Charles Scribner's Sons, 1938.

Silverstone, Paul H. *The New Navy 1883–1922.* New York: Routledge, 2006.

Smith, Richard K. *The Airships Akron & Macon: Flying Aircraft Carriers of the United States Navy.* Annapolis, Md.: Naval Institute Press, 1965.

Stephenson, Charles. *Zeppelins: German Airships 1900–1940.* Oxford, U.K.: Osprey, 2004.

Sweetman, Jack. *The U.S. Naval Academy.* Annapolis, Md.: Naval Institute Press, 1979.

Swinfield, John. *Airship: Design, Development and Disaster.* Annapolis, Md.: Naval Institute Press, 2012.

Toland, John. *The Great Dirigibles: Their Triumphs & Disasters.* New York: Dover, 1972.

Trimble, William F. *Admiral William A. Moffett: Architect of Naval Aviation.* Washington, D.C.: Smithsonian Institution Press, 1994.

Tully, Anthony P. *Battle of Surigao Strait.* Bloomington: Indiana University Press, 2009.

USS *Akron*, RG 24 Records of the Bureau of Naval Personnel, Logbooks of U.S. Ships and Stations, 1916–1940, box 1 A1, entry 118-G, NARA, Washington, D.C.

USS *Los Angeles*, RG 24 Records of the Bureau of Naval Personnel, Logbooks of U.S. Ships and Stations, 1916–1940, boxes 1–7, A1, entry 118-G-L, NARA, Washington, D.C.

USS *Macon*, RG 24 Records of the Bureau of Naval Personnel, Logbooks of U.S. Ships and Stations, 1916–1940, boxes 1 and 2, A1, entry 118-G-M, NARA, Washington, D.C.

USS *Shenandoah*, RG 24 Records of the Bureau of Naval Personnel, Logbooks of U.S. Ships and Stations, 1916–1940, boxes 1 and 2, A1, entry 118-G-S, NARA, Washington, D.C.

Wiley, H. V. "A Celestial Cruise." U.S. Naval Institute *Proceedings* (April 1925), 604–9.

———. "It's a Long Long Trail to Hawaii." U.S. Naval Institute *Proceedings* 63 (December 1937), 1737–52.

———. "Value of Airships." U.S. Naval Institute *Proceedings* (May 1934), 665–71.

Wiley, Herbert Victor. National Personnel Records Center, National Archives, St. Louis, Mo.

Winchester, Jim. *A Chronology of Aviation: The Ultimate History of a Century of Powered Flight.* New York: Metro Books, 2007.

Winslow, W. G. *The Fleet the Gods Forgot: The United States Asiatic Fleet in World War II.* Annapolis, Md.: Naval Institute Press, 1982.

Wood, Junius B. "Seeing America from the '*Shenandoah*': An Account of the Record-Making 9,000-Mile Flight from the Atlantic to the Pacific Coast and Return in the Navy's American-Built, American-Manned Airship." *National Geographic* 67, no. 1 (January 1925), 1–47.

Woodward, C. H. "The Navy's Participation at the Panama Pacific International Exposition." U.S. Naval Institute *Proceedings* 41, no. 1, January–February 1915, 167–72.

INDEX

Academy Practice Squadron, 14
Adams, Charles Francis, 92, 118–19, 124
aerology, 49, 65–66, 142–47, 155, 158–60
aerostatics, 49
Air Defense: on *West Virginia*, 252, 259
air photoreconnaissance, 28
air supremacy, U.S., 63
aircraft carrier, 28–29; airship docking to, 74–75, 83; development of, 33
airmail: first U.S. transoceanic delivery of, 58
airplanes: development of, 88; safety of, 88. *See also* HTA flight
airship design: effect on stability, 113; strength improvements, 113
airship development and U.S. Navy, 33–34, 39, 112
airship ground crew: training, 116; use of civilians as, 59, 116
airship ground school, 35–36, 49
airship hangar: specifications, 115
airship nomenclature, 37
airshipmen: self-concept, 70, 175
airships: advantages over airplanes, 41; as aircraft carriers, 86–87, 96, 113, 115, 122, 179–80; aircraft docking feasibility testing, 86–88, 95; ballast release, 43, 77; civilian passengers, 95, 97, 100; as command-and-control platforms, 113; commercial air service, 33, 53–54,

57–58, 68, 82, 96–97, 204, 221, 230–31; control car placement, 113; crew hardships, 97–98; crew size, 38; cruising range, 37; defensive weaponry, 113, 115; design modifications, 113; docking at sea, 74–75; effect of weather on, 51, 55–58, 61–63, 65–66, 70, 74–75, 77, 80, 82–83, 97–98, 126–29, 134, 140, 142–47, 157–61, 165–66, 173, 195–97, 207; emergency measures, 43–45, 75, 146–47; envelope breach, 43–45, 80; evasive maneuvers, 188; flight time, 35–36, 38–39, 47; fragility, 39, 41, 43–45, 47, 51, 55, 115, 231; generating lift, 39, 43; German leadership in, 76; ground crew, 38–39, 44, 50, 59, 75; hangars, 38–39, 134; in Herbert Hoover inaugural parade (1929), 84; hook-on device for airplane capture, 83–84, 86, 95, 113, 125–26, 138; innovations, 83–84, 96, 112–13; launching glider from, 98; load balancing, 50; and long-range reconnaissance, 113, 120–22; maintenance and repair, 39, 47, 51, 55, 76, 83; military applications, 31, 33, 54, 57, 112, 120–22, 132; mooring to high mast, 39, 41–42, 74; navigating geographic features, 50–51, 77, 134; negative publicity, 114–15, 119; in pilot rescue, 186; preparations for takeoff, 39,

ABOUT THE AUTHOR

M. Ernest Marshall graduated from the University of Virginia College of Arts & Sciences and the School of Medicine. He is a retired professor of medicine who devotes his time to historical research and writing. He lives in Charlottesville, Virginia, with his wife, Lisa.